Enigma Books

Also published by Enigma Books

Hitler's Table Talk: 1941–1944

In Stalin's Secret Service

Hitler and Mussolini: The Secret Meetings

The Jews in Fascist Italy: A History

The Man Behind the Rosenbergs

Roosevelt and Hopkins: An Intimate History

Diary 1937–1943 (Galeazzo Ciano)

Secret Affairs: FDR, Cordell Hull, and Sumner Welles

Hitler and His Generals: Military Conferences 1942–1945

Stalin and the Jews: The Red Book

The Secret Front: Nazi Political Espionage

Fighting the Nazis: French Intelligence and Counterintelligence

A Death in Washington: Walter G. Krivitsky and the Stalin Terror

The Battle of the Casbah: Terrorism and Counterterrorism in Algeria 1955–1957

Hitler's Second Book: The Unpublished Sequel to *Mein Kampf*

At Napoleon's Side in Russia: The Classic Eyewitness Account

The Atlantic Wall: Hitler's Defenses for D-Day

Double Lives: Stalin, Will Münzenberg and the Seduction of the Intellectuals

France and the Nazi Threat: The Collapse of French Diplomacy 1932–1939

Mussolini: The Secrets of His Death

Top Nazi: Karl Wolff—The Man Between Hitler and Himmler

Empire on the Adriatic: Mussolini's Conquest of Yugoslavia

The Origins of the War of 1914 (3-volume set)

Hitler's Foreign Policy: 1933–1939—The Road to World War II

The Origins of Fascist Ideology 1918–1925

Max Corvo: OSS Italy 1942–1945

Hitler's Contract: The Secret History of the Italian Edition of *Mein Kampf*

Secret Intelligence and the Holocaust

Israel at High Noon

Balkan Inferno: Betrayal, War, and Intervention, 1990–2005

Brad Lewis

Hollywood's Celebrity Gangster

The Incredible Life and Times of Mickey Cohen

Enigma Books

Enigma Books
580 Eighth Avenue, New York, NY 10018

www.enigmabooks.com

First edition

All photographs are from the Enigma Books archives.

ISBN-10: 1-929631-65-0
ISBN-13: 978-1-929631-65-0

Printed in the United States of America

Library of Congress Cataloging-in-Publication Data

Lewis, Bradley.
   Hollywood's celebrity gangster : the incredible life and times of Mickey Cohen / Bradley
Lewis. -- 1st ed.

   p. : ill. ; cm.

Includes bibliographical references and index.
ISBN-13: 978-1-929631-65-0
ISBN-10: 1-929631-65-0

1. Cohen, Mickey, 1914–1976. 2. Criminals--California--Los Angeles--Biography. 3.
Gangsters--California--Los Angeles--Biography. 4. Jewish criminals--United States--
Biography. 5. Organized crime--California--Los Angeles--History.

HV6248.C64 L49 2007
364.109/2

For Mr.

Acknowledgments

The book was considerably enriched by
Linda Lewis, Jack Scovil, Mario Mory, Allan May,
Jay Wynshaw, and Robert Miller.

The criminal has no hates or fears—except very personal ones. He is possibly the only human left in the world who looks lovingly on society.

—Ben Hecht
Screenwriter and author

Contents

Part Four
Mickey Redux
1955–1967

Part Five
The Survivor
1967–1976

Prologue

Mickey Cohen was a little man with a larger-than-life presence. His wardrobe and custom-built automobiles rivaled those of presidents, heads of state, and royalty. When he strolled into a room, his pervasive cologne, dazzling diamond pinky ring, solid gold watch, brand new sparkling shoes, and immaculately tailored suits compensated for his pugilist's countenance.

He would have objected to this book's publication. He always tried to control what was written about him, and brazenly fought all his critics. The underworld czar dogmatically denied his role in prostitution, illegal drugs, and sexual extortion rings. His blackmail targets included Marilyn Monroe, Lana Turner, and department store heir Alfred Bloomingdale. The most social of any mobster in history, he bridged the gap between Hollywood, Las Vegas, and Washington. Unlike many of his criminal predecessors, he had unique and likeable attributes that attracted movie stars, religious leaders, politicians, jetsetters, and international business moguls. He had the ear of many powerful people, including Richard Nixon, Reverend Billy Graham, and *Washington Post* columnist Drew Pearson. Enemies like Robert Kennedy were relentless in trying to topple him.

Mickey Cohen committed murder while still a young man. His explanation centered on his mixed moral perspective: "I have killed no man in the first place that didn't deserve killing by the standards of our way of life...in all of these...what you would call killings... I had no alternative. It was either my life or their life. You couldn't call these cold-blooded killings."

To live the maturing American dream fostered by the media and Hollywood, robbery became second nature, and extortion a means to an end. Jewish mobsters like Mickey developed their own moral codes, justifying their perverse approach to life, while embracing mother and siblings as taught in the Talmud. His puzzling moral compass couldn't be pinpointed as easily as that of other criminals; he openly bragged about his ability to judge those who deserved murder, while lecturing young men about respect for family and friends. His multilayered and conflicted personality allowed him to be generous with the poor and come to the rescue of the downtrodden, never forgetting his humble origins, despite his flamboyant personal choices for housing, dining, and clothing. His role in the history of this country can't be dismissed as either good or evil. Some tried to murder him for one or the other, in both reality and the court of public opinion, while others celebrated him with unabashed gratitude in a way that was and still is uniquely American.

We should not forget Mickey Cohen's America. Generations of amnesia-suffering witnesses have refused to admit that Jewish organized crime ever existed. The shameful portrait of Jewish gangsters is not something fearful parents and grandparents eagerly discussed with their offspring. Still, the Jewish gangster was as much a part of the Jewish-American prototype as a lawyer or doctor.

Private organizations and academia censored Jewish criminal history. Author Arthur Goren described the dilemma surrounding the censorship: "Widely publicized disclosures of vice and crime among Jews created dismay and then alarm in Jewish circles. Protests of innocence were now impossible." Yet, as a defense, Jewish leaders condemned the criminals, and cited that Jewish morality is far superior and removed from illegal endeavors.[1]

The mezuzah on doorposts reminds Jews to obey the Written and Oral Law. Author Gerald Krefetz noted the religious conflict: "The sociopathology of Jews is not an acceptable notion since it runs counter to both religious precepts, and preconceived ideas that Jews have of themselves." Mickey Cohen was aware of the moral difficulties: "Jews should behave differently and more correctly." Yet, because of his chosen occupation, he extorted and beat Jews, citing "business" as an explanation.

Krefetz reminded readers of the conventional Jewish parental guidelines: "...schooling was expected, intellectuality praised, and degrees and advanced degrees sought." With professional degrees, or plain hard work, "there is no need to steal or rob since normal Jewish upbringing establishes the belief that whatever is desired will eventually be provided."

Knowledge of those Judaic teachings did not deter Mickey's generation from organized crime, which presented a seductive dream shortcut to income and political power. Scholar Robert Rockaway discussed the basic attraction: "And crime was exciting, certainly more glamorous than the tedium of studying or the drudgery of working long hours in a shop or factory."

Mickey's birthplace, Brownsville, Brooklyn, took its cues from the Lower East Side of Manhattan, where fabled hoods like Edward "Monk" Osterman operated his Eastman gang from Gluckow's Odessa Tea House, downtown on Broome Street in the now trendy Soho district.[2] Relocated European Jews were easy prey—victims of con games and bullies. Jewish fagins (bands of pickpockets), prostitutes, opium-dealers, brothels, racketeers, and murderers filled Jewish enclaves run by thugs, not unlike their pirate predecessors. Mob language developed from Yiddish: "gun" was a general thief or pickpocket, derived from *gonif.*

The pervasive Shylock cliché spilled into academia. Here anti-Semitic scholars referenced criminal elements as examples of Jewish character, thus justifying college admission quotas.

Popular culture did little to dispel the anti-Semitism. The rough, uneducated Jewish gangster became a familiar American portrait in literature and movies. Like Mickey, the hero of Budd Schulberg's *What Makes Sammy Run?* and Harold Robbins' *A Stone For Danny Fisher* found little use in the business jungle for his immediate family and its Talmudic teachings. The depiction of criminals rarely dealt with the glamorous and privileged types like handsome and articulate mobster Arnold Rothstein.[3] F. Scott Fitzgerald's Meyer Wolfsheim (in *The Great Gatsby*), based on Rothstein, was a jabbering Yiddish-speaking Jew with a small flat nose, exposed nostril hair, and a large head. Voice artist Mel Blanc chose a Brooklyn accent for Bugs Bunny so that the audience would identify him as a crook or con artist; the popular cartoon character was a clichéd Jewish mobster hidden in rabbit drag.

Not until Sergio Leone's 1984 movie *Once Upon A Time In America* did anyone so vividly capture the crowded conditions and desperation in Brooklyn shtetls like Mickey's. Leone provided images of young Jewish boys trying to survive in a world not unlike the Wild West. Critic Vincent Canby likened the setting to "…the jungle where the five young friends, including Max and Noodles, learn their trade as petty thieves and arsonists."

Like the fictional movie characters played by Edward G. Robinson (Emanuel Goldenberg), and Max and Noodles in Leone's epic, Mickey was a product of the tough Jewish ghettos. His reinvented Hollywood life encompassed celebrity, fortune, violence, comedy, and tragedy, prompting him to peddle his life story to the movies.

He possessed a unique set of ambitions, similar to those of his political and entertainment acquaintances. A self-admitted hood, he often described himself in the most simultaneously vivid and degrading terms. Yet, he spent the majority of his life trying to shed the image of someone who could commit cold-blooded murder as easily as returning a steak at the fashionable Brown Derby, where waiters savored his regular twenty-dollar tips. Mickey's perverted sense of justice, a Robin Hood-like philosophy that the media endorsed, was a strange sensitivity for someone who dodged as many hits as he ordered. He preferred a philanthropic image, a crusader created by popular culture. He portrayed himself as a gentleman who neither smoked nor drank, and abstained from profanities in the company of women.

He was also a murderer but with a perverse code of ethics. He told writer Dean Jennings that he had murdered only once. Hecht had suggested that "blood lust" was the natural mixed morality "business equipment" of a criminal, "as a banker uses a frock coat."[4]

Author Jay Robert Nash had his own description of Mickey's public persona. "He [Mickey] was...a hot-headed, loud-mouthed goon...who enjoyed flashing his guns and frightening young girls and old ladies." Colorful Mickey rarely went anywhere without his thirty-eight a small weapon with less than a four-inch barrel.[5]

If asked about his threatening antics Mickey would respond, "That was me when I was a kid. I didn't know no better."

He received backhanded compliments from some authors. "Mickey Cohen, a bandit of unusual depravity and cunning" was Albert Fried's nod to a more complex interpretation of Mickey's character.

His unique and likeable traits attracted journalist Al Aronowitz: "...a spectacular clown who seemed to have stepped into real life right out of a Hollywood gangster comedy." Aronowitz, like many, admits that he was star-struck by Mickey: "...I liked Mickey because he was fun... Mickey could be as cold vicious as he could be witty and charming... The truth is I fell for him hard. Even today, I still have fond memories of him. To me, he was his own Billy Rose. He was a showman." Fans of all ages envied him.

On camera, Mickey appeared much like his executive counterparts in the movie industry, iron-fisted studio bosses, or street-tough producers. He spoke with a firm and direct delivery, always watched his diction, sometimes corrected his grammar while speaking, and portrayed a charismatic sense of humor.

He didn't possess movie star good looks like Bugsy Siegel. Mickey was short, perhaps five-five with his elevator shoes, stocky, and balding. Conservative Yalie Senator Estes Kefauver, an enemy of organized crime, once characterized Mickey as "a simian figure, with a pendulous lower lip...and spreading paunch." Author Ovid Demaris drew a more menacing portrait: "Pint-sized and pudgy, with simian eyes, a flattened nose, and a twisting scar under his left eye, he reminded Jimmy ["The Weasel" Fratianno] of so many punks he had known on the street and in prison." The FBI was less graphic: Mickey had a one-inch scar under each eye, and one on the inner corner of the left eyebrow. His nose had been broken, and he had a two-inch scar on his left hand.

He spared no expense when it came to his personal pleasures. He never dined at home without monogrammed linen and imported silver. Dandy Mickey's $20,000 wardrobe included 1,500 pairs of socks, fifty pairs of $50 silk pajamas, Chinese, Japanese, and Persian silk robes, silk underwear embroidered with his initials, never less than thirty pairs of sparkling shoes, and hundreds of ties. Kefauver took note of Mickey's wardrobe: "[Cohen] appeared before us in 'sharp' clothing, including a suit coat of exaggerated length, excessively padded in the shoulders, and a hat with a ludicrously broad brim."

His twisted symbiotic relationship with American journalism was groundbreaking. He commanded and received the front page; his flamboyant antics provided a never-ending supply of stories. Politicians, lawyers, business czars, and police—not always conscious of Mickey's insight into manipulating and currying favor with the media—fueled his extravagant life by increasing his publicity and power. This gave him a controlling entry to law enforcement and furthered his business moves. He became so influential that he only had to call one of his lobbyists in Sacramento to kill a bill outlawing slot machines in California.

Journalist Peter Noyes recognized Mickey's unique approach: "Day after day he was cultivating an image, and no other gangster in the history of this country has succeeded in doing that." Tinsel Town (Hollywood) was a good fit for Mickey; a place founded on myths and manufactured legends. He could not resist its seductive magnet.

He made efficient use of the syndication publicity available to him. He wrote flattering letters to journalists whose newspaper stories he enjoyed, while castigating his detractors. One fascinating exchange of letters illustrates his shrewd understanding of the media. He criticized *Journal-American* investigative reporter George Carpozi for not relying solely on his interview material: "But you went ahead and put your own answers to a lot of questions; not only that but you wrote on a lot of things which you did not discuss with me at all."

Mickey commanded networks of powerful and creative people, along with starlets whom he dangled as currency. He craved social acceptance at the highest levels, albeit often in the role of a Hollywood sycophant. "So where could I have had the opportunity to meet the people…? I'm talking about celebrities, politicians, people in higher walks of life and education... Where could I have ever come to meet this kind of people if I had gone into some other line of work than I did?" Despite his success, he suffered from low self-esteem, and was continually disappointed in himself.

The assessment of Mickey's overall intelligence varied. The FBI claimed that he had an average I.Q. of ninety-eight. When Senator Charles Tobey of New Hampshire interviewed Los Angeles Police Chief Parker, he asked, "Is he [Cohen] nimble-witted?" "No," answered Parker. "I would say he is essentially stupid. He is heavy-set and heavy-browed and quite ignorant. The private conversations we have been able to pick up do not indicate he is an intelligent or educated man." Mickey's lack of education did not prevent him from figuring out how to split up the money. The bills were stacked according to their value, and passed out one at a time.

His criminal character might be diagnosed today as a DSM-IV cluster A or cluster B personality disorder, characterized by irresponsibility, the inability to feel guilt or remorse for actions that harm others, frequent conflicts with people and social institutions, low frustration tolerance, and other behaviors that indicate a deficiency in socialization. Other labels include psychopathic personality, psychopath, and sociopath, all of which require fancy psychiatric medications.[6]

Germ-phobic Mickey would use up all the toilet paper and paper towels in a restaurant, and then request the linen napkins. In police custody or courtroom proceedings, he immediately demanded access to wash his hands. Macbeth theorists speculated that he was subconsciously trying to wash the blood off his hands. Others suggested that memories of his ink-stained hands as a newsboy led to his obsessive-compulsive disorder.[7]

Mickey sometimes enjoyed two- to three-hour showers, and caused his Brentwood apartment landlord to complain that the other tenants had no water with which to bathe. He liked to air dry himself rather than irritate his skin with a towel, which added to his multihour dressing schedule. The little emperor pampered himself. His slicked-down hair took hours to prepare, and he endlessly checked himself in front of a gilt-edged mirror. Writer and friend Ben Hecht once waited thirty minutes while Mickey pranced around nude, wearing only a hat, green silk socks, and maroon garters, "flicking the powder off his skin with a large Turkish towel. The sound effect is that of a busy shooting gallery." Hecht analyzed the moment: "It is Mickey caught up in a mood so deep, tossed around on memories so violent, high diving into day-dreams so vivid, that he has not the slightest awareness of darting around for an hour in a darkening room, naked and with a hat on... With Mickey, the fantasies share his day. He lives in them as actively as in the real world."

The dark shadows and bright lights of Hollywood distort the realities of Los Angeles criminal life. FBI files often differ from facts supplied by criminals and journalists of the same period. It doesn't matter who's telling the story—good guy or criminal; errors are common, accidental misstatements become accepted facts, while camouflage, varnish, and spin create new entertaining versions.

To compound the intrinsic problems of criminal research, criminals lie and descendants of mobsters sometimes prefer more flattering and protective melioristic biographies. Unique memoirs like Michael "Mickey" Cohen's 1975 attempt contain self-serving hearsay, predicated on shielding the author and his relatives, wisely fearful of offending living adversaries, and censored to accommodate certain politicians and celebrities. Rockaway praised Mickey's autobiography as "something of a classic," although skepticism should remain the rule of thumb for this type of material. Revisionist history told through sketchy timelines rarely provides an ironclad story.

Entertainment, popular culture, and politics are strange, yet permanent, bedfellows. Mickey's complex life links them all to crime. When the money and power-hungry entertainment industry developed, members of organized crime corrupted it. No other industry could churn money as fast, while perpetuating illusions about American life; how and where we eat, dress, and even talk are functions of show business.

Mickey was part of a unique American paradigm in which heroes were made out of bad guys.

"By any standard, Mickey Cohen was a piece of work," said *Life* magazine.

Part One

From Brooklyn to Los Angeles

1913–1938

1.

Once Upon a Time in Boyle Heights

Meyer Harris (Michael) Cohen was purportedly born in Brownsville, Brooklyn, during 1913, although he once admitted to the FBI that he was actually born September 4, 1911. Several modern archivists cite July 29, 1914, as his birthday; 1914 is the birth year on his burial plaque. Like many entertainment celebrities, Mickey enjoyed creating disparities about his age, always a little younger.

Brownsville is located in eastern Brooklyn, and was at the time a predominantly white, cold-water tenement ghetto known as "Jerusalem of America" because of its Jewish population, the largest concentration in the United States. The pleasantries of old Brooklyn, like the beach at Coney Island or the Nostrand Avenue trolley car, were not readily available to the Cohens. Even the immigrants in northern Manhattan and the Bronx looked down their noses at Brownsville, Margaret Sanger's choice for the nation's first birth-control clinic. Illiteracy was common and residents lived in fear. Violence is the reoccurring theme of writings about the dirty, tough, lawless community.[1]

The infamous ironfisted Shapiro brothers ran Mickey's neighborhood, and controlled the whorehouses and local merchants, who begrudgingly accepted Shapiro slots and vending machines. The local Jews who had departed Eastern

Europe had little to lose by becoming criminals. The old Five Points area of Manhattan had produced its share of Jewish gangsters, and rapidly spread to Brownsville.

Mickey's father Max, who died when Mickey was less than two months old, worked in the Brownsville fish business. He specialized in popular smoked varieties with unmistakable old-world tastes, a kosher staple in orthodox Russian-Jewish families like the Cohens. In his autobiography, Mickey dismisses his father with two sentences. He depicted his mother as saintly.[2]

Matriarch Fanny, originally from Kiev, Russia, had her hands full with a large fatherless family. Ben Hecht counted four sisters and a brother for Mickey. Redhead journalist Florabel "Carrot Top" Muir reported three boys and two girls. His lifetime of creating new versions confused journalists and close associates. The brood definitely included Louie, Harry, Sam, Pauline, Lillian, and Mickey. Yet the name Rose pops up in an FBI file as another sibling.

Fanny didn't speak English, but she understood the mechanisms for protecting her family in the new America. She knew how to keep food on the table, and utilized her survival sensibilities learned in the old country. Money was essential; it afforded protection as well as a means to secure staples in the concrete jungle. Mickey's mother wanted to keep her children, particularly her newborn and youngest, out of the worst environments. Writer Alfred Kazin knew Brownsville as "a place that measured all success by our skill in getting away from it."[3] Fanny headed west with daughter Lillian (Lillie) and little three-year-old Mickey in tow; due to financial restraints, she left the rest of the Cohen clan with relatives, but would reunite with them shortly. The New York that the Cohens left behind was aggressively anti-Semitic and a difficult place to raise a family without a father.

A steady Jewish migration to California and Florida had begun, and would continue for decades. Fanny chose Los Angeles, where the Jewish population had grown steadily from 500 in 1870 to 2,500 at the turn of century. Unfortunately, not all Eastern European Jews who moved west found the American dream so quickly attainable in the little pockets of a larger urban sprawl.[4]

Fanny sought refuge in another ghetto, Boyle Heights, and eventually sent for the rest of the family. Boyle Heights proved to be the Jews' little nirvana, at least compared to overly urbanized and crowded Brownsville. The sprawling provincial community in Los Angeles offered a warmer climate and relaxed atmosphere that fostered a seemingly easier way of life. Here the Jews embraced their culture and traditional values. The Breed Street Shul, opened when Mickey was ten, was on the corner of Brooklyn and Breed, and the Home of Peace Jewish cemetery was on Whittier Boulevard. Boyle Heights was a different kind of shtetl, where assimilation was available in the nearby world of the redesigned Hollywood Jews, many of whom had already abandoned the old ways.

Located on the east side of the Los Angeles River, Boyle Heights, named for Andrew Boyle, was undesirable property. No white men lived east of the river, where an acre of land cost twenty-five cents in the mid-to-late nineteenth century. After the completion of six bridges that connected Boyle Heights to greater Los Angeles, thanks to Mayor William Workman, land sold for $100 a parcel, large enough for a 1600-square-foot Spanish Colonial.

The almost identical homes lined street after street, with an occasional frame house, left over from the ranches, breaking the pattern. It was easy to grow roses, oleanders, and poinsettias in the southern California climate. Lemon, avocado, fig, and peach trees dotted the backyards. Even with some unpaved streets and an occasional hungry goat meandering about, this neighborhood appeared idyllic. However, this new kind of life had little appeal to the urbanized Jewish immigrant.

The frontier shtetl had its own Russian Town section, where the Cohens resided. The Los Angeles ghetto was not strictly Jewish like in New York: a mix of Italians and Mexicans lived in the same neighborhood. The provincial shopping area had dual-language signs outside the kosher butcher and poultry shops. The community had its share of little groceries and bakeries, a movie house, beauty shop, library, bank, and pool hall. By sticking with their little Boyle Heights pursuits, many English-speaking merchants and entrepreneurs eventually established dynasties in the recycling, meatpacking, garment center, aerospace, and furniture businesses.

People sat on front porches at night, particularly during the stifling summer. Children had full run of the streets; traffic was unheard of. Local blue-water beaches were only thirty minutes away.

One of the unlikely myths surrounding Mickey describes how at age three his mother got him a job selling newspapers, the *Los Angeles Record*, which later became the *Los Angeles Daily News*. Realistically, his first employment was to sit on the papers, to protect against the wind and petty theft, and likely nothing more.

Louie and Harry would drop an older six-year-old Mickey off on the corner of Soto and Brooklyn streets, the heart of the Jewish community, to sell the *Record*. His job was simple: collect two cents for each paper. The Cohens relied on the good will of local citizens to put the money in Mickey's hand, some even stopped to schmooze with the shy child who had little to say.

Mickey remembered: "It was a high box and my feet didn't touch the sidewalk. Women used to come by and kid me about eating things to make my legs grow longer... I used to stare at them blankly..."

Through his street exploits, he learned that it paid to be dishonest. Unfortunately, Harry, who was not as straight-laced or as religious as Sam was, became Mickey's surrogate father.

Mickey started his formal education at the Cornwall Elementary School. That lasted until second grade, when a federally sanctioned law unintentionally provided illicit work around the nation. Congress had passed the Eighteenth Amendment and the Volstead Act in 1919, which left the federal government responsible to enforce a dry country. Seven-year-old Mickey began his interest in bootlegging, fueled by most of his family. It was an easy way to make a buck, and a type of illegal activity easy to rationalize. Enter speakeasies and blind pigs, well-disguised drinking establishments that were precursors of the 21 Club, Stork, and El Morocco in New York. It was the time of flappers with Cupid's bow lips, F. Scott Fitzgerald and Zelda, Joan Crawford, and Al Capone's arrival in Chicago. Women drank spirits while they danced until dawn at speakeasies. Jewish gangs were in transition and began to carve out territories like any corporate entity.

"Organized crime was created by Prohibition. Before that there was just gangs beatin' each other up and minor shakedowns and heists...there were always crooked cops and judges... With Prohibition, crime became a business," was how Mickey summarized the changeover.

Writer Ben Hecht generously described Mickey's parents as "God-fearing and law-obeying"; perhaps an insight into the Cohens' mixed morality; Fanny overlooked her older boys' interest in bootlegging and late night gambling. Hecht's implication suggests that Mickey's older siblings benefited from their early years with a father who taught the difference between right and wrong.

God-fearing and law-obeying Fanny ran a gin mill out of their family-styled pharmacy/grocery store in the most Russian Orthodox section of Boyle Heights; Mickey would work the front, back, and knew how to operate the still. Harry and Louie operated a second location at Pico and Bond. Mickey described Harry and Louie's work as "pharmacists," but the local Board of Pharmacy also required a sanctioned "druggist" to be on hand.

A single parent like Fanny could not control Mickey, particularly after his growing street education and Harry's corrupting influence. He and the other uneducated Boyle Heights boys began making quick money in shady work. The American image was more than freedom; it was life on easy street, and crime was the easiest, and one of the few opportunities to make fast money.

The junior mobster spent his early childhood surrounded by bootleggers and the numbers racket. Trafficking in cocaine and alcohol provided the cash flow for strongholds in New York, while networks for gambling and extortion matured and extended to the West Coast.[5]

"I was really looking to make a buck at a very early age," Mickey once told Ben Hecht.

Newsboys fought each other for the best locations. By age eight, Mickey, who was good with his fists, had a highly desirable new corner at 7th and Broadway. He continued to sell the *Los Angeles Record* for two cents a sheet, and ran a dice game for the other newsboys in the alley behind the *Record* building.

He soon slept in the washroom of the *Los Angeles Examiner* so he would be available in time to sell the early editions, a courtesy of city editor Jim Richardson, whom Mickey sometimes helped sober up and find his way to his desk. Mickey was his own Horatio Alger, listened to any reporter who would speak with him, began to read the papers every day, and would continue to do so the rest of his life.

He was a quick study, despite his shoddy formal education; he became a student of the street. He wasn't good at numbers, but knew how many stolen papers would get him a "big Jew hot dog," a piece of bologna, or candy. He took a second job holding "little pieces of paper" for some of the older teenaged kids. According to him, the numbers racket netted him an exaggerated nickel per transaction.[6]

By age nine, Mickey graduated to delivering bootleg booze packages. One day when he was alone with an elder druggist, the police arrested him for throwing food at officers who came to inspect the family store. Of course they found the illegal bootlegging operation. He was too young to know about payoffs or other methods of dealing with nosy police. Louie's brother-in-law worked at the equivalent of the district attorney's office. Mickey watched as the judge chastised the police and threw out the case, a pattern that would repeat itself often during his life.

Brother Sam, an orthodox Jew, saved Mickey from reform school for stealing "this goddam Abba-Zaba candy made out of peanut butter, and I was nailed with a crate of it!"[7]

Mickey also ventured into the heist business. His target was the box office of the local Columbia Theater. Hecht found it surprising: "No Jewish morality, no family decency had touched his spirit. He launched his attack on society as if sired by a long line of pirates." The heist earned Mickey a seven-month stay in a reform school at Fort Hill in Los Angeles, where he received regular beatings with a bicycle tire. "For any old thing," recalled Mickey.

Once back in public school, Mickey had better things to do with his time than study his lessons. "I can't do a thing with the boy," lamented his mother when teachers complained to her about his truancy. He was too busy muscling in on the best street corners to pay attention to his education. He tried Hebrew school and only ended up in fights. Fanny placed him in a vocational school called the Alvarado, filled with tougher loudmouth kids. This too failed. He would become the only member of his family who didn't graduate college. He quit school well before age fifteen. According to Hecht, sometimes prone to exaggeration, Mickey was unable to read or count beyond five until he reached his twenties.

He hung out in pool halls with professional hustlers. He also learned how to handle dice like a pro mechanic; he could palm several cubes at once and make a switch. He became accustomed to a regular illicit cash flow.

Mickey mentioned his attraction to and problems with his unique early income:

> I got a kick out of having a big bankroll in my pocket. Even if I only made a couple hundred dollars, I'd always keep it in fives and tens so it'd look big. I had to hide it from my mother, because she'd get excited when she'd see a roll of money like that. One time when I was twelve, I left my pants hanging over the chair with three, four hundred dollars in my pocket—maybe a little extra than I usually had. So when my mother went to hang them up, this roll fell out and spread out all over the floor. She called in my brother Sam, and they must have thought I'd robbed a bank, because he kicked the shit out of me.

Big Brother Abe Roth, a popular prizefight referee, introduced him to more formalized pugilism. He met Roth at weekly luncheons, where he made mandatory appearances as part of his reform school probation. Mickey started boxing at age twelve, despite the known clichéd admonitions of Jewish mothers and grandmothers. It was a quick buck, and he decided not to tell his mother. Boxers Fidel LaBarba, Jackie Fields, and Mushy Callahan inspired him, while he fought four-rounders in Los Angeles at the Vernon and Olympic arenas, and illegal venues in Compton, Watts, and East Los Angeles.

Mickey's mother found out about his boxing from a local merchant.

> One day, the butcher stopped my mother—who didn't talk real good English—and said to her, "Mrs. Cohen, you must be proud your boy's boxing for the championship." So she says, "What's this boxing?"

He had always told his mother that he was going to the beach. According to him, boxing made no sense to her. However, her son was making money, and he loved the process: "...but my real pleasure was putting money together. Of course, if there was any way to steal the money, I'd steal it, too."

December 16, 1927, was a day that would change Mickey's life forever: he would learn the power of the press. A man named Hickman had kidnapped Marian Parker by claiming that her father, a bank clerk at Los Angeles First National Bank, had been in an automobile accident.

"I sold more papers on that day than I ever did before or since... We could sell papers then for whatever we could get, and people ate that one up. They couldn't read enough about it," commented Mickey on his windfall. The ultimate macabre murder and mutilation increased sales for three months.

He did have honest employment. His brother Sam suggested that he work for ladies dress manufacturers Hunt, Broughton, and Hunt. Mickey ran errands for Mrs. Hunt, sometimes to J. W. Robinson's department store. The Hunts liked Mickey, and brought East Coast buyers to see his fights. He proved to be a sociable young man, and people like the Hunts and their friends were his first introduction to a more educated and moneyed crowd. He began to make friends outside the limited shtetl, and developed a knack for ingratiating himself with distinctively different personalities.

Boyle Heights became a haven for drug gangs. The quaint City Terrace business area, with its red brick buildings, developed into a staging area for drugs smuggled from Mexico, particularly Tijuana. The local Mexican importers were no match for Mickey, who had his own little gang, and drove his own car, likely underage. It was easy for him to muscle in on existing territory, and skim out a living from the less organized criminals. He wasn't comfortable in a small-time operation, and let his aspirations guide him to some of the more established criminal areas in the United States.

Mickey, like so many other Jews who found the shtetl confining, made a decision to leave his Yiddish-speaking home and success-driven family in search of an affluent and bohemian existence. Harry, his mentor, had already left for greener pastures and larger opportunities.[8]

2.

Not-So-Famous Jewish Boxers

Tough Jews like Mickey battled through the Roaring Twenties and then the depression by relying on physical toughness in a syndicate-controlled world. Boxing offered the rough training ground for entry into the rackets, with the thinly veiled legitimate ring work as a backdrop, and, as did organized crime, it attracted Napoleonic personalities. Jockey-sized Mickey, Meyer Lansky, Lepke (*Lepkele*—Yiddish for "Little Louis") Buchalter, Genovese family luminaries Punchy Illiano and Quiet Dom Cirillo, all boxed early in their careers.[1]

Popular fighters from Mickey's era included junior welterweight Mushy Callahan, Olympic gold medalist Jackie Fields (Finkelstein), Charles (Bud) Taylor (the Blond Terror of Haute), Newsboy Brown, and Maxie Rosenbloom.[2] Future entertainment mogul Adolph Zukor also boxed. Sensationalist heavyweight Mike Tyson[3] has referenced this historic period as inspirational.

Mickey utilized boxing as a way up the criminal, social, and business ladders. Many of the fight managers were Jewish, easing his entry; Mike Jacobs was the most famous. Mickey knew that he appeared ignorant, coarse, and hardly good-looking. Boxing would provide his first big exposure to the public without concern for his diction or looks.

While he was still in his early teens, his mother had remarried, and this influenced his decision to leave home. Hymie Rudin, a friend from Boyle Heights, and later part of Mickey's mob, suggested that he try boxing on the East Coast, a more active venue filled with opportunities. At age fifteen, he chose Cleveland so that he could be near his brother Harry, who was promoting fights on the side.

Jewish boxers proudly wore the Star of David on their trunks. Insiders called Mickey "the Jew Boy." The derogatory distinction made him popular with the Italians. Harry, who also operated a small drugstore, managed him. Ed Bang, one-time sports editor of the *Cleveland News*, promoted many of Mickey's fights. He boxed flyweight, bantamweight, or featherweight, but most of the time flyweight; it afforded him plenty of fights. He was no Benny Leonard—whose hair never seemed to move out of place—or Barney Ross, but Mickey worked steadily, both in and out of the ring. He developed a reputation as a sturdy boxer.

Barred from society's upper anti-Semitic crust, Mickey made the most out of boxing, where beginners received a dollar a round. When careers washed up, and they were no longer contenders, fighters made the natural transition to the rackets, already firmly linked to the boxing community. When he wasn't boxing, Mickey concentrated on his criminal activities, under the watchful eye of the elder bosses. His muscle work earned him a regular salary of $125 a week and he also freelanced on demand for independent heists.

Moe Dalitz,[4] Louis Rothkopf,[5] Morris Kleinman, and Sam Tucker were in charge of Cleveland. The resourceful group grew from small-time hustlers by investing their earnings in new equipment and ingenuity, the backbone of any enterprise, and focused on smuggling Canadian booze over "Jewish" Lake Erie (nicknamed for the predominance of Jewish bootlegging gangs).

In Cleveland, Mickey learned the cardinal rules of stealing: "The two biggest sins among heist men are when you drop somethin'... No wristwatches on. Nothin' that could come off... When you come back...you dump everything on the table. If someone holds back...—that calls for the death penalty."

Mickey agreed to rob a restaurant manager's own establishment during dinner. It was across from the 105th Street Police Precinct. He was recognized—subsequently he wore a mask—and arrested, but survived through a series of fixes, allowing him to avoid prosecution.

He went on the heavy: "Pistols, shotguns, Tommy guns. Whatever was handy. We specialized in gambling joints, cafes, and whorehouses." He would raise the joints, and have the patrons line the walls with their hands high in the air. Mickey's gang, a subsidiary of the local Hill Mob, consisted of seven boys who supplied the muscle.[6]

During this period, Mickey bonded with Jacob Harry "Hooky" Rothman. Mickey said of his friend, "No two people were ever any closer than me and Hooky… He was my right arm. He weighed 190 pounds and was built like a bull." He also began a romantic interest with new girlfriend Georgia, a beautiful redheaded, dainty, and pleasant companion. They set up house on and off for eight years; she cooked, took care of his clothes, and accepted Mickey's line of work, which included a code of silence. He was fond of Georgia's spaghetti dinners whipped up for all the boys.

Toward the end of his Cleveland tenure, Mickey accidentally beat up the wrong person. He recalled:

> I can still hear his wife yellin', "You got the wrong guy!" I was so aggravated at the tipster who fingered the wrong person and caused an innocent man to be hurt that I took care of this fellow in the same way I had handled the innocent person.

It was during this period that Mickey received his first exposure to national politics, coupled with the idea that forces outside the government could influence world change. The American Jewish mob developed an early awareness of Adolf Hitler. Getting Hitler and his associates was on the mind of many Jewish gangsters, as well as their executive counterparts in certain mainstream businesses.[7]

The end of prohibition dried up most bootlegging profits, and Mickey concentrated on his heavy work. In 1934 he and pal Frankie Niccoli robbed a cafeteria cashier in Cleveland; the take was three grand. In their defense, the young thugs gave up the cashier who was in on the job. After receiving a two-year sentence, immediate parole, and probation, Mickey kept at his new line of work. Two months after this arrest, April 21, FBI reports show an embezzlement conviction, but could not corroborate his two-year suspended sentence, and orders to leave Cleveland.

With over two hundred heavy stickups and close to three hundred heists to his credit, the Hill Mob found the diminutive workaholic a liability. They gave him a letter of recommendation, and sent him packing with only a fifteen-dollar-per-day guarantee.

His ticket to New York came courtesy of Eddie Borden, a columnist for *The Ring* magazine, who suggested that Mickey become a regular contract boxer at Stillman's Gym in New York. Mickey refocused on boxing, weighed 117 pounds, and ran every day in Central Park. He lived at the Abbey Hotel, home of popular Club Abbey, where in 1931 the infamous Dutch Schultz gun battle took place.

Borden said of his early days with Mickey,

> He had a fighting heart and would tackle anybody. He wouldn't listen to me, and I quit managing him when he wanted to go up against anybody for the purse. He never had any idea of the value of money. He liked to dress well and would spend his last twenty dollars on a hat.

Eddie Borden remained a close friend.

Mickey felt at home with the New York mob; they served as surrogate parents; all his bills were paid. Despite a pocketful of cash and plenty of women, his low self-esteem prevented him from pursuing the nightlife just yet.

His entry to the New York organization came courtesy of Johnny Dio, a fight aficionado and labor boss, and his brother Tommy Dioguardi; the former went to jail in the early seventies for stock fraud. Mickey also met Frankie Carbo, who controlled some of the boxing, and Johnny's uncle Jimmy Doyle (James Plumeri), a name that would filter through JFK assassination conspiracy theories. The young boxer also palled around with fighter Sammy Dorfman, never a major contender, although he won his first forty-three bouts. Tony Canzoneri, another of his new acquaintances, was one of the best fighters of his era. He won two titles before the age of twenty-two, eventually becoming a three-division champion.

Mickey made the most of his New York contacts, including sportswriter Damon Runyon, who remained a lifelong friend. "Whenever I was out to the coast and Damon came out there, I would sit with him for an hour at a time, either at the Brown Derby or right across the street at Mike Lyman's." The cast of shared inspirations for Broadway characters included the real life High Pockets Farrinaci, Louie the Lip, Cheesecake Ike, and Red-Nosed Whitey.

Mickey always spoke affectionately of Owney "The Killer" Madden, a criminal who dressed in expensive suits, mingled in high society, and became his first mentor in organized crime.[8]

"Owney was really a guy to respect and admire… His faithfulness to his own kind is the strongest thing a man can have," he said of his idol.

Despite his upwardly mobile social calling and illicit day jobs, Mickey spent much of his time inhaling liniment mixed with sweat. Local newspapers in almost every state regularly reported on his boxing exploits. He maintained a respectable national ranking amongst the top in his weight. However, Mickey bashers insisted that he had a glass chin, couldn't take a punch, and gave up easily. Ben Hecht fondly remembers him as a decent prizefighter in the heavier 135-pound division, yet most of his fights in New York were in the 116–118-pound range.

Mickey's overall fight record included a few highlights. In 1931, he fought Buffalo-born Tommy Paul (Gaetano Papa), a featherweight titleholder, at the Equestrium in Cleveland. Paul, a hands-down styled boxer, defended his featherweight title ten times during an eight-month period—a record. He liked to say that Paul felled him with an early head butt that finished his boxing career, although records indicate that Mickey kept at it. He racked up losses to Jimmy Vaughn, Dicky O'Leary, Johnny Mitchell, Paul Dazzo, and George Annarino. In May of 1933 he fought featherweight champion Baby Arizmendi in Tijuana, a future world titleholder, but lost by a knockout in the third round. He faced future welterweight champion Freddie "Red" Cochrane two years later and lost in the second round. Although there is no general record of Mickey's health during his boxing years, the pounding had to take its toll on the young pugilist.

He would end his career with a record of sixty victories, twenty-five knockouts, and sixteen losses. He had six draws and eleven no-decisions. He would testify years later to Senator Estes Kefauver that he was the star of thirty main events. He recalled seventy-nine pro fights, with five against world champions, including Chalky Wright during 1933 in Los Angeles at the Olympic Auditorium.

"I didn't beat any of 'em but I fought hard," Mickey later told reporters.

Despite his highbrow contacts, Mickey's tenure in New York was shaky. Robbery arrest records made him a liability there too, a situation that did not please the local mob bosses. The FBI again could not corroborate his arrest record, but it remains the likely propelling force out of the Big Apple. Unpolished Mickey was a bad fit.

He was soon back in Cleveland, and part of an organized gang. During this period he became aware of Benny Siegel, as Mickey liked to call him.[9] Bugsy periodically sent him to do muscle work in Los Angeles, the beginning of a long association. Mickey's daily contact in Cleveland was Louis "Babe" Triscaro, who was the labor boss and reputed later to be germ-phobic Jimmy Hoffa's link to the Teamsters in town.

Mickey, still known as the Jew Boy, worked as a fulltime stickup guy, a rooter. The parent gang was the Cleveland Syndicate, whose members now included leader Moe Dalitz, Lou Rothkopf, Morris Kleinman, Sam Tucker, Sam "Game Boy" Miller, Thomas Jefferson McGinty, and Al and Chuck Polizzi. Critical author Ed Reid dismisses Mickey's work under Dalitz, since his gang controlled all the territory, and wouldn't allow someone like Mickey to chisel out a significant stake.

Mickey's unbridled ambition led him to hold up joints that were off limits, which incurred the wrath of some mobsters. Others offered him tolerance and protection, and admired his moxie.

As early as 1936, the mob sent him to Chicago to work with Jewish casino operator Joe Barron and lay low. The gambling joint had a pleasant restaurant as a front, where he enjoyed the Jewish cuisine, something he had missed in Cleveland. Napoleonic bully Mickey prided himself on slapping around guys in the card room.

Hecht wrote that the joint was crooked, a "flat store" or "bust out." Mickey's job was simple: watch the card room. It was an easy chore, until a hit disturbed the serenity of his workroom. A barrage of bullets riddled the plate glass windows, and when the smoke had cleared, the cops pinched him for murder.

He knew he was in deep trouble: "Jesus Christ, I certainly ain't going to get out right away."

He accepted his police station bunk as his new home. Spike Hennessey, owner of the Lincoln Hotel and leader of the St. Louis gang Egan Rats, saw to Mickey's release—no charges, no bail. Police connections could overcome anything, even murder.

Mickey also pulled jobs on his own with his black mask and Tommy gun. He would blow the money on fifty-dollar hats, sometimes two a day. He kept enough "case" money in reserve for food.

When Al Capone got wind of Mickey's audacious activities, he ordered happy-go-lucky Greasy Thumb Guzik to close down Mickey's craps game. "No dice" was Mickey's response to intimidation. Former bagman Jake Guzik, financial backbone of the entire Capone operation, whose money-handling talents earned him his nickname, was unaccustomed to any challenges and referred to Mickey as a "nervy young punk." Despite Mickey's and others' recollections, his relationship with Al Capone had to have taken place years earlier, as Capone was incarcerated.

Mickey described the resolution with Guzik and crony Michael "Hinky Dink" Kenna:

> It is now about five nights later, and I'm standing out in front of the joint waiting for any of the cop squads that would come by so that I could weed them…a ten-dollar or twenty-dollar bill would carry the coppers. The goddamn snow was up to my knees… I'm a son of a bitch if a black car don't come by with this machine gun and barroom! I had on a camel's hair coat that, boy, I was really in love with… I didn't even fall because I didn't want to get my coat dirty.

Others report that he soiled his new duds outside his favorite tonsorial establishment. He heeded the warning, but kept his craps game open.

Capone liked Mickey's flagrant independence. He could spot the ego-flattering similarities, and asked Mickey to stop by the Capone offices. Heartless, devoid of any conscience, and capable of murder were the right attributes for Capone. Journalist Bert Bacharach, father of popular music composer Burt, confirmed for Mickey that Capone was smitten by the personal similarities; they even looked enough alike.

Capone made over $100,000,000 a year and dominated Chicago in a way that was unheard of in other cities. The payroll was over $300,000 per week, and corruption was widespread; more than one-half of the Chicago police force worked for him. Mattie (Amedoe) Capone, the youngest of seven brothers, invited Mickey to Sunday dinner. Capone became another father figure for fledgling Mickey. He kissed him on both cheeks, complimented him, and stuffed money into his pockets.

Mickey jumped to the next level; he was boss of card operations and craps games. He and Mattie ran a new poker game in the Chicago Loop, and he became friendly with Capone brother Ralph, who ran much of Al's operations.

Mickey was enamored with Capone's opulent life. He had fifty elaborate rooms in the corner-property art deco Metropole Hotel, two floors with private elevators, service bars, twenty-four-hour gambling and carousing with women. Police, politicians, and attorneys waited their turn during business hours to make deals with the big boys. Mob life was full of empty suits.

Mickey had free reign, and gravitated toward boxing with Mattie's help. When Capone advised him against it, Mickey wisely stopped.

He exacerbated his Chicago problems by bludgeoning a man to death in a restaurant or drugstore. Hit man Katsy, also known as a goon taxi driver, had wounded Mickey, who beat him to a pulp.

"I had very poor control of my temper in those days, so I grabbed the gun out of this guy's hand and pistol-whipped him right in front of all the customers. He was a bloody mess," Mickey remembered.

Even mentors like Capone and Frank Costello, Prime Minister of the Underworld, had second thoughts about keeping Mickey in the Windy City. Following a trial for the beating, Capone's fixer advised Mickey to take a powder.

Years later, he would claim that the Chicago Loop operation was all his: "Nobody could understand how I was able to operate on my own." He had the help of a local police captain who "bent over backwards to let me do some good for myself. He was a great guy—a very honest fellow."

Girlfriend Georgia endured Mickey through his Chicago days; she eventually married, with his permission.

16

Several shootings later, he left Chicago. Some authors cite 1939, although several FBI accounts report Mickey sightings in Los Angeles as early as 1937, the likelier timeline, and more consistent with his peripatetic early criminal work.

Mickey did stopover to see his brother Harry in Detroit. He was still disillusioned with his mother's remarrying, an impetus to spend more time with father-figure Harry, with whom he pulled petty scams around town. At sporting events, they masqueraded as vendors, and talked workers out of their money and merchandise.

Detroit was always a Jewish town, run primarily by the Purple Gang and the Little Jewish Navy, and site of the most brutal Jewish-on-Jewish mob hit against the Purple Gang.[10] While there, Mickey remained a personal protégé of Rothkopf from Cleveland, who maintained a solid connection with Meyer Lansky. Lansky let Rothkopf know he needed someone to watch Bugsy Siegel, and Rothkopf, who had a lot of faith in Mickey, strongly suggested sending him to look after the mob's new investments. The top brass created a job for Mickey: keep an eye on Bugsy.

According to Mickey, Rothkopf told him on the telephone, "Look, Ben Siegel's out on the Coast and we want ya to go right out there as soon as you can."

The FBI reported that threats of dragging Mickey back to Ohio for parole violations motivated his move west. Author Reid maintained the unlikely scenario that Mickey was frightened of reprisal by the East Coast boys so he appealed to Bugsy and said, "I want to take a powder, come to L.A. and work for you."

Motivations aside, Mickey was off to Los Angeles during the inception of the syndicate's Golden Age.

3.

Tinsel Town

Twenty-five-year-old Mickey traveled west with a man identified as Joe Gentile, a career player for Capone. The young entrepreneur and his older domo pal established a base of operations at a modest Los Angeles hotel. Under the watchful eye of Joe G., as some knew him, Mickey initially supported himself with heavy work, the usual stickup activity. He was happy to be back with his remaining family in Los Angeles, and enjoyed the southern California climate while adjusting to the rapidly changing city.

When he arrived, Los Angeles was still raw, and made for criminals. Helen Gahagan Douglas, a former actress and representative from Los Angeles' Fourteenth District, knew the fragile landscape: "Frances Starr hadn't exaggerated when she said that Hollywood Boulevard resembled a movie set built to collapse the moment the stage manager cried, 'Strike it!'" The expansive locale was easy prey for Mickey and his East Coast contacts.[1]

Los Angeles was a town without rules, where bookmakers operated in the open and slot machines were rampant. A recall ousted corrupt Mayor Frank Shaw; he was replaced with Judge Fletcher Bowron. Shaw, who had been in the supermarket business with his brother Joe, operated with the local Sicilians, who ran an unsophisticated yet controlling interest in the West.

Some, like singer Lorna's father, producer Sid Luft, who favored a more provincial description of Los Angeles, were in denial about the criminal activities: "This was a very, very clean town. Nothing like Detroit or Chicago."[2]

In 1937, Los Angeles police squad cars responded to 83,315 calls that resulted in 17,529 arrests, too much for local jails. Sheriff Eugene "Gene" Biscailuz was pleased with his overcrowded operation at the Hall of Justice, and emphasized that any cook who worked for him had to be "proud of his [membership] card." During this period, Biscailuz began a relationship as Mickey's "father confessor." Mickey frequently flashed his own miniature Highway Patrol badge, supplied by the sheriff.[3]

Illegal gambling clubs, the principle form of entertainment, lined the Sunset Strip and nearby towns like Redondo Beach and Culver City, the latter home to MGM studios.[4] Tango parlors filled the adjoining beautiful Manhattan Beach, a community that boasted of its madam, who attended all the city council meetings. The police and local governments allowed the Hollywood mob full run of the little cities at night. The Los Angeles police had no rights on the politically independent Strip. Only Sheriff Biscailuz had jurisdiction over the bookmakers, madams, and after-hour joints. The symbiotic relationship between the sheriff and the mob had existed for years.

The misogynist Hollywood era was also in its heyday. Los Angeles was a Sodom and Gomorrah, filled with tens of thousands of girls who flocked to town to become the next Betty Grable, the sexy pinup with the sensational legs. Author Lee Mortimer described the city as an "Elysian fields for lonely-heart and introduction clubs, many palpable call services."

From the day he arrived, Mickey was all over town in fancy clothes and cars. He was out every night, playing the role of the consummate schmoozer; he knew how to work the glitzy crowd as well as anyone. He recalled: "I was out with ten different broads every night, and I was in every cabaret…"

However, he had practical business realities to overcome; he was technically working for Bugsy, with whom he didn't rush to solidify his relationship. "Actually we never even gave a fuck about Benny. We were just rooting, just taking off scores…" During his early tenure, Mickey learned that his former girlfriend Georgia, from Cleveland, had taken ill. He performed extra heists to send her money.

Handsome and somewhat smooth-talking Bugsy had started his operations at his sister's house at chic 721 N. Doheny Drive in Beverly Hills. He immediately held a meeting with all the top mobsters and brazenly let them know that he planned to organize their operations, and that he was the sole and final arbiter of anything illegal.

George "Les" Bruneman, part of the old-time Crawford-McAfee mob that operated gaming clubs in the resort areas south of Los Angeles, didn't agree with the new splits offered by Bugsy. Bruneman had aspirations of controlling all the gambling operations in southern California. On July 19, 1937, a little over a month after Bugsy had hit town, three bullets hit Bruneman while he walked on the promenade at Redondo Beach, forty-five minutes south of Hollywood. He stumbled into a local movie house and an ambulance was summoned. He remarkably survived a punctured lung, and defiantly announced he was going to reopen his clubs, after spending six weeks in the hospital. On October 25, eleven shots caught him while he drank at the Roost Café on West Temple Street. The five assailants also wounded his blonde nurse Alice Ingram and killed an innocent bystander, who had tried to record the license plate number on the getaway car. After Bruneman fell to the floor, two of the assailants drew forty-five automatics; one shooter handled two guns, and the duo pumped another five shots into Bruneman to guarantee the job. Bruneman, armed with two guns, had just bought a round of drinks for the fifteen patrons. Italian mob leader Jack Dragna and Bugsy purportedly paid off notorious hit man and future FBI informant Frank "The Bomp" Bompensiero three days later. Bugsy and Tony "The Hat" Cornero (Stralla) now had full reign in the little beach communities, something Mickey would capitalize on.[5]

The more macabre aspects of taking control slowly surfaced; the newspapers began to cover more murders and beatings. It wasn't all Mickey's doing or influence; some revisionists even link him to the Bruneman murder, but he spent much time answering questions at police stations. Within a year of his arrival, he and his ruffians pulled over eighty stickups without a single arrest. His later arrest record included three for bookmaking, two for cutting phone wires, assault with a deadly weapon, and vagrancy. Police released him the same day as most of his arrests. He had already learned the power of legal, police, and political connections.

Independent-thinking Mickey, of course, had checked in with Bugsy, as per the agreement with Lansky. He kept his distance, reserving judgment and comments on Bugsy's style and personality, while both dressed-to-the-nines newcomers ingratiated themselves with the movie stars. Siegel said of him, "I like his balls, and I think Mickey can be a big help to me." Once he and Bugsy had a working relationship, Bugsy would ask him to handle certain jobs, like sticking a joint on the Sunset Strip owned by Eddie Neales, who was a friend of writer

Milton Holmes, and played tennis at the Beverly Hills Tennis Club, to the dismay of many of the members. The club had accused Neales of skimming off the top of charity events held at the posh watering hole.

The stickup on the Strip was a classic Hollywood job. Mickey held a gun on the ritzy patrons while everyone handed over their money and jewelry. The miniature hardnose glanced over at a good-looking broad, but resisted temptation, since it was not polite to socialize while holding a shotgun. Outside one of his bruisers told him that they had just held up musician and bandleader Harry James and actress Betty Grable.

Years later when Mickey became one of the darlings of the social scene, he found himself at a gathering with Grable and his friend Florabel Muir, who thought the reunion with Grable was funny, and reminded him that he had once robbed her. Mickey, always conscious of his image, tried to apologize for his past, and said that perhaps he wasn't even at the scene of the crime.

Grable whispered in his ear, "We were insured anyway."

Bugsy and Mickey were not in Los Angeles to promote the heist business. Their larger job was to infiltrate the Italian mob and see how much they could carve out for the Jews. Mickey specialized in gambling, by now somewhat of an expert. The Sicilians were not pleased with Bugsy and Mickey's activities, and certainly did not want to share the movie business or gambling coffers. Mickey and Bugsy's formidable adversary was Jack Dragna, and he would play a significant role in Mickey's rise to power. Despite descriptions as an Italian relic, a Mustache Pete who was unwilling to flow with the new corporate tide, short-tempered Dragna was a big earner for the family and no pushover. The traditional ways of the Italian mob would prove an arduous challenge, but it appeared that he and the other Italians had underestimated the Jews.

Mickey, who had ties to both the Italian and Jewish mobs, was not afraid of Dragna. From his jail cell, Charles "Lucky" Luciano (Salvatore Lucania) sent word to Dragna to back off and let Bugsy and Mickey set up their operations. Luciano originally had said that Bugsy "was heading west for his health and the health of all of us."[6]

Before Mickey's arrival, Dragna looked to mobster Johnny Rosselli (Filippo Sacco) for regular advice and physical help in modernizing the bookmaking and gambling operations. Handsome, smooth-talking Rosselli had already established himself as a big player with the movie studios. He extorted millions from their coffers by providing protection to movie moguls. Rosselli was no fan of the new Jews, but he mostly stayed out of Mickey's way, and often cooperated.[7]

The criminal power transition followed a logical course. The new Jewish mobsters pretended to ingratiate themselves with the Italians, while their main goal was to diminish, partner when necessary, or eliminate them. To accomplish their goals, they needed strong liaisons with the growing legitimate businesses.

If Mickey and Bugsy were to move up, they needed to court the local luminaries on a regular basis .[8] The real power brokers in town were movie moguls like Louis B. Mayer, Jack Warner, and Harry Cohn, each with his own police force.[9] Bugsy's first substantial business contacts were Warner and Mayer, two of the most powerful Jewish studio bosses. Actor George Raft made certain that Harry Cohn was also accessible to Bugsy. (Raft lived in an old world luxuriously decorated apartment across the street from Romanoff's, a popular restaurant.)[10] The studio bosses appeared glad to have Bugsy in town, particularly after the years of Sicilian extortion. The moguls now had a direct pipeline at the local level to the growing national Jewish syndicate. In exchange for that luxury, Bugsy and Mickey controlled the extras who appeared in the movies, a nickel-and-dime extortion racket that added up. Mickey set up the more lucrative "insurance business," having the moguls fork over big bucks to guarantee smooth sailing on the elaborate sound stages.

Sam Giancana's nephew (godson) and half-brother, Sam and Chuck, acknowledged the movie business cornerstone and the symbiotic relationship with the mob: "Mooney [Giancana] told Chuck that the studios were too lucrative to abandon. 'We're not about to turn our back on so much money and power…they're our friends now. Rosselli's got them in his pocket.'" The list included Harry Cohn, Harry Warner, and L. B. Mayer—Columbia, Warner Brothers, and MGM. The mob boys had their fingers in a large pie.

Mickey would soon meet all the studio bosses, and he would do favors for them, particularly Cohn, who was a notorious bully, famous for his vulgar remarks and behavior: "If you've got talent, I'll lick your ass, but if you don't I'll kick it." He was one of the first Hollywood characters to use "fuck" in routine conversation.

Mickey initially was more comfortable with many of the studio bosses and their ilk rather than organization leaders or other legitimate industry owners, and capitalized immediately on the familiar speech patterns and prevailing business attitudes.

He quickly latched onto the parallels between organized crime and show business. The show business wannabees were bright, but didn't do well in school, and often shied away from books in order to favor their own creative fantasies. Entertainment and organized crime nurtured each other's business interests, and attracted a coterie of shady characters who legitimized their activities in the movie business with panjandrums like "manager" and "producer."[11] The mob easily exploited the creative pool. Many of them were fond of mobsters, along with everything else connected to the entertainment business, from theater tickets to transportation.[12]

Mickey and Bugsy acted swiftly to move in on all the ripe existing businesses. Like Bugsy, Mickey was a front man assigned to report on the prevailing attitudes and possibilities for the growing Jewish mob, which offered management advice. The concomitant political infiltration process required a lot of glad-handing and graft. The locals were already used to having thugs around, mostly of a less polished variety than Bugsy and even Mickey. For many, the new Jewish boys were a breath of fresh air. Having a ready supply of out of town muscle to back up threats of violence helped get the fledgling Jewish mob off the ground.

During Mickey's first year in Los Angeles, he met brown-eyed LaVonne, an Irish Catholic. Author Reid highlighted the love-at-first-sight romance:

> If Mickey Cohen ever loved anybody more than himself it must have been LaVonne Norma Weaver, a pretty little redhead and fashion model just out of high school when she met the hoodlum in the Bandbox Club in Los Angeles.[13]

The love-smitten Hollywoodite said this, and little more, about his first meeting with LaVonne: "She was some kind of dance instructor at some of the studios. She had me intrigued, because she also flew a plane and all that bullshit." (Since she was still alive when Mickey's scant autobiography finally appeared, he wisely felt protective of her, and supplied minimal personal detail about their relationship.)

LaVonne, who also modeled teen-age dresses, was going steady with a pilot, but Mickey soon changed all that. He knew he had to make a good impression. On his first date with her, he insists that there was no dancing, handholding, or passes. But he did arrive for the date at 11 p.m., four hours late. The couple stopped at his residence, smoke-filled by his waiting pals. After an hour of introductions, he treated her to dinner "at the best place at town."

Mickey craved respectability and social acceptance, and knew that a gun moll would dash his hopes. LaVonne fit his idea of a proper girlfriend; she quickly became part of his life. She could pass for a debutante or finishing school graduate, compared to most of the club girls. Her voice indicated a cultured background, and at least she spoke proper English. She was not shy about correcting his speech, or asking him to improve his diction.

One Passover after Mickey's arrival, he sent for longtime pal Hooky Rothman. "You gonna have it good here," Mickey told Hooky while he was still at the Santa Fe railroad station.

Not everyone shared Mickey's assessment of Los Angeles. He encountered many East Coast show business people who were initially disappointed in Hollywood dreamland, a place they had flocked to in order to beat the oppressive system found in more established East Coast cities. Los Angeles Jews were a subculture of dreamers, who had unrealistic expectations about the glamorous new digs. Hollywood life proved simultaneously to be the solution and the new problem; it required substantive socioeconomic adjustments. Mickey had one leg up on the bewildered East Coast crowd; he was already familiar with the expansive terrain, which was devoid of a cultural backbone. Intellectual expectations didn't encumber him; he was there to make the money.

Mickey's Jewish identity remained the foundation of his personal sensibilities. Larger Los Angeles was not a Jewish-friendly city. The prevailing attitudes toward Jews were negative, fueled by old political and social theories. Anti-Semitism ran deep within the Mafia, who often blamed the Jews for committing the crimes. Some theorists claim that the Mafia ultimately exploited the Jews for their age-old stereotypical financial skills. Regardless, legitimate Jewish and non-Jewish businesses increasingly embraced Jewish criminals for protection; mom-and-pop stores and restaurants had to show allegiance to either the Jews or Italians in order to survive.

Anti-Semitism was so pervasive that Jewish women lied about their religion in order to get employment; many corporations did not hire Jews. Areas like Beverly Hills and Brentwood, despite their growing Jewish populations, were decidedly Christian. All schools sung religious hymns at Christmas, and the Reformed Wilshire Boulevard Temple was a controversial example of assimilation, with its churchlike environment and choir.

Zionist-leaning Mickey shared Bugsy's interest in Jewish causes, particularly in view of the recent success of Adolf Hitler. Many Jewish syndicate executives paid close attention to overseas activities affecting Jews. Bugsy had his own brand of Jewish political activism. In 1937, he stayed at the same villa in Italy as two Nazi leaders, and promptly informed his hostess, Dorothy DiFrasso, that he was planning to knock off both Germans. DiFrasso, Count DiFrasso's wife, had invited him to visit at the same time that the Count was entertaining Joseph

Goebbels and Hermann Göring, respectively Hitler's propaganda minister and air force leader.[14]

"You can't do that!" replied the Countess.

Bugsy didn't understand and answered, "Sure I can. It's an easy set-up the way they're walking around here." Movie mogul Jack Warner was in town promoting *The Life of Emile Zola* and was privy to Bugsy's assassination plans. Bugsy called Lansky for permission to bump off Mussolini too. Lansky told him that he was operating independently, and not to contact any local Mafia. Warner single-handedly prevented Bugsy from breaking up the Rome-Berlin Axis. His take was all Hollywood: "I talked him out of it on the grounds we couldn't fix the local harness bulls if we got caught."

On November 9, 1938, Hitler put his political theories into practical use. Kristallnacht, the Night of the Broken Glass, witnessed the unleashing of Nazi mobs in Germany and in Austria, eager to torch synagogues, break shop windows, and beat anyone suspected of being Jewish. Over one hundred Jews died that night, marking the beginning of the Holocaust. Things would change forever, abroad and in the United States, inside and outside the mob.[15]

Mickey was not an observant Jew and had abandoned daily Jewish traditions. Nevertheless, the catastrophic event had a profound affect on his beliefs and he, like many Jewish mobsters, would keep a close watch on world Jewish affairs and future Zionist activities.

The raw Angeleno had to find a way to succeed during the worst of times for Jews, and his Jewish defense interests took hold early. He wrote of an episode with a man named Robert Noble, described as having "a lot of notoriety." Public figure Noble was notorious for his outspoken views as a Nazi Bundist, member of the subversive association Friends of Progress, and had the attention of radio and newspapers to spew his venom; Mickey called it "rabble-rousing anti-Jew" sentiments. During a temporary incarceration, which included lengthy questioning, he encountered Noble and another man. Recognizing them, he arranged to have the men put in a cell with him, and then he mercilessly beat both of them under the auspices of the police. The two men, face to face with snarling Mickey, tried to move toward the perimeter of the cell, which the police had locked.

Mickey's enthusiasm for these altercations comes through in his memoir. He was proud of his early reputation as a *bulvan*—Yiddish for "crude ox." "I started bouncing their heads together," recalled Mickey. "With the two of them, you'd think they'd put up a fight, but they didn't do nothing." Mickey's embellishments continued:

So I'm going over them pretty good. The wind-up is that they're climbing up on the bars...they're screaming and hollering so much everybody thinks it's a riot... The jail chief... Bright comes running down himself...he can't get in. These two guys are still up on the bars screaming about their rights and, "Why did ya throw us in with an animal, with a crazy man?"... I've gone back to my corner and picked up the newspaper... He comes over and says, "You son of a bitch, what happened now?"

Mickey remained calm, knowing that he had the cooperation of the police. "What are you asking me for? I'm sitting here reading the newspaper. Them two guys got into a fight with each other..."

Nothing came of it since he convinced the police that the men were anti-American and anti-General McArthur. In 1942, authorities put Noble in prison for sedition.

The undersized *shtarker*—"tough guy"—earned a reputation as an enforcer for politically correct causes. Mickey's strong political feelings were public knowledge, and he would continue his involvement as a lobbyist. Anti-Nazi activity was growing throughout the country, and he received requests from organizations like the Writers Guild for help in dealing with Nazi infiltrators. He and his goons assisted frightened local authorities in breaking up Nazi meetings. Since he had no interest in the civil rights of anti-Semites, he proved the right party for the job.

Hollywood and Los Angeles was his world to succeed or fail. With Bugsy taking the lead, it appeared Mickey had really struck gold.

Part Two

Headliners:
Mickey and Bugsy

1938–1947

4.

Setting up Shop

Word of Mickey's early business success naturally traveled east, and he became a host for the boys from out of town, many eager to meet the bosses in the movie industry. He didn't entertain in his home since his guests, "…wanted to see a broad." He had no problem in that arena: he had a stable of "…starlets—little broads—around. I don't mean whores, at times they were what you call, call girls…" Despite his and many of his friends' denials, he quickly established himself as a pimp. He also organized a unique welcome service for tourist mobsters: he would supply them with transportation and weapons.

Mickey emulated the conventional corporate style. He first treated a guest to dinner, and then they exchanged money. There were train junkets to New York, elaborate parties on their way to a prizefight or to nowhere. The boys played cards, often with some of the top business people and gamblers from Los Angeles.

Folklore credits gambler Nick "Nick the Greek" Dandolas for Mickey's lightning-fast entry into racetrack bookmaking. The well-read Greek was full of philosophical stories about long life, and told Mickey how a sect in India regularly lived to be 180 by eating certain breads and breathing correctly. Mickey stuck with ice cream.

"You're doing it all the hard way," said the Greek. "A smart kid doesn't have to go on the heavy to make a living."

The Brown Derby restaurant meeting with the Greek changed Mickey's life and business focus. He accepted the parental advice, and developed more businesses that did not require a financial exchange at gunpoint. Within three days, he set up shop as a bookmaker, only a few yards from the racetrack, in full view of Pinkerton detectives.

The nouveau bookie expanded his gambling interests to meet local needs and national plans. In 1938, he began an extensive betting operation in Westwood, the village west of Beverly Hills, and home to UCLA.

In order to monitor the boxing action, particularly ancillary gambling and fixes, Mickey hung out at Olympic Stadium in Los Angeles, located south of Pico Boulevard at Sixteenth and Grand streets, in an area known for its cheap bars and hotels. Whenever he frequented the bouts, an entourage of pretty women, bodyguards, and bail bondsmen surrounded him. Associate and bondsman Abe Phillips watched the count on the till and fixes, while Harry Pregerson, then a law student, would help keep Mickey out of jail.

The Phillips socialized frequently with Mickey. Abe's wife Helen knew that he enjoyed teasing and she joked at his expense, "Go out and kill me a couple of people." Mickey had already developed an unusual sense of humor for someone in his line of work, and appeared tickled by Helen.

While Mickey's short arms stretched into every aspect of gambling, authorities had to take a public stance to satisfy complaining constituents. Sheriff Biscailuz created a special vice squad to deal with the gambling boom, and made it mandatory for any raid to target gambling joints. The offshore gambling boat *Rex*, docked neatly beyond the three-point-one-mile offshore limit, coyly operated under Biscailuz's nose for a few seasons. The *Rex*, represented by attorney Sam Rummel, had its own horse room that paid track odds, luring customers away from the local racetracks. Former San Francisco cab driver Tony Cornero ran the *Rex* and would later build the Stardust Hotel in Vegas. Bugsy had fifteen percent of the *Rex* action.

State Attorney General Earl Warren declared the *Rex* inside California territory and not in federal waters. Police launched a well-publicized raid on the boat from coastline headquarters at the Santa Monica Del Mar Hotel. The sheriff and his staff enjoyed regular long stays at the beach to protect the interests of local citizens. The resultant Keystone Cop raid, with fire hoses streaming water down on the little police launch, ended with the beleaguered press receiving free imported brandy, thrown overboard to their hired boats. A few gambling devices were seized, and the reporters called it a night. According to Florabel Muir, who attended the raids, a more accessible offshore boat, the *Texas*, "got the works." By 1939, all the gambling boats were gone, and the mob concentrated on its land-based gambling enterprises.

Since Mickey had acquired an independent streak that was somewhat tolerated back east, he didn't waste any time establishing this same reputation in Los Angeles. He robbed one of boss Dragna's bookmaking operations belonging to Louis Merli (also known as Salvatore "Dago Louie" Piscopo), a partner of Johnny Rosselli. Author James Morton described Mickey in those early years as "essentially wild, a killer, and a freelancer."[1]

The heist took place while two sheriff's deputies watched the joint, a thirty-phone shop. A sawed-off shotgun and the requisite revolvers got everyone's attention. The take was about thirty grand and some jewelry. After the robbery, word got back to Mickey that he should check in with Bugsy, who had arranged a meeting with Rosselli at attorney Jerry Geisler's office in Los Angeles. Geisler always took care of Mickey and Bugsy, but according to Mickey, "I wouldn't really call Jerry Geisler a mob attorney."[2]

At the Geisler meeting, Bugsy made it clear that Mickey screwed up by robbing one of Rosselli's boys. Bugsy, in accordance with Rosselli, wanted Mickey to kick back some or all of the score. It didn't sit well with Mickey; mobsters didn't kick back score money to anyone. As a token gesture of respect, he returned a tiepin that had sentimental value, and avoided a battle with Rosselli and Dragna. Rosselli, unlike Dragna, let cooler heads prevail, preferring to build an alliance with his new colleagues, rarely appearing self-motivated. Although the anger simmered, Bugsy and Mickey worked harder to control all the action by muscling in on Dragna's territory.

New jugular blood spilled through the Hollywood area, while Mickey expertly played both sides of the mob. He diminished his stickup work, focused more on gambling, and came to the rescue of other businesses, particularly if run by Jews. He offered protection against other bad guys who were also trying to make a living like him.

One of Mickey's competitors, Irish Jimmy Fox, was harassing two small Jewish independent bookmakers, who ran a legitimate drugstore near Beverly Hills, at San Vicente and Wilshire boulevards. Fox, like his predecessors, made money by muscling small business owners to pay protection money.

Mickey particularly disliked Fox. "He was a two-gun son of a bitch, and he carried a lot of weight around here—kind of like a czar."

The two bookies didn't like Fox or his deal, and they complained to an intermediary who appealed to Fox. Mickey was all ears when the same source contacted him, and he met with the bookies at bandleader Mike Lyman's restaurant.

Because of his mixed morality and bias, Mickey defended the bookies, and told them, "Ya tell him ya spoke to me, and ya tell him I said to take a good fuck for himself, and tell him it come from me."

He arranged a follow-up meeting with Fox at the home of one of the Jewish bookies. Fox bellowed something about Mickey's brother Harry, who had stiffed him on a bootleg deal.

Following words to this effect, "My feelings towards you ain't so goddamn good anyway," miniature tough guy Mickey shot Fox.

According to Mickey, Fox's wounds were minimal. That night, the police arrested Mickey during a prizefight at the Olympic Auditorium, and led him to believe that he had killed Fox. The resolution was typical for Mickey: no charges filed. Fox lived on and never bothered Mickey or the two Jewish bookmakers again.

Local problems like Fox and Bruneman did not require national intervention, but occasionally the front office contacted Bugsy and Mickey to deal with someone of waning popularity. During the initial productive years of the Mickey and Bugsy Show,[3] Harry "Big Greenie" Greenberg's (George Schachter) mob value diminished on both coasts, and he was "going." He had crossed mob leader Lepke, and had threatened to talk with New York District Attorney Thomas E. Dewey. Mickey originally had orders to monitor Greenberg, but his career was no longer salvageable.

Popular movie culture displayed Greenberg as a cuddly teddy bear of a victim who naively felt protected by Bugsy. Big Greenie was not naive, but had mistakenly played the authorities against the mob.

The word was passed down: "Keep him in tow until we get a couple of boys out there."

First Lepke put a hit out on Big Greenie, but it failed. Greenie left New York following deportation to his native Poland, lived under his real name, Schachter, in Montreal, and ultimately fled to Hollywood. Everyone above Bugsy in the syndicate no longer saw Greenie as a threat, and decided to leave him alone, and "give him a pass." Bugsy still wanted Greenie out of the way and made up his mind to get rid of him. Mickey likely knew Greenie's schedule; he left the safe house every night to drive to the drugstore to get a newspaper. Forty-eight-year-old Greenie was a sitting duck the Wednesday night of November 22, 1939. Big

Greenie was peacefully reading the morning newspaper when he was gunned down in his car. Mrs. Ida Schachter dressed in black for the inquest when she stated that she was unaware of her deceased husband's past.

Bugsy's murder indictment materialized in August 1940, along with Frankie Carbo, Mendy Weiss (acting boss of Murder, Inc.), and Harry "Champ" Segal.[4] Brownsville-born Abe "Kid Twist" Reles had already given his deposition, and hoped for clemency. He had admitted being in on the hit, and planned to testify that Bugsy had grown impatient and fired on Big Greenie. Brooklyn District Attorney William O'Dwyer had publicized Reles' cooperation, thereby infuriating Bugsy. Worse, O'Dwyer's assistant Burton Turkus, hardly a politician like his boss, wanted to pursue the case. Somebody threw Reles from a hotel window in Brooklyn, resulting in a rash of jokes about the singing canary who couldn't fly. Police Captain Frank Bals was responsible for Reles' safety, and concluded that his death was an accident. Turkus knew that Reles would not have risked his life on a bed sheet and some wire—the reported material for his failed and deadly escape. Bals, rumored to be a bagman for the mob, was appointed deputy police commissioner by then Mayor O'Dwyer in 1945.

Bugsy remained in jail while he awaited the trial. He wore a custom-made denim jail uniform, had a private valet (another prisoner) who shined his shoes, and unlimited free phone calls. Ciro's owner Billy Wilkerson, jumpy, compulsive gambler, and Bugsy pal, saw to it that the Ciro's chef sent Bugsy his lavish meals of steak and pheasant.[5] During the forty-nine-day jail stint, Bugsy made eighteen visits to Dr. Allen Black, his Beverly Hills dentist. During one of his nights out, he dined at trendy Lindy's restaurant with English film actress Wendy Barrie. When Sheriff Biscailuz got wind of the rendezvous, he blamed the jail doctor Benjamin Blank, rather than face the corruption in his own sheriff's office. Dr. Blank wasn't so squeaky clean, on the take for over thirty grand from Bugsy, and lost his job, only to end up at MGM studios. He was well connected: he had gone to medical school with Bugsy's brother, Dr. Maurice Siegel! Dr. Siegel practiced in L. A. County.

Mickey claimed that Murder Inc.'s Allie Tannenbaum had murdered Big Greenie. Tannenbaum naturally testified that he was innocent, and pinned the whole thing on Carbo and Bugsy, whom he placed behind the wheel of the old Ford getaway car. The stolen hit guns originated at a cargo pier in New York, courtesy of Longie Zwillman, someone beholden to Bugsy.[6]

Bugsy wisely hired Jerry Geisler to defend him; everyone got off. Geisler received $30,000 from Bugsy, who had withdrawn the money from the campaign contribution to District Attorney Dockweiler's fund.

Not all Bugsy's problems with the law were as complicated or as serious as the Greenie trial. George Raft, who rivaled Sinatra for ties to the mob, appeared as a witness for Bugsy at a Beverly Hills trial, and put on quite a show. The judge reduced the felony charges to a bookmaking misdemeanor, a paltry two $250 fine.[7]

By this time, inextricable bonds linked Mickey and Bugsy's daily lives. The most unflattering version of their relationship describes Bugsy as Mickey's role model. Authors have called Mickey a shadow, bodyguard, chauffeur, gopher, and lieutenant. Underachiever Mickey saw himself as a lead player, albeit a character actor with a dangerous independent streak.

Nevertheless, Mickey and Bugsy worked together to insure their infiltration of the Sicilian operation. The takeover process was rocky, although the affable duo gave off appearances of an easy life; they were out on the town every night. Bugsy and Mickey were not shy about taking over, nor was either reticent when it came to establishing a classy public image. Many Italians didn't understand Mickey because he wooed the newspapers. That disturbed Dragna, who felt Mickey threatened everyone's success.

Dragna wasn't afraid and didn't back off as instructed by Luciano. On occasion he incorrectly described his position as secure:

> Meyer's [Lansky] got a Jewish family built along the same lines as our thing. But his family's all over the country. He's got guys like Lou Rhody and Dalitz, Doc Stacher, Gus Greenbaum, sharp fucking guys, good businessmen, and they know better than try to fuck us.[8]

Dragna became the butt of jokes, and proved no match for Mickey's tenaciousness.

To further irritate Dragna, and deflect public ire away from the Jewish mob, Mickey made statements to the effect that the Italians were ruining the neighborhood, and he was performing a public service through his adversarial activities. He told newspaper editor and old friend Jim Richardson, "The people of Los Angeles ought to get down on their knees and thank God for Mickey Cohen because if it wasn't for me the Wops would have this town tied up." He bucked the old world Sicilian system while currying favor with the public by pretending to ward off the elder Italian mob. Bugsy's attitude toward the local establishment, particularly Dragna, was "fuck 'em," and stood behind Mickey's every move.[9]

Mickey made certain that the newspapers printed positive quotes about his quick rise in the local business world:

Since I have been in charge of the program there has been a definite reduction in the crime of this city. All the types of people who would under previous conditions be bustin' heads in dark alleys and breakin' into respectable homes for robbery are now on my payroll... [He meant many of the Italians, too] ...and don't have to do that sort of thing to make a living. I've been a boon to this town. And I'll tell you somethin.' Despite the attitude of the police, there are a lot a people beginning to realize that fact.

He wasn't far off from the truth, since many local citizens accepted him, and he was already a Hollywood fixture.

However, certain national goals required a synergetic effort. A project brewed through the early forties that would revolutionize several industries and repaint the canvas of our country with an indelible vice-tainted patina. The growing Jewish syndicate needed Dragna's help with that new venture. Dragna was no beauty queen, and Bugsy was a good-looking, more articulate poster boy for gambling, someone the Hollywood crowd would follow to the proposed fantasyland. Dragna was incapable of providing public relations for the development of Las Vegas, so Bugsy used him principally for his California contacts and muscle.

The psychological and practical needs of Bugsy and Dragna initially complemented each other, and set the wheels in motion for developing Las Vegas. Both men envisioned themselves as leaders, a convenient stance for an awkward partnership. Neither party had much of a choice; both national mobs had an interest in expanding Nevada gambling. A unified commission on organized gambling had taken place in Atlantic City. Dragna attended the meeting and accepted his role, despite his distrust for the Jews, whom he thought were unorganized and uncontrollable.

The Atlantic City conclave had determined how to structure the Annenberg Nationwide News service (race wire) to benefit gambling. Bookies needed properly timed information on sporting events, particularly horse racing. One of the reasons Bugsy was sent to California was to help set up the race wire business, which was sorely lacking by East Coast standards. Securing the race wire became part of Mickey's job description. He made inroads to control the growing wire activity around Los Angeles. Many legitimate people owned a piece of the countrywide gold mine. The national and local fighting became extensive; local infighting resulted in beatings and murder, and until now did not attract much national media attention. Mickey grew uncomfortable with the wire service wars, but remained dedicated to developing gambling clubs on the California coast, and cooperated with national needs to secure the wire trade.[10]

At the same time, Los Angeles escalated its social and business transformation. Organized crime naturally moved in on the new theaters, restaurants, clubs, and movie business, creating a symbiosis that would continue for decades. Aside from influencing the talent bookers, the mob controlled the dinnerware, glassware, and napkins. Entertainment and organized crime learned to get along.

Nightclubs had become an integral part of popular culture in Los Angeles. Tuxedos were the standard attire for all employees. Sexy cigarette girls sashayed between the tables, while camera girls solicited business, too. A discreet "saw-buck" (ten dollars) slipped to the maître d' and he would open the velvet rope leading to the best tables. Money laundering and illegal gambling took place under the nose of politicians and police. Mickey saw nightclubs and restaurants as more than a place to socialize. He wanted, and ultimately received, a piece of the action.[11]

The Sunset Strip area was the hot ticket that provided a small-town feel. Never again would the country see the strange nighttime intermingling of movie stars, mobsters, politicians, restaurateurs, and the filthy rich. The extensive club scene helped fuel the development of the entertainment business.

Writer Lloyd Shearer detailed the odd mix of elements in a night out on the town:

> ...the studios were run by pirates, semi-illiterates, amoral immigrants, men who indulged in corruption, blackmail, sex orgies, nepotism, men who made exorbitant profits...and trafficked with the most despicable segments of the underworld.

Despite Mickey's East Coast tutoring and his hard-earned street education, he still had a lot to learn about Hollywood and its luminaries. An early lesson materialized about actors' unwillingness to pick up checks. His run-in was with Jackie Gleason (Herbert John Gleason), also from a crummy section of Brooklyn. During a party night at one of Mickey's new restaurants, big mouth funny lady Martha Raye, playboy attorney Gregson "Greg" Bautzer, and Gleason ordered everything on the menu. Mickey was happy because he had discovered how hard it was to make legitimate money in the restaurant business. When the sloshed group rose to leave, Gleason, "The Great One," merely signed his name to the check.

Mickey was livid. "I never heard of signing the check in my life."

It got worse as the group made its way to the front door.

"What is this bullshit? You come in here and eat and drink and you sign—who the hell signs a check?" screamed Mickey.

Gleason bellowed back, "Don't you know who I am?"

An argument ensued, and Mickey threatened Gleason. Martha Raye called Mickey every name in the book. When Bautzer stepped in to guarantee the meal with his check, Mickey held his ground and yelled, "Who the fuck are you?"[12]

The homunculus restaurateur liked to say that he slapped around former boxer Gleason, who once took on the Joe Louis adversary Tony Galento in the streets.

The Strip became Mickey's roving office. Anytime he showed up out on the town, owners feared a problem, but most were happy to have a customer who spread around cash as if he was printing it at home, a business he always personally avoided. During these late night jaunts, he claimed that he rarely had a drink, despite conflicting reports about his alcohol consumption. Certainly, heavy drinking did not cause his rabble rousing; he didn't need booze to make a stir.

Mickey fancied himself a knowledgeable food critic, and enjoyed the steadily improving Los Angeles cuisine. Writer Ben Hecht echoed the self-appraisal: "Mickey was a gourmet. Food can make him almost as fretful as the police, especially the wrong kind of ice cream." Yet, detractors like Reid minimized Mickey's culinary tastes. Reid pretended to be shocked that a Jew would eat ham and eggs in public, instead of keeping strictly kosher.

Mickey's close friend, nightlife companion, and constant publicist was Florabel Muir, who wrote for the *New York Daily News* after stints at several major West and East Coast newspapers. The FBI would label Muir "notorious" in their files. The notorious reporter helped define Mickey's career. Journalist Peter Noyes recognized the close bond between Mickey and Muir: "She covered the Sunset Strip beat; she went everywhere with him; she reported on him daily. She was part of the reason that he became a legend."

Mickey became a regular at popular Ciro's, with its wedding-cake-frosted second story and a missing slice. According to author Sheila Weller, he never paid a tab in the legendary nightclub, but was welcome nonetheless at a ringside table.[13]

Juxtaposed to Weller's claim, Mickey was quick to whip out a roll of bills; he was an obscene tipper. To make sure that everyone would remember him, he tipped five and ten dollars, huge sums in the late thirties and early forties. Former boxer Art Aragon recalled in one interview that Mickey was not a ten-dollar tipper, but a regular one-hundred-dollar tipper. "I don't know where he got this money...he bought everybody," said Aragon.

Managers and maître d's, at places like the lavish Coconut Grove inside the Ambassador Hotel, have said that Mickey routinely peeled off a roll of fifties and one hundreds whenever he arrived with his entourage. He loved to pay his way, and three hundred bucks a pop was nothing to him. Headwaiters couldn't wait to see him. Many friends and associates have stated that he went out of his way to take care of everyone's bill, as many as fourteen guests at a time. He never went out alone, and usually had a minimum of eight to ten dinner guests. Writer Dean Jennings knew him to be a "chronic check grabber." Mickey, often seen in the company of mobster actors George Raft and Edward G. Robinson at the Hillcrest Country Club, would leave fifty pairs of shoes for polishing in the men's locker room. Ray Fulce, a locker room attendant from 1956–1959, and now a caddy at the prestigious club, had always marveled at "Mr. Cohen's" generosity. Joe Patti, owner of the former Rat Pack hangout La Famiglia in Beverly Hills, said that Mickey was a very generous tipper, particularly when he was club hopping with beautiful women. When Joe was the bartender at Beverly Hills' other Rat Pack hangout La Scala, non-smoker Mickey gave Joe one of his expensive personal cigarette lighters as a gift.

Mickey had invested in several lawful businesses, prompting the FBI to list his occupation in 1940 as a "gas station owner." Gas-station-owner Mickey was now also the boss of West Coast bookmaking. He ran an army of muscled employees who helped him rake in millions for Bugsy and the mob. Anytime the FBI came calling, he remained fearless and sarcastic, perhaps accounting for the numerous occupations reported on his records. He had already developed a strong power base, yet some writers who perhaps took "gas station owner" and future occupation listings more literally, labeled him a minor player.

On the social front, LaVonne had been dating Mickey for two years when he arrived with Tuffy (his Boston terrier) and announced immediate marriage plans. Folklore enthusiasts prefer to believe that he was late for most of his dates because of his primping, so he often had one of his bozos pick up LaVonne; he even missed the scheduled time for his wedding.

On October 15, 1940, Tuffy witnessed the middle-of-the-night brief wedding ceremony, despite the minister's complaints. The wedding chapel was located on S. Western Avenue, and the minister maintained affiliations with the Temple of Divine Wisdom. Mickey was twenty-seven and LaVonne twenty-three.

"You can't bring that animal into a wedding!" the minister exclaimed.

Mickey did not acquiesce, and had to rely on LaVonne's charm to persuade the minister. Human witnesses included Mickey stalwarts Joe Sica and Mike Howard.[14] The best man was William "Stumpy" Zevon, who joked with Mickey about the minister's large feet. (Father of future rocker/songwriter Warren Zevon, Stumpy would remain friends with Mickey. On occasion the two men would treat Stumpy's relatives to ice cream on visits to the old Brooklyn neighborhood. During one brief sojourn, an irascible fountain owner made the mistake of not opening up for Mickey and the boys. Mickey changed the owner's mind—some say by merely offering to buy a whole tub of ice cream.)[15]

Mickey's local commitments and growing conflicts over the race wire did not permit a honeymoon. Lavonne's early relationship with him developed during Hollywood's exciting halcyon days, ideal for a young couple on their way up. The Cohens were entrenched in one of the most productive transitions in American business and popular culture, when the entertainment business defined the social lives of locals who had cash to burn.

In keeping with his wife's consistent wishes, Mickey hired a tutor to help with his diction and table manners. His accent and ability to string together sentences improved dramatically. He became more comfortable dining where he bumped into people whose speech implied proper education. He was hell bent on molding himself into another persona, and fought hard to avoid his character defects. Hollywood gave him all the room to grow out of his brusque, hood's background.

LaVonne grew accustomed to tons of cash and Mickey's peculiar and unscheduled business life. She accepted the double standard; Mickey did whatever he wanted, whenever he wanted, while she led a conventional life, including an overblown conservative profile. She learned to embrace the most prude outlook toward stylish unrefined items like sexy clothing and flashy makeup.

LaVonne knew that his business required him to be out with women, a problem in any marriage. Since the backdrop of the entertainment business and its social Hollywood mores supported risqué behavior, it defined his marriage style. Nobody raised an eyebrow. Like his show business mogul counterparts, seen all over town with starlets, Mickey used women to compliment the schmooze. Mob visitors also expected evening escorts, since social perks usually accompanied deals.

Because of the wire service wars, and the already large number of Mickey enemies, everyone agreed that the army would be a good place for him to hide. As an alternative, the mob had links to protective havens like the Bahamas and parts of the Caribbean. His attempt to enter the service proved foolhardy.

When he registered on October 16, 1940 (the day after his marriage), the draft board decided he was "morally unfit for military service." They told him that he was already registered 4-F due to a psychiatric examination he had received years back by order of a judge who deemed his courtroom behavior eccentric. Mickey's brother Harry tried to have him reclassified as "of good character and reputation," but the local police would not supply the selective service with enough information to invalidate their negative character description.

Mocambo, the Brazilian-themed club filled with glass-caged macaws, parrots, and cockatoos, opened on January 3, 1941, and had a nearly twenty year run. At the height of the its popularity, Mickey and his strong-arms commanded a ringside table.[16]

One night the famous columnist and Hollywood powerhouse Hedda Hopper noticed that all the guys in Mickey's entourage had bulges, and she was not referring to the legendary Mae West line, "Is that a pickle in your pocket, or are you just glad to see me?" type of bulge.

Hedda saw guns; her response was not phallic. She told the management, "Move him or move me. I won't sit next to this bum." Polite managers escorted Mickey to another table.

While the gang boss was away from his table, likely washing his hands, pal Florabel Muir warned the headstrong Hopper, "You'd better be careful. He'll wipe you out." Muir had a sense of humor; Hopper didn't.

"Wipe me out? He wouldn't dare," Hopper nervously replied.

Walter Winchell took another approach one evening at Ciro's. He, attorney Art Crowley, and private detective Fred Otash, who had a hard-on for Mickey and his delinquents, were dining when Mickey and his entourage arrived, trailed by the Los Angeles Police Department's gangster squad.

Winchell pulled out a gun, slid it across the table to Crowley, and said, "Jesus, with all these different groups in here, there might be some shooting tonight." Otash recalled "nut" Winchell's plan: "Look, if there's any shooting, we'll all duck under the table and start shooting back." Otash didn't say how many guns tough guy Winchell carried.[17]

The FBI believed that Bugsy intended for Mickey to be the next boss, and began a grooming program as early as 1942. Bugsy fancied himself more of a sportsman and personality, and deferred daily business decisions to Mickey, who proved ideal because he had demonstrated his willingness to "kill whenever necessary to get results," an undeniable attribute in his business. Tested employees at his level were scarce. Mickey, despite his independent streak, was still a favorite of the boys back east, and they counted on him to insure a complete takeover.

The FBI account of Mickey's and Bugsy's antics offers a simplistic overview of a more complicated national process. FBI files fill hundreds of pages concerning Mickey's extensive gambling interests, but nobody challenged him. The FBI ignored Lansky's power and control; Lansky pulled all the strings. Bugsy left a lot of the muscle work to Mickey, but no records exist of Mickey's personal participation in hits. He succeeded due to his own persistence, the absence of FBI plans to intercede, excellent attorneys, and corrupt political cooperation. Like one of his lifer employees known only as "Nate S" boasted, "I have been thirty-five years in organized crime—and never a black mark against me." Like Nate, nothing seemed to tarnish Mickey's quest to take over.

Dragna now appeared comfortable with Mickey's takeover of all the gambling. The old-time Italian only wanted to maintain the distribution rights to the Continental Wire Service's racing sheets. Continental's Russell Brophy and James Ragen wanted no part of Mickey. When Dragna met with Bugsy, Mickey, and Joe Sica at a Hollywood drive-in on Sunset and Vermont, he agreed that Mickey was gambling boss and Sica was the narcotics king. Rosselli had already agreed.

In July 1942, as an example of Mickey's early contributions to securing the race wire service, he and Joe Sica beat up non-cooperative rival Russell Brophy. The brutes tore out the telephones and hit him on the head with a gun. He complained to the police. Sica paid a $200 fine to Mickey's $100; the erroneous charge of murder having been reduced to a simple assault.

"I guess I only beat him a hundred bucks worth," was Mickey's quip years later.

Through Mickey's strong-arm antics, all the local bookies begrudgingly acquiesced to the national reorganization, and Mickey and Bugsy took further control out West. The war of the wire services had also taken its toll nationally, and most small-time operators no longer cared whom they were associated with, as long as no business interruptions occurred. One by one, the bookies fell into line when muscled by the new race wire syndicate, and the country was poised to offer expanded national betting services.

Even though Mickey did not serve his country, there was more illegal work at home because of the war. A secondary market developed around ration stamps and any item that was in short supply provided an excellent opportunity for the racketeers, in effect creating a "black market" in the U.S. They jumped on the swag, and sold everything they could get their hands on. Mickey entered the black market as soon as World War II started. He made a ton of money; it was easy for him. Rationed food items included butter, sugar, coffee, chocolate, and red meat—all to help accommodate the troops. The government set the standards for basic food requirements and issued rationing stamp booklets. Even infants had to be registered. Tires and gasoline were always in short supply.

The mob stumbled into a ready-made business. The syndicate saw to it that these items were always available at a premium, and often insisted that a customer buy some extra bootleg booze along with his purchase of staples. One of the largest secondary markets was nylon products, which made stockings a hot item. Even before the war broke out, silk imports from Japan had stopped. The War Production Board controlled silk supplies in America, and commandeered what was already in short supply for parachutes. This set off a run by women on the remaining silk stockings, and an instant black market item that everyone demanded. A male suitor or apologetic husband could do no wrong with flowers and a pair of silk stockings. The government eventually stopped DuPont from manufacturing any nylon stockings. It was another gold mine for the syndicate, and the boys cornered the market.

The Cohens would move several times in the early years of their marriage in order to accommodate Mickey's growing wardrobe, as well as his passion for more luxurious accommodations. Until 1942, he maintained a residence in Burbank, a city that would become a consistent source of revenue. During the mid-forties, he lived at 9938½ Robbins Drive in Beverly Hills, adjacent to the central restaurant and shopping area, and later in tony Brentwood. One of his main offices was located at 141½ North La Brea Avenue, a few miles east of Beverly Hills, and close to the Strip.

The upscale moves resulted in another naïve FBI report: "Cohen had attracted the attention of the No. 1 Gang Lord in Los Angeles, Benjamin (Bugsie) [*sic*] Siegel, and as a result of their association he was soon able to move into more pretentious quarters in Los Angeles." The in-denial FBI acted as if Mickey and Bugsy operated independently. Even though Mickey contended that he was standoffish in the beginning of their relationship, both men had to answer to Lansky. Organized crime was already nationally controlled, and modeled on American corporate structure. Lansky would one day boast, "We're bigger than U.S. Steel."

Mickey enjoyed his Beverly Hills digs, and the protection that the insulated city afforded him. New Beverly Hills police chief Clinton Anderson made it difficult for any driver to stop a car for five minutes after midnight. The fervent night patrols proved successful, and made it tough for any outside criminals to hang around Beverly Hills after hours.

Chief Anderson appeared impressed when he described the affluent neighborhood:

> White-pillared Colonials, tile-roofed Spanish homes in pinks and blues, glass-walled moderns and low-slung ranch houses border winding streets lined by palm trees 60 feet in height…artificial waterfalls, indoor fountains, private

trout pools, inlaid marble floors transported from European castles…gold-plated bathroom fixtures and private motion-picture projection booths for home screenings.

It was also a nice environment for mobsters to socialize. Thanks to the police, Mickey had less fear of a hit in Beverly Hills, and became a regular in the little burgeoning city's nightclubs and restaurants.

LaVonne was not immune to Mickey's way of life; she lived in constant fear of his demise, and a normal family life was out of the question. He and LaVonne had planned for children, and eventually considered an adoption. Mickey vetoed it, citing problems once the war had begun. He knew he couldn't provide a proper life for a child.

One night he instructed LaVonne to pick him up after a card game. She couldn't find him until midnight, staggering down the street with his hands supporting his head with newspapers to stop the bleeding. Someone at the game had hit Mickey on the head with an iron pipe, and he was able to escape the card room by jumping out of a window.

Another time he arrived home to the sound of machine guns. Still in his car, he sped away, while she anxiously called all over town, and finally located her beloved at Neddie Herbert's, a former New Yorker and close confidant of Mickey's.

LaVonne once told Florabel Muir, while sitting with Mickey in the breakfast room,

> I wonder what it would be like to sit in a room with the lights on and all the shades up. I drive past other people's homes and see them sitting there in front of their windows not worrying about somebody shooting at them.

Mickey complained, often in the form of teasing: "That's why I wish I'd never got married…"

LaVonne pinched Mickey's ear and chirped, "You wouldn't be alive if it weren't for me looking out for you. You don't need to worry about me…"

In 1943, the frustrated authorities finally took on the mob in court. The sensational Hollywood Extortion Case took seventy-three days and resulted in multiple guilty verdicts. The Hollywood unions, including the Stage Handlers Union and the Movie Projectionist Union, had had enough members to entice the Chicago mob to take control. Frank Nitti and Paul Ricca were able to extort large sums of money from MGM, Paramount, Twentieth Century Fox, Columbia, and

RKO. On March 19, after Willie Bioff and George Browne had ratted him out, Nitti shot himself in the head. Rosselli would serve three years in Leavenworth prison. The case proved to be an isolated attempt to control the West Coast mob.

Mickey's business profits escalated, payrolls increased, and cash flowed from the illicit faucets. Several of his hoods made $1100 per week. Neddie Herbert was at the top, and with good reason. FBI files listed him as an ex-killer who worked for Bugsy. He was always much closer to Mickey, and some report that Mickey grew up with him. Neddie never impressed journalists as the murder-for-hire type. Most found him funny, although he was mechanically proficient with a machine gun.

"He could take a machine gun apart and put it together again in record time, better than any U.S. Marine expert's time. And he was also a crack shot with the same type of weapon," was Mickey's proud take on Neddie's skill.

Neddie was fearless; he once spit into the face of mob leader Joe Adonis. The verdict of the syndicate Round Table in New York was humiliation; Neddie's own brothers would beat him to even the score. He loved animals, and once shared his New York apartment with a gorilla. The boys called Neddie "a card"; he kept them in stitches. He always substituted the word "prostituter" for "prosecutor." Anytime Mickey finished squeezing into his third tightly fitting pastel suit of the day, Neddie would look him over, feign hunger, and ask, "Hey, Mickey, you got an orange on you?" Neddie was a man with a unique and fearless sense of humor— Mickey's court jester. He was always on Mickey's side, and remained second in command while providing comic relief like any good sidekick.

Other employees garnered five hundred per week. The lowest rung on the payroll was two hundred—plus all they could steal. The FBI was aware of the unreported cash changing hands, but did not interfere.

Mickey made the most of Hollywood's ability to pamper its citizens; he took advantage of his shopping opportunities, and continued to fill his obscenely vast wardrobe, which was essential to his approach to work. He, who always wore new suits and ties (sometimes never wearing the same suit twice), was a regular at Bullock's Wilshire department store. He liked to mingle with the wealthy Jewish shoppers, purchasing the fanciest items in town despite the outrageous cost of imported goods. He thought nothing of shelling out three hundred bucks for a Panama hat. He was conscious of which gangsters dressed the best, like fashion plates Frank Costello, Luciano, and Bugsy. (Bugsy always wore cashmere suits, something Mickey didn't like for himself; cashmere wrinkled too easily, and he wanted to have a clear crease in his trousers.)

Mickey's view of his trappings was simple: "If you can't live well, you might as well be out of it altogether, you know what I mean?" He wanted all the nice material things that went with success.

He and Bugsy liked to have their hair cut at Gornik and Drucker's in Beverly Hills.[18] Columnist Steve Harvey relates that founder Harry Drucker became concerned when rival gangs started hanging around at the same time. The manager alerted Drucker that customers were afraid to visit, and feared that the adversaries would shoot it out like in the gangster movies. That never happened, and mob influence in Beverly Hills continued.

Mickey realized early on that the fancy cars and clothing did not entirely make the man. He was still crude, a rough character, and he knew that it put some people off. He couldn't accept that and craved assimilation with people he considered to be of a "higher element." He didn't see himself as gangster, but rather an entrepreneur.

Some upper-echelon mobsters echoed his feelings and encouraged him to stay away from the violent end of the business. Many of the Jewish mobsters already had established themselves in legitimate businesses, and paved the way for their descendants to lead respectable lives, like the bootlegger Bronfmans[19] and race wire Annenbergs.[20] Even Frank Costello had suggested a legit life to Mickey, and now Bugsy whispered in his ear about diversifying his regular business investments. He obliged and began to buy up real estate on the Strip, increase his splits in fancy supper clubs, and establish more ventures for the East Coast mob.

In the process, he became a constant fixture on the Strip's social scene, one that now existed only with his and Bugsy's imprimatur, since their influence had infiltrated all the top clubs. He furiously made the rounds at night, hell bent on establishing himself as a Hollywood celebrity by hobnobbing with the rich. Social climber Mickey would develop long-standing friendships with Robert Mitchum, Sammy Davis, Jr., Errol Flynn, and Ben Hecht. The future Rat Pack needed a place to play, and he helped provide it. Without him, perhaps the Rat Pack phenomenon never would have happened. Despite his character and reputation, he had no problem fitting in with the Rat-Packers-in-training and their business and social entourage. Entertainers loved the mob—where else could they gamble in the days before Vegas?

The higher ups on both sides of the legal divide had one thing in common— they wanted to attend black tie dinners with famous producers and beautiful actresses. Just as Mickey had, national politicians and corporations courted Hollywood for its ability to sway public thinking. Washington and Hollywood have always made strange alliances, and created a growing web that connected show business, organized crime, and politics.

The Golden Age theatrics of the Los Angeles mob had arrived; the opening act of the Mickey and Bugsy Show was a hit. Without them, organized crime could never have developed so swiftly around Hollywood. This network would continue for decades. The national mob set the stage for the big move to Las Vegas. Showstoppers, a series of macabre events that even the best playwrights could not have imagined, filled the remainder of the production.

5.

The Jews Return to the Desert

Mickey combined his burning desire for social acceptance with the nuts-and-bolts of running a growing organized business, while becoming the first in his profession to develop a crafty public image. "If you lived in L.A. in the forties and you didn't know who Mickey Cohen was you had to be in a mental institution. He was everyone's ideal of a gangster, in this town," boasted journalist Peter Noyes.

Mickey's varied business interests soared, supplying him with an enormous cash flow to support his flamboyant lifestyle. He remained beholden to higher ups like Lansky, who supervised the growth of a tiered corporate syndicate. While the pint-sized entrepreneur was always tempted to make money in legitimate businesses—he now owned several—crime proved his only consistent and reliable means of income.

He controlled most of the gambling in Los Angeles. The national syndicate knew that he could immediately lay off bets of between fifty and one hundred thousand dollars. Americans loved to gamble, and were ready to bet off track at a moment's notice, a phenomenon that solidified his position. "For every person that went to the track there was a hundred that went to the bookies," noted crime historian James Johnston. Mickey's casino and bookie interests expanded further, thanks to a blossoming following of movie stars and rich locals. His early experiences with bookmaking helped him establish a pervasive syndicate throughout greater Los Angeles. "Nothing went unless I O.K.'d it," were his own words.

Cash also spilled from businesses tied to public consumption. He provided protection for large operations, owned and distributed cigarette vending machines, resold stolen liquor, and sold drugs. Nothing was off limits, so long as it brought in money, and some appeared very legitimate. In 1944, Mickey's pal Charlie Shuster, who fronted for him as a fight promoter,[1] built the first commercial building near the Los Angeles Airport, a Jim Dandy Market in Westchester.[2] Many suspected that Shuster's chain of supermarkets was a front for gambling operations. While money laundering and stolen goods, particularly during the wartime rationing, were associated with illegal fronts of this type, authorities never linked either to Jim Dandy.

Despite favorable accounts written by sympathetic journalists, some employed by Mickey, he was indeed involved in narcotics. Mexico provided a steady flow of drugs into California, under the auspices of Bugsy and Mickey. The supply lines were originally organized and managed through Al Capone's reign.

Gary Wean, an L.A.P.D. detective sergeant and later a Criminal Intelligence Investigator for the L. A. district attorney, often tailed Mickey around town. One night the first stop was the Pink Pagoda in Chinatown's tourist trap. He later met with bondsman pal Abe Phillips and legal beagle Harry Pregerson at the South Gate Arena. They all ended up at another Chinese joint, Tangs, near City Hall. Mickey dropped off a man in Chinatown named Abe Davidian, who was tracked down by police, and found heading north with millions of dollars worth of narcotics. Davidian would never testify in court because he was found shot to death before the trial.[3]

Mickey's social life rivaled that of any celebrity entertainer, a combination that allowed him to continue nurturing his playground for junior Rat Packers and their coterie, while he mingled regularly with the entertainment power base. His contribution was always making a market in prostitution; one employee source was his Hollywood talent agencies that maintained rosters of young people from all over the country.[4] Sex for gangsters was a given, an intrinsic recreation and concomitant venerable form of illicit revenue. Mickey made the most of his free social time, and combined the latter financial aspect of sex with pleasure. In May of 1944, the FBI surveillance teams watched him and his boys set up "a large seven-room mansion located at 9100 Hazen," today home to actor Hal Holbrook,

48

with neighbors *Dynasty*'s Linda Evans and *Star Trek*'s Jonathan Frankes. The FBI made no effort to interfere with the luxurious brothel on Hazen. The Feds felt that the responsibility lay with the local authorities, many of whom benefited from Mickey's sexy playground establishments.

Soon completed, the fancy joint was a spectacular party house where a special list of Mickey's friends could spend the night in "wild all-night orgies, and party-girl bouts." The FBI further described the location as a meeting place for "Hollywood personalities." While popular Mickey was host of "commercial sex parties" catering to the rich and famous, what many of the celebrities didn't know was that he would never hesitate to use his knowledge of anyone's sex life for extortion and blackmail; candid movie footage and snapshots materialized as needed. The Hazen house was Mickey's private sexual sound stage.

He once told Ben Hecht, "I never entered a whore house, except to heist it." Hecht never shared Mickey's purported lascivious reputation: "The Jew Boy was not only virginal toward sex, but also toward booze, tobacco, and drugs." He felt that violence delighted Mickey more than sex. By his own admission later in life, Mickey concurred: "To tell the truth, I don't go for it much... Girls very often like me and seem attracted to me, and I find them also attractive, at times."

Despite his later contrition, he still bragged that during his tenure in Los Angeles he had sex two to three times a day. A steady flow of striking actresses, models, and professional ladies dined regularly with sociable Mickey, more likely for his power and growing celebrity, than for his debatable carnal prowess.

By 1945, Bugsy raked in over $25,000 a month, mostly thanks to Mickey, who in addition to controlling the basic gambling had a leg up in the important race wire. With all the illegal gambling action and maneuvers into legitimate business, the authorities occasionally had to make it seem that they were trying to fight organized crime, but the grandstanding efforts were minimal. Los Angeles appeared resigned to accept its criminal partners, this despite the scrutiny of John Hansen, head of the L.A.'s FBI.

The top brass in Cleveland had told Mickey that it was necessary for him to participate in the developing Las Vegas project. He and Bugsy often traveled to Vegas, while most of the gambling action at the time was in Reno. The wartime economy brought in defense workers and soldiers—hardly the high rollers. Occasionally, some flamboyant visitors dropped between $700 and $1400 during their stay.

Bugsy and his partners Gus Greenbaum and Moe Sedway (Morris Sidwirtz) bought the El Cortez Hotel from Marion Hicks, and promptly sold it for a profit of nearly $200,000.[5]

Greenbaum was a successful Arizona bookie, who would prove to have a knack for managing casinos. During one meeting, he beat up Mickey. "Greenbaum reached across the table and grabbed Cohen by the tie and began to kick him under the table…until his shins bled…he gave a shove and Cohen's chair flew back, spilling the little mobster on the floor." According to Mickey bashers, Moe Sedway witnessed the event, and he and Greenbaum resumed their conversation while Mickey limped away.

The initial visits to Vegas by Mickey and Bugsy were to make certain that the new Trans America wire service, headquartered in Phoenix, ran properly; it was essential for the entire Vegas operation. This vast company leased 23,000 miles of telegraph circuits from Western Union, and cost the syndicate $1,000,000 per year. Moses Annenberg, who had worked as a circulation manager for Hearst newspapers, under pressure from the federal authorities—income tax fraud—had given up his own Nationwide wire service in 1939, and paved the way for the smooth operation of third competitor Continental. Al Capone was ultimately not very happy with Annenberg's operation, and likely influenced his decision to quit; Annenberg feared for his life.

Many people close to Bugsy have said that he actually hated the desert, and despised having to spend so much time in Nevada. Mickey was no tagalong either when it came to heat and sand; he thought Vegas was a lark, and wanted nothing to do with it. Despite his distaste for Las Vegas, he regularly accompanied Bugsy on the desert trips. His bookmaking business was a cash machine, and he was pleased to focus on that.

Mickey's favorite and only hotel in the underdeveloped desert was the El Rancho Vegas. The other small hotels and properties away from the strip offered him few of the amenities he needed. He liked to reside in one of the hotel's casitas. The only problem was the trek from the little bungalow to the main building. Since he always liked to show off his wardrobe, he unhappily risked dirtying his fancy duds in Vegas windstorms.[6]

Mickey commented on his dislike for the new venue: "Vegas and I disagreed, so I had to push myself to go there." He had no reason to suspect better times ahead, but he cooperated with the Jewish Desert Storm. He, self-admittedly, could not have been more wrong about the potential of Las Vegas. Many in both the Italian and Jewish mobs had shared his initial opinion. On the other side were visionaries to fuel the phenomenon. Examples included Roger Leonard ("Kallman de Leonard"), a pal of Mickey's and Joe Sica. Leonard and Sica insisted that they get in on the Vegas operation.

During the period of the Vegas jaunts, Mickey introduced new friend Frank Sinatra, who always called Mickey "Michael," to James Tarantino. Sinatra was building his close social coterie, which the newspapers then called the Varsity, the forerunner of the Rat Pack.[7] Tarantino wanted to publish a scandal sheet, *Hollywood Nite Life,* to blackmail celebrities. He immediately became part of Sinatra's group. Sinatra gave him $15,000 to set up the magazine; Mickey had pressured him personally, and extracted $5,000 from him on three separate occasions.[8]

Bobby Garcia, who ran the Cover in Palm Springs, an illegal club frequented by Sinatra, commented on his customer's new pal: "Frank was so enthused about meeting Mickey Cohen, the big shot of the underworld." Garcia warned Sinatra: "They are going to keep five-thousanding you to death, you stupid son of a bitch. I'll tell you what I'll do. I'll tear up your marker if you quit gambling." Garcia claimed that Sinatra reformed after that.

Anytime after that when Tarantino was short of cash, he came to Mickey, who knew about all the proposed articles and offered editorial opinions. He always represented that he had protected his Hollywood friends from the scandal tabloid. He threatened Tarantino after he published negative press on Louella Parsons, someone who took every opportunity to mention Mickey in her gossip column. Later, after a tiff over a proposed series of critical articles on Judy Garland, including her drug use, Mickey claimed that he was instrumental in shutting down *Hollywood Nite Life.*

His power and notoriety attracted more unlikely liaisons, and he began a perverse relationship with Richard Nixon, one that lasted a lifetime. Early in his career, Nixon began taking money from Mickey.

"I always had a bad feeling about Nixon, though," Mickey revealed years later.

On the surface, the relationship might appear to be a strange match, a social system gone awry: why would a Southern California boy like Nixon want anything to do with a Brooklyn-born hood? One of the few things they had in common was their published year of birth, 1913.

Late in 1945, Republican leaders chose Nixon to run for representative from the Twelfth District against popular New Deal Democrat Jerry Voorhis. Nixon knew he would lose the election without Mickey's help and imprimatur: Los Angeles was a Mickey stronghold; he controlled the territory that Nixon sought. Ambitious Nixon had no interest in returning to law practice in provincial Whittier. In order to run for the House seat, he surrounded himself with local powerhouses. To ensure Mickey's backing, he wisely asked for a meeting.

Author Anthony Summers described the somewhat clandestine meeting: "It took place, Cohen said, at Goodfellow's Grotto, a little fish house where the politicians met and where they pull the screens across the booths for these kinds of talks... The meeting was arranged by Murray Chotiner." Chubby, cigar-chomping Chotiner was an attorney who liked his silk ties, monogrammed shirts, and jeweled accessories.

Mickey's other recollections were more casual and slightly different:

> I first met Nixon when he started running for Congress in 1945. It was a matter of one situation leading into another. Like somebody would say, "Well, ya ought to get together with Dick," or "Ya ought to know Dick."

The little politician even recalled a contradictory venue:

> He [Nixon] was just starting to get his foot into the door, and Orange County where he was from was important to my bookmaking program. I met Nixon there in a coffee shop. I think all I really said to him was something like "We got some ideas, we may put some things in motion."

Nixon cared very little about bookmaking or Mickey's criminal activities; his aspirations were more grandiose. Mickey's interest in politics at the local level wasn't very complicated—he was always looking for another politician to put on his payroll.

Mickey could not have done a better job for any politician.

> For his campaign I gave a $5,000 check which I used to have a copy of. My friend Myford Irvine of the Irvine ranch family was my man in Orange County on certain propositions. The contribution was important for me and for the country. It was also Irvine's wishes. Irvine was powerful, as far as he was instrumental and a part and parcel of me running out there, so when he asked, I gave. In fact I think a bigger amount was asked, but I Jewed him down to $5,000.[9]

The FBI knew about Mickey and his new pal Nixon, but had a policy that precluded any intervention: "It was diplomatically, but very firmly, re-emphasized...that the Bureau would not become a party to political activities in any form..."

Nixon told a cheering crowd during the Voorhis election, "I want you to know that I am your candidate primarily because there are no special strings attached to me. I have no support from any special interest or pressure group." Nixon ran a dirty smear campaign, called Voorhis a Communist, won the election, and remained friends with Mickey. Their paths crossed many times.

Rowland Evans, Jr., and Robert D. Novak shed some light on why Nixon played ball with Mickey. "Richard Nixon's personal reputation was that of a hard man, bordering on meanness." A common ground existed for conducting business. Mickey and many mobsters shared Nixon's ill temper and skill as a master at manipulating mass communications. "He [Nixon] was always a man alone," understood biographer Richard Reeves. So was Mickey.

When back in Hollywood, sometimes a bullet was necessary to reinforce business interests. Mickey's description of his relationship with the competitive Shaman brothers was graphic. He didn't like them because "they thought they were real tough." He felt that the Shamans were insignificant talent, part of the hoards of lower strata criminals he had to step over after moving west.

On Monday, May 14, 1945, Mickey beat up Max Shaman's older brother Joe at the newly opened La Brea Social Club. According to Mickey, he wasn't responsible for the fight with the Shaman boy, who was disturbing the peace in the restaurant. "So Hooky broke a chair over his head and bodily threw him out of the joint—slapped the shit of him, you know, gave him a deal, gave him a going over." The La Brea Social Club was a well-known Hollywood hangout that featured a fancy craps table above the home-style restaurant. Actor George Raft had given Mickey $100,000 to invest in the club.[10] Hooky Rothman, Mickey's lifelong friend, helped run the elaborate La Brea Club setting, while host Mickey enjoyed the fruits of his most recent labor. The customer base featured gambling pros like Nick the Greek and Sacramento Butch. The upstairs area handled everything illegal, including sports betting. Mickey was boastful of his housekeeper's cooking talents; she even baked on the premises. He understood his restaurant didn't rival the new Chasen's restaurant, which he referred to as "gourmet cooking," but it was popular nevertheless.[11]

The next day Shaman brothers Max and Izzy announced that they were going to give Mickey "the beating of his life." They advertised their intentions by searching for Mickey at his La Brea Social Club and Santa Anita Park. Mickey also operated a paint store, actually a gambling front, at 8109 Beverly Boulevard; it stocked as many scratch sheets, racing forms, and bookie junk as it did paint supplies. Izzy waited in the car while Max checked the store. Izzy heard shots, ran to the door, and heeded warnings not to enter. Then he heard three or four more shots and ran back to his car for his own gun.

That Tuesday afternoon, when twenty-eight-year-old Max Shaman had come in screaming, Mickey—as they whispered in the gangster movies—already had the drop on him. He always kept a pistol on or in the desk and fired before Shaman could pull the trigger on his own gun. The featherweight bookie had shot Max Shaman to death with a thirty-eight. When Izzy returned he found Max dead. Since Mickey was the only one in the store, he had to confess to police. The authorities marked off the confrontation as revenge.

Estes Kefauver, chairman of the Senate Committee on Organized Crime, wrote extensively on his interviews with Mickey, and referenced his menacing past. Kefauver's version of the entire Shaman incident conflicts directly with Mickey's; however Mickey did corroborate the shooting. He explained to Kefauver:

> ...he reaches toward me with a gun. He was going to shoot me. So that was it. I blew my top. You gotta remember, I was different than I am now. I was a wild-haired kid. I blasted him with a piece I had in my desk.

For legal help after the Shaman shooting, he turned to reliable attorney Jerry Geisler, who told Mickey to get him $25,000 right away and he would take care of everything. Geisler received the money that night. Frank Costello sent an extra $100,000 to Los Angeles to ensure Mickey's fair treatment.

The coroner's jury inquest insisted that police hold Mickey for murder.

In court, he flatly stated, "I shot in self-defense, Your Honor."

District Attorney Fred Napoleon Howser, who replaced deceased John Dockweiler, part of the Artie Samish political machine, was easily convinced of Mickey's innocence.[12] His 1944 appointment materialized under suspicious circumstances: the Board of Supervisors approved him before the public had any inkling, or the proper burial of Howser's predecessor had taken place.

After a private court conference with Geisler, Assistant District Attorney William E. Simpson agreed that Mickey acted in self-defense, "protecting himself from bodily assault by a larger man." Six-foot Max Shaman weighed 230 pounds to Mickey's undersized five-three, only 145 pounds.

The judge accepted Mickey's self-defense plea, "justifiable homicide," dropped the charges, and dismissed the case. His arrest is not on the record.

Mickey knew that the Shaman killing left many people unhappy. He told reporters that mysterious cars had begun following him and cruising around his Robbins Drive home. To satisfy him, police investigated and sent protection, headed by Detective Lieutenant L. R. Veit. Mickey made sure that reporters printed that he was leaving for a month's vacation.

The police raided the La Brea Club twice in November 1945, the first time with twenty arrests. On November 20, police arrested the "31-year-old Hollywood sporting figure" and twelve other men. They held Mickey briefly on felony charges related to robbery and guns found at the location. The police admitted that the raid was an ordinary "vice shakedown," forcing the Deputy District Attorney Don Avery to refuse the complaint.

Mickey was now as prominent as Bugsy in Los Angeles. His bad-boy status was firmly elevated to the national level. He developed entire geographical areas, almost at will. He found a significant weak spot in the policing of the San Fernando Valley, an expansive underdeveloped area north of Beverly Hills. The soft city beyond the Canyons was Burbank, where he had resided.[13]

Mickey set up a gambling operation on a horse farm called the Dincara Stock Farm, at 806 S. Mariposa Street, now part of artsy NoHo (North of Hollywood). He had craps, chemin de fer, blackjack, and slots. He gave away food and drink, something casinos would learn to do when the legalized gambling business grew. He employed a string of Filipino houseboys whose number rivaled the roster of his equestrian stables. Service was first class, and so were the customers.

He boasted, "It was the goddamdest joint you ever seen. You'd come in there in the afternoon and you'd think you was on a movie set, because there was everybody from Warner Brothers and other studios." Actors still in their soldier or cowboy outfits headed in for lunch, sometimes just to "kibitz with the guys around there."

He led the life of an English squire. He learned to ride, complete with the fanciest garb, including the shiny boots, and hobnobbed with the society set that preferred English to Western riding. Mickey, by his own admission, was a fish out of water, with his crude Brownsville/Boyle Heights mouth, spewing profanities from up on his horse, decked to the nines like a British gentleman. He visited friends in his new outfit, always arriving with gifts, such as French pastries. The rich ladies found him amusing, and he rode alongside them with funnyman Neddie Herbert.

The police ignored his Burbank takeover. He had a key man inside the department, and paid huge sums to keep the force in tow. He paid the higher-ranking officials $1000 per month. He also hired Blanie Matthews, the chief of police at Warner Brothers Studios. Jack Dineen, a retired police captain, oversaw Mickey's entire operation. The FBI rightly blamed the local police cooperation for Mickey's success. He confessed, "My horses was an operation which I done for my own personal entertainment. But you realize that none of these things would operate for five minutes if it wasn't for the cooperation of the powers." Even with multiple raids on the ranch in the late forties, the gambling joint would reopen.

On January 10, 1946, over three inches of snow uncharacteristically stalled the city of Burbank and the surrounding ranches and orchards. The extremely rare weather served as a natural metaphor whilst a white blanket covered the soiled city, whose slogan, "People, Pride, and Progress," should have included gambling, movies, and Mickey Cohen.

Police harassed him regularly in Beverly Hills and Hollywood. When private detective Fred Otash had worked for the police department, his regular orders had included rousting Mickey. "When I was a cop our orders were to get Mickey Cohen on anything we could. I went after him tenaciously." He would later work for Mickey and supply him with "lawyers with facts that made him look good."

Future nemesis vice squad Officer Rudy Wellpott and partner J. G. Fisk picked Mickey up at his club on North La Brea Avenue. This time the officers dug up the old 1934 embezzlement charge from Cleveland, and arrested him for not registering as an ex-convict. The papers again referred to him as a "Hollywood sporting figure." Attorney Sam Rummel filed a demurrer—a claim of insufficient legal basis—against the petty January 31, 1946, arrest. Mickey was back in action quickly after posting a $500 bond.

Even with extra police protection and tails, on March 15 someone robbed Mickey's apartment of over $10,000 in furs and jewelry. The FBI surmised that he had his wife's things stolen because he was short on cash. He refused to sign a complaint with the Beverly Hills Police Department, and they dropped the matter.

During 1946 Mickey became acquainted with Jack Ruby (Rubenstein), who years later would kill JFK's assassin Lee Harvey Oswald. Then a Los Angeles detective, author Gary Wean still followed Mickey all over town. He has written extensively about the connection between the former Jack Rubinstein and Mickey. Unsavory Ruby, who started out as a punchboard-gambling salesman, led a degenerate life. He liked to brag about his contacts with the mob, and one of the names he mentioned most often when he tried to impress someone was Mickey, who was one of his idols.

Wean first encountered Ruby inside Mickey's black limousine; Mickey's boys chauffeured Ruby all over town.

I was working University Division. The Inglewood Police Department would hire off-duty L.A.P.D. officers to help them direct the heavy traffic to the Hollywood Race Track. It was there I became acquainted with Mickey Cohen and his hoodlum friend, Jack Ruby, from Chicago.

Through Mickey, crime voyeur Ruby was privy to the developments of the West Coast operations. His eventual rise to power thoroughly impressed Ruby, who was already enamored of Mickey's associations with Hollywood moguls and movie stars.

Wean observed that Mickey "had several talks with Jack Ruby who was managing Harry's Place on Main Street." Ruby and Mickey would hang out at Harry's and another location named the Red Devil.

The years 1946–47 saw the elimination of many Mickey rivals. The *Evening Herald* reported that "…two men in a swift black car" killed major bookmaker Pauley Gibbons as he returned to his Beverly Hills apartment at 116 North Gale Drive."

It was 2:30 a.m. on May 2, 1946. The forty-five-year-old Gibbons, who had thirty arrests to his credit, bit the dust. Seven bullets felled him, and he yelled from the sidewalk, "Don't kill me! Please don't kill me! Help! Help!" as nervous neighbors peered through curtains. The assailants had waited near Wilshire and Gale until they spotted him. Earlier that evening, he had asked his brother Myer for money. Myer promised to help, but not soon enough. Gibbons wore a gold diamond sapphire ring and a gold watch at the time of his death. The assassins removed neither.

Beverly Hills Police Chief Anderson said that he could have easily supplied a dozen motives for the murder. Police questioned liquor storeowner Harold Marks, who had previously threatened Gibbons for welshing on a gambling debt. Marks also owned the Fair-Bev club where Gibbons played cards, and did so just before his death.

Months later Gibbons' partners Benny "The Meatball" Gamson, a suspect in Gibbons' own death, and George Levinson, "his torpedo," were also knocked off while inside their Beverly Boulevard residence on October 3, 1946. Gamson was bestowed his less-than-flattering moniker because he looked like a meatball on spindly legs. The *Evening Herald* referred to him as the current "No. 1 bookie." *Life* humorously reported that he died of an occupational disease—"gunfire."

Gamson's death netted Mickey 10,000 new bookies. By then he was taking in over $80,000 per week in protection money alone. The FBI suspected that he was behind the Gibbons hit, as well as others. Everyone who was a threat to his eventual rise disappeared.

After years of conflict with Mickey in Los Angeles, Dragna acquiesced to muscling in on the local Vegas bookmakers. He provided the armor that controlled the fledgling Vegas hotel operations, then nothing more than mom-and-pop motels with gambling. The Vegas activity only angered Dragna, since Bugsy and Mickey excluded him from the detailed talks about expansion. He was already disappointed with the Bugsy-Mickey takeover of the West Coast and Los Angeles, and was less excited about his new role as the muscle to pave the way into Vegas. Regardless of the friction, Dragna helped eliminate local competition in order to perpetuate a national gambling syndicate.

The Vegas operation now needed firmer control of the wire service in order to succeed. Bookies paid the service up to $1200 per week for the gambling information. James Ragen, national head of Continental Press Service, was one of the first competitors to feel the pressure of elimination. He knew he couldn't last, even though Dragna and Rosselli backed the Continental.[14] Ragen, whose son-in-law Russell Brophy had taken the beating from Mickey, spoke with the Chicago FBI agents, and hoped for protection. He pushed for Capone's old Chicago mob-backed Trans America, as agreed at the national level. Bugsy, Mickey, and Joe Sica were the strong-arm, and all focused on one goal: get control of the wire.

Senator Estes Kefauver considered the Continental Press wire service "Public Enemy Number One," and knew that the wire service ensured continuous Vegas business for the mob. Yet, he appeared somewhat naïve when he painted a picture of the then current state of criminal affairs:

> When the "noble experiment" [Prohibition] ended, the gangs had to look for a new and equally lucrative racket. Organized prostitution had already been made difficult by passage of the Mann [White Slave] Act. Narcotics was profitable but definitely limited as an operation of universal appeal.

The Los Angeles office of the FBI bugged Mickey's home beginning May 24, 1946, and periodically attempted to bug his offices. The surveillance was particularly unsuccessful regarding the syndicate's elaborate Vegas plans; nothing turned up about the wire wars either. The new bugs were part of a program entitled "Reactivation of the Capone Gang," and included Bugsy and Dragna.

On June 24, Harry "Red" Richmond, a Chicago bookie, was gunned down in front of his home after switching back to Continental.

Eleven days later James Ragen barely escaped a drive-by shooting, which included a fifteen-mile, sixty-miles-per-hour chase. The Chicago police gave him protection only after he ran into a precinct.

An old beat-up delivery truck loaded with orange crates turned out to be the next hit vehicle. Two gunmen flipped the tarpaulin and opened fire on Ragen. One record indicates that he may have died from mercury poisoning, rather than his multiple shotgun wounds received on August 14, 1946. Mickey and Bugsy had likely set up the Ragen hit to the chagrin of Rosselli and Dragna.

The competition had become a prestige issue with Dragna, who took out his frustrations on Mickey, and targeted him for hits. Prospective assassins turned down offers flat, like one to Mocambo-robber Robert Savirino, who told police that his offer to bump off Mickey was a paltry $2,500 and not worth the risk. More attempts to get Mickey loomed on the horizon.

When all the dust settled, the wire was in place, headed on the West Coast by Bugsy and Mickey.

Bugsy was obsessed with Las Vegas and had Lansky's approval. He envisioned—but not quite the same way as depicted in the movies—the potential in the desert, and perceived that Beverly Hills residents were an easy mark for cash on junkets there. Popular culture has extensively explored the folklore surrounding the discovery of Las Vegas. Bugsy, obviously overtaken by the desert sun, stands in barren sand dunes and spiritually envisions a casino. Actor Warren Beatty, portraying Bugsy in the movie, shouts, "I got it! I got it! It came to me like a vision! Like a religious epiphany." Witness Harvey Keitel (as Mickey) wonders if Bugsy is speaking about God. At least critic Peter Travers inserted a jab regarding the historical inaccuracy and sentimentality of *Bugsy*: "Siegel had vision. At least this movie thinks so."[15]

Insiders knew that Bugsy did not have the temperament or creative initiative to have come up with the Flamingo Club idea on his own, nor did his harsh management style fit the proposed image of the casino. Mickey identified the personality defect, and warned him, "In the East, people are kind of abrupt and brusque, particularly in the racket world, but you don't do that out here." He had learned to tone down his East Coast gangster moxie when it came to corporate business.

It was Lansky's idea to place Bugsy into a project that had already begun; Bugsy was not present at the inception of the Flamingo. The new bandwagon was composed of an ensemble of creative criminals and the best available companies in corporate America. It was not smooth going; problems continually cropped up, from the simple objective kind involved with building to the intervention of many powerful personalities.

Dragna's own attempt to shake Lansky down for a piece of the Flamingo ended with a whimper. Jimmy "The Weasel" Fratianno reported that Lansky asked

Dragna to come up with $125,000 for a piece of the action. Lansky knew that was out of his league and the request wouldn't materialize a second time. Dragna proved again to be an ineffectual leader, never truly feared, and therefore unable to control future activities in California and Las Vegas.

To build the Flamingo Club ("Flamingo" was his girlfriend Virginia Hill's nickname, after her deep throat fellatio talents) Bugsy actually collaborated with quirky Billy Wilkerson. Bugsy had nothing to do with the purchase of the land. Margaret M. Folsom sold a thirty-acre plot off the strip to Wilkerson. Attorney Greg Bautzer brokered the $84,000 deal, and acted as the owner. Wilkerson hired daring Del E. Webb, co-owner of the New York Yankees, to head the Flamingo construction.[16] Surprise partner Bugsy showed up at the construction site a month after the groundbreaking, and brought gifts for Wilkerson.

U.S. Senator Pat McCarran and the movie studios helped supply Webb with the building materials. Items like steel girders and copper tubing were restricted at that time. Neither the Civilian Production Administration nor the Veterans of Foreign Wars could stop this massive undertaking. Many of the hotel builders "suggested" that their suppliers take stock in the new companies, instead of cash.[17]

The design of the Flamingo was derivative of the Beverly Hills Hotel, a main building with a series of thirty-six luxurious private bungalows. Wilkerson initially hired architect Richard Stradelman, and Virginia Hill was the interior decorator. Bugsy wanted the best and Hill wanted to change everything. Tons of marble, tile, and statuary arrived from Italy. The high-end merchandise needed to satisfy the design was extensive; everything Los Angeles had to offer was purchased at a premium. Nothing came cheap, not even the labor, but black market items helped reduce costs. In addition, the plumbing had a million-dollar price tag thanks to private sewer lines for each room. The original heating and air conditioning had to be rebuilt; the housing structure was too small and the system had improper outlets. Funding became an issue as the project escalated. Lansky authorized Harry Rothberg to sell off sixty-six percent of the Flamingo to cover cash flow problems.

Fights ensued between emotionally unstable Wilkerson, Lansky, and Bugsy, who threatened Wilkerson in front of attorney Greg Bautzer: "And before I go, you're gonna go first. And don't take that lightly. I'll kill ya if I don't get that interest."

Fearless Bautzer told Bugsy to pipe down, or else affidavits outlining the meeting would shortly be in the hands of the police, the district attorneys in L.A. and Vegas, the attorney general, the FBI, and that furthermore Bugsy should personally make sure that nothing happened to Wilkerson. Bautzer additionally advised the boys, "And if Mr. Siegel is wise, or his associates here are, they'd better make sure Mr. Wilkerson doesn't accidentally fall down a flight of stairs. They'd better make sure he doesn't sprain an ankle walking off a curb..." Wilkerson received an initial pay off—$300,000.

The Flamingo's final cost was $6,500,000—five million more than the original budget. Vendors had resold stolen deliveries, and the project became a victim of the mob's own vices. Bugsy had to borrow $1,000,000 from an Arizona Bank to pay Del Webb's construction fees.

Wilkerson thought it was absurd to open so soon and on December 26, 1946, the height of the holiday season. The bedrooms weren't ready, and the guests had to stay at the El Rancho or Last Frontier, one more reason to leave the casino early.

The Flamingo Hotel proved a disaster, despite an opening night with toastmaster George Jessel, George Raft, Sonny Tufts, Jimmy Durante, Xavier Cugat's band, and Rosemarie; perhaps too few stars for the celebrity-happy crowd. Bugsy had wanted Sinatra, who declined, and was exploring opening his own casino. Virginia Hill and Bugsy greeted their guests—who paid fifteen dollars each, including dinner—like royalty; she wore a white crepe formal gown with sparkling gold sequins; he, a tuxedo adorned by a striking white carnation. The high rollers were all in town with stacks of $100 black chips. The tables were hot, the gamblers won early, and they left with their winnings. The casino owners had not yet learned the art of keeping people inside by creating certain moods with sounds and lights. The show budget ran $35,000 each week, with $4,000 extra skimmed from the casino for Cugat. Lansky knew the score by two in the morning; he looked more like a sucker than the people he had hoped to lure to the tables. The hotel lost between $100,000 and $300,000 in its first two weeks. Cugat limped through a five-week run, and the hotel closed. Wilkerson returned to Hollywood.

Things were not looking good for Bugsy.

6.

Goodbye Bugsy

B ugsy's brash approach alienated many mob figures on both sides of the ethnic divide, and he ferociously fought Lansky over control of the Flamingo.
Author Hank Messick delved into the inside exchanges:

> "Shit on them," said Bugsy. "The Flamingo is my baby. You said so yourself. They'll get their cut, but I don't want them butting in on my territory. Let them go to Reno if they want to." The face of Meyer Lansky went blank, took on a pinched and hungry look. "I didn't hear that," he said in a cold voice. "I hope I never hear it. This is syndicate money you're spending, Ben. Don't forget it." Suddenly aware he had gone too far, Siegel made a visible effort to control himself.

It was too late.

Following the altercation Lansky called Lou "Rody" Rothkopf at the Hollenden Hotel headquarters in Cleveland, and complained about the Bugsy problem.[1] Rothkopf offered this interpretation to Lansky: "It's that bitch. She's driven him out of his mind." Virginia Hill had not curried any favor with the East Coast leaders, and only irritated an already touchy relationship with Bugsy.[2]

"Get word to Mickey," ordered Lansky. "I want a close watch on Ben, night and day." Lansky knew that he could trust Mickey.

When the Flamingo reopened March 27, 1947, everyone already knew about the hit on Bugsy.

Virginia, secretly married to Bugsy, was making travel plans for Paris, a convenient distance from Beverly Hills. Police Chief Clinton H. Anderson cautiously concurred with her knowledge of the hit: "Virginia Hill is alleged to have been familiar with the entire operation …she was aware that the killing was to happen…" She picked a fight with Bugsy, justifying her flying into the Parisian arms of a champagne dynasty heir.

Bugsy was aware, too. "There's no doubt that Benny felt there was some kind of come-off going to take place," acknowledged Mickey.

Bugsy's independence had clashed with the national crime syndicate. Colleagues like old pal Lansky linked his flawed personality traits to the Big Greenie murder, something that rattled the syndicate. Nobody thought it was worth all the trouble it had caused. Lansky had had talks with him, but he continued to blaze his own reckless path.

Mickey knew it was too late to change Bugsy. "Benny taught me a lot about diplomacy, but he couldn't teach himself."

He was also stealing too much from the wrong people, and that objective fact was crucial to any business decision made by the mob bosses. The hotel was still millions in the red as Bugsy scrambled to raise $1,500,000 in thirty days. He had bounced $150,000 in Bank of Nevada checks made out to Del Webb Construction.

Following a heated meeting with Lansky in Las Vegas, the two agreed to meet again on June 21 in Beverly Hills. Lansky was spotted there the day after the Vegas meet. Bugsy had hopes of maintaining a share in the Flamingo, after turning over the bulk of operations to the mob, or so Lansky would later disclose to insiders.

The day before his demise, Bugsy flew in from Vegas at four in the morning to have Mickey secure more armaments. He wanted to be prepared, and ran down the roster of local muscle who worked for Mickey.

Bugsy spent his last day on earth making the rounds in Beverly Hills. First lieutenant Allen Smiley chauffeured him to Drucker's for a haircut, to an attorney, and later to the Coldwater Canyon home of pal George Raft, who was raising money for his own motion picture production company. He ended the day at Virginia Hill's sixteen room rented home in Beverly Hills.[3] He treated Smiley and houseguests, twenty-one-year-old Charles "Chick" Hill (Virginia's brother) and girlfriend/secretary Jeri Mason to a trout dinner at Jack's in Ocean Park, a seaside town.

On June 20, 1947, at 10:45 p.m., as forty-two-year-old Bugsy sat in Virginia Hill's home reading the *Los Angeles Times*, a long-range sniper hit him in one of his baby blue eyes with a thirty-caliber high speed carbine bullet (the embellished popular culture description). A proper autopsy revealed that the bullet actually entered the back of his skull, and exited through an eye socket; investigators found the eye across the room. The cause of death was cerebral hemorrhage. It was one of the most gruesome and famous mob murders of the era. According to Florabel Muir, "Four of the nine shots fired that night destroyed a white marble statue of Bacchus on a grand piano, and then lodged in the far wall."

The corner of the newspaper had a tiny advertising sticker that read, "Good night, sleep peacefully, with compliments of Jack's."

The assailant had hid in the shrubbery near a rose trellis and fired nine shots through a fourteen-inch square in the terrace window. Five hit their mark—two in the head. Bugsy remained upright on the flower-patterned, chintz-covered sofa as the blood poured from his face.

Smiley had directed Bugsy to his final seat—the only angle visible from the window. Charles was upstairs with his girlfriend Jeri at the time of the shooting. When they came down, Smiley, sprawled on the floor, yelled, "Douse the lights. They're shooting through the window," and to call the police. A bullet had passed through his coat.

Virginia Hill, identified as an "Alabama Heiress," wouldn't show her face in Beverly Hills after the shooting. Upon her return from abroad, she spent most of her time in Mexico.

Moe Sedway and Gus Greenbaum were inside the Flamingo within one hour of the shooting. Charlie Resnick, Morris Rosen, and Davey Berman also had a future hand in operations. The bosses calmly announced that the hotel was under new ownership.

The day after Bugsy's death, Mickey called Drucker's to make an appointment for a haircut.

Chief Anderson appeared at Mickey's Brentwood home—its value now estimated at $200,000—to ask him who shot Bugsy, although he makes no mention of this in his own book published in 1960, when Mickey was still very much alive and in power.

Mickey appeared visibly shaken and answered the Beverly Hills police chief, "I wish I knew."

To show how upset he was, Mickey drove his fancy Cadillac throughout Los Angeles, and made sure that everyone knew he was looking for Bugsy's killers.[4] Crime mythology bathes in how he pretended to act on news that the killer had decided to hide in the posh Roosevelt Hotel, a place where any action would surely make the papers. The Lilliputian boss pulled a stunt out of the Wild West, and hustled in with his guns brandished, and called the bad guys out. He fired from two forty-five caliber automatic pistols, and made a nouveau design in the ceiling of the already elaborate foyer. Mickey's friends deny that this took place, citing that it was out of character.

Hits were part of the business, and Mickey had to look the other way when the Bugsy plan materialized—likely based on an understanding between Lansky and Dragna.

> People in my line of work always had a reciprocal agreement on certain matters. Like if something had to be looked up or taken care of out here, I was called on by somebody in Chicago or Philadelphia or Boston... If the request went very far, naturally, it would have to get a real good clearance.

Many people had a lot to gain by eliminating Bugsy. Sedway and Greenbaum were among those who didn't weep over his demise. Weeks before the hit, a worldwide summit meeting took place in Havana, Cuba. Lucky Luciano held court, and discussed the Bugsy problem, which included his skimming on Mexican narcotics points. Theorists suggest that he then privately had called for Bugsy's demise. Some thought that Dragna was in on the hit. Those who knew him better said that it was unlikely that the mediocre career criminal had any direct connection. Lansky tried to pin the rap on Dragna, despite attempting to broker a peace between Dragna and Mickey, who wanted to "hit" his Italian competition. Others claimed that it was Frankie Carbo. Mickey suggested much later that it might have been Frank Costello, who had backed off from business in Los Angeles, opting to let Dragna fight it out with Mickey, who renounced any ties to the Italian operation.

Columnist Sidney Zion was convinced that Lansky had Siegel killed and, of course, that meant that Mickey was in on the hit—he had the most to gain; many thought he had the hit arranged for personal reasons. Newspapers all over the country raised suspicions about him. It was front-page news with scenarios fueled by classic Shakespearean tragedy motivations. Stalwart Fred Sica spoke years later of his conversations with Mickey: "...a little bit longer, maybe, and you might be the boss, eh?"

People all over the country feared that the Bugsy assassination would stir up gang wars in every city, and pressured politicians to act. During interrogatories by the city, state, and federal authorities, Frankie Carbo and others who didn't want to accept Mickey as the new boss blamed him for the Bugsy set-up. H. Leo Stanley, chief investigator of the Los Angeles district attorney's office, was one of the prominent proponents of "Let's blame Mickey." His boss, D. A. William E. Simpson, would have loved to pin anything on Mickey. Simpson's office was convinced that he had Bugsy killed, and based its theory on surveillance conversations recorded in his Brentwood home, particularly remarks made to Alfredo (Fred) Sica.

Stanley hyped what he had for all it was worth:

> In those transcripts, as well as in the tapped phone talks… I understand there are certain references to conversations…arranging release from jail in Fresno…certain individual on $50,000 bail.

Stanley was convinced that the bail money was for the shooter.

Mickey responded to investigator Stanley and others by going public: "I never said anything incriminating." He knew that enough evidence didn't exist. He had copies of all his surveillance tapes—nineteen wax transcriptions—so it was impossible to bluff him. The police eventually backed off, and cited publicly that they did not have the proper evidence to proceed. The FBI corroborated that the local police had nothing on him.

According to Mickey, he had stepped in right away to take over all of Bugsy's operations "on instructions from the people back east." Years later, he waxed emotional for a moment: "Naturally, I missed Benny, but to be honest with you, his getting knocked off was not a bad break for me…"

New boss Mickey had some substantial challenges in Los Angeles. The upcoming battle for control of the Sunset Strip and all it represented would become the bloodiest in the history of Los Angeles. Frank Costello, who liked Mickey, stayed out of it.[5] Once Johnny Rosselli was imprisoned for parole violation charges, only Dragna and Mickey were left to fight for control. Rosselli had made it clear to him that Mickey had to go. Mickey's grandstanding had a sour effect on Rosselli, who confided in a girlfriend, "That Mickey Cohen. He's a disgrace to the underworld."

7.

Hello Mickey

With Bugsy out of the picture, Mickey received all the public attention. He was the most powerful and visible mob influence on the West Coast. The press enjoyed his antics, and reported on him regularly. Hollywood and its surrounding areas became a city of vice, and he "a gang lord without peer," according to *Life*. He ambitiously wrote editors and journalists, a habit that he would continue the rest of his life; he felt that if anyone printed something about him, he had a duty to let him or her know if the information was "fair and objective." Of course, he would deny that he had anything to do with criminal activity. If a writer questioned his motives or suggested something about his religion, the offending office would find reams of mail from Mickey; some letters were over seventeen pages long. He was as relentless in his journalistic and literary pursuits as he was in his business ventures.

Moe Sedway and Doc Stacher now handled daily operations at the Flamingo, while Mickey took his orders from the national leaders. An FBI report noted that Dragna was leaking information about Mickey's plans to kidnap Sedway, who was in the hospital. He claimed that Mickey was going to hold Sedway for a $100,000 ransom. While nothing materialized, Mickey didn't waste any time taking over the race book at the Flamingo Hotel in Vegas. Even though it was beginning to turn a profit, the casino skimming was too much to handle, and the whole situation looked like a sure loser to insiders. Four months after the grand opening of the hotel, Mickey's cut of the income was $1500 to $2000 a month and his main job was to be certain that the gambling debts were paid.[1]

His success in Los Angeles continued its dependence on a cadre of dishonest politicians who were able to wink and sleep comfortably at the end of the day. Artie Samish, the man who never met a meal he didn't like, helped Mickey every step of the way. He and Mickey backed Fred N. Howser for attorney general in 1947. Howser, who had an impeccable record, had worked for Governor Earl Warren, who saw him as the wrong man for the job because of his mob associations; a Warren-Howser feud persisted for years.[2]

Howser assigned Detective Harry M. Cooper from the Hollywood Bureau to hang around with Mickey and act as a bodyguard, a courtesy of Samish's appeal to Sacramento lobbyists. Mickey did not want any protection from the police; he felt it was more of a liability. With his own coterie of enforcers, the last thing he needed was police interference.

Attorney General Howser had told the police to "lay off Cohen for the time being," according to the FBI. The *New York Times* called the Howser investigation "extensive...pertaining to gangsters and hoodlums, race wire services, the murder of Benjamin (Bugsy) Siegel and other interests of the office pertaining to the Los Angeles vice inquires." The article referred to Mickey as a "key witness in a county grand jury investigation of sustained corruption in the Los Angeles police department." Despite all the publicity, no indictments from the investigation reached Mickey.

The *Nation* reporters were never shy about the realities surrounding Mickey:

> ...everyone is morally implicated in the situation which creates Mickey Cohen and corrupt police departments and does strange things to the press...the general social situation is so corrupt that a modicum of force and bribery...makes it possible for the hoodlums to take over.[3]

Gambling continued to grow, despite the cries by politicians to eliminate it. The State of California, which received revenue from tote machines at the legal tracks, contributed to Mickey's success by assisting in the expansion of wire services, which needed the legal betting operations as much as they did Mickey's bookmaking services. Over 8,000 legal slot machines operated in California alone, and owners paid a $100 federal tax on each device. A sergeant in the Los Angeles

Police Department ordered 500,000 punchboards, essentially lottery boards, similar to today's scratch-off versions.

Money and banging heads together didn't satisfy the local gang lord, although he was proud of his success at the latter. Despite his entry into a variety of regular businesses beyond Hollywood's financial trappings, Mickey was dissatisfied with his fronts and had an undying need to be part of the show business milieu that surrounded him. Tinsel Town's pervasive atmosphere proved a more powerful aphrodisiac than politics. Since he was able to maintain a glamorous reputation thanks to those—and there were many—who wanted to embrace gangsters, his access to the inner workings of show business was limitless. Like posh Manhattanite criminal Arnold Rothstein, he wanted to be a patron saint of the arts, thereby solidifying his place in popular culture.[4]

Almost everyone within Hollywood's creative boundaries imagined that he or she could put on a show. Each one, from parking attendants to accountants, had a screenplay in their back pocket. The celebrity-driven environment likewise seduced Mickey, and he made a concerted effort to become a legitimate player in the movie business. He became as interested in promoting a creative property as he was in collecting his Vegas money. Hollywood drove him; it became his ticket to immortality.

His movie and literary interests grew out of his friendship with Ben Hecht, another tinsel town convert.[5] Mickey had already settled in as a celebrity in 1947, when Hecht took him under his Hollywood wing. Hecht had a diverse background, despite having never attended college, which may have accounted for his willingness to embrace someone like Mickey. Their shared interest in Jewish politics would bring them together; Mickey maintained a strong interest in Palestine.

He initially had no idea who Hecht was, but after intermediary Mike Howard, "manager and bodyguard," explained further, and with some convincing by Neddie Herbert, he grew excited. After he and Hecht spoke on the telephone, Mickey agreed to a meeting at Hecht's Oceanside, California, home.

Hecht recalled his first vision of Mickey: "...he had put on weight as an 'underworld king' due to his passion for ice cream and French pastry. He ate little else."

Mickey's demeanor amongst Hollywood elite was nothing like his purported police profiles. Hecht portrayed him as a man at peace: "Outwardly he was a calm, staring man in a dapper pastel suit." Mickey never came on strong in the company of people he respected. He had learned how to carry himself with a quiet dignity within the limitations of his conversational skills and street education.

He was most afraid that Hecht would swindle him and wanted to be sure that he represented only kosher interests in Los Angeles, unlike the "phony Jews" as he called them.

Mickey and Hecht would learn that they were both ghetto children; Hecht had attended Broome Street Number Two public school in one of the worst sections in Manhattan, which is now part of the chic SoHo district.

Hecht observed the gangsters' response after finding out about Broome Street: "A wave of relief seemed to come over them [Howard and Mickey]."

Howard tried to break the ice at the meeting by relating a recent mishap in which Mickey bought a Palestine bronze plaque from a Jewish patriot. The man turned out to be a Chicago con artist, and got away with two hundred of Mickey's cash. Howard then awkwardly presented Mickey's political position to Hecht:

> As soon as Mr. Cohen's friends catch this thief, they will break his head. In the meantime we would like to be of some help to the Jewish situation—if we can be assured we are not goin' to be trimmed. So Mr. Cohen would be obliged if you told him that's what with the Jews who are fighting in Palestine. Mr. Cohen is sorry for the dead Jews in Europe but is not interested in helping them.

Hecht's "outfit" still did not appear legit to them, and they insisted on detailed explanations from him.

Howard further confronted Hecht, one of the highest paid screenwriters in town: "I can't understand why you are having any trouble raising finances in Hollywood for your outfit. The movie studios are run by the richest Jews in the world. They could underwrite this whole Irgun matter overnight." Howard had nailed the political dilemma in Hollywood: local Jews possessed a mixed morality when it came to the Irgun.[6]

Hecht did his best to explain the different strata amongst Jews; many preferred to stay out of international politics. The wealthy Hollywood Jews wanted nothing to do with the fighting, and publicly opposed his American League for a Free Palestine. He explained that he was unable to get a nickel out of Hollywood for the Irgun.

Mickey resented what he called a "highfalutin Jew," and was aware of his effective role as its counterpart. He spoke up: "Knockin' their own proposition, huh?" He decided that he could help, particularly with the backing of the Jewish mob on the national level. He cautiously told Hecht, "I'd like to see you some more. Maybe we can fix up something."

Out of those meetings, Hollywood and the criminal underworld forged another strange bond. Mickey would meet Hecht frequently at his home.

Hecht recalled that he was "diverted, relaxed, even pleased" to have Mickey as a new friend. He described Mickey's life as representing "a certain sanity in a lunacy-whirling world—the sanity of the criminal." Mickey didn't present a hidden agenda, and was a refreshing change to many of the jaded locals.

During the new pals' travails, Hecht introduced Mickey to Otto Preminger, a former actor, and now a well-known producer and director who, Mickey recalled, later needed information for the edgy movie *The Man with the Golden Arm,* which would star Frank Sinatra as a heroin addict.[7]

Mickey and Otto spoke about the horse racing business during a party in Mickey's backyard, a Sunday ritual of Italian food. During his conversation with Otto Mickey received a phone call from Rocky Paladino, and Otto overheard him use the word "laid" in conjunction with "horse." He asked Hecht, "What kind of man is this? What does he mean, he lays horses?" Otto expected the most perverse explanation.

Mickey "humbly" felt that he was an asset to Hecht.

> The writer Ben Hecht was always bringing people to meet me. I guess he thought I was some sort of strength that could help certain people. I don't know how he learned about me or anything, but I guess there was always a lot about me in the papers.

Mickey and Hecht would take long night drives along the coast with Neddie, and sometimes stopped at an all-night ice cream stand Mickey owned. Hecht was sensitive to his complicated and privately sullen friend, and knew that Mickey's life offered little diversion from his conflicted and stressful activities.

During the period of Mickey's initial friendship with Hecht, the FBI listed his illicit income sources as gambling, shakedowns, proceeds from robberies, payments for strong-arm jobs, and prostitution, something he always denied. His gambling interests included an elaborate betting pyramid centered on the racetracks. Prostitution was something the boys from back east continued to expect when in town, and a cornerstone of Las Vegas.

It grew in Los Angeles, ranging from the low-end burlesque houses and bars, catering to intoxicated servicemen and husbands eager to arrange an assignation at one of the local hotels, to fancy call girl services. Many semi-pros were employed by movie studios as bit players, but had larger assignments that included socializing with visiting exhibitors, executives, and local politicians. The party girls could also find extra income by frequenting bars where the bartender could arrange dates by phone. All this took place while most of the country was gearing up for one of its most provincial decades. The freewheeling attitude toward sex in Los Angeles was practically unheard of in other major cities. The homosexual population grew, and would find a comfortable nightlife at places like the Maxwell Café and the local Flamingo. Authors Jack Lait and Lee Mortimer would blame "the impressionable youth of both sexes, which reflects the manners and mores of the movie colony…quick to take up filth as a fad." The naïve authors remarked how husky cowpunchers, rugged U.S.C. football stars, middle-class homeowners, voters, Negroes, Mexicans, Chinese, Japanese, important politicians, leading industrialists, and too many movie personnel could all be taken in by the increase in local perversion, including the questionable sexuality of the new "great wave of fairies and lesbians."

Misogynist Mickey regularly set up famous actresses, including Marilyn Monroe and Lana Turner, with many of the young men who worked for him. He filmed them having sex, so that he could sell the movies on the black market. If he wanted to influence an actress's activities, he would threaten to make the film public. He was involved in regular shakedowns of local prostitutes; he "borrowed" almost $10,000 from a relative of one girl. Other times he played the role of benefactor, more consistent with his projected public image. The local environment and the social permissiveness of Los Angeles enhanced his lascivious activities.

Mickey socialized with many women, countless of whom thought that his show business connections could help them. One nefarious girlfriend was Elizabeth (Beth) Short, the "Black Dahlia," who fancied black outfits with fire red lipstick and nail polish. A calculating sexual tease with show business aspirations, she finagled her way into the lives of well-known movie and mob people who paid her way. Many, like movie star Franchot Tone, struck out when it came to sex with her. Speculation on her sex life ranges from prostitute to seductive virgin, the latter based on autopsy reports. Mickey and Short liked to hang out at the Spanish Kitchen on Beverly Boulevard. Popular Short became a brutal murder victim in 1947; her body, severed in half, had the appearance of a well-planned scalpel murder. The notorious and ghastly murder remains unsolved.

Routine rousts took place, like the one on November 15. Mickey gave his word that Jimmy Fratianno, Nick Satullo, James Regace, Harry Brook, Samuel Bontempe, and Sidney Dine would all leave town. Fratianno had already served eight years for robbery in Ohio, and Satullo had served six years for murder. Regace gave his occupation as a haberdasher. The police claimed that this was the beginning of a national push against criminals.

Mickey's most famous legit business was his elegant men's clothing store on Santa Monica Boulevard, Michael's Exclusive Haberdashery, which opened in 1947. Reporters liked to chide him by writing that all the suits in the store were his size. Since the mugs needed a hangout, the haberdashery was open twenty-four hours a day. The FBI and Los Angeles police all knew that it was Mickey's headquarters, but nobody under his tutelage was ever seriously pinched, indicted, or prosecuted for any activities stemming from inside the haberdashery, despite the FBI's 1947 claim that he was personally responsible for no less than seven murders. His other businesses now included a jewelry store and several supermarkets. The FBI confessed that he was the quintessential entrepreneur of his generation; he had his hand in anything that made money.

Many investigators, including the California Crime Commission, and several reporters who fought against Mickey's takeover, paid no attention to the developing mobster hierarchy and its rapidly changing structure. While he continually moved up, some refused to accept the obvious: he had made it to boss. Former Brooklyn prosecutor Turkus, who was not alone in his thinking, despised Mickey's manipulation of the media and his success:

> ...the small shot who goes for the sandwiches when the big boys have their hotel-room sessions... His efforts appear to have been about as weighty as Mickey Mouse... It is just that Mickey revels in getting his name in the papers; Dragna hides from a headline... There have been some recent news-wire stories, attendant on attempts on his life, which sought to picture the undersized loudmouth as Bugsy's heir... Mickey Cohen thought he was just the man to fill Bugsy's shoes... The real power, though, appears to be Dragna—and no one knows it better than Mickey."

The last part of the evaluation was true, and Mickey clearly had ideas about how to resolve the future in his favor. He was determined to prove wrong anyone who had completely misjudged the balance of power after Bugsy's demise. His methods were way ahead of his time, and he had developed unique communication skills that few public figures possessed.

Despite his own self-doubts, he had become an international celebrity. His activities provided a steady stream of headlines. "The fastidious little gambler had captured the imaginations of people all over the world," wrote journalist pal Muir. People who read about him wanted to protect him, and lived in denial when it came to his detractors. Muir confessed that he fascinated her and she took full advantage of his insatiable need for publicity, which didn't hurt her regular readership, while she enjoyed countless nights out on the town with her subject.

He wasn't quite inside the Varsity, Clan, or, later, Rat Pack. He could not garner the public's worship that was reserved for the most celebrated entertainers. Despite his less-than-handsome physical appearance, he did cut a dashing figure in extraordinarily tailored suits, which helped him assimilate further into the entertainment crowd. He continued to lead the fantasy life that the public suspected of entertainers. He shopped in the right places, tended to his hair and nails at the fancy establishments, and mingled with celebrities. He also became a fan of some entertainers, and influenced their careers.

Mickey's criminal instincts would always keep him in his own special category of celebrity, and in trouble. Ironically, by breaking the law, he received the fame he desired from those whom the laws protected. Despite his tiny number of convictions, the local police regularly rousted him without due process and the FBI tracked his every move. Considering his control over illicit businesses that had expanded well outside the provincial boundaries of Los Angeles, it was remarkable that he continued to survive without prosecution and permanent incarceration.

Part Three

Mickey, the Celebrity

1947–1955

8.

The Fundraiser

Mickey's relationship with Ben Hecht led to his continual involvement with Jewish causes. Beginning in 1941, Hecht had developed firm relations with the Irgun, an Israeli defense organization. Peter Bergson, Samuel Merlin, and Yitzhak Ben-Ami had asked him to help in their project to create a Jewish army in Palestine and to make American Jews aware of the Holocaust.[1]

Mickey became directly involved with Menachem Begin and the Irgun. The future of Palestine (Israel) became an obsession for him:

> Now I got so engrossed…that I actually pushed aside a lot of my activities and done nothing but what was involved with this Irgun wars… There were dinners held in Boston, Philadelphia, Miami. And plenty of armament and equipment was collected that you could possibly get.

The neophyte Zionist wanted to influence Jewish politics at the international level, and like everything else he attempted, he was fearless when it came to Palestinian politics. Despite his business success, his personal net worth had more to do with being a Jew than the balance in his bank account. Because of his torturous mixed morality, he remained Jewish first and mobster second, and Jewish leaders, including rabbis, knew they could count on him for help.

The Jewish mob and their business associates were an enormous help in solidifying the future of the soon-to-be Israeli state. None of the underworld activities involving Israel could have taken place without the help of ex-haberdasher President Harry Truman. Mickey had open run on the docks, and was able to get supplies, even government surplus, ready for shipping. The East Coast was in full swing via Albert Anastasia and Charlie "The Jew" Janowsky. Meyer Lansky orchestrated a significant amount of gun hustling from New York. In New Jersey, Harold "Kayo" Konigsberg was on call for the Irgun.

Writer Sidney Zion lamented the overall lack of cooperation in the United States: "...that scores of Jewish outlaws were busy running guns around Mr. Truman's blockade while their liveried Jewish cousins shook their heads in shame or sat in those Frank Lloyd Wright temples rooting for the English." History showed that "the American Jewish leaders raised hardly a peep while their brothers were melted to soap." American Jews at the time were preoccupied with their daily lives, and hardly paid attention to the initially sparse reports of horror coming out of Europe, downplayed by the American media. Assimilation proved more important than separation, while many, concerned for their own security, did not want to become the focus of growing anti-Semitism in the U.S.

Irgun leaders asked Mickey for advice, and he made suggestions on how to handle the politics with the British, whose position remained cold: they didn't care how many Jews died, so long as the Arab oil survived, and the Jews stayed out of Palestine. He suggested hanging British officers in a public area during the worst part of the conflict. The gruesome advice was nonetheless effective and contributed to the British ultimately leaving Palestine.

In June 1947, just prior to Bugsy's murder, Mickey headed up a fundraising drive for the Irgun. "Through my connections I made everybody throughout the country—the Italians, the Jews, the Irish—set up whatever positions there were to be helpful to the Israel cause."

The top mobster brass attended a gala, and didn't quibble. Mickey was powerful enough to throw a benefit with a significant turnout. Slapsy Maxie's Café, the famous off-Sunset Strip club run by Mickey, hosted the lavish affair. The front man/manager, Max Gould, lent the club free of charge for the event. Borscht belt entertainer Lou Holtz was the master of ceremonies for the criminal and show business royalty.

Jimmy "The Weasel" Fratianno recalled the unique dinner:

...The place's packed. I've never seen so many Jewish bookmakers in one place in my life. Abe Benjamin's there, Morey Orloff, Ben Blue, Martha Raye, Danny Thomas. Sitting at our table's the chief of police of Burbank and his wife, Mickey and LaVonne. Neddie Herbert and his wife, and me and Jewel. And I'm sitting next to Mickey.

A weakened Ben Hecht (he had a recent hospital stay to remove his gall bladder) "addressed a thousand bookies, ex-prize fighters, gamblers, jockeys, touts, and all sort of lawless and semi-lawless characters; and their womenfolk" for forty-five minutes.

After a few more speeches and remarks by Mickey's own rabbi, Menachem Begin—on the lam for the King David Hotel bombing in Israel—stood before the throngs of criminals to add authenticity to the cause.[2]

Mickey had plugged into a fundraising system that had existed for generations. The tradition goes back as far as biblical Isaac, who was the first man to give up one tenth of his earnings for charity. When the pitchmen had exhausted the introductions, Holtz looked to Mickey to make the first pledge, a tried and true method of fundraising to solicit higher or matching pledges.[3]

The methodology arranged by Mickey and his partners had its own demanding twist. Cohort Howard had told Hecht that the fix was in: "Each and everybody here has been told exactly how much to give to the cause of the Jewish heroes. And you can rest assured there'll be no welshers."

Mickey started the ball rolling at $25,000, a substantial amount. "Angels" Bugsy and Samish quickly pledged $10,000 each.

Fratianno recalled the chaos:

> After that, forget about it. Everybody's pledging thousands. Even the bookmakers are pledging five and ten grand. They know Mickey's running the show and they're going to have to pay. I see all this shit going on and I ain't going to pledge nothing. So Mickey kicks me and says "Pledge fifteen thousand."

Fratianno answered, "You're fucking nuts."

Mickey made it clear that he would cover the money.

The apprentice fundraiser gave Hecht a shot in the arm and told him to "Make another speech and hit 'em again."

Hecht declined, citing his recuperation.

Mickey next pushed Howard towards the stage and told him to make an announcement. "Tell 'em they're a lot o' cheap crumbs and they gotta give double."

The estimated amount raised at a series of benefits taking place during that brief period reached well over $1,000,000. The single fundraiser estimates covered a wide range, from $200,000 to $800,000. Many raised eyebrows focused on the take—as much for the huge sums as for who had orchestrated the on-demand drive. Finger pointing and false accounting accusations ran the gamut from total swindle to authentic generosity.

Despite all the good will, Fratianno came away claiming the whole thing was a fraud. Perhaps it does take a thief to catch one, but he was no pal of Mickey's, and never hesitated in later years to diminish him. They worked and occasionally hung out together, but he wouldn't have minded if Mickey suddenly vanished or ended up in a coffin. Fratianno, a product of Cleveland's Little Italy, could not relate to the Jewish mob, many of whom grew up in places like Brownsville or the Lower East Side of Manhattan, nor what it was like to be a Jew and to have just lived through the Holocaust.

He confronted Mickey directly.

The next day I see Mickey and I says, "What's the scam all about?" He says, "Jimmy, this ain't no scam. This money's for the Jews." I says, "Mickey, don't give me this horseshit. There's no way you're going to let eight hundred grand slip through your fingers. Not in a million fucking years." But he swears it's on the level and now I'm wondering how this guy's going to pull it off.

Months after the fundraiser, Fratianno, who said that Mickey was sitting on a million dollars, claimed that a story appeared in the *Herald* that delineated how the boat carrying the supplies for the Jews had sunk. This added fuel to Fratianno's claim. His paranoia ran so deep that he suggested that Mickey had a plant at the newspaper, someone he saw socially, and she would print whatever he wanted. He believed that the reported sinking of the supply ship for Israel was all part of a grand plan, beginning with the fundraiser.

Fratianno outlined the scenario for author Ovid Demaris:

I think to myself, "You cocksucker, I know your game." The way I see it, Mickey made up a story about buying guns and ammunition for the Jews with the million raised at the benefits and then said the boat sank. A few unknown people died, some were saved, and it gets printed in the press. I says, "Mickey, congratulations. You've just pulled off the biggest, cleanest fucking score I've ever seen made." And he looks at me, just squinting, you know, and for a split second there's this big shit-eating grin on his face. But he says, "Jimmy, you've got me all wrong. The story's right here in the paper." I says, "Mickey, with your bullshit you better hold on to that paper, it might come in handy when you've got to wipe your mouth."

Yitzhak Ben-Ami, who headed the Irgun's European-based illegal immigration operations, took issue with Fratianno. In 1947, the Irgun sent Ben-Ami to the United States to assist the American League for a Free Palestine, the Irgun's funding and propaganda arm in the United States. According to him, Fratianno did not know the amount of money raised or the national distributions.

Herb Brin, former investigative reporter for the *Los Angeles Times*, disagreed emphatically with Fratianno's critical appraisal of Mickey's sincerity. "I knew how he [Mickey] was and what he was. But when we talked about Israel, he was a different person. He had tears in his eyes once when we talked about Israel."

Journalist Al Aronowitz felt that his relationship with Mickey had as much to do with their own religious backgrounds as anything else:

Oh, I know he killed people and he was a Yiddish *momser* [bastard] and he was just plain no good. But I was a kid writer who loved colorful characters... I also related on the level of our Jewishness in the same way African-Americans call one another "Bro." Mickey and I both grew up in immigrant Orthodox Jewish households and, in my heart of hearts, I was rooting for Mickey as a Jew who had achieved gangster stardom in an Italian underworld.

The facts surrounding the ship story also do not support Fratianno's critical claims. A ship later chosen for the delivery of supplies was the *Altalena*,[4] the pen name of writer Vladimir Zeev Jabotinsky,[5] who had helped create the Jewish fighting brigades in both World Wars, and the Irgun Zvai Leumi militia.[6]

Modern Hecht biographer William MacAdams and others accepted Fratianno's critical description, and treated the matter as if two ships existed— Mickey's mystery ship and the *Altalena*. Despite all the contrary information, Fratianno remained hell bent on characterizing Mickey as a thief[7] and a liar, and the Jewish fundraising effort as a fraud.[8] That didn't stop him from attending Mickey's weekly bagel-and-cream-cheese brunches.

However, Mickey's fundraising methods would cost him his standing in the eyes of influential Jews. Many respectable leaders were uncomfortable with his addition to the international political mix. Jewish circles tried to drum him out of his political relationships. His character was too extreme for scores of upper-crust Jews, many of whom were against the Irgun anyway, and others simply wanted nothing to do with him because of his criminal background.

Mickey's response to his diminished Jewish social standing was logical and businesslike. The unhappy Jewish groups contacted attorneys Sam Rummel and partner Vernon Ferguson, and asked if they could intercede and convince Mickey to curtail his activities.[9] The Jewish leadership made it clear that they would see to it that he would go to jail, but he paid little attention to the threats, which ultimately amounted to nothing.

Most people in the Jewish-cause trenches did not have a problem doing business with Mickey. Yehuda Arazi was the arms buyer for the Haganah, and made the realistic position of his organization crystal clear: "In my business we can't be too fussy who we do business with. Sometimes they're not nice people."

Mickey's activities were not limited to fundraising, and he later recalled some of the details: "Through my connections, I was able to send armaments to Israel. There were a couple of Irish kids, expert in dynamite. They went over as a favor to me and taught those young Israel soldiers how to use the stuff. And I sent over three pilots."

Due in part to their efforts, many Jewish gangsters lived to see the creation of Israel and its survival as a strong Jewish State; it was a rewarding victory for the Jewish mob. Years later, Mickey would proudly display a silver cigarette box engraved with, IN GRATITUDE, TO A FELLOW FIGHTER FOR HEBREW FREEDOM "MICKEY COHEN," FROM THE HEBREW COMMITTEE OF NATIONAL LIBERATION, awarded June 1, 1958.

9.

The Virtuoso

Mickey's long-standing relationship with Sinatra, ultimately the Rat Pack, and their entourage, highlighted the perverse intermingling of entertainers and mobsters that took place every night in his clubs. Sinatra's manager George Evans was forever trying to squelch stories linking Frank to Mickey. When detectives found Sinatra's phone number in his address book Mickey answered simply, "Why, he's a friend of mine."

While Sinatra had always been cool to Bugsy, he remained close with Mickey and respected his power and social opinions. Sinatra had immense popularity, charm, charisma, and a questionable high-class reputation—all things Mickey desired. He was a new breed of Hollywood mobster, as vibrant and flamboyant as any entertainer. Each one wanted a piece of the other.

During the period of Mickey's fundraising efforts, Sinatra[1] asked him for help with his social life, in particular his soured relationship with Ava Gardner. The two industry powerhouses met at night in Mickey's luxurious Brentwood home. He knew that his house was under surveillance, but it did not deter either one of them, and a one-on-one personal talk ensued.

Sinatra appealed to his unlikely dating advisor to intervene. "Lookit. I want you to do me this favor. I want you to tell your guy Johnny Stompanato to stop seeing Ava Gardner."

Sinatra didn't know that he had little to worry about when it came to Stompanato, who made the Hollywood rounds, dating many aspiring and already famous actresses. He was aware that Mickey could control Stompanato.

Mickey responded cordially, "I treated him like a friend." He told Sinatra that he didn't like to mix into anything having to do with broads, and advised Sinatra to return to his family.

Mickey saw himself as an advisor for the lovelorn. "I actually felt at all times that Frank was going to go back to Nancy where he really belongs. I love Frank and I have a very great respect for him, and even when he was at his worst, I was his best friend… I mean, that is what a friend would say. Besides, I had troubles of my own."

Sinatra chose booze, mostly at Ciro's, to soothe his eventual loss of Ava Gardner, the only breakup that showed his sentimental side.

Mickey's relationship with Sinatra solidified further when times became difficult for the singer in the late forties and early fifties, a period that included serious vocal problems and a decline in popularity.

He provided a resurrection testimonial dinner at the Beverly Hills Hotel; he had the clout to bring out the big names. Because he liked Sinatra, Mickey spent a great deal of time and effort organizing the dinner and made sure the place was packed. It was an impressive tribute.

Mickey later reflected on the troubled times for the crooner: "When Frank was going pretty bad, when he was kind of discouraged…I brought in his father and mother, and they put their arms around me and kissed me the same as they did Frank. His voice was even faltering a bit at the time… I was close to tears myself because his voice was really bad… A lot of people who were invited to that Sinatra testimonial, that should have attended, but didn't, would bust their nuts in this day to attend a Sinatra testimonial. A lot of them would now kiss Frank's ass… I really felt that he just had to find himself again."

Mickey's club operations included the Rhum Boogie on Highland Avenue—the club's name likely copied from the Chicago version associated with boxer Joe Louis. Run by Mike Howard, the club featured popular black acts. Mickey was proud of the fact that John Barrymore was a frequent customer. Barrymore liked to pick up washerwomen who were working the night shift in nearby office buildings and take them all out to dinner.

Mickey's Slapsy Maxie's was located near cross street La Brea in the Miracle Mile district on Wilshire Boulevard. Boxer-turned-actor namesake "Slapsy" Maxie Rosenbloom, nicknamed by Damon Runyon, was the source material for the Big Julie character in *Guys and Dolls*. Now the Beverly Cinema, the 4,000-square-foot Slapsy Maxie club helped launch the careers of Jackie Gleason, Phil Silvers, Danny Thomas and Joe E. Lewis, the latter famous for having his throat slashed by the mob over a contract dispute, and ultimately receiving a testimonial dinner by the Friars in 1950. Lewis was famous for his lines, "Behind every successful man is a surprised mother-in-law... Behind every great woman is a great behind."

The other fronts for the Slapsy Maxie club were clothiers Charlie and Sy Devore, who dressed the soon-to-be Rat Pack in sharkskin suits, and provided the wardrobe for many future television shows. Mickey claimed to have only lent the Devores some cash to get started, perhaps twenty-five thousand dollars. Despite his denials, the cocky impresario maintained a certain number of investment points in Slapsy's and other clubs, as in any structured investment. That number was always subject to change, particularly if the headliners increased nightly revenues.

Mickey helped launch the careers of several popular entertainers. The Devores liked the Martin and Lewis act enough to ask him to finance the venture. Dean Martin and former Brownsville resident Jerry Lewis made their first appearance on the West Coast on August 9, 1948, at Slapsy Maxie's, after a huge splash at the Copa in New York. Before the Copa, Martin and Lewis had appeared at the Five O'Clock Club in Atlantic City, owned by Skinny D'Amato,[2] who never charged admission to celebrities. They had played all the mob-run joints: the Riviera in North Jersey, and the Chez Paree in Chicago.

Mickey also helped by filling the club tables with his on-demand entourage. The audience, which needed little coaxing to see the most remarkable act in show business history, included Barbara Stanwyck, Humphrey Bogart, Lauren Bacall, Jane Wyman, Ronald Reagan, James Cagney, Clark Gable, Donald O'Connor, Debbie Reynolds, Gene Kelly, Fred Astaire, Rita Hayworth, Orson Welles, Harpo and Chico Marx, Edward G. Robinson, Bob Hope, Bing Crosby, Carmen Miranda, Al Jolson, Mel Tormé, Count Basie, Judy Garland, Mickey Rooney, Spencer Tracy, Greer Garson, William Powell, Billy Wilder, June Allyson, and Gloria DeHaven. At a pool party at George Raft's house earlier that same day Martin and Lewis had met Loretta Young, Edward G. Robinson, Veronica Lake, Mona Freeman, William Holden, William Demarest, and Dorothy Lamour.

Guy and Angela Crocetti, Dean's parents, were ringside.

The magical act debuted with the energetic Dick Stabile orchestra, a perfect match for the zany Martin and Lewis. Slapsy Maxie bartender Dick Martin was inspired to copy Dean's act; the timing and character he created would carry him to *Laugh-In* fame with partner Dan Rowan.

Joan Crawford was also in the audience the night Martin and Lewis brought down the house at Slapsy Maxie's, and remarked, "That Dean Martin is rather attractive," but she made it clear to her journalist friend Larry Quirk that wild and screwball Jerry Lewis would probably make a better lover.

Sinatra's first take on Martin and Lewis was not entirely enthusiastic: "The dago's lousy, but the little Jew is great."[3]

Martin[4] and Lewis[5] negotiated a movie deal with producer Hal Wallis, a record contract with Capitol, and a television show with NBC. Mickey used his power in the entertainment business to help the funny duo join the professional unions. It was easy for Mickey to ask for favors; he controlled goon squads working at a number of unions, including A.F. of L., which paid big protection money.[6] At first comedian Lou Costello balked, and complained about an unpaid debt from Martin. Mickey maintained a close enough relationship with Costello, who also maintained ties to New Jersey mobster Willie Moretti, to have him step aside and not hinder the careers of Martin and Lewis, who gave a command performance at Moretti's daughter's wedding in New Jersey.

Despite all the occasional grandstanding by the authorities regarding Mickey's hard times, he and his troublemakers were doing well. A new, more luxurious haberdashery was in the works at the 8800 block of Sunset Boulevard, and Mickey couldn't wait to permanently move to the hot Sunset Strip address near Ciro's and Mocambo.

The topping on this eclectic period was another hit—August 18, 1948. This time it was more public, at Mickey's haberdashery. The folklore surrounding this hit typified the multiple versions of mob events reported by newspapers, authors, eyewitnesses, and Mickey himself. Cursory details of the Fratianno version sound surprisingly realistic, since it involved one of the many benefits of mobster life: a never-ending ticket source for sporting events and shows. *Annie Get Your Gun* at the Greek Theater was the hot ticket that year. Mickey had seen the show and was recommending it to his associates. Fratianno brought his wife and daughter with him when he visited Mickey's shop to pick up tickets for the show. Fratianno, recently released from the Ohio State Penitentiary, suffered from tuberculosis, and Mickey had paid his hospital bills at a sanitarium in the San Fernando Valley.

Mickey boasted to Fratianno, "Be my guests. They don't cost me nothin' anyway. I can get all the free tickets I want. Best seats in the house, too. I got you third row, center aisle."

Fratianno's version of the shooting contradicts what the police and crime researchers had surmised. While the innocent ticket exchange took place, a hit squad was waiting outside. If this story was true, Fratianno exercised poor judgment when he shook hands with Mickey, who quickly headed off to the washroom to disinfect, a scenario that somewhat corroborates several creative memories of the incident.

Frank DeSimone waited outside for the signal from Fratianno. Once Fratianno's family was out of range and well down the boulevard, Frank "The Bomp" Bompensiero joined DeSimone outside the shop. The Bomp resembled a B-movie version of a Los Angeles hit man: he wore a white Panama hat and sunglasses and he had a reputation as one of the most feared hit men in the country, which made him a popular choice to kill mobsters. Fratianno said that The Bomp "had buried more bones than could be found in the brontosaurus room of the Museum of Natural History."

From the sales floor of the haberdashery Hooky Rothman spotted the gunmen and rushed outside to confront the two plug-uglies. When they tried to push past Rothman, he took a swing at The Bomp's sawed-off shotgun; The Bomp fired and blew off part of Hooky's face. Hooky was shot a second time as he struggled to his feet.

The *Los Angeles Times* stated simply that Hooky "was blasted fatally with a shotgun by gunmen as he *opened the door* of Cohen's newest shop at 8800 Sunset Blvd" and referred to the larger haberdashery location as "in the luxurious office of Michael (Mickey) Cohen's…heart of The Strip." The entrance to Mickey's office was actually around the corner on side street Palm Avenue, below the street level of the Sunset Boulevard haberdashery. (Italics added.)

Police officers found Hooky in a pool of blood; his bloody handprints marked the wall above him, and another trail of blood lined the stairs to Mickey's office. Revisionists love to create the image of him felled amongst the fine silken menswear. Doctors at West Hollywood Emergency Hospital pronounced thirty-six-year-old Hooky dead.

During the fracas, two of Mickey's thugs, Al "Slick" Snyder and Jimmy Rist, initially reported to have been watching television, were also injured. Rist was a jack-of-all-trades member of the group. Snyder's role was always a mystery, although every gang tolerated soldiers, hangers-on, or gofers who remained faithful to the cause.

Mickey had originally told journalist Florabel Muir that *he* had been making a long distance telephone call when the hit began. He had handed the telephone to Snyder, and instructed him to wait until the party on the other line answered, while he went to the washroom. When he heard what sounded like shotgun or machine-gun fire, he stepped from the washroom and saw a man running out the front of the building. Hooky was already wounded, slumped on the sidewalk, and Snyder hid under a desk, where he was shot.

Mickey's later revisionist version was no Annie-get-your-gun: "Hooky got killed one night when I had been home late for dinner. I pulled up to the temporary haberdashery, and I looked through the big window where Slick Snyder was sitting at the desk. As I got out of the car, Slick is on the phone and I can see he's telling the operator, 'He just pulled up,' or something like that. Hooky took the car and I jumped into the store." He corroborated that Hooky had tried to grab the shotgun, but contradicted himself further by telling Muir that he had slammed the washroom door shut after the first shots, and laid down on the floor with his feet braced so the door couldn't open. He summarized: "They shot Slick first because when he was at the phone, they thought he was me…" He also later claimed that he saw Rist tackle the gunman who fired on Snyder. "Then I heard another blast outside. It was Jimmy Rist that got hit. They thought they hit him in the head, but they just shot off a piece of his ear."

Sheriff's deputies arrested Mickey, Rist, Snyder, Sol Davis, a "store clerk" who returned from a drive-in diner across the street, and Meyer Horowitz, manager of the haberdashery, for suspicion of murder. Walker Hannon of the Sheriff's Department first took Mickey's statement. The police later tracked down Mike Howard, who allegedly also acted as a store manager and buyer for the haberdashery. Authorities soon released the boys from County Jail.

Chief of Sheriff's Detectives Norris Stensland dragged Mickey to a local West Hollywood substation for a quick interview. Mickey's version on the whereabouts of Hooky before the hit differed from Rist's.

He initially told the detectives, "They were out to get me."

When police grilled Slick Snyder inside General Hospital, he refused to tell them anything, except that he was a haberdasher. Mickey tried in vain to have Snyder moved. Doctors said that his shoulder and right arm would not tolerate the trauma, stating that they hadn't eliminated the possibility of amputating his arm. His doctors requested that the police at least release him from the prison ward.

Mickey told reporters at the hospital, "I have no idea why anybody would want to bump Hooky or me off."

Reporters hypothesized that Mickey's poachers had held up too many competitor bookies, and compared the shooting to Bugsy's demise, which remained unsolved.

The talk of the town became, *Why didn't they get to Mickey?* Many authors accepted the simple answer: he had hid in one of the lavatory stalls. The convenient take was somewhat unrealistic, because trained hit men weren't shy when it came to aiming a few blasts at john doors or breaking them down.

Mickey explained why the shooters left without being sure that they got him: Rist was able to get control of a pistol, and the shooters were amateurs. He told Muir, "If they had been real operators and not such cowardly rats they could have walked up the alley and stuck their guns in through the window and blasted us all. I got a good look at the face of the man who came in first, and as long as I live I will never forget it." Most reports say that the room was dim, making a hit from the outside difficult.

Ballistics experts Sergeant James Layne and Lieutenant Fred Wolfe studied the thirty-eight caliber slugs, and concluded that the bullets matched those of the assailant's gun supplied by Rist.

Groman's Mortuary, 830 W. Washington Boulevard, housed Hooky's body. His brother Louis planned for services the next day, as soon as relatives could arrive from the East Coast.

Mickey detractors claim that he had Hooky set up, and their friendship was questionable, more Shakespearean tragedy than a Norman Rockwell painting. The California Crime Study Commission was also convinced that he had it in for his pal. The Commission claimed that he had ordered Hooky beaten in the past and concluded that the bookie boss had set up the hit. Mickey's friends said that it was unlikely that he would harm Hooky. Fratianno and Dragna, the notable people behind the attack, were not fond of Mickey, and the hit likely had nothing to do with Hooky.

Hooky's surviving brothers did not hold a grudge. At the funeral his brother Babe nodded to Mickey and murmured, "You don't have to say anything. Hooky died the way he wanted. He lived for you, and he died for you the way he wanted."

The experience shocked Mickey, who had been in high spirits pending the completion of his new haberdashery.

He became a hot news item. The FBI commented on the headline attention: "He received sensational publicity in August, 1948, following the assassination of his bodyguard Harry (Hooky) Rothman, supposedly by rival gangsters, and the wounding of two other associates at Cohen's place of business on Sunset Boulevard, Los Angeles."

Police seized Mickey's "bluebook," essentially a list of contacts. Lieutenant Garner Brown of the sheriff's homicide detail began a tedious process of calling and questioning everyone whose name appeared in the book. The list also contained all of Mickey's celebrity contacts, the unlisted telephone numbers of politicians, prizefighters, newspapermen, and Hollywood stars, creating an awkward set of circumstances for the investigators. Chief Detective Norris Stensland reassured the public that no wholesale arrests of names listed in the bluebook would take place, which reduced rumors that had appeared in the papers and alarmed Mickey's celebrity circle.

The local police arrested Mickey three separate times in conjunction with the hit on Hooky, suspicion of murder, suspicion of conspiracy to commit murder, and conspiracy to obstruct justice; assault with a deadly weapon; and robbery. Even with the piling on of charges, nothing harmful to him materialized; his legal team proved successful again. The FBI also begged off the situation.

Mickey established extra security precautions at the haberdashery. He installed bulletproof doors, steel walls, and an elaborate burglar alarm. He stationed an around-the-clock guard on the premises. A steel-plated door separated the sales floor from his office, which was finished with walnut paneling, a ceiling-suspended television, and indirect lighting. He usually sat at a circular desk in an oversized swivel chair, under a picture of President Franklin D. Roosevelt.

In a new roust on September 2, 1948, police arrested Mickey's friend, actor Robert Mitchum, who was charged with possession of marijuana while in the company of two sexy employees of madam Brenda Allen[7]: twenty-five-year-old dancer Vicki Evans and twenty-year-old actress Lila Leeds.[8] Real estate agent Robin Ford was also at the West Hollywood Hills Ridpath Drive bash.

Mitchum told reporters that his career was "all washed up."

Mitchum biographer Lee Server discussed the famous case in unflattering terms for Mickey: "...was widely understood that Mickey Cohen, king of the dope, prostitution, and gambling rackets, had a sizable percentage of LA city and county law enforcement in his pockets..." Mitchum never outright accused Mickey of a setup, but Server was clear: "a connect-the-dots conspiracy theory; that the events leading up to Ridpath Drive were engineered by a vengeful ex-associate, mobster Mickey Cohen, and some corrupt faction in the Sheriff's department ready to do Mickey's bidding."

The D.A. was convinced that madam Brenda Allen, herself a shapely redhead, was helping Mickey use the call girls for blackmail by recording and photographing the sex action with unknowing johns. He had several young men in his employ who helped set up these salacious sessions and sexual blackmail provided a steady stream of cash from distraught husbands, caught in the act with Allen's bevy of young beauties.

Mickey's boys were frequently in and out of trouble. On November 1, 1948, Lieutenant William Burns' special gangster unit jailed Mickey and five pals. Officers picked up the gang at the haberdashery and whisked them off to the Central Jail on violation of Section 137 of the Penal code, which "prohibits influencing of witnesses' testimony by threat, violence, or bribery." The arresting officers threw in a narcotics charge for Max Rothman. Others arrested were James Regace, Sol Davis, and Davey Ogul. Police later grabbed thirty-five-year-old Jimmy Rist at Mickey's Café Continentale on Santa Monica Boulevard.

The officers nearly fell to the floor when the guests surrendered their pocket cash. Mickey removed slightly over three thousand dollars from his custom-tailored trousers. Max Rothman had forty-one hundred and change, while impoverished Regace barely counted to three hundred and fifty, Ogul nearly one hundred, Rist a few cents shy of sixty bucks, and pauper Sol Davis had only ten dollars and fifteen cents.

The new arrests related to gambler William Petroff's beating on August 30. Police suspected that Joe Sica and Robert Iannone had roughed up the card player. Nothing transpired because the victim later told police Lieutenant Burns that it was all a big mistake and that the beating was part of a drunken brawl.

Then Petroff flipped, and told Chief Deputy D.A. S. Ernest Roll that Mickey and his goons had threatened him. He told the authorities how he had earlier met with Mickey, Regace, Rist, Davis, and one of Mickey's attorneys at a ranch home near Malibu.

In order to insure Petroff's cooperation Mickey tried to pay him off, saying, "Don't you know I can have you killed in five minutes? You'd better keep in line. Don't you want to stay alive around this town?" Mickey gave Petroff fifty dollars and emphasized that he was to repeat the drunken brawl story to the grand jury.

Mickey naturally denied the whole episode and told reporters, "This is a crime against humanity. I've got all the facts, and this is the worst double cross I ever got. Petroff tried to shake me down for money. Burns thanked me when I turned him in. They must be doing this for publicity."

The Petroff beating was typical of many incidents reported in the newspapers. Mickey would always deny the circumstances, and the story would peter out as soon as someone lit a flame under a new one. His schedule included many appointments regarding indictments and grand jury requests, some involving him directly, but more often, anyone remotely connected to his operations. Litigious

Mickey, armed with the best attorneys that money could buy, also contributed to his hectic court calendar by initiating lawsuits.

During all of the legal and political wrangling, Mickey still had to contend with local competition. Some authorities wrongly identified James Francis Utley (Squeaky), a partner in the *Lux* gambling ship, as the heir apparent to the Los Angeles throne, which now stretched to burgeoning Las Vegas. Mickey did not perceive Utley or anyone else as a permanent threat. He ran an abortion clinic in Los Angeles that catered to women from the Pacific Northwest.[9] Perverse Utley would dress up as a doctor to attend the operations, and insisted on conducting his own personal examination that included sex. He also owned a few gambling traps, ran bingo games, and used hockshops as fronts.

Mickey's take on Utley did not include leadership potential: "I don't think Dragna realized it, that this guy Utley was an out-and-out stool pigeon for the D.A. and attorney general's office." Mickey admitted that Bugsy had once asked him to refrain from attacking Utley, citing that Utley's business with the police was part of regular activities. If that was true, the California Crime Commission was not spilling what they knew to the public.

Jim Richardson of the *Los Angeles Examiner* reported that Mickey confessed to him that he had considered killing Utley, but the boys took a vote and decided that a beating was sufficient.

"Utley's rise spells more trouble for Mickey," naysayer author Turkus advertised incorrectly. He continued: "…the noisy hoodlum and a strong-arm aid barged into Utley's restaurant to settle a difference of opinion. In his typically show-off style, Mickey picked a busy noon hour. They gave Utley a savage pistol-whipping, while some one hundred luncheon customers looked on."

According to Mickey, the incident took place in front of the famous Brown Derby on Vine Street.[10] Mickey had left Champ Segal's barbershop at lunchtime. Utley was talking to a "copper" named Roughhouse Brown; Mickey assumed Utley was doing some of his stool pigeon work, and he nonchalantly continued on his way. Utley spotted him and walked over, which didn't sit well with status-conscious Mickey, who didn't want to be seen in public with Utley and a cop.

The retired pugilist remembered: "So I went over and I give him [Utley] a few backhanders—beat him up pretty badly." He admitted that there were a few onlookers. "We didn't try to kill him." He likely had clubbed Utley unconscious with a pistol butt.

Mickey understood how to use Hollywood, the media, and politicians to his benefit. Yet Turkus predicted his demise after the Utley incident: "It is just such flamboyancy that stamps Mickey as a plug-ugly who seeks to blow his importance up to the stature of a ranking boss of the Syndicate. It is notable through the years, none of the big-shot moguls ever went around attracting attention in public, anywhere. They have, in fact, shunned all such antics. Lucky and Lepke and Frank Costello and Joey Adonis and the Fischettis and the rest—it is their very aversion to the public exhibitionism Mickey displays which has made them powerful."

Many writers didn't see Mickey's manipulation of the media and the public as a tool and maintained that he was naïve. Most gangsters, before and after him, publicly belittled their personal intelligence and diminished the size and success of their ventures when speaking with the media. The East Coast brass were both admonishing and admiring of his consistent public style. Frank Costello was baffled by him: "Jesus Christ, Mickey, that publicity is going to kill ya." Lucky Luciano always had said of the publicly demure Costello, "…now there is a man who knows how to keep his mouth shut and tend to business."

Mickey was in flux, and took personal stock of his position. He was aware that his celebrity status might interfere with his ability to make an illegal living. He still had a steady flow of cash, and his envious empire had a national following, but the recent wave of publicity cut his profit margins, and he questioned the benefits of such overwhelming publicity and concomitant fame. He craved the attention, but liked the money more.

The ballyhoo also had a negative effect on his social life, and contributed to a mild depression. When his nefarious exploits repeatedly hit the papers, many celebrities who had become accustomed to his habitual presence in the clubs, and were never shy about using his promotional or financial resources, began to distance themselves from his exploits and turn down his social invitations.

He was suddenly afraid to contact people that he had previously felt were his friends. Florabel Muir characterized him as a man who "leads a lonely life surrounded only by those whose reputations can't be damaged by association with him."

It was a turning point in his life. He became aware of the duality of celebrity. His public image, always something that inspired him, had now become a source of isolation.

Like anyone addicted to fame, Mickey could not stop. He decided to stay the course. He knew he had already crossed the line and later concluded, "I sometimes think that I've always been too friendly with reporters." He was smart enough to realize that his lifelong association with reporters and the newspaper business provided insight not available to most criminals, and served as a business advantage. He also knew that his background from the wrong side of the tracks was a hindrance to reputable assimilation. He still hoped that his celebrity could overcome his shortcomings.

Mickey continued his avid newspaper reading and was ready to refute articles to control the damage to his reputation, while he kept abreast of current events. He expanded his contact with journalists and sports writers, and became a consistent pundit.

He had his limitations, and once told Muir, "I love you like a sister, Florabel, but even for you I ain't going to talk to no cops. If I knew the killers were in the next room I wouldn't turn them in to cops."

He surged ahead, despite continued police and FBI surveillance. Some surveillance teams complained of their fruitless labors because all they listened to was bickering between Mickey and his cronies. The FBI would soon temporarily close its surveillance and phone tap operations on him. But that didn't stop the local police from continuing their daily harassment tactics.

Mickey's next year would bring him even more notoriety, while raising his public image as a local savior.

Mickey testifying.

Mickey as a young
boxer, 1928.

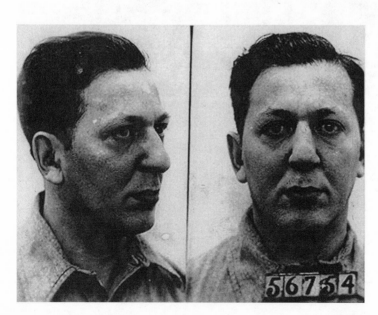

Louis "Lepke" Buchalter.

Happy Meltzer, Mickey, and Big Jim Vaus with his recordings.

The Brown Derby in 1941.

Meyer Lansky.

Bugsy Siegel.

George Raft.

Vito Genovese in 1945.

Lucky Luciano in 1947.

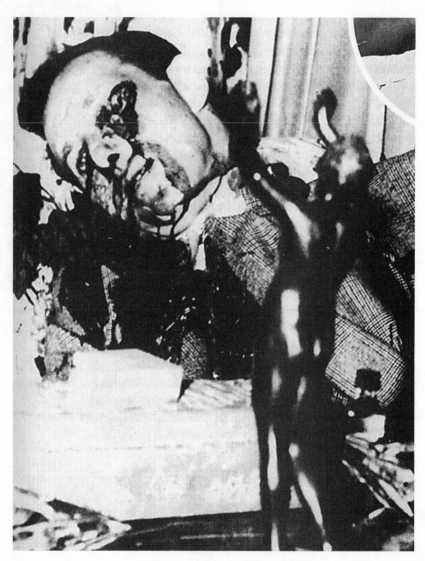

Bugsy Siegel dead, June 20, 1947.

Frank Costello, 1947.

With attorney Sam Rummel, who had Mickey released after a writ of habeas corpus in the Pearson trial, March 25, 1949.

With bail bondsman William Lewis. Judge wants Mickey to find Little Davey Ogul, January 17, 1950.

Sam Giancana, mob boss of Chicago.

Mickey on trial for cursing a cop, September 20, 1949.

Carlos Marcello, mob boss
of New Orleans.

Mickey and LaVonne at the first tax trial, April 1951.

Mickey after his house was bombed.

Johnny Rosselli.

10.

Mickey and the Seven Dwarfs

Mickey spent most of his office time at his new haberdashery headquarters at Sunset Boulevard and Palm Avenue, the site of the Hooky Rothman murder. After his emotional stumble, brief isolation, and coming to terms with his knavish celebrity, his vision was to move up. He went about it carefully.

By January of 1949, the daily gross from the single Flamingo location was over one hundred thousand dollars. That year Moe Sedway would personally take out nearly four hundred thousand dollars. Mickey was making tons more money than the FBI estimated in its scrupulous but un-incriminating files. Trans America wire service had folded in 1947, and the surviving Continental Press, self-described as a news provider, reported a yearly income of nearly two and one-half million dollars. It was the number one betting system in the country. It hooked up all the top bookies, providing off-track information for the casinos.

Mickey's power and business interests were now so pervasive that he often knew the time and location of police raids, which were intended mainly for show. He had some of his gambling locations customized, much like in the popular Abbott and Costello movies, where a whole room could mechanically change at a moment's notice. When word arrived concerning the phony raid, a manager only needed to push a button and all the gaming tables would vanish. Mickey had such a disappearing hideout in Midland, Texas[1] (President Bush's current hometown). The entire casino, including the card and craps tables, would disappear into the concrete floor of an automobile garage.

It was his job to keep the expanded gambling locations running smoothly and to insure that celebrities and wealthy locals could gamble at will. Despite all the public warnings, droves of suckers packed his establishments, allowing him to provide the national syndicate with a constant gaming cash flow. Most experts reported that all the games were fixed, which is more likely true than not. He had the skill to fix the casino games, mostly with marked cards and trick dice.

At a meeting at Mickey's bugged house, Mike Howard, one of his own boys, was quoted in police reports when he outlined the wise man's logic regarding games of chance: "It ain't gambling if you play gin and pick up pat hands, or if you roll the right dice. It's business. You must wind up a winner every night. Don't be a gambler—be a businessman. Get the dough, if you got to take it away from them, knock 'em down and put a gag in their mouth. You got to figure what is going on. You go to the ball game, you come back with some money...don't make a damn who wins; you win anyway. For my dough, you can take those honest games and stick them. I go to the races, and sit there for five races and drink ice tea, and bet on the last race, because it's fixed and I know it. That's not gambling; that's business. To hell with luck."

Mickey was very protective of his turf, and wasn't afraid to personally confront the competition. One example involved a tip-off indicating that a couple of thugs from St. Louis were planning to heist one of his joints. He waited for the thieves outside.

The stunned gunmen exchanged pleasantries, and then apologized to their host: "Jeeze, Mick. We was misinformed. We wunt touch no joint of yours."

He loaned each of the hardworking looters two grand for making the long trip and returning shorthanded. They sent the money back a few weeks later.

He commented sarcastically, "I guess they must of done another piece of work."

On January 15, 1949, two police officers stopped Mickey's pal Harry "Happy" Meltzer[2] (Happy Freed). Inconsiderate Meltzer was supposedly carrying a gun without a permit. Florabel Muir, who covered the ensuing debacles in a series of articles for the *New York Daily News*, marked this per chance rousting as the beginning of a year that she enjoyed calling the "Vicecapades of 1949," named after the immensely popular Ice Capades shows that played at venues like Madison Square Garden. She recalled the incredible year: "The curtain went up on a year's run of comic and dramatic skits." *Nation* contributor and future editor Carey McWilliams labeled the upcoming bizarre events a "complete paralysis of law enforcement."

The day Meltzer was pinched he was driving a Cadillac behind one driven by Mickey. The two vice squad detectives who stopped Meltzer were Mickey enemies Detective Lt. Rudolph Wellpott and Sergeant E. V. Jackson.

Since the detectives could not produce a gun, the defense charged them with an unfounded shakedown and spiteful arrest. At this trial, attorney Sam Rummel played a tape of Sergeant Jackson talking with high-profile celebrity madam Brenda Allen, an incriminating scenario that certainly diminished Jackson's testimony. By the time the defense finished all of its shenanigans, Jackson faced charges of extorting twenty grand from Mickey, perjury, living with prostitutes, running a house of ill repute, and murder.

Thanks to a tip off, police surprised the head of the vice squad during a dalliance with Brenda Allen in a parked car. The cops were regular customers; they would stop by Allen's place to collect bribes and "engage in immoral relations" as described by the *New York Times*. No vice operation functioned successfully without the cooperation of the local police.

Meltzer's arrest had backfired. Instead, the arresting officers and the head of the vice squad were publicly humiliated. The police force became the butt of newspaper criticism, and the ensuing grand jury investigated Chief C. B. Horrall and Deputy Chief Joseph E. Reed.

National audiences watched the soap opera play out between Mickey and squeaky-clean embarrassed Mayor Fletcher Bowron, who pledged to clean up the city again, and began a publicity campaign touting the merits of the government and police.

The ongoing Brenda Allen case (she was the target of a vice sting operation) complicated Bowron's attempts to sway the public. The vice department had consistently looked the other way when it came to Allen, but now felt that they could make a case against her. Some authorities hoped that they could incriminate Mickey in the city's attack on her prostitution ring. He went on the offensive and publicly accused vice squad Sergeant Stoker of protecting Allen's "swank house of prostitution and assignation." She had regularly paid Stoker one hundred dollars per week. The obvious turn-the-tables ploy took the heat off organized crime, and increased the public's scrutiny of the police. Straightlaced journalists cringed when Mickey accused Bowron's cops of being crooked. Unbeknownst to the authorities, the exhibitionist hoodlum, as the papers called him, had orchestrated the entire

Brenda Allen affair. Even though the FBI was aware of Mickey's police payoffs, he continued to manipulate the situation to his advantage.[3]

Heavyset J. Arthur "Big Jim" Vaus' recordings (he was an electronics maven) clearly incriminated Sergeant Stoker, who bossed Brenda's operation. The topper was the court's initial rejection of Mickey's generous offer to provide the tapes, citing the source as unreliable. The recordings, including telephone calls, materialized later and were played before a grand jury.[4]

Mayor Bowron began his version of damage control, and accused the Los Angeles Grand Jury of soft-pedaling the investigation. The mayor wanted the public to believe that Mickey had paid for the incriminating wiretapping solely to have the goods on the police. The public was on to the police, didn't buy Mayor Bowron's spin, and sided with Mickey.

Mickey's future nemesis William Parker, who then worked as an overzealous inspector, stepped up the action and threatened to expose the entire history of city corruption. He zeroed in on Sergeant Stoker, who had enjoyed a long career playing both sides of the legal fence and was surprisingly sympathetic to Mickey, and publicly supported his claims of corruption in the police department. Stoker, who was in deep financial trouble, cooperated with the press, was suspended, and charged with attempted burglary in relation to a home improvement loan.

Despite all the threats and legal hullabaloo, the only arrest and conviction belonged to Brenda Allen. However, factions developed within the vice squad, and increased Mickey's enemy list. He still traveled with his own extra bodyguard, Sergeant Cooper. The FBI believed that he was concerned about his own vulnerability, and that he, as Bugsy had been, was in danger from the east coast enclaves.

Despite Mickey's growth, many crime historians confused the issue of his power and diminished his role. An FBI file dated March 3, 1949, observed that, "prominent criminal operators...have been forced to leave Los Angeles," suggesting that Mickey was succeeding. One agent reported that, "Mickey Cohen is definitely on an offensive in this area and has ambitions to replace Benjamin 'Bugsie' [sic] Siegel as the criminal boss of the Los Angeles-Las Vegas area." The FBI soon acknowledged, "Mickey Cohen is the principal criminal figure in the Los Angeles area and heads a gang of hoodlums and alleged killers who dominate racketeering activities in the Los Angeles area." However, the FBI continually ignored his national connections.

Mickey's antics became the focus of Governor Warren of California. On March 7, he released a second report of the Governor's Commission on Organized Crime, which detailed the use of the Continental Wire Service, still operating out of Cleveland, and its illegal and incestuous relationship with Western Union. Western Union distributed the race wire information to eight major drop-off points, which, in turn, supplied Mickey's bookies with timely betting information. It naturally denied any culpability, as well as the existence of Mickey's cartel. The governor asked Attorney General Howser to intercede, but he refused, despite a court order, and continually denied the existence of bookmaking.

Mayor Fletcher Bowron of Los Angeles, instead of asking city officials to cooperate with state and federal authorities, went out of his way to elevate Mickey to a public crusader. The office of the police commissioner called Mickey, didn't disclose the nature of the call, and only said that it was important that they talk to the gambling boss in person. Mickey had contributed regularly to the mayoral campaigns through attorneys Sam Rummel and Vernon Ferguson; a call from the commissioner on behalf of the mayor was understandable.

Fish restaurant Goodfellow's Grotto, home to the Richard Nixon kick-off campaign, was the location chosen for the special meeting. Mickey joined Captain Harry M. Lorenson, a top-ranking chief investigator for the police commission, and clothing manufacturer Burton Mold, a political activist. They wanted to talk to him about a litigious radio repairman named Alfred Pearson, who had a shop at 5120 West Adams.

The police were upset about Pearson suing Elsie Phillips, a little old lady customer, over an inflated $8.95 repair bill that she had refused to pay. Fifty-three-year-old Pearson had also sued the city regularly. This included Police Captain Lorenson for $45,000, alleging that he was trying to put Pearson out of business.

Pearson had received an inflated judgment against Elsie, and with the help of a potentially bribable city marshal sought Elsie's home as payment. He won the $4,000 home for under $26.50. Under the law, Pearson immediately charged Elsie ten bucks per week rent, which the outraged police investigators gladly paid for her.

Mayor Bowron passed down very explicit instructions at the meeting with Mickey: it was okay to bang Pearson around, but not to kill him. The mayor mentioned that it would be good to send him to the hospital, and even suggested the best day and time for a hit.

Mickey offered the smart way out, kill the bum, but acquiesced to Bowron's plan. Consumer advocate Mickey sent seven of his hooligans to rough up Pearson. Initially posing as reporters, they spoke to Pearson's daughter-in-law, sometimes rudely, only later having their "editor" apologize by phone.

A Keystone Cop scenario unfolded. On March 19, 1949, the skullduggery contingent arrived disguised as pickets and nearly killed Pearson. He suffered a cracked skull and a fractured right arm after the do-gooders went at him with fists, iron bars, feet, and pistol butts.

Two rookie cops, Allen Rubin and W. S. Carey, were conveniently in the area, along with amateur photographer Roy Diehl. The officers watched as the departing bad boys rushed into a sedan.

The perpetrators made an illegal U-turn, headed west on Adams, and the police gave chase. Rubin and Carey radioed for additional patrol cars, brandished their weapons, and forced the sedan to pull over at 2124 Orange Drive. Other patrol cars arrived; officers cuffed the scoundrels. The police found several pistols under the car seats, and recovered a riding crop and a tire iron that flew out of the fleeing vehicle during the pursuit. Without further delay, the officers issued a traffic ticket.

The seven perps arrested were Neddie Herbert, Frankie Niccoli, Davey Ogul, Happy Meltzer, Eli Lubin, Lou Schwartz, and Jimmy Rist. The list of defendants, dubbed the "Seven Dwarfs" by the *Herald*, would later grow to thirteen.

After the radio police took the boys into custody, Wilshire Bureau Detective Lieutenant Jack Swan promptly ordered their release. One of the dwarfs warned the police, "…you square this beef, or we're going to shoot the works against the department." Lt. Swan claimed that he didn't know who the boys were; he thought that they were local businessmen who had formed a picket line, and had legal gun permits.

Out of jail, some of Mickey's' Disney characters absconded to Oracle Junction, Phoenix. Mickey recalled that the *Examiner*'s Jim Richardson offered the corporate plane to fly at least three of the dwarfs to Phoenix so that they could hole up at Stumpy Zevon's residence. Judge Schweitzer sentenced a missing Davey Ogul to ninety days in jail after his attorney Joseph T. Fornow told the judge that Davey had telephoned to say that he was ill.

Sergeant Winfield Scott Wolfe had told the rookie police Officers Rubin and Carey, and traffic officers William Hinkens and Doyle Crowder, to tear up their notes and not discuss the case, and treat it as a routine shakedown, citing a need to protect the department.

The *Herald Express*, a Hearst-controlled newspaper, ran this March headline: SEEK COHEN POLITICAL LINK IN POLICE HUSHUP SCANDAL. The column head read, HEARING OF BOSS IS SET.

Mickey laughed off the whole situation. "They say they're lookin' for some of my boys, well I don't have any boys anymore." The *Express* called him "affable" in its article.

According to him, he had arrived at Pearson's shop with only little Davey Ogul and Jimmy Rist, a three-hundred-pound *shtarker* and former fighter. The embellishment mentions that three hundred onlookers applauded the event from outside the store.

After the beating, while Mickey waited at his office in Slapsy Maxie's, he found out about a technical problem—Pearson had recorded the beating. He had snapped on the recording device as soon as Mickey's boys had entered. He also had recorded prior telephone calls from the phony newspaper reporters. Mickey sent dainty Jimmy Rist back to get the device. The FBI was livid: they overheard the plan to retrieve the recording tape.

Mickey also secured the negatives of amateur photographer Roy Diehl's photographs taken during the arrests. Bob Will, the police reporter for the *LA Times*, acted as an intermediary. Mickey failed to buy the newspaper prints from editor Chester "Smokey" Hale.

The new champion of civil rights became an overnight cult hero. Because of conservative public pressure, the police pinched Mickey, and he posed for an ominous-looking photo trailed by one of his henchman, forty-one-year-old Solly Davis. He and Davis were booked separately on suspicion of conspiracy at the county jail. Bail for each was set at a monstrous one hundred thousand dollars.[5] Bail bondsman Glasser Brothers posted the money for Mickey, but Solly remained in jail. Superior Judge Charles W. Fricke, contacted at home at 9:00 p.m., signed the writ for Mickey's release.

Unshaven Mickey, dressed in a zippered golf jacket, v-neck sweater and wide-brimmed hat, asked his captors in front of the press, "What is this, anyway?" while he waited for his release.

He confided with reporters, "What can I say? I guess they just need publicity for the elections, or something. I knew it was going to happen, I knew they would get me before the election."

LaVonne picked him up at the police station and they went to dinner at a Vine Street restaurant in Hollywood. He told reporters that after dinner he intended to head home.

This time Mickey was unsure if the FBI would play ball with the local authorities, so he opted for a safe haven within short flying time of Los Angeles, and left for Mexico until things died down, leaving Frankie Niccoli in charge of Michael's Haberdashery. Mickey knew that he had nothing to fear from local authorities, but wisely waited to see what the FBI would do, but their informants came up with little, often spying on the personal lives of Mickey's employees and associates, who boasted of windfalls from the past such as the illegal nylon business. Agents knew that it would be difficult to make a case against Mickey, but trudged onward with their flimsy informant program.

Three days after the beating, local authorities asked for FBI assistance in bringing the stray dwarfs back home. Assistant U.S. Attorney Ray Kinnison had wired Attorney General Tom C. Clark in Washington because this whole episode was a civil rights violation. The FBI did not confirm the request, and therefore kept their usual distance from Mickey and his gang.

A grand jury convened to look into the role of the police in freeing Mickey's boys. Mayor Bowron and Chief of Police Horrall tried to control the situation in the media. The D.A. charged Lt. Swan with releasing felony suspects without knowing the facts and ordering the release of potential evidence without a full investigation. Sergeant Wolfe had one additional charge, instructing officers to withhold and destroy evidence.

Bow tied D.A. Simpson asked jury foreman Harry A. Larson to schedule a special panel for the Friday after March 23 to review Mickey's indictment. Simpson later talked tough to the newspapers: "We have asked that all available evidence be delivered to us…no one will be spared and that the chips will fall where they may."

Bulldog Assistant D.A. John Barnes echoed the sentiment: "No punches will be pulled."

Simpson later admitted that it would be tough to get Mickey. Everyone was convinced that he had orchestrated the scenario but evidence was lacking. The D.A. backed off. "… But it's pretty hard to put the finger on the person in back of a web."

Chief Horrall still wanted the book thrown at Mickey and the dwarfs, including robbery, burglary, and assault with intent to commit murder.

Mayor Bowron supported Horrall, but needed to reassure the public in the newspapers. Bowron mimicked the still popular nineteenth-century Ivory soap advertisement, assuring that the police department was "99.44% pure." Mickey controlled many cops in the infinitesimal "56%" portion.

The Pearson saga continued to make regular front-page news. The publicity rivaled anything previously recorded, and the newspapers further christened Mickey and his gang, Snow White and the Seven Dwarfs. A popular cartoon depicting the gang in Disney drag filled the newspapers.

"Mickey was treated as the patron saint of the disenfranchised in Los Angeles," said journalist Pete Noyes.

The media played up Elsie-the-widow as a victim, embellishing that she was caring for her son's child while he was off in the military, preparing to fight in Korea.

Good Samaritan Mickey returned to town, and latched on to his new image expressed in the *Examiner*, a "hounded Robin Hoodlum fighting off the scheming minions of the law."

Prosecutors charged Snow White with assault with a deadly weapon, murder, and obstruction of justice. Attorney Sam Rummel headed Mickey's defense team with the cooperation of local police and politicians. Desperate fishing-expedition-styled prosecutors indicted clothing manufacturer Burton Mold for obstruction of justice.

The convened grand jury reviewed the tangled legal process, beginning with when the police returned the gang's weapons and let them off the hook without charges. They focused on the subsequent police suspensions.

Captain Harry M. Lorenson somewhat sided with Mickey: "The only thing I am interested in is legal action against Pearson. I do not approve of gangster methods such as Cohen's. I think the parties responsible for this should be apprehended immediately. I have accused Pearson of being the most dishonest businessman in the city...one and two calls a day from people Pearson gypped... We have hundreds of witnesses to testify against him." He told suspicious reporters that he had never met Mickey.

Pearson continued his legal quest to convict Lorenson for malicious prosecution and civil conspiracy, claiming that he tried to destroy Pearson's business, and ridicule him publicly in the process. A recuperating Pearson told Chief Horrall, "I may be laughing now but the next time you see me I may be in a morgue. That's where I'll be. And I ain't kidding."

The FBI informant was still in place and concentrated on Niccoli's relationship with an unnamed female in the hope of digging up evidence against Mickey. The plant reported Niccoli's interpersonal fights, as if his social break-ups had an impact on Mickey or the case. One FBI agent gingerly wrote that the informant wasn't giving them much, but he remained on the payroll anyway. Another agent begrudgingly wrote that based on what he could assess from the local police informants it would be difficult to make a case against Mickey.

On March 28, 1949, the FBI finally installed their new microphone surveillance, after several failed attempts having to do with "leased wire" problems. By May, they gave up on interfering in the Pearson case, and again dismantled their new high-tech devices. They received tip information from columnist Walter Winchell on April 18 that proved of little help.

In early May, an ambush took place while Mickey drove his car home to Brentwood. The modified car could travel at higher speeds than most street vehicles. He was under fire for several blocks, and dodged bullets from shotguns and Tommy guns, much like the gangster movies. Lying on the front seat, he managed to steer the car along main drag Wilshire Boulevard, while he dodged the crossfire. Like movie stars Cagney, Raft, or Robinson, he drove through the deluge unscathed.

He supplied this account of his behavior during the fusillade: "I'm probably at my coolest in an emergency. The minute I sensed what was happening, I fell to the floor and rode that goddamn car all the way down Wilshire with one hand. I probably couldn't do it again in a thousand times... With all the shooting, I only got hit with the flying glass, but I must have had fourteen, fifteen, sixteen little pieces of glass in me."

When Mickey arrived home, his dinner guests were waiting for him, including mob actor George Raft! Nobody was able to sit down to eat except Mickey, who enjoyed his strip steak and Cherries Jubilee as if nothing had happened. Raft was in no mood to consume his favorite apple pie after seeing his bloodied host, who, for the moment, minimized the event.

The whole town was edgy. Another incident took place in a hangout called Plymouth House, which catered to both the police and the mob. Fred Otash, working for the police at the time, related how two of Mickey's bodyguards heckled him and his partner Rudy Diaz when they had entered the restaurant. When the bad guys spat on the floor, Diaz went to work on one of them. As Eli Lubin came to the bodyguard's aid, Otash tripped Lubin and hit him in the back of the head with a gun.

Mickey ran out of the dining room, with his napkin still neatly tucked inside his vest, and yelled, "What the hell's going on here?"

Otash replied, "Two of your seven dwarfs think it's cute to spit on cops and no sonofabitch is going to get away with that. Take these idiots back inside and give them their pablum. They're not ready for steak yet."

The following week Mickey and his gorillas ducked raining bullets as they exited the same establishment. The reporters, who knew about the previous fight, suspected the cops, particularly because the recovered buckshot looked like the police issue variety. Otash had an alibi, telling the FBI that the alleged assailants had been fishing in Malibu with many witnesses, and things cooled down.

Toward the end of May, Los Angeles police concentrated on locating Mickey's missing dwarfs. One lucky search tip forced a "flying squadron" of police to head to balmy Palm Springs to search for anyone associated with the Alfred Pearson beating. The *Los Angeles Times* described how a sweep of the area took place, something hard to accomplish in a sprawling desert.

The big plans of Sergeant John J. O'Mara of Los Angeles and the local Palm Springs Chief A. G. Kettman resulted in a series of low-level arrests of ex-cons and party girls who knew Mickey. While sweeping sunny Palm Springs, Sergeant O'Mara suggested that Eli Lubin and James Rist were more likely in Phoenix.

Back in town, the nightclub scene could sometimes become a little raucous, irrespective of mob business. The morning hours of May 31, 1949, witnessed trouble at popular Charley Foy's Supper Club, 15463 Ventura Boulevard, in Sherman Oaks. Mickey and LaVonne were out for dinner with the Rummels. One of the patrons was tablehopping after one in the morning. When the likely inebriated guest starting flirting with Mickey and Rummel's wives, Rummel gave the man a good shove and said, "Get going."

The man started a fight at the adjacent table and then everyone got into the act. Fortunately, heavyweight boxer Lou Nova, who at one time had gone up against Joe Louis, stepped in while Mickey and his group made for the door.

Sam Rummel said, "I told Mickey it was time for us to get out. In a half second all hell broke loose at our table..."

Captain Charles Stanley arrived to find a quiet restaurant, a cooperative Lou Nova, and some broken glass. Nova gave police a calm explanation: "I walked in and saw a gray-haired man about six feet tall, and a lot of people milling around. I quieted them down and tried to help a couple of screaming women who were nearly hysterical. Later I saw the man being escorted from the room. I don't know who he was."[6]

Lt. William Burns, chief of the police gangster squad, told reporters that he would question Mickey and Rummel.

Walter Winchell supplied the FBI with a note concerning actress Peggy Ann Garner.[7] She had opened in a new Broadway show in May "and Mickey Cohen, the West Coast gangster, is backing it with $75,000." The blacked-out names of the people who had passed the information to Winchell were probably the producers, intent on drumming up publicity by supplying him the information. His intentions remain unclear; the information is hardly incriminating. A personal notation from him, "To Hoover," indicated an ongoing familiarity between the reporter and the FBI czar, although some called Hoover "Edgar."

The FBI focused on every step Mickey took, despite having given up surveillance at his home and places of business. They claimed that one of his attorneys talked him out of participating in a *Collier's* magazine first-person story.

Collier's instead ran with a story on the powerful lobbies that influenced state politics.

Agents questioned the legality of the fight game in Los Angeles, and considered that Mickey was fixing fights. They wondered, what were Mickey's connections to the local tracks like Santa Anita? What did the local specialized Gangster Squad have on Mickey? Many exchanges between Washington and Los Angeles resulted in the same foregone conclusion: "case closed…not under our jurisdiction." The FBI forever provided Mickey with a free ride.

The feds barely recognized the expansiveness of Mickey's ventures, although they acknowledged that he was no longer a local phenom: "…Mickey Cohen is presently engaged in major criminal operations involving interstate enterprises and that he definitely plans to expand in the future." The agent who wrote it suggested that they bug Mickey's office again. FBI boss Hoover granted the request in 1949, and the agents started over.

They also tried to monitor a series of Mickey's phone numbers, as if linking the numbers could provide a national crime pattern. The list that surfaced is somewhat laughable. Joe Glaser, president of Associated Booking Corporation, was one contact detailed extensively in a memo titled, "Michael Cohen, wa. Mickey Cohen." Glaser booked bands, and Mickey or his club employees had many reasons to talk with him.[8] The FBI agents checked Glaser's corporate stock registration, his banks, and business contacts, but nothing turned up in the feds' New York office.

Another report mentioned that a series of phone calls indicated Mickey's ties to organized crime in Arizona, but the FBI still ignored his national tutelage.

Information about Sergeant E. V. Jackson and Lieutenant Rudy Wellpott filled the papers again, and the public had a peek into the Brenda Allen back-story—how Mickey had pulled all the strings. Jackson wanted to take Mickey on in the newspapers. By outlining his perspective as a victim, he claimed that Mickey had threatened him with telephone records of conversations with Allen, because of Harold "Happy" Meltzer's gun toting charge. Mickey had approached Jackson at Temple and Broadway, and threatened him with problems if he made any trouble for Happy Meltzer. Mickey called Jackson a "sucker" in the matter, and suggested that he agree to let Meltzer plead guilty with a reduced penalty, the usual offer. When Jackson and Wellpott refused, they knew that Mickey would discredit them.

Jackson publicly pleaded, "If…I was unable to take criminal action against an associate of Mickey Cohen because I feared exposure by evidence he had collected, I would never have allowed myself to be placed in my present condition… It is also unfortunate that certain of the press have by speculation and inference purported these charges to be unquestionably true."

The press sided with Mickey's campaign of maligning the police, but Jackson still tried a final impassioned plea: "I ask the people of this city to support and assist Chief Horrall…," and blamed Mickey for all the public ill will toward the authorities.

Mayor Fletcher Bowron, who ran on the slogan of having "kept the city clean," was re-elected by a landslide for his fourth term on May 31. Many citizens thought that Bowron had the mob under control. The in-denial residents believed that the mob was nonexistent, merely an exaggeration of pulp fiction writers and eager journalists. Some mob critics presented the diametrically opposed view— that the dirty mob profits actually drained the local economy. Two days after the city of Los Angeles confirmed Bowron, local newspapers began an investigative series of articles dealing with police department scandals, despite the former support of the *Los Angeles Daily News* during the mayoral election.

On June 17, 1949, the FBI noted that they had been monitoring Mickey's business contacts, Oak Valley Farms, Jay Lord Hatters, Jayne Thomas (a woman's hat maker), Jay Hatters, and Jay Lord Manufacturing, a series of companies that sold "a general line of men's furnishings and haberdashery." Despite his haberdashery, and his own personal collection of over twenty boxed hats, the information on his clothing exploits continued to fill FBI files. Granted, mob influence in the garment industry was no secret, and ranged from ownership to delivery trucks, but the FBI made no allegations regarding Mickey's garment center associates, nor mentioned the fact that he utilized a loan shark bank for the garment center operated by Neddie. By June 21, the naïve FBI finally realized— again—that they weren't going to get anything on him by bugging his house, clubs, or haberdashery. The eavesdropping was discontinued on June 21, "inasmuch as same has proved unproductive." Top brass ordered the agents to destroy all handwritten logs; the information was useless and embarrassing.

Local authorities still wondered if Burbank was home to illicit activities, like gambling. The 1949 county grand jury decided to reopen the matter after chairman Harry Lawson of the Criminal Complaints Committee received a request to investigate on June 29. The 1948 grand jury had previously reviewed the same matter, and focused on Mickey's Dincara Stock Farm. Burbank City Prosecutor William Taylor had had no choice but to originally dismiss the charges. A rabbi had signed an affidavit certifying that the alleged gamblers had attended a charity event at Dincara to raise money for the Palestine war. He stated that Mickey had lent the facility for the affair. The current anonymous complainant still had his suspicions, particularly after Burbank police released three men on gambling charges back in May, even though officers found the most modern gaming equipment valued at over twenty-five thousand dollars. Police always released Dincara gamblers for lack of evidence, and confiscated none of the equipment, not as much as a deck of cards, to the dismay of grand jurors.

Mickey received a subpoena to appear at the Mitchum marijuana trial in July 1949. The Los Angeles *Herald Express* and other newspapers eagerly covered every move of the sensational celebrity-driven circus. A photo of police officer Audre Davis outside the grand jury room, replete with Hollywood sunglasses, purse, and scarf, appeared in the July 11 issue.

The newspapers helped promote Mickey's ethical perspective. "I have never mixed with prostitution or neither did I mix with narcotics," was always his stance. "I got certain traits and ethics that I lived up to, and I followed them to the letter."

Nothing linked him to the Mitchum case, and the prosecution could not produce a single witness to testify against him. The D.A. dismissed the case; no charges filed.

Mickey's joints couldn't be touched, and certain authorities spent a large part of their lives trying to topple the reigning king. On July 19, good-guy police Lt. Rudy Wellpott raided Mickey's private club on La Brea and came away with a hundred decks of marked cards, worth about a thousand dollars. Mickey claimed that he only used the trick equipment on pros who were trying to set him up for a big loss. Wellpott also found two thirty-eights in the office desk, allegedly belonging to Mickey.

Wellpott now publicly advertised his hatred for him: "Mickey knew I intended to kill him."

When he heard about it Mickey's reply was simple: "Tell him the feeling is mutual."

Wellpott followed him around; supposedly hoping Mickey would pull a gun on him, so he could accomplish his braggart goal.

Everyone was talking about Mickey, thanks to his close relationship to journalists and recent events. The newspaper love affair with him continued, particularly with the Hearst press, which liked to describe Mickey as a "gambler." He had a cozy relationship with many Hearst employees. At the suggestion of old friend *Examiner* City Editor Jim Richardson,[9] Mickey had the attachment removed from widow Elsie Phillip's home, and he returned the house to her with a tidy profit. William Randolph Hearst had personally called Richardson to tell him to lay off Mickey and give him a "fair break" whenever Richardson grew critical. Hearst, who would die in 1951, was fond of Mickey, understood him as a unique character, and suggested to him that he didn't have to be a gangster, that he was capable of running other businesses.

Mickey didn't know what to make of Hearst. His low self-esteem prevented him from appreciating and acting on Hearst's perspective. Hearst was similarly unable to recognize Mickey's incurable social impediments, which locked him into his lifestyle.

Journalist Muir was more candid than Richardson about her tight association with Mickey: "…his [Mickey's] confidence enabled me materially to get accurate information on the many headline scrimmages in which he was subsequently involved…a benefit to us both. It gave me a wealth of information." She saw herself as Mickey's "mother-confessor."

If a newspaper didn't show love, Mickey would personally burst into the editor's office. *Los Angeles Mirror* editor J. Edward Murray took Mickey's challenge to examine the haberdashery business in order to see if he was legitimate. Murray concluded that his salespersons weren't moving the several-months-old stock. He loved to needle Mickey with character assassinations like "pipsqueak," but confessed that he used Mickey just as the other journalists did—to sell papers. (*Daily News* editor John Clarke ended up drowning; whether he jumped or fell from a boat remains unknown.)

As Mickey's celebrity climbed to new heights, his enemies grew more uncomfortable.

11.

Shootout on the Sunset Strip

July 19, 1949, would be another long night out on the town. Detective Harry Cooper still escorted Mickey. As per Cooper's even newer agreement with Attorney General Howser, he had been everywhere with Mickey the prior week. Mickey had acquiesced to the cozy night escort with the condition that the city and county police reduce their regular harassment, which included a lot of frisking. Money was pouring in regularly from the Sunset Strip clubs, and he needed assurances that his police protection wouldn't interfere with his cash flow and normal operations.[1]

Mickey had dinner at his home with Cooper and sexy Hollywood starlet Dee David of 1545 N. Las Palmas, a very popular social companion who made the rounds.

He had plans to later meet Florabel Muir, who now went everywhere with him. She wasn't shy about her motives: "That's why during the month of July 1949, I was following Mickey Cohen around the gay night spots on the famous Sunset Strip in Hollywood, watching and waiting for someone to try to kill him and hoping I would be there when they did."

The growing eclectic entourage spent several hours at the Continental Café, one of Mickey's joints, before heading over to Sherry's. He also had met earlier with rotund Artie Samish, the powerful state political figure, at the Charochka Cafe.

Muir recalled that she first attended a party in the Hollywood Hills to celebrate Gertrude Niesen's joining the cast of *Annie Get Your Gun*. Louis Sobel of the New York *Journal-American* declined to go on with Muir; he knew that a cup of coffee with Mickey meant a long haul, and he needed a good night's sleep. On her way in to Sherry's that night Muir joked with police sergeant Darryl Murray and Detective Harry Cooper, "What are you standing out here for? Trying to get yourself shot?"

Sergeant Murray had supposedly been present early because he was working undercover to protect Mickey from Eastern gangsters who might be muscling in on the local rackets. Murray's boss, Deputy Chief of Police Thad Brown, thoroughly milked his concerns for Mickey's protection. Chief Brown wanted the public to know that he had a dual responsibility to protect all citizens and Mickey. He went to great pains to publicize that Murray and his squad followed Mickey home every night, and waited until he was safe inside his Brentwood home.

Sheriff Biscailuz had jumped on the polarized political bandwagon by helping protect the citizens from Mickey, sometimes enlisting support from Santa Monica chief Joe H. McClelland and Long Beach chief William H. Dovey. Biscailuz never felt that it was his job to protect Mickey, and this night there wouldn't be a single sheriff near Sherry's or the Strip.[2]

A former New York City detective named Barney Ruditsky owned and ran Sherry's, as well as Plymouth House, where Detective Otash had slugged Eli Lubin. Ruditsky fared better as a restaurateur but had his complaints: "Every night that Mickey Cohen came in, for the protection of my customers, I sort of watched the place and walked around outside and inside." Ruditsky thought that Mickey was a pain in the ass, and he particularly didn't like it when the spiffy ice cream junkie showed up late with his entourage. Despite his bickering, Ruditsky knew the nature of the business at that time—you accommodate the Strip traffic or post a closing sign.[3]

Fratianno recalled the night matter-of-factly: "It had been a slow night at Sherry's until Mickey Cohen arrived with his entourage for their usual coffee and pastries."

Mickey sat inside Sherry's with *Los Angeles Times* reporter Ed Meagher and cameraman Clay Willcokson. He signaled for Muir to join the table. All the journalists wanted to hear what Mickey was willing to say about his being the target of a hit. Who was trying to kill him? Was it only Dragna? Why did he now need local police or state-sponsored federal protection?

Brave Mickey said that he didn't need the protection, and tried to diminish his audience's anxieties. The headline-happy celebrity told the reporters that he had no fears: "Not as long as you people are around. Even a crazy man wouldn't take a chance shooting where a reporter might get hit. You're too hot." Mickey's logic had always worked in the past. Surrounded by columnists with famous bylines, actors, and politicians, he felt safer nightclubbing than he did in his own home. He insisted that the only problem was Biscailuz and his nonsensical frisking stunts; his officers still had instructions to stop and pat down Mickey's men on sight.

When Neddie Herbert joined the bull session, the banter switched to the old days in New York. He talked about how his family survived in the poultry business. Max Annenberg, circulation director of the *Daily News*, "was like my rabbi," he told the enraptured audience. "He used to kick me in the pants and tell me to get on home and stay off the streets so I wouldn't get in no trouble."

A few weeks prior to that night, Neddie was the victim of an assassination attempt outside his apartment. He had just come home from a night out on the town with Eli Lubin, who still appeared around, when he dodged eleven bullets fired by two men lurking out of sight. He pretended to be cool when the journalists questioned him. "I gotta instinct for danger... I didn't even see them two guys, but I sensed 'em before I heard 'em. I dropped to the ground and crawled onto the stairway, and their shots fall all around me," Neddie said moments before the evening died down, and the Sherry's horde adjourned to the street.

The clique now included Johnny Stompanato, identified as a jeweler,[4] Frankie Niccoli, Jimmy Rist, Eli Lubin, and Florabel Muir's husband Denny Morrison (a freelance writer/publicity man), as well as Dee David, Muir, and Detective Cooper. The tired and well-oiled group meandered outside and waited for the valets to return with their cars. An *Evening Herald* reporter described the unlikely congregants as, "...a gay sidewalk throng." Muir's husband stopped to talk with Charlotte Rogers, the press agent for the Mocambo. According to conflicting reports, it was at this moment that Sergeant Murray appeared at the scene.

Ciro's showgirl Beatrice Kay, who had dropped by after work for a bite to eat, left first, followed soon by the *Los Angeles Times* reporter and cameraman.

At between three-thirty and four in the morning on Wednesday, July 20, shots came from behind an embankment on a vacant lot across the street next to crooner Bing Crosby's building.

Ruditsky ran outside from the kitchen when the shooting started. "It sounded like firecrackers and everyone hit the walk."

One of the first shots went through a car window, missing a valet attendant's head by inches.

Inside Sherry's, Muir, who had bent over to retrieve the Los Angeles *Examiner,* turned to Sally Ventura, the hatcheck girl, and exclaimed, "Those bastards are throwing rocks in here too."

Moments later Muir found a flattened half-dollar-sized deer slug on the floor.[5] Another bullet whizzed past them and struck a glass door. Muir ran outside. She had taken some shotgun pellets in the rear.

A blast nipped the ear of vaudeville piano player Margaret Padula, who had a regular gig at Charlie Foy's Supper Club in the Valley.

Cooper yelled, 'I'm hit.'" The hoods had shot Agent Cooper twice in the stomach. It was less than twenty-four hours since Attorney General Howser had publicly disclosed Cooper's new night assignment.

Mickey was easy to find but hard to kill. The shooters struck him in the right shoulder, but he worried more about hitting the pavement in his Al Pignola suit, and tried to keep his balance, or so he claimed years later.

Neddie Herbert's luck would run out, and he fell to the pavement, shot.

Dee David caught pellets in the rear and groin.

The Sherry's shooters also hit an unnamed girl in the back while she stood outside.

Muir, pleased with her exclusive, later provided a moment-to-moment account of the action: "...saw Mickey jumping out of the car driven by his friend Frankie Niccoli. His right arm hung limp, and blood was spreading over his coat near the shoulder. He ran to Cooper, the state police officer, who was clutching his stomach with one hand and waving his pistol with the other. As Mickey grabbed him he began to sag. Blood was spurting down his pants. 'Get in the car,' yelled Mickey, but Cooper couldn't make it. Then with his left arm the little gambler hoisted the six-foot-six officer into Niccoli's car." Muir's heroic depiction has its detractors. Folklore and Mickey-hater Fratianno have it that Mickey bent over to check a scratch in his Cadillac, and the shooters missed badly, but the car took a few hits.

Sergeant Murray was no help. He gave chase, but didn't catch up with anyone.

Niccoli, Mickey, and Cooper left a trail of blood as they rushed for cover, and made it into their cars.

Dee was in severe pain and Johnny Valentine carried her back into Sherry's. Waiters and patrons yelled, "Get out of the way," and tried to make Dee comfortable until the ambulances arrived twenty-five minutes later.

Muir listened to Neddie as he lay motionless on the pavement: "My legs are paralyzed... If Mickey makes it, he's going to go to work with a Mixmaster" (any rapid-firing weapon). The newspapers would run a picture of Neddie lying on the ground in front of Sherry's, and another when medics hoisted him into an ambulance.

After urging later by Muir, since the late-arrival sheriff's deputies refused to look at the vacant lot, Ruditsky found two twenty-gauge shotguns near the scene of the shooting behind a signboard. Muir also found some sardine sandwiches, the obvious dining selection of discerning shooters.[6]

Neddie and Dee initially arrived at Citizens Emergency Hospital on Santa Monica Boulevard, not far from the Strip. The treating doctors were Ray Richmond and Robert Nichols. At the hospital, he repeated the Mixmaster remark, this time substituting "I" for "Mickey." When he was switched to Queen of Angels Hospital, calls went out for extra transfusions.

Mickey and Cooper drove to the same hospital, Hollywood Receiving.

"They almost missed me," Mickey said at the hospital. He handed his "pocket change" to the treating doctor—his version of a co-payment. It consisted of a thousand dollar bill, twenty hundreds, and small bills adding up to an additional sixty-nine. Dr. D. C. Dickey accepted the money from Mickey, who said, "Keep it for me, doc."

Cooper had three abdominal wounds. The early papers said that the doctors expected him to die.

Physicians initially exaggerated Mickey's condition as serious, telling reporters that his shoulder was shattered. Three hours later he was at Queen of Angeles Hospital with all four victims. He had a slug removed, which doctors reported nearly reached his lung, followed by plenty of morphine. He ultimately got off easy with one arm out of commission and a ruined suit jacket. The *New York Times* reported that his injury was slight.

LaVonne, touted as a former showgirl, arrived at the hospital in her Cadillac convertible. When she saw her wounded husband, she fainted; the doctors medicated her with sedatives. The newspapers ran a picture of her escorted out of the hospital by Johnny Stompanato.

An anonymous call came in to Mickey's hospital later that night: "Be on your guard. We're going to come down and get Mickey tonight." A sedan came to a screeching halt in front of the hospital not two hours later. Four men and a woman ran past guards who chased the intruders through the hospital. They never reached Mickey, exited through a side door, made it to the getaway car, and sped off.

The longer-term care for Cooper was provided by Dr. Joseph Zeiler, who almost one year later removed the final bullets from his liver. Doctors initially released him from the hospital on July 30. When he left for the final time on Friday, May 12, 1950, he had major plans the next day. He married Dee David, whom he had met at Mickey's house the night of the shooting! All the victims of the shooting were under constant police guard. Still, because of the media demand for news, photographers had full access to the injured before and after they received treatment. The papers proudly displayed macabre hospital shots, including some victims receiving plasma. The tabloid-style ghastly stuff, the kind true crime fans loved, was big news, the biggest since Bugsy's murder.

Mickey announced the day after the shooting, "I'm scared not only for myself but for everyone around me, my wife, my friends, and even the law. I don't know what to expect next."

When reporters pressured Mickey about the kind of work Neddie performed, he simply answered, "Everybody keeps askin' me if Neddie is my pay-off man for the cops. That's ridiculous. He's only been in town seven months—he hasn't even had time to get acquainted with the cops—let alone pay 'em off."

The papers were full of Mickey's racketeers, some carrying bags of cash into the hospital. A few days after the shooting, the local papers published sympathetic pictures of him lying in the hospital bed. One caption read that a "heavy deer slug" had hit him, invoking the image of an innocent hunted animal. His narrow escape with death aroused sympathies in unexpected places, and his worldwide fan mail became extensive.

Three days later, silk-pajamaed Mickey was angry about all the speculation and spoke to reporters while sipping a glass of ice coffee. "They want me to sit here and lie—just to make it look like they're getting somewhere. Well, I don't lie. I don't drink… I don't smoke… And I don't lie. I lead a real pure life." The purist had ordered filet mignon for his supper; he had the local restaurants deliver all his meals.

The newspapers played up Sergeant Murray's heroic timing, and, once in the spotlight, he later claimed to have been a guest at Sherry's: "I was leaving with my wife, behind Cohen's crowd, when the shooting started." When challenged by the press, Deputy Chief Brown revealed that Detective D. L. Murray had been following Mickey that night, but not as a member of the Sherry's entourage. Both

Brown and Chief Worton made it clear that it was not Murray's job to protect Mickey.

Muir had received her wish to be in on the action, and reported in the *Mirror*, "If I hadn't stopped to buy a newspaper last night I would more than likely be lying in a hospital today with the rest of the victims of the 'mad dog' gunman who fired seven shotgun blasts across Sunset Blvd. at Mickey Cohen and his henchmen as they were about to get into their cars in front of Sherry's restaurant on the Strip."

Mickey continued to do his best to manipulate the public. "It's hard to believe we live in a world of killing. Whoever done this must be dope fiends."

Muir contradicted the other papers and the FBI, which said that only her clothing was damaged: "...I was hit in the derriere by a deer slug that had luckily struck something else first, all my friends told me I was crazy to be around where guys with shotguns were trying to polish off the famous Hollywood gambler, Mickey Cohen, and his pals."

Another day under her byline, "Florabel Muir Reporting," she elaborated: "...police and sheriff's deputies have been shaking down Mickey Cohen and his henchmen...it looks like they've been shaking down the wrong guys." Muir reminded the readers of the old days when Owney Madden was shot at by Vincent "Mad Dog" Coll, who killed innocent bystanders.

Mickey agreed with Muir's passionate take and told reporters, "How any human being can fire into a crowd of people beats me. They're animals...they ain't humans."

The *Los Angeles Evening Herald and Express* was way ahead of its time when it came to reality shots. They published a reenactment of two men brandishing shotguns pointed at Sherry's. The picture, taken from behind, gave the reader the shooter's perspective just before the attack.

Follow-up stories indicated that a tip-off call came to police at ten-thirty the night of the shooting, allowing them hours to prepare. The woman caller said that there was going to be a shooting in the 8800 block of Sunset, where Mickey had his men's store. Police drove over to find hefty Jimmy Rist listening to the end of a baseball game on the radio. The deputy sheriff called it a night, and figured all was secure on the Strip. He did not attempt to locate Mickey.

After the hit, the police investigators rounded up everyone, from Sinatra associate and Mickey-friend thirty-eight-year-old Jimmy Tarantino to barber Joseph Messina. The FBI interviewed Sherry's owner Ruditsky, even though they knew he couldn't be helpful.

On July 23, authorities also released two Tarantino employees, Hy Porter and Joseph Tenner, both of whom worked in San Francisco. James English, the San Francisco chief of inspectors, had proceeded originally on evidence that Tarantino was overheard saying in a local bar, "I'll take care of Mickey Cohen." Editor Tarantino naturally said that the whole thing was ridiculous, and that the police had acted on a vendetta because of criticism in Tarantino's magazine.

According to Jimmy "The Weasel" Fratianno, Jack Dragna had ordered the hit: "The next time Mickey goes to Sherry's, Happy will call Louie [Jack Dragna's nephew] and we'll hit him with twelve-gauge shotguns when he comes out, which will probably be when the joint closes. By then the whole street should be deserted." What sounded easy had proven more complicated. Fratianno later identified Dominic Brooklier as one of the shooters. However, Brooklier was a good shot and usually didn't screw up when it came to hits.

A rumor popped up that Frank Costello, whom the FBI said was "recently in LA holding secret meetings," gave the order to get Mickey, but Mickey denied that Costello had anything to do with the hit. He certainly didn't want reporters printing anything like that. Instead, he played the public perfectly: "I dunno this Costello, I never met him, never seen him, never spoke to him in my life. So how could anyone say I been keeping him from muscling in on my territory?"[7]

Edward Johnson, a sporting goods dealer who had sold one of the shotguns used in the shooting, disappeared.

"I don't know him," was Mickey's response regarding all the suspects and leads. "Never met him at all."

The speculation on the identities of the shooters continued for many years. Mickey figured that competitor Jimmy Utley had arranged the hit; something safe to say when his publisher released his revisionist memoir.

When stabilized, Dee David, who had suffered perforated intestines and a torn kidney from four .38-caliber slugs and at one point was reported to be near death, insisted to police that she had just happened by the restaurant, and had no idea that Mickey Cohen was dining inside. She also added that she was no longer associated with MGM, and now worked as a nurse. But everyone in the restaurant knew that she was Johnny Stompanato's friend, and no stranger to Mickey. A photo of Mickey visiting Dee appeared around the country; his arm was in a sling, and he wore a plaid robe.

Dee later told the papers, "I think I screamed. I don't remember. I was in intense pain. I remember trying to move my legs, to see if I still had them." The papers ran glamour shots of her.

Carl Earn, a fabled Jewish tennis pro, visited Dee in the hospital, and had chatted for some time with Mickey. Consequently, the police followed peripatetic Carl around for about one week, and wondered what he was doing at all the ritzy homes in town. "I'm here to give tennis lessons," he politely told the suspicious officers. They continued to follow him anyway.

Neddie Herbert, hit in the spine, would die a week later from uremic poisoning secondary to his kidney injury. The bullets had shattered his backbone. The comedic sidekick was only thirty-five.

Mickey later questioned Neddie's actual cause of death. Few close to him knew that he had only one kidney, caused by what Mickey called "secret drinking." Mickey was certain: "By the time he told me about it; it was too late. The wrong medicine had been given out to him." He wanted to blame the doctors, and would not accept the fact that his lifelong friend had died because of their shared chosen profession.

Now the Sherry's story and investigation had snowballed and Mickey had created a media feeding frenzy (years before the expression materialized to indicate overzealous and tiresome reporting). The usual political rambling ensued about who was at fault for allowing such a horrible and violent event to take place in the pristine world of Hollywood.

"Mickey's going to get his and he knows it because I told him so," said Inspector Norris G. Stensland. He had told Mickey "he was on the spot" the preceding August, and therefore he should have known better. In one of the articles about the warning, the reporter referred to him as "the little fat mobster…escaped a gangland ambush in his Sunset Strip "haberdashery."

City Councilman Ed Davenport was livid about tax dollars going to support Mickey's bodyguard. He reminded the voters how Howser had told the police and sheriff's department to lay off Mickey: "Cohen got a bad bargain when Howser agreed to protect him. Look where he is now."

Biscailuz, Simpson, and Police Chief Worton, who served the LAPD during some of the Vicecapades 1949–1950, all begrudgingly told reporters that they knew about Mickey's relationship with Howser, and all had agreed to play ball with him and reduce their harassment of him.[8]

Mickey refused to discuss the reason for Cooper's existence. "Hell, I don't know. All I know is suddenly there's this guy with me all the time."

He intimated from the hospital that the hit was all part of an elaborate plan. He could not resist his ego and described himself as a willing victim, deliberately exposing himself as a target in order to help the authorities find his enemies. When asked why the maneuver was necessary, he declined to reveal details. The

New York Times corroborated the concept by calling Harry Cooper a "decoy." Mickey was a key witness in the minds of grand jury investigators, but no sensible person could have thought that he was going to spill anything about Bugsy's murder or the race wire.

Mayor Fletcher Bowron didn't get excited over the incident. He cited that the shooting was under the county's jurisdiction, and contradicted reports that the attorney general had asked the police to back off Mickey. Bowron referred to him as "small fry."

Police Chief Willie Worton said that the directive to lay off Mickey came from Ralph Davis in the attorney general's office. "I can't see why police should furnish a bodyguard for a character like Cohen," Worton said. He clearly knew his position: "I can't trust a soul in the whole department."

Mickey then decided to stir things up, and told reporters that he had inside information. The *Mirror* headline based on his public campaign read, MICKEY SAYS HOWSER KNOWS WHO SHOT HIM. Howser, in response, now played up the angle that he had assigned Detective Cooper to protect Mickey after shootings on San Vicente Boulevard near his Brentwood home and outside Neddie's apartment.

Mickey made certain that everyone looked to Howser for answers: "Howser must have had a red-hot tip to want to give me a man to watch me."

His corrupt mentor Sheriff Biscailuz, protecting his turf, said that he had had two men assigned to follow Mickey, one a Sergeant Brown. Insincere Biscailuz promised to follow up with his men, and find the shooters. Under public pressure, he vowed to "clean up the case," and assigned six extra deputies to patrol the Strip. In answer to what Sergeant Brown was doing during the shooting, Biscailuz said, "Somehow he got out of the line of fire. He must have ducked." Biscailuz advised the public that they shouldn't be concerned about Mickey and Neddie Herbert. "They asked for it. They sleep all day and prowl at night."

D.A. Simpson chimed in, "My office will give every assistance to the law enforcement agencies in an effort to solve the crime."

Howser further covered his rear by telling reporters he was going to "fully accept the challenge" to unravel the mess. A few articles appeared that named the human resources that Howser had shipped in from other cities to help with the investigation. At the same time, exasperated politicians and constituents called for an investigation of his "hands off Mickey" message to the police.

Howser later claimed that the hit was a result of Bugsy's assassination and the race wire battle. He said that Mickey's attorney, Rummel, had asked for help since Mickey feared for his life. He expounded on his previously duplicitous remarks: "We had specific information as to the sources which might attempt to assassinate

Cohen... We are not at liberty to divulge any other details at this time... Cooper was given the assignment both for the purpose of carrying out the investigation...and to prevent, if possible, any killings." That covered everything, all angles.

The Sherry's shooting infuriated the public so much that a veterans group formed a vigilante committee to get rid of Mickey. The *Washington Star* carried a quote from a wisely unnamed spokesperson: "Mickey Cohen is merely a Mickey Mouse for the real vice overlords. We are determined to find out who these vice lords are and name them publicly."

On Wednesday July 27, Sheriff Biscailuz released the last two suspects in the Sherry's shooting, Tony Brancato, thirty-four, and Anthony Trombino, twenty-nine. Mickey was still in the hospital, and reporters mentioned his larger room and separate television for his guests. Dr. Joseph Zeiler had seen to it that he had a separate wing on one floor, while the nuns at the hospital baked a variety of chocolate treats for the pint-sized wounded gangster.

When things died down, Muir chided Mickey about how he had felt protected around reporters. His cynical answer was, "You didn't show 'em your press pass. How did they know you was a reporter?"

Fratianno later spoke of the difficulties involved with eliminating Mickey: "I was talking to Johnny Rosselli...and he was telling me that Cohen reminds him of Bugs Moran in Chicago. Capone tried to kill him a dozen times. They never laid a glove on that guy... It's the same with Mickey."

It was true; they couldn't get him. But it wasn't over.

The Sherry's shooting remains unsolved. It was one of the most famous bungled rubouts in gangland history, and became the most sensational story of the era.[9]

The complicated year rolled on, filled with bathos and pathos of an unparalleled variety for such a short time span. The community remained polarized regarding Mickey and the police; it appeared that the majority of the local citizens had lost confidence in the chief, sheriff, and mayor. Federal investigators would not give up trying to incriminate him.

12.

More Vicecapades

Everyone had lied about his relationship with still-jailed Brenda Allen or the fact that she had employed police.

Vote-seeking politicians had to rake the Brenda Allen situation for all it was worth. A new indictment surfaced barely six hours after Neddie's official death announcement on July 27. Superior Judge Robert H. Scott charged Chiefs Horrall and Reed, who had officially retired, with one count of perjury each. Captain Wisdom, a former personnel director, received one perjury count, Lt. Wellpott, one count each for perjury and accepting a bribe, with right-hand man Sergeant Jackson receiving the same. The investigation revealed that Wellpott and Jackson had received information from Allen on gamblers, dope peddlers, and gem and fur thieves in exchange for looking the other way. The charges included, "to collect bribes and engage in immoral relations." The verified bribes amounted to nearly one thousand dollars.

Brenda Allen spoke out from jail, and threatened to "blow the lid off" the entire police department.

"I would be willing to testify as a character witness at their trials," said the naive Mayor Bowron when asked about the indictments of Horrall and Reed.

Mickey did not leave Queen of Angels Hospital until July 29, against the wishes of Dr. Zeiler, who had concerns about Mickey's healing shoulder. The propelling reason to leave the hospital was Neddie's funeral. Before leaving, Mickey paid the hospital tab for everyone, a balance of fifteen hundred dollars for himself, plus all of Neddie's and Dee David's expenses.

Mickey had arranged a local funeral for Neddie at the Willen Mortuary, 7700 Santa Monica Boulevard, in Hollywood.

Four sedans with "hard-eyed henchman" escorted Mickey to the "Jewish conservative services," according to the *Los Angeles Times.*

The first arrivals at the funeral parlor were a young blonde and brunette in the company of Max "Killer" Gray, who had visited Mickey frequently in the hospital.

Blue-suited Mickey arrived with Mike Howard, Davey Ogul, Johnny Stompanato, and Cliff Bruno. Attorney Sam Rummel arrived later with bail bondsman Irving Glasser.

Six sheriff's patrol cars cruised the streets as less than ten mourners entered "the chapel to chant the traditional El Moleb Rahamin," a memorial prayer for the dead that speaks to the immortality of the soul.

A dozen deputies patrolled the surrounding streets on foot. Two Department of Justice agents mingled inside during the service. Reporters were not welcome.

Neddie lay in a copper casket estimated at several thousand dollars. Howard had paid for a large rose and gardenia floral heart.

. Rabbi Varuch Rabinowitz delivered the sermon that included, "I considered him a good boy." He mentioned Neddie's help in the underground Palestinian movement, lending both his talent and money.

Moments after the funeral, sheriff's Lieutenant W. R. Tiernan handed out subpoenas to Mickey, Mike Howard, Frankie Niccoli, and Dee David, demanding their presence at the coroner's inquest for Neddie.

Mickey left in a two-car caravan, followed by the same number of sheriff's vehicles. He stopped at the haberdashery before heading home to Brentwood.

When he arrived at home, he posed for reporters at the front door with happy Tuffy, apologized for his prior lack of attention to the press, and behaved cordially.

Deputies made it clear that they had completed their job, had no interest in protecting Mickey, and left promptly.

Mickey had booked a flight to New York for a second funeral with Neddie's extended family the next day, but when it was time to board the United Airlines red eye, his seat was vacant. "I called it off," he told reporters. "It would cause too much commotion. It wouldn't do any good to go east now." Instead, he spent a quiet evening at home to nurse his mending shoulder.

A United Airlines cargo plane delivered Edward Neddie Herbert's body to New York on July 30. The heavily insured casket arrived at Newark Airport early in the evening. Undertaker Jack Vogel, an old friend of the family, claimed the body.

Mickey had arranged for a five-hundred-person funeral at the Park West Memorial Chapel, 115 W. 79th Street, in Manhattan. The chapel secretary told reporters, "This is a very hush-hush affair."

During the period of the Sunset Strip wars, Mickey also spoke regularly with Howard Hertel of the *Los Angeles Examiner*, Joe Ledlie and Sid Hughes of the *Mirror*, and Gene Sherman of the *Los Angeles Times*.

He was also tight with popular Agnes Underwood of the *Los Angeles Herald-Express*, whom he met when she was switchboard operator at the *Record*. She gave Mickey one of her books, inscribed, "For Mickey Cohen. If you are going to continue to make headlines, please make them on *Herald-Express* time." Underwood liked him: "I get along well with the little guy because I try to play fair with him. He just wants his side told, too, and I have never known him to lie to me."[1]

Underwood invited the Cohens to a Paramount press premiere. Afterward, the entourage headed for dinner when a car with dimmed lights skidded around a corner. Mickey jumped between Underwood and the purported threat. Nothing happened, but the war wasn't over.

On three occasions, Dragna likely gave the orders to blow up Mickey's house in Brentwood. He publicly denied any connection to hits on Mickey: "Mr. Mickey Cohen can stay alive as long as he wants. It doesn't bother me to have him around. He has nothing I want. I'm an old man and all I look forward to is raising my family and giving them a chance to have things easier than I ever did." It was far from the truth.

Sometimes former employees tried to kill Mickey. Dominic Brooklier was one of the recalcitrant mob bosses in Los Angeles before Mickey arrived. Unimaginative Brooklier concentrated his efforts on pornography and extortion. Once Mickey had set up his gambling operation, Brooklier found himself working for him. Dissatisfied, he ended up switching allegiance to Dragna, and helped him try to eliminate Mickey.

Dragna had elevated the gang status of his nephew Louis Tom Dragna and Louis Merli, the latter hardly a fan after Mickey had robbed him years back, and assigned both to daily business operations that included Mickey's elimination. The Sicilians had a few plans.

A *Time* article aptly named "Clap Pigeon" appeared on August 1, 1949. Survivor and "sad-eyed little Mickey Cohen became the undisputed boss of Los Angeles gangdom," an expression that would be repeated. It didn't take long before his competitors tried to curtail the described gloomy survival.

At two in the morning on August 2, 1949, an explosion rocked the street across from Mickey's house; the jerky *cafones* who had planted the pipe bomb had the wrong address.

The neighbors were fed up. Mickey had become a liability to his community, and local citizens complained vigorously to the police and attorney general. The cries reached the mayor.

Mayor Bowron made a clichéd radio challenge to Mickey: "We are coming after you and we are going to stay after you. We are going to put you out of business if you engage in any form of criminal activity within the City of Los Angeles, regardless of where your base of operations might be, or who your cohorts of mobsters might be." This August 4 broadcast came on the heels of a clean bill of health for the police department. Leo E. Hubbard, of the county grand jury, had said on the radio that the department was "essentially clean, well organized, and efficient," with no trace of "payoff or protection."

In contrast, newspapers published new details of the recent grand jury testimony surrounding the Brenda Allen case. The publicity reminded the public of its less than squeaky-clean police. The August 10 story reviewed the grand jury's last try to nail Mickey on his role in the Allen matter.

Mickey had previously made sure that Lt. Wellpott knew that they had the goods on him. Mike Howard had phoned Wellpott and invited him to the fundraiser for Israel at Slapsy Maxie's. While attending the function, Mickey and the boys made it abundantly clear that it was in Wellpott's best interest to show up at the office of Marvin Kobey, president of the gambling front Guarantee Finance Company, a continual focus of the governor's Crime Commission.

Lt. Wellpott related the details of his awkward confrontation: "After being there for a while it was interesting to notice who some of the people were that were present. There were some judges, assemblymen, congressmen, some people from your office. And finally, Mickey Cohen made his grand entrance. He expressed his appreciation for my having accepted the invitation, trying to impress the importance of my being there…."

Wellpott said that Kobey had been drinking and told him that they "really had something" on him. Wellpott was only then aware that Brenda Allen's establishment had its own surveillance bugs, and that Mickey had bugged Wellpott's own phones as well. It was quite the reverse sting.

The blackmail call played for Wellpott came from a young girl who complained that he had neglected her. Why hadn't he called? She sprinkled the phone call with endearing expressions.

Wellpott had also heard phone calls about Jimmy Utley and gambling games organized around town.

The lieutenant said how the boys revealed more information: "…Mickey Cohen was supposed to have records in his possession where informants had informed me as to what was going on on the West Side."

Mickey's name came up frequently during new grand jury testimony from forty-eight witnesses. J. Arthur "Big Jim" Vaus, "electronics engineer," admitted that Mickey had originally called him for help after police arrested Harold "Happy" Meltzer on the gun charge. Mickey had asked if Vaus had any of the Brenda Allen recordings. Vaus affirmed that he had made them, and Mickey asked him to bring the recording machine, not the tapes, to Meltzer's trial. Vaus admitted that he had an ongoing relationship with Mickey, but did not receive any compensation for his help.

Mickey had told Vaus, "If this all works out the way we think it will you'll never have to worry."

Vaus had suggested that he also tap the telephones of Chief Horrall and Mayor Bowron, according to Sergeant Guy Rudolph who worked for Horrall. Vaus did not bug the offices once word leaked out regarding his intentions.

Lieutenant Wellpott and Sergeant Jackson successfully defended perjury charges, and everyone else on the long indictment list received acquittals.

That did not preclude new grand juries, local police, U.S. Attorneys, or the FBI from going after Mickey. With more hits on the horizon, this had been some year for the flamboyant clotheshorse.

On August 18, an accusatory story broke regarding Bugsy's murder. The police had taped one of Mickey's phone calls three days before the Bugsy hit in which Mickey had told Jackie Richards about an eight grand payoff with a promise of the balance in "ten or fifteen days." Sheriff Biscailuz had a fit when he found out that the police knew about this for two years. Investigator Leo Stanley, Attorney General Howser, and Councilman Ernest E. Debs all pronounced their criticisms. Mickey's attorney Sam Rummel threatened to sue. (The same day U.S. Attorney James Carter dropped false citizenship charges against Harold "Happy" Meltzer.)

The night at Sherry's, Mickey had had every reason to fear for his life, yet no one present ever picked up a tad of anxiety. He had shown tremendous restraint in refusing to mention what had recently happened at his home. U.S. Attorney James Carter broke the agreed silence and told the public about another whack attempt on Mickey with a M1A1 Bangalore torpedo from World War II. The explosive device was designed to destroy antipersonnel mines and barbed wire obstacles; it can clear a path over five feet wide. This was not an easy device to plant under or near Mickey's house; each Bangalore weighs at least thirteen pounds, of which nine pounds is the explosive, packed in a fourteen-inch-long, five-inch-thick iron pipe. The deadly goomba muscle hired to pull off the stunt had had their difficulties; the device never exploded. Had it gone off, the house and everything in it would have been flattened.

Shortly before his murder at Sherry's, Neddie Herbert had discovered something fishy at Mickey's house. He asked wiretap expert Vaus, "Did you leave a funny wire under Cohen's bedroom?"

Vaus clipped off a piece of wire that led to a hole in Mickey's bedroom screen. He lit a match to it, and it ignited. He traced the rest of the fuse to the Bangalore and dismantled it, but could not tell if someone had already tried to detonate the bomb.

District Attorney William Simpson, who had cooperated in keeping quiet about the bomb until now, challenged Mickey to come in and discuss all his recent problems. He claimed that he had recordings of Mickey discussing national gambling deals, his relationships to movie stars, Bugsy, and Frank Costello. What irritated him is that he knew that Mickey had copies of the same recordings, and he even told reporters that Mickey had likely paid twenty thousand dollars for them. Nothing came of Simpson's public posturing.

A memo dated August 22, 1949, dismissed any reason for the FBI to increase its involvement in Los Angeles organized crime, particularly anything related to Mickey. "I wanted you to know that I have personally made a survey of the situation and have determined that there is no information indicating a violation of Federal law within this Bureau's investigative jurisdiction. This Bureau can and will not be brought into this investigation in the absence of an appropriate basis for such investigation."

J. Edgar Hoover sent the memo to the attorney general, signed only as the Director of the FBI.[2]

Another message from Hoover, this time to a local agent, stated that the agent should not be concerned about Mickey's asking for the repayment of a thirty-thousand-dollar gambling debt. Someone in West Palm Beach, Florida, owed the money, and since there was no evidence of a threat, it wasn't an extortion problem. Hoover essentially had told the agent to leave Mickey alone.

The FBI received an invitation by telegram on August 23 to help get rid of Mickey: "Vigilantes respectfully requests your participation at citizens mass meeting Patriotic Hall, 8 PM. Thursday August 25th. Please wire." The agents had filled dance cards, and declined the invite. A local grass roots organization proved no match for Mickey.

Chief Worton took this moment to renew the faith of his constituents by proclaiming a "revived war on hoodlums." The big effort resulted in one arrest: Mike Howard, one of Mickey's scoundrels, on suspicion of violation of the state narcotics act. Officers also found a gun in his home. The ho-hum efforts tickled the readership of local newspapers, who knew from experience that Mickey was invulnerable.

Mickey remained adamant regarding his unfair treatment by police, particularly a claim that he had disturbed the peace. He was already upset about Mike Howard's arrest, the night Worton sent Detectives James E. Barrick, A. M. Barr, and Oscar W. Poluch, a federal narcotics agent, to Mickey's house. He was dining with Earl Brown, a famous crime writer for *Life*, Gene Cook, Ed Clark, who also worked for *Life*, and Al Ostro of the *San Francisco Daily News*. The police insisted that Mickey leave his guests and escort the officers to the haberdashery to check on two illegal guns that they claimed Mike Howard had purchased. A verbal pissing contest ensued, short of a physical altercation, and resulted in Mickey's arrest.

His trial attracted much attention, and he enjoyed every moment of it. He entered the courtroom on August 31 dressed in his finest lightweight tweeds and a "red-splashed blue tie," according to *Los Angeles Times* reporters, sat in the back of the courtroom, and remained silent while mouthpieces Rummel and Ferguson gave the audience an earful.

All the journalists thought it was a hoot, and the educated dinner guests testified that their generous host had impugned the ancestry of the police, a heinous crime. Rummel and Ferguson put on their usual show, and condemned the city and the police force, while neatly painting Mickey as a victim.

"The police department is in complete intellectual confusion," declared Ferguson.

Vernon Ferguson, a dapper man in his own right, roared back at Glendale Judge Kenneth White in Municipal Court, "This campaign of harassment has gone too far! The murderers are still at large. Instead, the police are harassing Cohen, who has been a sick man ever since and who has been staying at home most of the time."

He criticized the police force, and attorney Sam Rummel added, "The police are frantically trying to divert attention from pending criminal cases involving police officers."

The tall attorney Ferguson continued. "This thing has gone on and on and on. Mr. Cohen was the victim of a murderous assault last July 20"—the Sherry's shooting.

Mickey had previously apologized to the arresting officers at his house, Captain Lynn White of the new intelligence division, and Officers James Barrick and A. M. Barr.

"I lost my temper," Mickey had later said after peeling off a "C-note from his bankroll" to pay for his bail.

Ferguson reminded the judge that Mickey had other pending legal matters, and asked for the return of his one hundred dollars since he had already posted over one hundred thousand dollars in the Pearson matter, which was now set for trial October 3. He also took the police to task for directing "vile and filthy" language at his contrite client.

Mickey received an opportunity to describe pal Mike Howard as an "absolute angel" and Solly Davis as "too stupid to be a bookmaker."

The logic of Mickey's defense included: why can't a haberdasher named Cohen call police unkind names if President Truman, an ex-haberdasher, can call a newspaper columnist like Drew Pearson an S.O.B.?

After four hours, the sympathetic and thoroughly entertained jury acquitted Mickey. He wasn't a villain in the eyes of the public. Thanks to the Pearson case and the Sherry's shooting, his "polls" remained favorable.

However, the judge kept Mickey's one hundred bucks.

Chief of Police Worton refused to comment on the alleged harassment and simply stated, "It was done on my orders." The former Marine general repeated his admonitions regarding Mickey and any of his gang; Worton was out to get them.

The confusing 1949 Vicecapades baffled the FBI, local police, politicians, and reporters. Nobody had a handle on anyone's political perspective, right up to the federal level. Through the summer, the newspapers carried stories indicating how active the FBI was in taking care of the organized crime problem in Los Angeles.

By the end of August, FBI agents noted that the phone surveillance still hadn't turned up anything: "The Bureau will be advised of any pertinent facts developed." They had occasionally received tip-off letters about stolen goods. Still no action against Mickey.

When the FBI became aware of all the competitive bugging and surveillance attempts by the local authorities, many grueling interrogation sessions ensued. Why didn't the local D.A. tell the FBI about its own involvement in the bugging? Why didn't the FBI receive copies of the recordings? Did Mickey really have his own records? How corrupt were the local authorities?

Mickey surely had his own records. Somebody had periodically removed boxes of files from the City Attorney's office, which prompted an FBI agent to write, "…and the funny part was it was always connected with this gang of Mickey Cohen's activities." Someone in the offices of U.S. Attorney Carter or special assistant Max Goldschein had given the city's and/or FBI surveillance tapes to Mickey. Goldschein had a reputation as a rackets buster, would fly in and out of Los Angeles, and exaggerate his probe into the dark underworld of Hollywood.

Published stories stated that U.S. Attorney Carter was ready to indict Mickey based on incriminating information saved from old wiretaps, and again how he had supposedly paid the police for copies of all his phone calls. Carter now had new information to move against him utilizing income tax laws, the Mann Act (white slavery), the Dyer Act (stolen cars), the Stolen Property Act, federal gun laws, customs laws, and the "very far-reaching and comprehensive False Information Laws." He assigned fifty treasury agents to pay strict attention to the mob's cash flow, particularly its bookmaking operations, which included the suspicious Guarantee Finance Corporation. "The only solution to the gangster problem is to go into the income tax angle," said Carter. Reporters reviewed the history of Al Capone, and his prosecution for tax evasion. If Mickey or his advisors took note, it was never mentioned.

Carter denied the information contained in the articles when asked for more details by an FBI agent. He eventually confessed to the FBI that he had limited jurisdiction and essentially no case, despite the wide scale assault in the media. The best he had had was the failed false citizenship claim against Meltzer.

What did humorously leak out to journalists was that Mickey regularly made many bets from his residence, mostly on horses, some on other sports, occasionally kissed his cockatiel when he came home, and sometimes told his wife to go to hell.

The convoluted efforts of the FBI reached President Truman, who stood by the strict legal doctrine: no process existed for federal involvement in local matters. Mickey received yet another pass, and this time from the president! He had every reason to believe that he was immune from federal prosecution.[3]

13.

Bad Boy Mickey

Mickey received his regular public attention and tried to regain his momentum in business despite his recuperation, assassination attempts, and the stealthy James-Bondish undermining of the police department.[1]

The diminutive gambler's success and new cult status did little to change his low self-image. While basking in all the guru-like publicity he realized that he still hadn't reinvented himself sufficiently, and hadn't overcome his deep-seated deficiencies. Writer Jennings once unflatteringly labeled Mickey semiliterate and agonizingly insecure. Jennings, like others who were able to get close to the emotionally riddled leader, also understood the angst and loneliness that filled the voids in his oft-joyless periods, particularly after a year like the proceeding one. Mickey never pursued a systematic way of desensitizing himself to his own character flaws or helter-skelter existence. He never sought professional help, and relied on personal contact to reflect upon his life.

Business was full speed ahead, and he accomplished the difficult balancing act with aplomb, while adversaries still preferred him dead. He coasted and controlled most of the local action, while the city, state, and federal authorities watched. Los Angeles was still in transition and served as an easy mark for the expanding East

Coast mob. Even with the growing influence of the mob in Vegas and Los Angeles, authorities still viewed Mickey as a sole entity, rather than part of a large organized crime machine.[2]

His holdings were now extensive, and stretched well beyond the local boundaries of Hollywood. He still, of course, denied any complicit role in criminal activity, and insisted he was just another entrepreneur with a wad of cash. Jimmy Fratianno loomed large in some of Mickey's dealings. The most famous was the Turf Club action in Del Mar, the celebrity-driven racetrack not far from the ocean, just north of San Diego. Fratianno, Jack Morton, who was close to actor Cary Grant, and Mickey started a new business there with fifteen thousand dollars each. The purpose was to take the bets directly from celebrities who frequented the Del Mar track. The list was impressive: Grant, Mike Todd,[3] Harry James, Al Jolson, and J. Carroll Naish. In order to run that type of operation Mickey relied on intermediaries to pick up the action. Mac Gray, who worked for George Raft, was one of the regulars.

The county grand jury still focused intently on little Burbank, home to Mickey's posh equestrian playground. Everyone in the movie business knew that Mickey's Dincara Stock Farm was a great place to eat, drink, ride horses, and gamble, but nobody in the government was able to prove the latter. On September 16, 1949, the probing grand jury interviewed Burbank's finest, Captain Clark Duncan, Officers F. G. Walizer, Harry Strickland, and a former Burbank peace officer named Phil Foy. They mulled over the present investigation, and after reviewing the failed raids of the last three years prepared for a long haul.

Juxtaposed to Mickey's protecting damsels in distress, his often heinous sexual activities became public. During September, a story broke about his pervasive shakedown operation. The newspapers spoke of dapper Mickey as a prostitution extortionist who paid a harem of lovely ladies to "inveigle rich victims" into compromised situations. Inveigle they did; Mickey had tons of recordings and black and white photographs.

Paul R. Behrmann, a Hollywood business agent (he had represented Robert Mitchum) spilled the beans. Without revealing his sources—"a lot of people would be killed"—Behrmann contacted District Attorney William E. Simpson with information regarding one of the largest sexual extortion crime rings in existence. When Simpson learned that Mickey Cohen was the purported head of the extensive blackmail set up, Behrmann was quickly in front of a grand jury. The former actors' agent insisted that Mickey ran an elaborate scam with his stable of escorts targeting eager businessman. The hookers were knockouts, some disciples of French love teacher Claude Marsan. Behrmann knew of one wealthy

Hollywood figure who had to fork over seventy-five thousand dollars for the purchase of an indiscreet recording. Sometimes an incriminating photo in the hands a *shtarker* was enough for the horny sap to fork over the extortion dough. Mickey kept sixty percent of the money, a tax-free swindle with little overhead— only hookers and cameras—and the typical male libido supplied the rest. Behrmann mentioned favorites Lila Leeds and Vicki Evans, the Robert Mitchum friends tried on narcotics charges, as two members of the licentious ring.

D.A. William Simpson, who had once reprimanded the police for withholding wiretap recordings of Mickey, had to drop the case because Behrmann was not a credible witness, and was out on bail after his own three-count larceny conviction.

Mickey was happy to tell reporters, "Anyone...knows I never mix in anything of that kind."

Vicki Evans still had to answer questions from the district attorney in New York; the main issue of the interview was Mickey's Hollywood shakedown racket. Police mentioned that she had applied for a permit to dance in a Greenwich Village nightclub under the name Florence Fedele, a specialty dancer.

She told reporters, "They asked me if I knew Mickey Cohen and I said, 'No.'"

The D.A. also asked her about *Hollywood Nite Life* publisher Jimmy Tarantino.

Evans, who remained protective of Mickey and anything related, was clear: "I ain't' no stool pigeon."

During this time, Mickey began one of his many unlikely relationships—with the Reverend Billy Graham. Electronic wizard Big Jim Vaus, the son of a minister, introduced Mickey to Graham. Vaus had been in the process of illegally slowing the Continental wire service, so that bets could be placed on sure winners. He had abandoned his cheating efforts, claiming to have given up his life of crime, and now worked for Graham fulltime.

Mickey acknowledged Vaus' influence: "From 1949 on, Jimmy was all over me about going straight. He said Graham had changed his life and I should meet Graham personally."

During the last few months of the year, Graham complained about the resultant negative publicity surrounding his relationship with Mickey. The suddenly religious gambler publicly denied that he knew Graham. The duo would take a respite from the spotlight, but their relationship would continue.

The public continued to lambaste the State of California for not having control over crime in Los Angeles. In response to the outcry, Attorney General Howser told reporters that Governor Warren's Commission on Organized Crime was "not a law enforcement body, but merely a study group." He professed to know nothing about the committee's crime work in Los Angeles. When asked on

October 6 about Mickey's intrusion and control over certain aspects of police work, Howser responded, "Let me say I am wholly convinced of the honesty and integrity of the Los Angeles Police Department, the Los Angeles Sheriff's Office and the District Attorney's Office."

The difficult year began to take its toll, or so Mickey publicly represented. He began to complain to reporters about his cash flow problems, and ultimately advertised the sale of his haberdashery in late November 1949.

"That's true, I'm trying to liquidate. I'm stuck with a big lease and I must raise cash."

It was not actually possible to sell the lease, but Mickey enjoyed the publicity. He insisted that he would liquidate his entire stock, citing his recent forfeiture of $75,000 bonds for Frankie Niccoli and Davey Ogul in the Pearson matter.[4]

Honest Mickey told reporters, "I can't let anyone else take over that debt... I'm the loser and I have to pay. I ain't no welsher."

Mickey certainly acted as if he needed money, despite numerous reports of his enormous cash flow. He had recently sold the Café Continentale at 7823 Santa Monica Boulevard to Leo E. Tomcray of Culver City, a move he cited to emphasize his financial problems.

Despite the banter about money problems, Mickey pal Louis Schwartz was able to post fifty thousand dollars bail from the Cantillon Bond and Insurance Agency. (Four of Mickey's remaining Pearson muggers had gone to jail on October 13. Since Neddie died, only twelve defendants remained in what newspapers touted as a "conspiracy.") Schwartz got into a scuffle with reporters when they tried to take his picture leaving jail.

Mickey voluntarily appeared before a federal grand jury on November 30, 1949, after attorney Sam Rummel had promised to produce his famous client. Max Goldschein, special assistant to U.S. Attorney Carter, had flown in again, this time from Kansas City, to ask Mickey about his pervasive connections to the rackets and gambling in Missouri. Goldschein had also previously pressed the issue of the Hollywood extortion ring, in which he had tried unsuccessfully to get Mickey on mail fraud violations.

Goldschein pursued his new angle. Mickey had sold the La Brea Social Club to Gus Klein, who now operated the club as Tobi's Café. Klein's sister, Mrs. Tobi Klein Prensky, from Kansas City, acted as hostess. Goldschein was acting on surveillance information he had gotten from Mickey's house, including Kansas City telephone numbers. Enemy Lt. Rudy Wellpott had supplied Goldschein with transcripts obtained from hidden microphones in the La Brea Club.[5]

Mickey naturally denied having any connections to illegal activities in Kansas City: "I don't know anything more about this than you fellows... I don't know Klein by name, but I might know him by sight. I don't know anything about Kansas City gambling. I have no business connections there and I've never been there except while passing through on a train."

Former Kansas City insurance man Sam Tucker said that he had no idea why Goldschein had subpoenaed him, admitted having owned a nightclub, and denied any connection to Mickey.

Mickey's tax returns also received a going over by Goldschein's staff, a financial roust that did not sufficiently attract Mickey's or Rummel's attention, not even after U.S. Attorney Carter's public statements. Mickey's poorhouse act may have been designed to deflect the publicized tax scrutiny.

The independent reprobate's home life with LaVonne remained private, thanks to the media's cooperation. He did not reveal personal data about his marriage to reporters. The mob also cooperated with the unwritten rule to avoid immediate family, excepting the abortive bomb hits on Mickey's home. The fundamental design of the mob system also worked to benefit his extracurricular sex life, and he continued to make the most out of socializing without his wife.

He reinforced the concept of LaVonne's independent role: "LaVonne wasn't dumb by any stretch of the imagination—she could read the newspapers and she knew what was going on—but I never told her any of the details, and she never asked." LaVonne wisely left the business to him; it eliminated any possibility of her complicity, and any time that she had to appear in court prosecutors promptly dropped the charges.

Mickey's glamorous social existence with LaVonne was the focus of a well-orchestrated *Life* pictorial. By this time, the Cohens claimed that they had been married in 1941. The information in the article is at once both comical and revealing.

"Mickey believes her maiden name was Brenf but isn't sure. Mrs. Cohen lives very inconspicuously, rarely accompanies Mickey and 'the boys' to Hollywood nightclubs."

The Ozzie-and-Harriet pictorial showed LaVonne watching Mickey play with the dogs at "their Brentwood home," and a shot of LaVonne as she "knits and nicens up." (Having children was no longer an issue. After Mickey watched Bugsy's two daughters growing up without a father, he dropped any further discussion.)[6]

LaVonne was a petite woman with a shy smile and a short, conservative hairdo parted down the middle. A full-page shot of her sitting at a queen's vanity displayed a collection on the ruffle-encased table that could have belonged to the wife of a doctor, lawyer, or CEO. Nearly thirty perfume bottles, a collector's array of elaborate crystal, atomizers, and other decorative pieces filled the counter. The bathroom had pink furniture and "the luxuriant pile of the carpet was almost ankle-deep" as described by author Ed Reid.

The dinner table was set every night, but Mickey preferred a nightclub or casino. When he was sometimes available to eat at home, dining at the Cohens was one of the hottest tickets in town, and many mainstream businessmen dined there often. Mr. and Mrs. Cohen operated inside the Hollywood social loop, a much sought after position, particularly since Mickey's connections were invaluable when it came to sports or theater tickets, and dinner reservations at popular nightclubs. The next morning after dinner with the Cohens, local executives likely boasted on the country club golf courses, first namedropping Mickey, and then adding any one of the numerous Hollywood celebrities, politicians, or reporters who dined or dropped by the house.

Mickey was acutely aware of the underworld appeal to the straitlaced; a concept fueled by the mystique presented in movies and pulp fiction paperbacks. Despite his uncouth ghetto upbringing, he possessed a charismatic offbeat sensibility that cut through any cloak of social dishonesty. Many actors, including some who played gangsters on the screen, preferred the company of mobsters. George Raft and Lawrence Tierney, who was famous for playing public enemy John Dillinger in the movies, sought out Mickey and other mobsters as friends. Raft was closer with Mickey now that Bugsy was gone.

LaVonne frequently stayed at home. Mickey slept most of the day; his bedroom was lightproof. When he didn't appear for dinner, that didn't stop LaVonne from serving dinner for his bodyguards and cronies. She and Johnny Stompanato watched movies outdoors during the warmer weather.

To add dignity to her life, LaVonne maintained a separate membership at the Brentwood Country Club, a distant cousin to the more fabled and popular Hillcrest Country Club, home of the entertainment roundtable. LaVonne spent many weekends golfing at the Brentwood Club without Mickey. He rarely showed up, and often left town for the weekend.

Life magazine recognized the local police conflicts: "There is little effective cooperation between city police and Sheriff Eugene Biscailuz' deputies and independent municipalities like Gardena ignore both agencies." Gardena was one of Mickey's gambling strongholds.

During early 1950, the FBI watched Mickey carefully. They reported on his efforts to secure gambling debts.[7] On one occasion, under pressure from Mickey, his goons had his debtor flown in from Las Vegas in order to pay his tab—something that perversely irked FBI agents, who labeled the gambler a "victim" and mentioned how Mickey had chartered a plane on Desert Skyways, a subsidiary of Western Airlines, to make certain that the man found his way to Los Angeles.[8] He unwisely had been hiding out at a fifth-rate hotel called the Charleston. Fearful of his position, he had already borrowed the money to pay Mickey; he hocked a three-stone man's ring, a fountain pen, and gold Rolex. Once the mystery gambler realized that he had committed a mortal sin with the mob, he inquired through the criminal grapevine about his safety. The word out was that Mickey only wanted his money and that no harm would come to the debtor. The man originally had told friends he was contemplating suicide. It made the FBI wonder why he had bothered to pay Mickey.

As an example of ongoing fruitless efforts, the FBI laboratory tried in vain to make the case that one of Mickey's checks might have been a forgery. On January 2, 1950, the FBI called off the lab: "A definite conclusion was not reached."

The relentless pressure continued. The *Los Angeles Times* reported Mickey's links to gambling in Hawaii. Sergeant Joseph Jones of the Honolulu Police Department told reporters on January 4 that four men suspected of running a full service sports book worked for Mickey. Morris Cohen, no relation, pled innocent to running a lottery that took bets on football, baseball, and basketball.

Mickey replied to the charges: "I don't know anyone operating a gambling syndicate in Honolulu. My wife and I have a friend over there, but I don't know anything about this. She has nothing to do with anything like that."

Honolulu police speculated that Frankie Niccoli and Davey Ogul were alive and well.

Mickey begrudgingly admitted to reporters talking to him about Honolulu that he had gotten into a fight with Ogul and Meltzer. It was a few months back, over the possibility of their turning State's evidence against Mickey. He had jumped out of his fancy Cadillac, and with a fast left floored Ogul, who was standing in front of the haberdashery. He then walked to a nearby jewelry store and punched Harold "Happy" Meltzer.

When asked about the incident Meltzer had replied, "I got nothing to say, whatever."

Mickey was still having problems with his cash flow, or at least that's the impression he wanted to give to the authorities and his public. He followed through and advertised an everything-must-go sale of his haberdashery stock. The highly publicized event attracted many curious fans and the usual schadenfreude voyeurs.

In its January 16, 1950, issue *Life* magazine ran a half-page photo of the outside of Mickey's haberdashery when he liquidated his stock. The sign on the store window in big letters read MICKEY COHEN QUITS! Giant Hollywood beams from the Film Ad Corp illuminated the street like a movie premiere. The caption read, "Famous for its grand openings, Hollywood has a grand closing, complete with searchlights, as Mickey Cohen sells out his haberdashery stock." Cynical author Reid commented on Mickey's purported financial woes with his own caption of the same photo: "A haberdasher named Cohen must sell his swank Hollywood emporium when two of his henchmen skip, forfeiting Cohen's $75,000 bond."

Mickey may have appeared weakened to his enemies. Dragna had not given up on the idea of assassination. It was four-twenty in the morning of Monday, February 6. Mickey was in the midst of the ongoing Pearson trial. The Cohens had returned from a birthday party at about three o'clock. An alarm sounded at Mickey's home, and he reflexively grabbed a gun. After inspecting the inside of his property, he concluded that smoke from an incinerator had triggered the alarm. He looked outside the windows for prowlers. Perhaps three minutes later, a bomb went off inside the house. The FBI estimated that Dragna's men used eighteen to twenty-four sticks of dynamite.

Mickey ran to the rescue of his pet terrier Tuffy, who by now must have sensed that it was a liability to be Mickey's favorite dog.

Police heard the explosion at the station three and one-half miles away. The force of the bomb blew a man across the street out of his bed.

One side of the "Brentwood mansion" (really only seven or eight rooms) was completely demolished. The downward force of the dynamite left a six-by-three hole in the foundation of the house. The roof was gone, along with Mickey's flashy wardrobe. The front door had split down the middle.

Fortunately, Mickey had a modern view of marriage; his wife LaVonne had her bedroom and lavish dressing area—Mickey bragged that he had shelled out twenty-five thousand dollars for it—on the other side of the house. The separate bedroom arrangement saved his life, because when the dynamite exploded he was on LaVonne's side of the house. The entire house would have blown up if not for a specially constructed vault inside the foundation. Dragna's crew had not investigated the house design thoroughly before planting the dynamite.

Sergeant R. W. Killion of the West Los Angeles Police Department told reporters, "If Cohen had been in the front bedroom it probably would have killed him." Mickey remained inordinately lucky. The only report of a casualty was the daughter of a neighbor who suffered cuts from the flying glass. Nobody in the house was hurt, including Tuffy and the maid Kathryn Jones, who had put in a hysterical phone call to the police.

Tuffy had left his miniature bed, a copy of Mickey's, the moment Mickey moved to the other side of the house. Tuffy did suffer some emotional damage, not unlike any transplanted New Yorker. His former owner, manufacturer Samuel J. Kaufman, phoned Tuffy regularly to encourage him about adjusting to the West Coast. Tuffy never did return to Manhattan, despite the traumatic episode.

The police questioned Joe Sica, then under indictment for narcotics charges, and Salvatore Piscopo. The FBI knew that it was a routine roust. Satisfied, the police quickly released the naughty locals. By this time, Sica had developed his own national reputation. Mickey's friend, *Washington Post* columnist Drew Pearson, in "The Washington Merry-Go-Round," described how Sica rose from Mickey's bodyguard to "Southern California's No. 1 hoodlum." Sica ran his own haberdashery "under the sovereignty of good-natured Sheriff Gene Biscailuz, rather than the tougher Los Angeles police." He also operated a health club that was a "blind" for his bookie operations. Pearson went as far as to say that Sica, "narcotics king," had taken Mickey's place as the star hood in town.

Police also arrested James Basil Modica and Martin Fenster, but couldn't connect them to the bombing. They were held instead on suspicion of violating the Deadly Weapons Act, since the police had found bomb construction materials in their possession. Police cracked down on Dragna's mob, and arrested Max Shaman's brother Moe on a misdemeanor charge. They could not find Jack Dragna, now fifty-five; authorities suspected that he had taken a banana boat to Nicaragua. The roust continued with his twenty-six-year-old son Frank Paul, and Jack's brother Tom, sixty-one. Police then arrested Girolamo Admao, Dragna's banana trade partner.

Assistant City Attorney Perry Thomas had warned Frank Paul to register as a sex offender, and cited him for a misdemeanor. Police suspected that Moe Shaman was in on the bombing of Mickey's home. To the dismay of William A. Smith, (chair of the Board of Supervisors and who pushed for a showdown with Admiral William Standley, the retired chair of the governor's Commission on Organized Crime), none of the arrests resulted in anything consequential.

Florabel Muir, like many others, did not take the event as casually as Mickey. She was up for the two days following the hit, and with Joe Ledlie of the *Mirror* conducted a progressive live radio show from Mickey's den. The journalists assured the local residents that the bombing was an isolated incident and not the beginning of another gang war. Muir also reported the news on her own afternoon television show that aired on KFI.[9]

Mickey made the most of these episodes. He was always available for interviews, which fueled his rivals' jealousy of his success and apparent immortality. He even wrote his neighbors a lengthy letter, editing out expressions like "nobles oblige" [*sic*], which he had picked up from Muir's husband Denny Morrison.

On Monday morning, my home was bombed. Though this outrage constituted a great threat to my wife and my neighbors and has deprived me of the sense of security and sanctuary that every man feels when he steps across his home doorstep, it didn't make me nearly as unhappy as the action, today, of some of my neighbors...those who are trying to push me out of the community. Guided as I was by the kindly statements of those in the neighborhood who apparently took only into consideration the fact that Mrs. Cohen and I are going through a very rugged and painful period of our lives, I took it for granted that if I could expect no breaks from the mad beast who bombed me I would certainly have no reason to fear hurt from my neighbors, whom I have never molested in any way. In fact, I still have faith in them, I still feel that they will respond to the logic of the situation, and the human factors involved. I feel sure that they are aware that despite much adverse newspaper publicity not one single iota of proof has been brought forward that would show that I have done anything to draw the kind of savagery that occurred last Monday morning, and before. I am hopeful that some of the more well-informed are aware that I have done nothing in self-defense... though the opportunities were open to me...that would endanger my neighbors in any way. I have even sent away friends who would have stood by to help me. I did not want to incur the possibility of wrong and unsavory appearances. I have confidence that most clear-thinking people will realize that my position has been well represented. In the words of some of the wild-eyed characters who have written about me for the public, you have been 'bum-steered' and I have been 'bum-rapped.' Let's both stop being victimized. I am a gambler and a betting commissioner; no more, no less. I'm not a mobster, a gunman, or a thug. I leave such antics to Mr. George Raft and Mr. Humphrey Bogart, who make money at it, or to be certain other local actors—bad actors—who make the penitentiary at it, ultimately. I am not in the dynamiting business, the shooting business, or in any of the other varied forms of homicide. I sell shirts and ties, and sometimes I make a bet or two. That's being on the level with you. I would like to go on living quietly amongst you...if for no other reason than that if I were to go elsewhere the same situation might arise, if there were enough intolerant people in that community. I have faith that the regular authorities will take steps to prevent any possible recurrence of Monday's incident. And I have faith that most of my neighbors will go along with me in this belief, as they will with me in my desire and determination to preserve my home. And if for no other reason, I believe that my neighbors will stand by my right to live in Brentwood because to do otherwise would be to play into the hands of the fiends who lit that fuse last Monday morning... I don't think anyone in this little community of ours wants to give them that satisfaction.

The letter was signed, "Very sincerely, your neighbor, Mickey Cohen."

While playing gin rummy with Johnny Stompanato and Joe Ledlie a few nights later, Mickey finally let Stompanato win a hand.

Stompanato was mystified and asked, "Why did you do that?"

Mickey made Ledlie's jaw drop with, "Noblesse oblige."

When Stompanato queried his educated boss he received, "Something a peasant like you wouldn't understand."

Some neighbors initially complained about the bombing, particularly actor Dean Jagger. Mickey eventually sent Jagger a funny telegram: "...Let's hope no further bombings will knock your little gold statue off the mantel." It amused Jagger enough to let Hedda Hopper print the exchanges, but things did not quiet down in the upscale neighborhood.[10]

The humorless Brentwood Terrace Property Owners Association sent a letter to the City Council: "The presence of Mickey Cohen in this neighborhood represents a continuous and increasing hazard to life and property, and constitutes a menace which we can no longer tolerate...immediate steps be taken to eliminate this menace." The group warned the city that they wouldn't give up easily, and that Mickey should be declared a "public nuisance."

Mickey remained nonplused by the whole event, even when reminded that this had been the sixth attempt on his life in three years. "Even in those days I slept very well. A lot of people wuz, er, were, wondering if I were in my correct mind."

On Tuesday, February 7, Governor Warren claimed that Mickey knew who had bombed the house and said, "...knows as well who is trying to kill him that way as he knows the address of his home."

Mickey replied, "I'm too small a guy to get involved with any discussions with the governor of the State of California."

Repairs started on the house, attracting hundreds of people who watched the contractors work. Police Chief Worton ordered twenty-four-hour patrols. He made a point that the protection was for the citizens and not the Cohens.

The ongoing Pearson trial—still in Mickey's life after what seemed like an eternity of assassination attempts, fights with the police and city, prostitution stings, and courtroom appearances—revealed that Alfred Pearson's less than desirable reputation extended to his family. Mrs. Hazel Pearson, his daughter-in-law who had worked in the Adams Blvd. shop for seven years, called Pearson a gyp artist.

On February 9, Hazel Pearson answered attorney Rummel directly, "I've never really liked the man."

In court, sign painter Roy L. Wolford described how Rist had ordered the decoy picket signs needed to traipse around the Pearson shop. Wolford displayed the red, white, and blue signs that read, DO NOT PATRONIZE THIS RADIO STORE. HE TAKES WIDOW'S HOMES FOR $8 BILLS.

The trial uncovered "startling" information: Mickey met almost every night at the 8800 Sunset Boulevard haberdashery with James Rist, David Ogul, Harold Meltzer, Louis Schwartz, Edward Herbert, and Frankie Niccoli.

"Some nights a few might be missing. Other nights a few others would be added," wrote a diligent *Los Angeles Times* reporter.

The infamous group would sneak off to a lavish dinner in either Beverly Hills or West Hollywood. The list of trendy and expensive eateries included Ciro's, Romanoff's, King's, Sherry's, and the Continentale. Hardly the greasy spoon choices of someone short on dough.

The Pearson saga finally ended and the jury acquitted Mickey on March 7, 1950, one year after its inception. The police never reinstated the suspended Pearson cops, but their acquittals held up.[11]

Mickey still could not recoup the bail money associated with his gang, since he couldn't prove that any of the muggers who had disappeared were dead. When Niccoli and Ogul vanished, the city had permanently pocketed the money.

"There just ain't no justice," said Mickey.

Bill Howard, another Mickey pal, suspiciously disappeared in the ocean; Mickey forfeited another twenty-five hundred in bail money.

Mickey never balked about the money: "I knew they were six feet under."

Chief Worton disagreed and claimed that he knew that Niccoli and Ogul were in Chihuahua City, Mexico, and had been seen crossing the border into El Paso. Niccoli had dyed his hair blond and used a device to enlarge his nostrils, popular amongst those on the lam.

Mickey's reply: "Anyone that wants to bet they are [in Mexico] can get 10-to-1 from me." Several reports said that four of Dragna's men likely strangled Niccoli after he refused to jump ship and work for Dragna. Niccoli was not afraid to tell Dragna, "I love the guy," referring to Mickey, who later claimed that Dragna's men had gunned down Niccoli and Ogul, and buried them in a lime pit, making all the investigations and speculation a waste of time.

14.

Federal Heat

The public remained fascinated by Mickey's life, particularly his ability to survive so many well-publicized assassination attempts. He became the master of the sound bite, long before it turned into the annoying staple of radio and television journalism. He had an audience that clamored for him, and he continued to entertain them through his exploits and willingness to speak openly. Journalists enjoyed quoting him because he was always willing to offer controversy, often with a sense of humor. "If I see a guy a couple of times the press calls him my henchman. What the hell is a henchman, anyway?"

The *Nation* estimated that Mickey's bookmaking business had grown to seven million dollars annually, with pay-offs to a single person totaling $427,000 per year. Police officers helped collect his gambling money. Still, local city officials wanted no part of seriously investigating him. The *Nation* asked the obvious question: "Why do the law-enforcement agencies fail to clamp down on it if they are really interested in Mr. Cohen's activities?"

Writer Carey McWilliams explained the country's attraction to Mickey: "...he is a fascinating figure to all sorts of people—columnists, politicians, movie actors, society figures, and others—who are drawn to him by stories of his power and wealth, his fabulous hospitality, and above all by the curiosity that people have about a man who moves about under the shadow of a death sentence." McWilliams compared Mickey to hopeless romantic Jay Gatsby of the novel *The Great Gatsby*. He wondered if Mickey's success wasn't proof of brilliant insight into the mind of author F. Scott Fitzgerald, and offered a brief bio of Mickey that concluded with "Lord of Sunset Strip."

Stories like these indicated that Mickey's public cash-flow escapades were only grandstanding. He wanted his public to think that the city had harmed him by keeping his Pearson case bail money. He already had a reputation as a soft touch for anyone in need, and as one of Hollywood's most generous hosts. He still traveled with an entourage that often numbered fifty, all driving Cadillacs.

Mickey was still haunted by the feeling that he wasn't accomplishing enough socially or politically. He always needed something extra, any activity that would help diminish his own low self-esteem and help solidify his public status as a decent person. He fought against those who dismissed his life ambitions as being only ego driven. He remained devoted to Israel, a deep-seated responsibility that was unrelated to his personal achievements. He continued his quest to right all the wrongs written in the newspapers. He complained bitterly about the local police and claimed they were out to ruin him. He took on the city, and his political activism convinced enough people that the local government was corrupt.

"Honest" Mayor Bowron, ironically first elected on a recall, was now himself the victim of recall petitions. People in town carried brooms to "sweep Bowron out." The "Ordinary Citizens Committee" to recall Bowron quickly collected 130,000 signatures.

The troubled Mayor claimed that "...gamblers and others of the underworld who have the cooperation of Communists" financed the dump Bowron campaign. Present circumstances forced him to base his re-election campaign on a simple unconfirmed fact: Mickey was a "small-time punk," a creation of the media, and Los Angeles was "still the city of angels," as reported in *Life*.

He proved neither argument.

To illustrate Mickey's pervasive power, late Friday on April 14, 1950, Thomas C. Cheetham, who had worked for Warden Clinton Duff at San Quentin prison, resigned from his position with the Department of Corrections, and accepted a demotion to assistant captain. He had taken vacations in Los Angeles, and allowed Davey Ogul to pay his Knickerbocker Hotel bill with one of Mickey's checks; Mickey had also sent him some sport shirts. Ogul's brother Leo had wanted a transfer to the Chino facility. Cheetham met socially with Mickey, LaVonne, and the Burbank police chief, to help facilitate Ogul's requests.

Mickey's cozy relationship with the Los Angeles police would abruptly change. Chief Worton retired, and the new chief, William H. Parker, stepped up efforts against him. Chief Parker, wanted nothing to do with him, and polarized the department against him. He created an intelligence division that would only answer to the chief. Mickey was the central target. Police regularly harassed him, and arrested him for petty citations, like jaywalking.

Retired L.A.P.D. detective John O'Mara confessed that they had violated Mickey's civil rights, but "civil rights wasn't a great thing in those days, you know, and how the hell's a gangster gonna say his civil rights were violated?"

Mickey tried to reduce his difficulties with the police by appealing to the public through the newspapers, but it was to no avail with the new chief.

Things were brewing in Washington. On April 21, a Senate commerce subcommittee listened to retired Chief of Police Worton and Capt. Lynn White of the L.A. police discuss interstate gambling, gang wars, and killings. Mayor Bowron let the committee know that bookies were "the most menacing in the entire field of organized crime." The committee became educated in the way of bookmaking, the "package sale" promotions of the Continental News Service, and Mickey's dozens of handbooks that linked New York, Chicago, and Florida. The committee also learned how men at Florida Gold Coast Hialeah racetrack wore women's girdles that hid radio transmitters with antennas.

On May 3, 1950, the Senate Select Committee on Organized Crime in Interstate Commerce, also known as the Kefauver hearings, began its long dark journey into the underworld. The unique committee, made up of senators from around the country, was a clear departure from the status quo. The goal was to expose mobsters and organized crime in front of the American public. Fourteen cities would host the first such hearings of this magnitude to be televised nationally. To the dismay of children nationwide, popular shows such as *Howdy Doody* were preempted. The final hearing was saved for New York, where interrogators hoped for a knockout.

It shouldn't have surprised anyone, but when the Justice Department reported gambling links between Florida's Gold Coast and California, the May 30 story appeared in major newspapers as if *they* had discovered gold. The story coincided with Kefauver's Miami stop, where he revealed that he had information on Mickey, Frank Costello, Joe Adonis, and Florida/New York bookie Frank Erickson. Mickey's named also turned up again when Kefauver delved into a Broward County Florida sheriff's gambling associations. Mickey had inquired about laying off horse bets at the popular Boca Raton Club, something he did routinely around the country when the local demand for bets ran high.

145

On June 7, 1950, the Missouri Highway Patrol raided a Western Union office in St. Louis that did bookmaking business with Mickey. During July, government investigators mentioned his connection to a one million-dollar federal loan for the owners of the Mapes Hotel in Reno, who were expanding, and were now technically in business with a government agency.

An FBI report in June named Mickey as the "key underworld figure in Las Vegas." They were still investigating his activities with the gambler who had flown in to pay off his debt and labeled them overt "kidnapping," even though there was no indication of violence. Mickey apparently had help from the LAPD in finding his "victim," which annoyed the FBI agents further, many of whom blamed local authorities for thwarting FBI activity. Over one hundred pages of reports dealt with the single incident, with much of the information supplied by informants. Despite all of their efforts, the FBI came up short: "Interviews with fight managers and confidential informants negative." They even fished around with employees of the trendy Copacabana in New York and the cruise ship staff of the luxury ocean liner *Queen Elizabeth*.

The "victim" obviously had felt that it was in his best interest to pay up, but he also took a series of cooperative steps to disarm any police action. He said he was an old friend of Mickey's, and claimed that no debt had existed—Mickey merely needed the money, and as a friend, he had initiated a loan. The "victim" turned out to be a bookmaker who had initially run out on Mickey. The bookie had specialized in boxing matches, and either he or one of his associates owned a piece of the sports book at the Desert Inn in Vegas. This mystery man was New Yorker and *Ring Magazine* writer Eddie Borden, Mickey's old pal. The FBI couldn't have been further off in its secret investigation and depiction of Mickey's relationship to Borden.[1]

The FBI had bigger ideas about frying Mickey, although they had wasted significant time on his ability to track down Borden in Vegas. The mix to get him now included agents who assisted the Internal Revenue. The IRS watched all of Mickey's activities, including his travel expenses on trips to New York.

During one trip to Chicago with Johnny Stompanato, the duo spent a precautionary night in jail. Police had arrested Mickey and Stompanato at the seventy-five-dollar per day penthouse of the Ambassador East Hotel, where Mickey had registered as Michael Cain. The Ambassador was not Mickey's first choice; several hotels either asked him to leave once they had identified him, or simply initially refused him a room. Jack Kearns, who had managed Jack Dempsey, was also present during the roust.

The police knew that they had no charges, but proceeded anyway. Attorney Charles Bellows asked for a writ of habeas corpus, a determination of lawful imprisonment vs. release, forcing Criminal Court Judge Julius H. Miner to tell the police to either back off or charge Mickey with a crime.

Los Angeles Times reporters wrote, "Promptly at 3 p.m., the jail doors opened and the moon-faced gambler walked out a free, but most unpopular man."

Police released "gambler" Mickey and "jeweler" Stompanato on August 4. Chief of Detectives Andrew Aiken told Mickey that it was likely that he would be killed hanging around Chicago, and that would soil the neighborhood.

Aiken told him to get lost: "We don't want your scar tissue messing up the place. We don't want to find your body on a street here."

"I'm goin', I'm goin,' Mickey replied. "Just as soon as I get out of this police house I'm headin' for other parts."

Aiken, convinced that Mickey was hiding something, tried to diminish his public stature and said, "He's got the reputation now as a no-good guy and anybody who puts up with him will get the same reputation among the hoods. He's a real Homeless Hector."

Mickey insisted that his arrest in Chicago was a fluke. "I shouldn't have no enemies anywhere. I've never been bothered in California." When questioned about all the shootings back home he replied, "Just playing, I guess. Nothing else to do."

He told the reporters that he was on a three-week cross-country tour with Stompanato, and that his purpose to visit Chicago was to "square myself" with the Chicago national bosses.

On August 8, Chicago police arrested Mickey's brother Harry. Years back, Harry, also known as Harry Colen and Harry Sheridan, had been up to no good in the war surplus business. He had taken eight thousand dollars in 1946 from two unnamed men for the delivery of upholstery tacks, which never materialized. Since he smartly refused to waive extradition, the case flipped back to Los Angeles, where the outstanding grand theft warrant had originated. At his appearance in court, Harry said that he was innocent and had been living with his wife and two children in Chicago for six months. Authorities released him on five thousand dollars bail, the outcome left in the hands of Los Angeles police.

Something new was taking place at the federal level. The FBI sent out memos in November 1950 advising all agents to keep every morsel of information for use as evidence. They made records of all Mickey's West Hollywood State Bank checks, and hoped that the laboratory would find a forgery. Agents interviewed women who had worked for him, and kept a list of pimps. The FBI stepped up its attention on national work, and followed people associated with him in New Orleans and Miami. The agents intermingled with the vacation crowds at the Flamingo and El Rancho, and nosed around smaller Vegas businesses, desperate for any incriminating information. They also confronted some extremely popular and successful club owners in New York. Los Angeles agents hung out at the Olympic Arena and Hollywood Legion Stadium boxing arenas. The FBI questioned anyone remotely connected to Mickey, including apartment landlords and hotel employees. The agents traced Mickey-money to companies like the True Value Beer and Ale Company in Washington, D.C., but investigations of these smaller connections turned up little impropriety.

The full-scale attack continued, but the obsessed FBI refused to give up on the Borden kidnapping angle. After reviewing the entire case, one agent wrote that the "kidnapping" idea was weak, although it may be a violation of some law. The agents reconsidered all the facts; perhaps Borden had owed over four thousand dollars, something Kefauver already knew. Even though the whole process was a timewaster, agents scoured over the exchanged checks many times, and interviewed banks and businesses. If the FBI wanted to take action against Mickey regarding the Borden kidnapping, they had to do it before November 1, 1953, under the current statute of limitations.

Mickey still had time for his political interests, despite the surrounding tumult. With Mickey and others in tow, Richard Nixon made a bid for the Senate in 1950. He ran against beauty Helen Gahagan Douglas, one of the most popular Democrats of the era, a former opera singer and actress. She had held the seat Nixon sought for the last six years.[2]

Author Anthony Summers quoted Mickey on his new travails with Richard Nixon:

> "I was again asked by Murray Chotiner to raise funds…we had to… See, Chotiner had a brother, Jack, that was a lawyer, one of the guys with the programs with the bookmakers, that also defended some of my guys… I reserved the Banquet Room in the Hollywood Knickerbocker Hotel for a dinner meeting to which I invited approximately two hundred and fifty persons who were working with me in the gambling fraternity… Everybody from around here that was on the pad naturally had to go to the dinner. It was all gamblers from Vegas, all gambling money; there wasn't a legitimate person in the room."[3]

The guest list at the hotel fundraiser included a solid array of bad guys: Joe and Fred Sica, the latter known for his narcotics connections; George Capri; Hy Goldbaum; and Jack Dragna all came out to help Nixon. The Sicas remained part of Mickey's local mob, while Capri and Goldbaum ran different casinos in Las Vegas. They both worked for Lansky, who continued to control much of the Vegas action.

Summers continued:

> "There was a certain figure we had to raise for that night," Cohen recalled; "$75,000, a considerable piece of money in those days... I'm sitting at the affair with a group of my guys from Vegas when my business manager, Mike Howard, says, 'Mickey, we didn't raise the quota. We're short $20,000.' I said, 'Tell ya what ya do, Mike.' There were three entrances to this banquet room. I says, 'Close them.' Then I got up and I said, 'Lookit, everybody enjoyed their dinner, everybody happy? Well, we're short for this quota, and nobody's going home till this quota's met'"... According to Cohen, the mobsters quickly rediscovered their generosity. "All the guests seen the doors were being closed, so the quota was met over and above, and that was it."

Nixon could not have been more pleased; he made a short thank you speech like a pro, and let Murray Chotiner handle the rest.

Rabid anti-Semite Gerald L. K. Smith, a Huey Long fan, campaigned for Nixon by urging California voters "...further the ideals of Christian nationalism, and this is not to send to the Senate the wife of a Jew."

Columnist and showman Drew Pearson described the political play-by-play as "one of the most skillful and cut-throat campaigns I have ever seen." Nixon ran a dirty anti-Semitic anti-Communist smear campaign against her—he called Douglas the "pink lady"—using the mob's money and won the election.

Mickey's quirky attraction to Nixon required overlooking his entire package. Since Nixon was really no friend of the Jews, it didn't make complete sense for Mickey—who operated on Lansky's approval—to bend over backwards for him. Both he and Lansky recognized that Nixon's potential political power and consistent cooperation in their syndicated endeavors outweighed any political or social positions that conflicted with their personal beliefs. Mobsters usually didn't support politicians for social reform; they did it to make money and afford themselves of another protective veil.[4]

Not only did Mickey raise considerable sums of money for Nixon, he also "leased" him his campaign headquarters in the downtown Pacific Finance Building on Eighth and Olive streets, prime business real estate. Attorney Sam Rummel handled the arrangements, and Mickey bankrolled the operation. Nixon's people didn't have to pay a nickel for any printed materials.

Aside from the large fundraisers, Mickey arranged to funnel money to Nixon on a consistent basis. To avoid scrutiny, the money came through a variety of sources including Artie Samish, who was still one of the most powerful lobbyists in California.[5]

Authors like Anthony Summers point out that Nixon was a very calculating politician, and knew exactly how to deal with people like Mickey. Yet, Summers also questioned the relationship: "However damning, is this account by a criminal really credible? Did Nixon and Chotiner ask one of the leading mobsters in Los Angeles, a man notorious for his crimes even then, for cash contributions—and in not one but two election campaigns?"[6]

During the first week of November 1950, ads filled the pages of newspapers, including the *New York Times*, touting Florabel Muir's biography *Headline Happy*. The celebrity-driven copy let readers know that for three bucks they would get the "inside stuff" on Bugsy Siegel, Charlie Chaplin, Errol Flynn, Mary Astor, and Mickey Cohen.

Crime instigator Kefauver took a publicity-enhanced trip to Las Vegas on Wednesday November 15. When word got out that Kefauver was actually spending time in the area, local mobsters suddenly came down with everything from nervous breakdowns to coronaries. Kefauver subpoenaed everyone from Desert Inn owner Wilbur Clark; managing director of the Golden Nugget; Guy McAfee, the Flamingo's Gus Greenbaum; and Executive Director William J. Moore at The Last Frontier; to A. E. Cahlan, executive editor of the *Las Vegas Review Journal*; the lieutenant governor; police chief; and tax commissioner. Author Shawn Levy evoked the mixed emotions on Kefauver: "This wasn't the first time the government had made a grand posture of busting up the Vegas Rackets…sniffing around and making noise so he might get nominated for president."

The Kefauver noise was music to the ears of the national mob leaders, who had always felt that they had nothing to fear from him. He frequented racetracks; young ladies who played the field were often in his company, a public image that made him appear like a grandstander, not someone who was serious about his political ambitions. The mob bosses were only partially right: Kefauver would not focus on Vegas, but he was still out to make a name for himself on the backs of the syndicate leaders.

His Las Vegas showboating unwittingly provided a priceless advertisement that lured every unhappy low and mid-level gangster to Las Vegas. Why fight politicians and local police if a new legal enterprise had received a free pass from the Senate committee?

While Kefauver continued his now popular and televised hearings, the mob focused on the great expansion of legalized gambling. This included prostitution and narcotics on a national scale. To the average frat boy, Vegas symbolized sexually the worst and best of America. The repressed country was unable to come to terms with its future. Betting Commissioner James Carroll typified the parochial approach to reality when he told Kefauver that gambling "is a biological necessity for certain types…the quality that gives substance to their daydreams." The mob supplied those daydreamers with slot machines, punchboards, cards, dice, roulette, wagers on sporting events, the numbers, and many beautiful party girls.

When Kefauver visited the LAPD after Las Vegas, he tried to gather as much information as possible on Mickey. Police Chief Parker told Kefauver that legal muscle Rummel was the brains of the outfit and that Mickey's operations were ineffectual without him. Kefauver did not plan to make longtime mobster Dragna a significant target of the extensive hearings that tracked and attacked the criminal organization in Los Angeles.

Despite all the new scrutiny, Mickey had ordered one of his many special automobiles. This model was a better copy of the one used by the president, a $16,000 bulletproof Cadillac—a 1950 Series 60S (50-6019X Fleetwood) V8 Cadillac. He paid Hillcrest Motors in Beverly Hills the base price of $7,000 for the custom-built vehicle. Work had begun on the extraordinary car while Mickey traveled around the country with Johnny Stompanato. (Rumors surfaced that Mickey might have a hard time securing a permit for such an elaborate street limo. He also applied for a permit to build a special steel fence around his Brentwood home.)[7]

The *Los Angeles Times* pictured the car simply as a "custom-built armor-plated Cadillac" and mentioned that Coachcraft (8671 Melrose Avenue) designers Burton Chalmers and Rudolph Stoessel would handle the special details. Chalmers was naturally overjoyed to get the order: "We even figured out a way to make the new curved windshield bulletproof—and that's never been done before…. I can tell you this job is far superior to anything they've got in Washington." His separate bill for his limousine work amounted to eight thousand dollars.

Mickey was as status conscious as he was concerned for his safety. The unique and futuristic vehicle had bombproof flooring and eight-inch-thick armor-plated doors (carbon steel) that weighed one hundred pounds each. Inside each door was a slab of bulletproof fiberglass. The bulletproof windows could withstand armor-piercing bullets, hand weapons of any kind, and consisted of two separate chunks of one and one-half inch plate glass. A hinged windscreen provided a venue for inside weapon firing. The tires were also bulletproof: Goodrich Silvertown Seal-O-Matic puncture-proof models. The fully air-conditioned vehicle weighed close to five thousand pounds and featured a built-in bar. All Mickey's cars had customized compartments so he could hide money—"when I collected so much dough that I couldn't stuff it all into the secret pockets, and there was fifty-dollar bills flying all over the inside of the car."

He was proud of his multi-ton acquisition. "It felt like a tank. Way before air conditioning was in many other cars, you could stop in the desert and have icicles on the hottest day. The glass was made where you could shoot out, but they could be sitting there shooting at you and nothing would be coming in."

Public comments fueled by the newspaper scrutiny brought too much attention to his new toy. It soon turned out that he was unable to obtain the proper registration. The Highway Patrol refused the permit; only accustomed to issuing armored vehicle permits to institutions like banks. The initial position of the police was, "there'd be 10,000 armored cars on the road, and the police would never be able to stop them."

While attorneys Sam Rummel and Vernon Ferguson appealed for Mickey to operate his car on the streets of Los Angeles, the limo remained in storage for months. The attorneys claimed that he needed it to protect himself and his family. The judge who eventually granted the license for street use was more curious as to how Mickey was able to get the L.A.P.D. to road test the vehicle for him.

The FBI kept in regular touch with Mickey's attorney Sam Rummel. He, naturally, could not provide the FBI with any information to help them make a case. They still had fantasy hopes out of making a witness out of the "kidnapped bookie" Eddie Borden. During one further interrogation by the FBI, Borden blamed the whole incident on the Rams football team. If only they could have won the game none of this would have happened—and the FBI would have saved a ton of taxpayers' money.

The federal authorities had never spent this much time or money watching Mickey. The extensive and repetitive work included lining up dozens of minor witnesses. Now the federal authorities focused even more intently on Mickey's daily activities. Yet, there was still dissension among the principal FBI agents as to Mickey's importance and capabilities. The current push could have been a ploy designed to have him and his attorneys think that this kind of trivial material was going to be the focus of the upcoming Kefauver Committee. All the action appeared part of an effort to ready the playing field for Kefauver, but the only thing they had at the time was the possible kidnapping charge. Either the FBI was kidding itself, or the thousands of pages available on Mickey didn't tell the full story. Kefauver knew that Mickey was too popular to convict in Los Angeles—the city did little about all the shootings. However, he remained determined to get Mickey.

The publicity hound kept on his local rounds. Mickey continued to make headlines, complicating Kefauver's task. He had opened the Carousel ice cream parlor in Brentwood (which his sister would manage), with celebrity host Walter Winchell christening the first-day festivities, and adorned the walls with photos of celebrities like Sammy Davis, Jr., Pat Morrissey, Mike Wallace, George Raft, Audrey Totter, Leo Diamond, and Kay Cee Jones. It was a perfect place to congregate for Mickey; he easily consumed a couple of pints of ice cream at one sitting.

According to Mickey, Edmund "Pat" Brown, the district attorney and future governor, and the rest of the attorneys on the prosecutorial sixth floor were beholden to him. He shuffled between a quarter of a million to six hundred thousand dollars per day in cash and commissions. Not only the attorneys, but also the police firmly supported his antics and business. He would make sure that police officers tailing him would eventually catch up with him so they would be able to make a report. "They had to make a living too," was his generous rationale. Everyone seemed to be on his payroll.

Despite the heat from the police and honest politicians, he operated at will and expanded his operations to the disdain of Dragna, whom Mickey described as "kind of lackadaisical." Mickey knew that the East Coast mob supported him, although many authors portrayed his current activities as those of a minor operator. He wasn't naive, and since he had already outlived many of his critics on both sides of the law, he felt secure in the process that had led to his takeover.

The fastidious mobster had every reason to be confident, and he continued to speak defiantly to reporters.

15.

Showtime

Estes Kefauver, the Democratic majority pick to run the investigatory committee, pursued his indelible mark on American history and challenged organized crime in America. His efforts marked the first time that the country paid any significant attention to organized crime's national syndicate. Ninety-two consecutive days of televised hearings became the reality television show of the era, and marked the beginning of television as a powerful media tool.[1]

Author Kitty Kelley recognized the new format: "Viewers saw gangsters like Meyer Lansky, Frank Costello, Mickey Cohen, and Willie Moretti dressed in shiny double-breasted suits take the Fifth Amendment—'I decline to answer the question on the grounds that it might tend to incriminate me.'"[2]

Kefauver forcefully educated the people of the United States by testing "the medium is the message" for the first time and well before Marshall McLuhan coined the phrase. Television was in its infancy. People had heretofore mostly watched wrestling. Since the hearings appeared during the inception of the television boom created by Milton Berle, the majority of people still didn't own television sets in 1950 and were therefore unable to see the unusual event unfold; perhaps thirty million watched, less than twenty percent of the population.[3]

The public imagination focused on the spectacle that unfolded. Old news became new again, and an entire country began to believe the stories about an organization of criminals that existed in the underbelly of Ozzie-and-Harriet cities and towns. The media, a McLuhan term, was collectively influencing the country's thinking.

Massachusetts Democratic congressman, future senator and president, John Kennedy was startled by the effect of television and later wrote, "These hearings, the Kefauver crime hearings, the McClellan rackets hearings...political TV spectaculars have given the American public new ideas, new attitudes, new heroes, and new villains."

The Associated Press marveled at the new phenomenon: "Something big, unbelievably big and emphatic, smashed into the homes of millions of Americans last week when television cameras, cold-eyed and relentless, were trained on the Kefauver Crime hearings." Those who didn't see the televised proceedings heard the interviewees on radio and listened to them deny the existence of the Mafia. Few witnesses admitted that they had ever heard of it.

The syndicate brass must have had a few hearty laughs at Kefauver's expense during those tedious three months. Even the name of the committee sounded laughable to the mobsters, "Senate Select Committee on Organized Crime in Interstate Commerce."

From Mickey's criminal perspective, knowing how to run a shady business amidst all variations of political frameworks, the committee was "a joke, a gimmick for the furtherance of a politician."

Kefauver knew his target: "The Mafia is a shadowy international organization that lurks behind much of America's organized criminal activity... It is an organization about which none of its members, on fear of death, will talk... The Mafia, however, is no fairy tale...it has scarred the face of America with almost every conceivable type of criminal violence, including murder, traffic in narcotics, smuggling, extortion, white slavery, kidnapping, and labor racketeering."

The Kefauver Committee was also well aware of Carlos Marcello ("Googy Eyes") and wisely profiled him during the investigations. Marcello, always a friend to Mickey, would later run into him during the McClellan hearings, where both mobsters answered to Robert Kennedy.[4]

News of Mickey's scheduled appearance before the committee naturally made headlines. "The Senate's Kefauver investigating committee visited the City of the Angels last week and sought out its most aggrieved, blue-jowled cherub, roly-poly gambler Mickey Cohen," was how *Time* began its two-column report.

Mickey was flattered. "I guess the Kefauver committee decided to see me because I was reputed to be the boss gambler in this part of the country." He felt that the whole process was an exaggeration, and Kefauver was showboating. Mickey and his attorneys were predisposed to the idea that the senator's efforts would prove futile. However, records indicate that attorney Rummel had advised Mickey that it was in his best interest to cooperate.

The day before Mickey's appearance, the federal committee looked into the Guarantee Finance Company and its alleged bookmaking. The senator grilled Undersheriff Arthur G. Jewell, a stand-in for Sheriff Biscailuz, who would testify the next day and answer questions about the suspicious company. Jewell couldn't recall a thing, and contributed to the conclusion that the California crime commission appointed by Governor Earl Warren operated with apathy and collusion. The Kefauver Committee commented that the California commission accomplished nothing with regard to Mickey.

The committee criticized John W. Snyder, secretary of the treasury, for not handing out indictments as suggested by Mayor Bowron, who said that no major hoodlum "however great his income" had ever been convicted of tax evasion. The committee called Bowron "accurate and fair" and noted the problems between State Attorney General Howser and the governor.[5]

In gearing up for Mickey, the committee spent a considerable part of the day looking at "gambler" Mickey's books. The *New York Times* reported financial gaps of $210,000 in his records. Something was up, and it wasn't Mickey's bookmaking, prostitution, extortion, or drug associations.

True to form, the fearless cartoon-embellished celebrity was late for his committee appearance on November 17, 1950; he had been preoccupied primping and preening himself because he was going to appear on television. He was unaware that two of his security guards at the time were paid informants for the police. (Barney Ruditsky of Sherry's would testify the same day and tell reporters, "Same old thing, New York stuff.")

When the elevator-shoed witness entered the crowded courtroom, he was the star of the show. He wore a natty brown suit, brown tie, and "deep black scowl," observed a reporter for *Time.* A battery of reporters, photographers, movie cameras, and tape recorders filled the arena in Los Angeles' federal building.

Mickey knew and appreciated the power given him by the committee. He made the most of the ideal venue; he worked without notes, and hardly conferred with his lawyers. He had become a pro at manipulating the media; his style magnified the ineptness of his interrogators, and gave the public a taste of the absurd. The politicians questioning him sounded scripted or stilted in their initially polite interrogation.

He supplied his interrogators with a brief bio, including his boxing exploits, adding "but I wasn't very good." He answered that he worked as a tailor, and that five years had passed since his bookmaking days, when he was "a bookies' bookie, a layoff man."

Mickey mentioned some of his associates: Rocky Paladino of Boston, Jake Kaplan of San Francisco, and a man named Rogers from Asbury Park, New Jersey.

When Senator Tobey asked, "Is it true that he [Artie Samish] is a strong-arm man in California politics?", Mickey replied demurely, "I believe he is well respected in the community."

He went with his usual flow: "I could spit on the sidewalk, and it would make headlines."

Mickey told the enraptured officials that he was the "best newspaper copy in town."

He was at the top of his game. He raised his eyebrows, expressed hurt on cue, and was never shy about denying the charges, offering his own spin when questioned about Pauley Gibbons, Max Shaman, and overall nefarious behavior.

"I ain't never muscled no one in my life… I ain't never offered no policeman a bribe… I never pistol-whipped anyone… I ain't never been with no prostitute… I never had no part of a fix… I never strong-armed nobody in my life; I may have beat up some people… I've been arrested so many times, I can't remember all of them."

When asked if his line of work would lead anyone to want to kill him, Mickey answered, "I can't picture anyone who would want to do that." He explained that he had utilized his own private investigators to visit cities around the country to see who was after him. "I don't have nothing that anybody could muscle away from me. I don't have any places they could take over," he added, to minimize his role.

His colorful demeanor was a hit with television audiences; he remained comfortable and fearless.

For hours, committee members delved into his businesses. The Kefauver report treated his legit business interests as if they were sets on a movie lot: "Mickey always seemed to have either a paint shop, a jewelry store, or a haberdashery on his string and some investigations are unkind enough to believe that he used these businesses as a front for his bookmaking operations."

Rudolph Halley, chief counsel for Kefauver, received nothing substantial from Mickey, who he remained one of the most uncooperative witnesses. Halley became frustrated and began rattling off long lists of names, some of which were low-level operators dug up by overzealous investigators for the committee. Mickey had never heard of many of the people so it was easy for him to smirk and say, "No sir."

The core of the questioning centered on his ability to move money around the country. He cleverly used many different accounts for each casino; he ran seven, making it virtually impossible to trace his money. He did admit that he lived in a $40,000 home with $48,000 in furnishings, owned a few Cadillacs, and an armored car.[6]

Mickey expected his interrogators to believe that he was penniless and insisted that in order to survive he had borrowed hundreds of thousand of dollars. He stuck with his story about being broke and living off the kindness of others, and eventually stated that he probably owed closer to $300,000. He reached in his pockets and removed $268 to indicate his net cash worth.

The answer was probably closer to the truth than anything else he would say. Since he didn't keep books, he wasn't lying about being broke on paper. His entire operation ran on cash—it was always available—and no records were required. Relatives and friends had lent their names for ownership purposes, and could exchange cash or checks with Mickey, who was sometimes listed as an employee. Money was also stashed in safes hidden inside clubs.

Senator Tobey, another interrogator, inadvertently gave Mickey further control by supplying him with the straight line, "How do you maintain that kind of credit?"

Mickey smiled, and relished the question like a contrite Lou Costello answering to Tobey's Bud Abbott, "It's getting very weak, Senator."

Tobey and counsel Halley grilled Mickey with questions like, "Is it not a fact that you live extravagantly, surrounded by violence?"

Mickey acted confused. "Whaddaya mean 'surrounded by violence', people are shooting at me?" He drew more laughs with lines like, "I've been arrested so many times I can't remember them all."

The frustrated senator eventually admonished him, and insisted that he answer the questions directly.

Like a schoolboy dressed down by his teacher, Mickey became sullen. "I don't like the way he asks them questions, There's two ways to ask a question and I say he isn't asking them right."

The fun and games dissipated when Mickey lost his cool on more than one occasion. "I remember the old senator kept calling me a 'hoodlum.' He really used some terms that were uncalled for, for a senator in that type of thing," he said years later. He maintained an "honor among thieves" mentality; he perceived the senator as a slightly different version of himself.

Kefauver had done a lot of homework before tackling Mickey, and stacked the deck against him. One of the key witnesses against him was John O'Rourke from West Palm Beach, Florida. Ironically, this key witness had never met Mickey. O'Rourke had entered into a real estate deal with Mickey valued at three million dollars. Profits materialized in cash, with an option for partners to take shares in new deals. Money never changed hands unless a point or share hit a predetermined amount. Disbelieving prosecuting attorneys and investigators listened to the unorthodox-but-effective business structure that eliminated personal contact.

In July 1950, O'Rourke had told Senate crime investigators that Mickey had won more than fifty thousand dollars in phone bets on Florida horse races. He testified that he was a bookie and ran the fancy Boca Raton Club and two other places in tony West Palm Beach. Mickey's lucky run was "disastrous" for O'Rourke. Myer Shine, wealthy hotel and theater chain owner, told authorities that he had sold the concessions at the Boca Raton Club and Roney Plaza to O'Rourke and his partner New York bookie king Frank Erickson, a partner of Frank Costello.

One of Mickey's "marks" named Seltzer unexpectedly testified that he had never loaned Mickey the twenty-five thousand dollars previously stated in a signed letter. He had relied on witnesses like Seltzer to testify that he had borrowed money to pay his bills.

West Hollywood State Bank president Harold W. Brown had loaned Mickey thirty-five thousand dollars in the form of a personal loan. The authorities estimated the number at fifty thousand dollars, and Neddie Herbert had acted as the bagman. Mickey kept several accounts at Brown's bank for each card club.

Senator Tobey remained baffled and asked how Mickey moved money around the country so easily. "How could a man of your reputation OK from 3,000 miles away for a bank president to give another hoodlum this type of money...when I go to a bank in New Hampshire—and I'm a senator, an honorable senator, a property owner—to borrow $500, I have go through hell and high water to get it?"

Mickey controlled his laughter, and supplied his consistent retort that people simply liked him. He played out the hearings by utilizing his ability to improvise with humor; he performed for the reporters, while irritating the hell out of the committee members with his wise-guy bravado.

Kefauver asked him why everyone was so nice to him, especially when it came to money.

Mickey repeated, "I can't answer that; they must like me."

Kefauver concluded later, "In exploring the financial operation of the little gangster, the committee had uncovered some interesting facts on Mickey's method of reporting income to the government. It consisted of supplying a few unsubstantiated and undocumented figures to his accountant, Harry Sackman, of Beverly Hills. Some items as large as $10,000 were described merely as receipts from "Various Commissions."

Sackman had reported, "I always ask him each year to give me the detail and he says, 'here is the figure and this is the only thing I can present to you.' If the government accepts the figure, that is their responsibility."

Mickey's unresponsive style resembled that of white-collar criminals today. He claimed that he really didn't make any money, and that a running tally of commissions determined profits. As mentioned, a business only kicked off payouts when income reached a predetermined profit, usually equal to the unit investment—put in fifty thousand, get out fifty thousand. To complicate the accounting, Mickey gambled with business partners, and sometimes exchanged large sums equal to investment points. His defense was that the money exchanged would often balance out over time, and therefore he had no income to report.

When asked about race wire rival Russell Brophy's beating with Joe Sica, he said that it was "purely a personal dispute." He again denied any "strong-arm" activity or "muscling in" on other people's businesses. He said that he was not acquainted with the transcontinental race wire.

When Eddie Borden's name came up Mickey claimed that the whole issue was a complete fabrication of the Los Angeles Police Department to divert the committee's attention from "dirty work." He said that he was worried about Borden, who had suicidal spells, and had seen him recently to show the local police that nothing had happened to him.

Mickey did not dispute his arrest record, and the committee fished all the way back to his embezzlement in Chicago, for which he had received a pardon. He told the committee that his current problems stemmed mostly from "police harassment."

The grilling concluded with the usual list of suspects, the do-you-know list compiled by "experts," including names like Frank Costello, Joe Adonis, Meyer Lansky, Jack Lansky, Ralph Capone, "Little New York" Campagna, Murray

Humphrey, and Charlie and Joseph Fischetti. Mickey continued to insist that he didn't know most of the names, although he did know all of the big boys. Anyone he knew was merely one of his "very good friends."[7]

The hearing lasted five hours. Mickey eventually called Kefauver a liar and, of course, it made headlines. When Kefauver dismissed him after a long, hard afternoon in front of the microphones, Mickey faced his adversaries and sneered, and held the grimace until he left the courtroom. The *New York Times* called him a "dapper saturnine man."

Senator Tobey had the last word: "The committee must go into this matter further at a later date."

The media had unintentionally elevated Mickey's national status. The one-upmanship game played out to the advantage of the mob, like a rigged reality show. The event provided television laughs, drama, and something decidedly new to do before the days of Berle and Sid Caesar.

Despite Kefauver's positive take on the outcome, the *New York Times* reporter who covered the hearings said that Mickey "gave the fanciest sparring exhibition of his career."

When the committee interviewed Jimmy Utley, he denied that Mickey had anything to do with the beating incident two years ago, which was now described as a pistol-whipping. He had no recollection of his assailants.

On November 18, the committee grilled Frank "The Bomp" Bompensiero, characterized as a business partner of Dragna. The implications of the questions linked Mickey, Dragna, and dozens of others to drug trafficking from Mexico. The Bomp liked his bullfights and Mexican food, and sometimes spent three nights a week in Tijuana at Caesar's Restaurant.

Four days later, Mickey, under advice from attorneys, agreed to an FBI interview. He acknowledged that he had known "the bookie" Eddie Borden, who owed him money for over twenty years, but denied that the man was involved with taking bets in Vegas.

He was candid, described Borden as a "sucker gambler," said that he bets "every possible thing there is," and laughed it off.

Mickey, very comfortable at the interviews, explained to the Feds that he didn't understand what everyone was so worried about. Borden wasn't hurt or killed or "something." He denied everything except meeting Borden in Las Vegas at the Mayan Hotel. Nor did he enter into discussions about cashing checks; his version differed markedly from the FBI's, and included different amounts paid to him by deadbeat Borden.

He insisted that he was Borden's friend, and expressed concern about his depression.

The result of the FBI kidnapping angle turned up a list of many people who said that he had tried to track Borden down. Many said that Mickey had been agitated and aggressive, and said things like "you can't go to sleep until you get him."

The FBI copied polite Western Union messages sent to Borden:

> This is positively the last request and I wish you can mail without delay to M. Cohen 513 Moreno Avenue, West Los Angeles. I am leaving for Las Vegas tonight where gambling is legal and nothing can happen. It is very vital that he gets that money because he has been hounded to death for no reason and the lawyers must be paid or they don't take the case. I know you understand and won't fail me because it is of great importance to me and other party. You will be getting back installments very soon. Thanks and regards.

The business as usual approach appeared no different from anyone else trying to collect money. The FBI concluded that Mickey worked by "implied intimidation" and that he could get people, even the police, to do things against their will.

The FBI accrued an additional one hundred pages of interviews with informants, croupiers, United Airlines staff, airport parking lot attendants, Yellow Cab drivers, hotel personnel at the Desert Inn, Flamingo, and the Park Sheraton in New York, bank employees, tellers, and managers at Manufacturer's Trust Company, Security First National Bank, and West Hollywood State Bank. Even gas station attendants at the popular Standard Oil Station in Beverly Hills received a visit from the FBI.

The Lockheed Air Terminal police guards didn't recognize a single photograph agents showed them. The usual number of clandestine female companions and sheepish clerks gave no information to the FBI. One femme fatale called Borden "a Broadway character who was mixed up with the fight crowd," and added a Runyonesque touch to the already bizarre investigation.

By the end of November 1950, Eddie Borden was the object of a national search; reporters appeared to know more about him than did the FBI. He traveled by train from Los Angeles (where he had been visiting with Mickey), to New Orleans, and calmly strolled into an FBI office. The agents gave him a subpoena to appear at a federal grand jury in Los Angeles. They treated him to a free train ticket and expenses to hurry him back to Los Angeles.

Borden could not have been more pleased: "Boy, this is something. They're giving me money just like that. They're sure trusting. What would stop a guy from going somewhere else?" He took the whole thing lightly, and added, "Don't worry, I'll be there."

The grand jury wanted to talk to Eddie about his kidnapping, even though he denied that it had taken place.

Mickey told the *New York Times* reporters, "It's stupid. Eddie's my best friend. I've known him since I was 16. Sure he's loaned me dough."

Borden had previously been in Los Angeles with Mickey, who claimed that both local police and FBI were present when he saw Eddie. Borden said that he left Los Angeles because authorities consider placing a bet there a crime worse than murder. He made sure to joke that his Los Angeles plane trip two weeks earlier with Mickey associate Eli Lubin was purely voluntary.

The *Times* also mentioned that the grand jury was looking into a possible tax evasion case against Mickey, something that should have been obvious by now to him and his attorneys.

In court on November 30, Borden again denied that Lubin had kidnapped him and forced him to fly on the original Desert Skyways charter plane, almost a year earlier. Grand jury foreman Roy McLeod concluded what the FBI had known for some time: "got nothing definite from Borden." Lubin was described by the *Times* as "a former Cohen henchman."

That same day Texas Rangers escorted Mickey out of Wichita Falls, Texas. Police director Homer Garrison, Jr., said that he acted on information that Mickey was there organizing his gambling rackets. Unshaven Mickey grumbled about the poor hospitality in Texas, and claimed that he was looking into new oil leases.

Mickey was traveling with Florabel Muir's husband Denny Morrison and Harry Brook; the latter took off promptly for Cleveland. Morrison defended Mickey to reporters and stated, "I know for a fact Cohen has not placed a bet in three years." Morrison and Mickey headed back on American Airlines, but not before Mickey threatened to sue everyone.

During December 1950, according to author Kitty Kelley,[8] when Senator Kefauver turned the questioning over to attorney Joseph L. Nellis, Frank Sinatra was unclear about whether he had paid Tarantino anything to help start his blackmail rag sheet *Hollywood Nite Life*.[9]

Kelley knew the truth: "Frank had invested...which ensured him good publicity in it."

Sinatra never mentioned Mickey. "Jimmy called up...he had an eyewitness account of a party...in which some broads had been raped or something... I told

Jimmy that if he printed anything like that he would be in a lot of trouble." The rest of Sinatra's interview sounded like he received his information from reading newspapers, and knew little about mob life.

Mickey attorney Rummel's own problems materialized at the worst possible time for the FBI. While Rummel was trying to enter his fashionable Hollywood Hills, Laurel Canyon, home, a sawed-off twelve-gauge double-barreled shotgun felled him at one-thirty in the morning, December 11, 1950. Jimmy Fratianno labeled the 1910 model weapon a Remington. He said the triggerman was Angelo Polizzi.

Rummel survived the blast to his neck, only to die the next day. He had been involved in trying to silence witnesses who could help Kefauver's anti-crime investigations. His intentions appeared duplicitous to mob members, even though Kefauver did not call him to testify. The night of the shooting, he had met with a captain and sergeant from Sheriff Biscailuz's vice squad. They looked at files from a grand jury probe of the Guarantee Finance Company, the alleged source for some local police payoffs, and a front for an extensive bookmaking operation. Nothing materialized and the California Crime Commission chastised the police.

The *New York Times* quoted Mickey after news of Rummel's demise. "Oh, God—it's not so!" he exclaimed, and then pointed out that he had lost six "intimates" in the last four years.

Mickey rushed over to Rummel's house where Chief Parker presided over the crime scene. After a few minutes of condolences for Mrs. Rummel, Mickey was in a fistfight with three-hundred-pound Detective Jack Donahue, who had always made Mickey's life miserable with petty arrests. This time Chief Parker sent a cursing Mickey home.

Rummel's death did not faze Mickey or his operations, as Chief Parker had earlier intimated. Kefauver may have believed that Mickey's operation would fall apart without Rummel, who owned a five-percent interest in the Gardena and surrounding poker clubs. (Mickey described Rummel as more of a partner, and that Rummel had made his own side deal with the Gardena club. He had often taken shares in lieu of fees.) Thinking that Mickey's operations were in shambles may account for the delays and repetitive work by the FBI, and no action at the federal level.

16.

The Fighter Stumbles

Chanukah and Christmas 1950, and New Years 1951 rolled around without any action by the federal authorities regarding Mickey. The U.S. Attorney's office grew skittish with its informants, and considered making the case without federal intervention. Several doubtful FBI agents thought success was unlikely.

Mickey was one of the insiders, and pundits wondered why the Kefauver committee had wasted so much time asking him questions without any incriminating evidence. Some marked the events off to fledgling inexperience; the committee couldn't do any better.

The answer soon materialized: the authorities had another angle all along—they were out to get Mickey on tax evasion. The tax years in question were 1946–1948, and additional charges included making false statements to I.R.S. agents.

Many periodicals joked about Mickey's car and his loss of control of his empire. An editorial in the *Nation* referred to him as the unseated boss of the bookies. The periodical stated about the Cadillac, "Mickey, momentarily bereft of his empire, has announced it for sale." Possible buyers were Presidents Alemán of Mexico and Perón of Argentina. The writer joked that Spain's Franco might be a better candidate since the United States had agreed to loan Spain money. The *Nation* also upped the price of Mickey's new acquisition to $20,000.

After a few exchanges with Los Angeles agents, the FBI concluded that Mickey had no respect for the truth and was "evasive, misleading, ingratiating, and two-faced." After many years of successfully manipulating the FBI and the newspapers, he had no reason to cooperate.

The local police had it in for Mickey, particularly when authorities released news of his tax problems. He threatened officers who had stopped his Cadillac tank at four-fifteen in the morning on January 3, 1951. Patrolmen T. U. Hutton and A. L. Santor wanted to ticket him for not moving on a green light at Hollywood and Vine, a five-dollar infraction. Mickey threatened to punch everyone, and ended up getting the ticket. He had innocently stopped for a newspaper. Witnesses claimed that the officers were rough and dragged him from the vehicle. Things had changed.

The *New York Times* reported that Hutton had criticized Mickey's way of life, with Mickey responding, "Take off that badge, you punk, and I'll stretch you out."

Mickey told reporters of his disdain for the police: "…worse than a bunch of Nazis, always tryin' to get their names in the papers."

Journalists Lait and Mortimer wrote Mickey off in January 1951: "Mickey Cohen, a peewee character, became an eminent citizen after his arrival with Benny "Bugsy" Siegel, who moved to California for his health when Brooklyn became too small to hold him and his sawed-off shotguns. After Benny was rubbed out, Mickey, who had no weight and no protection, was a clay pigeon until he became a stooge of Sammy Rummel, the underworld lawyer. Rummel was murdered last year."

By February 7, 1951, the newspapers regularly reported on a probe of Mickey's tax affairs, and threw his sudden and apparently unexpected dilemma into the court of public opinion.

The FBI abruptly dropped all Mickey investigations, pending the outcome of the Kefauver Commission and the IRS. The myopic FBI finally admitted that the Mafia existed, but clung to the archaic notion that only decayed relics like Jack Dragna remained in charge. Most reports still ended up in the GIIF (General Investigative Intelligence File), which included Mickey's no-action investigations.

Mickey's worst-case scenario materialized and was the direct result of the Kefauver Commission and the IRS. Kefauver had naturally turned over his records to the IRS, which was on Mickey the second the hearings had concluded.

Mickey told *Los Angeles Times* reporters he had other plans and was "tired of all this notoriety." He flew to Tucson to investigate new businesses. He spoke about plans to sell his customized car. He told others that he wanted to jerk sodas rather than have anything to do with the rackets.

Brother Harry Cohen announced that he had negotiated the purchase of a drugstore in Tucson. He proudly told reporters, "Mickey will manage the store." He said that he would sell his Chicago construction company and move to Tucson with the Mickey Cohens. The money for the drug store was already in escrow and he outlined his ambitions: "I plan to eventually expand the store into a chain…"

Mickey added, "Everything is going to be legitimate… I'm tired… I want to keep things peaceful."

The money for the stores, more accurately listed as a one-quarter interest and registered in Phoenix, came from the sale of Mickey's customized armored Cadillac to J. W. Jenkins for $12,000. Jenkins, manager of the Texas Stock Car Racing Association, planned to display the car at Fort Worth's Riverside Drive Speedway.

Mickey's deal included plans to rename the two-store drug chain, "the Mickey Cohen Drug Stores."

Publicity-savvy Mickey spoke about the nice people in Tucson: "We went to an art show there and bought a couple of paintings and everybody treated me lovely."

Local reporters asked LaVonne about Mickey's interest in drug stores and a linoleum company that belonged to an old Chicago friend, Ralph Sills, who had known Mickey when he boxed. She happily replied regarding the new opportunities, "I'd like that very much. I've wanted him to get into a nice business. We want to get along peacefully and without notoriety. The past few years have been a nightmare. We don't enjoy it." She said that Mickey was not stopping in Texas and she was unaware of any details of his business activities. She also added, "If any transaction is completed he'll probably call and tell me about it… In that case we'll probably sell our home and move to Tucson. We'll start to relax—and begin life anew." LaVonne said that she didn't know anything about the possibility of a car sale, but added that she was happy about it nonetheless.

The state of Texas began to focus on Mickey, and perhaps rightly so, based on the Cohen family's rosy plans to relocate and invest in other states. He had flown to El Paso to attend the funeral of Detective Ralph Marmolejo, Jr., a twenty-eight-year-old victim of a gun battle in a railroad yard. Marmolejo had met Mickey when Texas Rangers rousted him on a prior trip to the Lone Star State. While in El Paso, Mickey received a subpoena to return for questioning by the Texas House of Representatives.

He spoke with reporters at the airport in Los Angeles after he arrived on American Airlines. He whined to them, "…those people in Texas will do practically anything for publicity," while he posed in a fancy suit with a shiny tie clasp, holding a newspaper. He focused his discussion with them on the deceased detective and lamented, "A terrible thing… He was one of the few nice coppers I ever met. He was a good friend of mine."

Texas may have jumped on the national bandwagon. U.S. District Attorney Ernest Tolin had gone public with discussions about Mickey's tax returns. Authorities in Washington called him part of the hierarchy of national crime figures in the United States, namely because he had mailing addresses in Los Angeles, Chicago, and New York—the old axis of evil. The only other Angelino mentioned was Harold "Happy" Meltzer, who was in a New York jail awaiting a hearing on March 28 regarding opium smuggling charges. Authorities had named Meltzer on March 6 in two indictments, linking him to an international narcotics ring.

Texas Rep. Fred Meridith, chair of the committee, was at least candid about the witch-hunt, unaware of specific questions to ask Mickey. Meridith told reporters, "I have to advise myself on what connections, if any, he has with Texas crime." That said despite newspapers playing up Mickey's generic bookmaking, numbers, and slot interests in Texas.

Smart money knew that Mickey wasn't about to kiss up to local politicians in Texas. He was often right about the grandstanding, something he was accustomed to wherever he appeared. He couldn't be bothered with Texas politics—he knew the high level of corruption that existed in the state and the ineffectual police work to control it. He said that he would have an attorney check into the Texas matter. He appeared more upset about his travel costs, since the state had no system for subpoena expense reimbursement.

Texas Rep. Clyde Whiteside, architect of the new Texas anti-crime initiative, knew Mickey would flick off attempts to interview him at a hearing. Whiteside insisted anyway. "But if he fails to appear, I think we can get Gov. Warren of California to agree to extradition—assuming that Gov. Shivers [of Texas] will go along with us."

In the midst of the all the difficulties, newspapers ran stories on Mickey's continued relationship with the Reverend Billy Graham, who had founded his own evangelist association the prior year. Neither he nor Graham denied that they had been spending time together again.

Mickey replied to reporters who had suggested that he had plans to convert to Christianity, "In the first place, I'm a Jew. I go to the synagogue once in a while."

He and Graham had dinner together at a nightclub on Sunday and Monday, February 18 and 19, 1951. They visited private homes along with guests like actress Jane Russell, who refused to tell reporters about anyone else in the evangelist duo's entourage. Mickey denied rumors that he was off to a Fort Worth, Texas, revival meeting. Some understood that he and Graham were planning a vacation with their wives at a Texas ranch.

Mickey added, "I don't want Billy to get in any jam over me."

Graham played his regular role and concluded with, "After all, Jesus visited Zachaeus of Jericho, who was a tax gatherer of shady reputation."

Mickey remained in close contact with Graham.

On April 3, 1951, the Texas House of Representatives cited Mickey for contempt of court. He refused to appear before the House Crime Committee; he had told them he didn't have the money for the trip. He later recanted, headed for Austin, and instead finalized the deal on the two drugstores in Tucson, Arizona. The FBI took this as an indication that Mickey was seriously going legit and looking for some place to retire, ignoring the obvious criminal benefits of prescription pharmaceuticals. Newell Stewart, secretary of the State Board of Pharmacy in Arizona, pledged that he would not grant Mickey a license.

When pressed by Representative Meridith to return to Texas, Mickey said, "I don't have any plan to go to Texas now."

A damning official indictment came down on April 6, 1951, at 9:15 in the morning. Agents wrote, "…and a month after our final hearings Cohen and his blonde wife LaVonne were indicted for alleged income tax evasion over a period of three years." It was ironic that the government caught up with Mickey for a white-collar crime. The next day newspapers contained articles about him, tax evasion, and general malfeasance in government. Reporters anticipated a new public awareness that would pressure the government for reform.

Mickey was able to persuade United States District Judge William Mathes to reduce his initial bail to only five thousand dollars. Confidant Mickey had strolled into the hearing without an attorney, and frustrated Assistant United States Attorney Ray Kennison, particularly when the judge cooperated with Mickey. He was still unaware of the gravity of the investigation and figured his high-powered attorneys would take care of everything as they had done in the past.

Mickey had signed a net worth statement indicating a taxable income of about $250,000. (Some years Mickey had reported income of $6,000 or less.) The IRS easily produced evidence to show that he had spent over $350,000 for the same year. The math betrayed Mickey, since he couldn't claim that the extra money came from savings—he always maintained that he didn't have any.

The Cohens had underpaid their taxes by $156,123. The government claimed that they owed over $300,000 with penalties. The *New York Times*, which referred to Mickey as "Los Angeles' most prominent underworld figure," detailed the indictment: false declaration on $172,000 borrowed, false declaration on $250,000 borrowed, false declaration on $244,163 disbursed, while disbursing $343,139. The numbers thrown around in the press seemed just as nebulous as those Mickey had made up.

The IRS could no longer accept Mickey's life as a poor haberdasher—the occupation listed on all his recent tax returns. Many had wisely told him that the publicity would be his downfall; his media hype had only fueled the IRS case. No haberdasher lived in a home in Brentwood, with a fancy soda dispenser, a cook, a housekeeper, beautiful gardens, two customized dressing rooms, and a special third bathroom for the shower maven and his talcum powder. Unbeknownst to him, local politicians, police, and a few members of the IRS had already made careers out of Mickey's expenditures. The agents knew that they would eventually catch him.

Dan Goodykoontz was the agent who had done the incriminating calculations. He became a popular speaker at business luncheons after the publicity surrounding Mickey's indictment snowballed.

Bugsy had warned Mickey early on about taxes: "You sonofabitch, you gotta pay taxes."

"What the hell, you're gonna heist it and pay taxes on it," was Mickey's thinking, but he began paying.

Bugsy forgot to tell him not to cheat.

Mickey blamed Bugsy's old financial advice as the source of his trouble. He felt that if he had not paid any taxes his potential sentence would be less—the sentence for non-filers was only a year and a day.

Out on bail he insisted to the public that he lived on borrowed funds. He said that his personal indebtedness was one-half million dollars, all in the form of unsecured loans, with no receipts. Unfortunately, most of the people that he owed money to had died.

He told the press, "What hasta be hasta be. What can you do? It ain't the end of the world."

At the time of the tax trial, George Raft introduced Mickey to Dean Jennings of the *Saturday Evening Post*. Raft interrupted Mickey's breakfast at Linny's deli to ask him if he would meet with Jennings, who was writing a book about Raft.[1]

Mickey's first meeting with Jennings took place at the fabled Brown Derby.[2] Jennings, on advice of his friends, had a loaded gun in a leather holster prepared, but after consults and deliberations, wisely chose to leave it in his hotel room.

Mickey arrived at the Derby with two lawyers and a bail bondsman. The three were helping him prepare for an upcoming assault trial. Jennings took note of a purple scar under his left eye, his shiny brown eyes, a thick gold watch chain that held a mezuzah, a gold watch with solid gold stars instead of numbers on its sky-blue dial, and a diamond ring.

He and Jennings initially hit it off.

"What kind of story you gonna write?" Mickey asked.

Jennings answered, "You won't like this one. It won't be a puff piece, and so you may not want to talk to me."

When Jennings confessed about the gun idea, Mickey nearly fell out of his chair with laughter.

He paid the check from his three-thousand-dollar roll of one hundred dollar bills. When they left the Derby, a woman asked him for his autograph, and he obliged.

Mickey once sailed from fancy Tiburon in San Francisco right past Alcatraz with Jennings and columnist Herb Caen.

Caen appreciated Mickey: "...the only true gentleman at the party was hoodlum, Mickey Cohen."

In response to his tax troubles, Mickey again planned to sell the haberdashery and inquired about an auction to sell his personal possessions. Many subsequent reports said that he had sold his home, which was not the case. He continued his claim that he was broke and still needed money for lawyers. He called around to ask for loans, and even dialed Ben Hecht, who, living in Nyack, New York, said that he was broke too, and unable to raise the five thousand dollars for Mickey.

"That's O.K." said Mickey. "Good luck."

Nevertheless, Mickey remained close to Hecht.

He wasn't the only one of his gang on the hook. On April 25, 1951, Federal Judge Sidney Sugarman held Harold "Happy" Meltzer in lieu of a $100,000 bail. The papers related how the perps had brought opium for conversion into heroin via Mexico, using private planes and fake gasoline trucks. United States Attorney Irving H. Saypol, who would become famous during the trial of Julius and Ethel Rosenberg, was aware that the extensive ring had operated freely since 1945. Meltzer's attorney asked for leniency because the defendant had saved the government the expense of a trial by cooperating.

In May of 1951, Marvin Newman, a specialist in movie star auctions, wasted no time or expense in setting up a highly publicized auction of Mickey's personal property in Beverly Hills. *Newsweek* covered the celebrity event: "Mickey Cohen was unhappily auctioning off the 'complete and luxurious furnishings'..." (The Brentwood home was now valued at only $75,000.)

When asked why he was having the auction Mickey never missed a beat: "Why am I selling this stuff? I have to have the dough. I never realized how expensive it is to fight Uncle Sam." He told his followers that Kefauver was "a contemptible little punk."

Auctioneer Newman took out ads in the *Los Angeles Times* for "The Year's Most Interesting Auction Event... Furnishings from the home of Mr. and Mrs. Mickey Cohen, Nationally Prominent Personality... Naturally, expense was no object and every piece of furniture was custom designed."

Newman knew how to work the crowd. Over ten thousand people showed up to attend a sneak preview of Mickey's possessions staged behind police lines. The icing on the cake for the gawking throngs was the possibility that the rich owner might really be broke.

Newman was proud of the spectacle and declared, "It beats Jimmy Roosevelt's, Marlene Dietrich's, and even Rita Hayworth's. Mickey outdraws them all by thousands." The statement said as much about Mickey's popularity as it did about the changing state of celebrity in America.

A picture in *Newsweek* captured a dapperly dressed Mickey holding one of his long-barrel handguns tagged for sale, while a similar weapon rested on his lap. Auctioneer Newman would sell three dozen weapons, and Mickey's king-sized bed with foot-high monogrammed letters. The advertised *objets d'art* didn't net all that much, although the auction lasted three days. Mickey's dog Tuffy's mahogany bed sold for $35.00.

Sixty-one-year-old Harry Sackman died of a heart attack on May 31 before giving more extensive and official testimony regarding Mickey's finances. Like any good mob accountant, Sackman had insisted that he had informed his client of the law and could only file financial reports based on the figures presented by his client. He had also juggled the books for the Guarantee Finance Company, the multi-million dollar bookmaking front. (His brief business associate was retired IRS officer Donald Bircher, who denied doing any of Mickey's creative accounting.)

The tax trial would come to fruition and begin on June 3, 1951. The maximum sentence carried a fine of $40,000 and 20 years in prison. The FBI was hoping to turn Mickey into an informant. Even in-the-dark LaVonne faced an aggregate penalty of 15 years and $30,000 in fines, unheard of for mob spouses.

Jury selection took the attorneys only an hour and a half to complete. Federal Judge Harrison ultimately released petite LaVonne from the tax evasion case on motion of the government attorneys.

Mickey said that LaVonne "knows as much about my business as a day-old baby." He bragged to reporters that he was confident he would "beat the rap." He had told a grand jury that he would plead guilty if the government could show that he had $50.00 of unreported income. He added, "It's a pleasure to walk into the courtroom with a clear conscience... We're ready for trial and it will turn out all right."

The trial revealed that Mickey rented safe deposit boxes all over town under the names Allan Weiner and Donald Duitz. U.S. Attorney Ernest Tolin called bank employees like Miss Aurora Lenci, who had known Mickey from several banks. He also called former Hollywood State Bank president Harold W. Brown; he had resigned after the going over by Kefauver and Tobey.

Bail bondsman Louis Glasser testified that Mickey's house was worth a quarter of a million dollars, with a collateral value of at least $100,000. He estimated Mickey's additional collateral net worth at $150,000.

Famous local furrier A. Lipsey testified that he had delivered a $3,000 mink coat and a $2,400 marten cape to LaVonne in 1947.

Mickey was uncooperative during the trial and never recanted his original testimony, but still drew compassionate remarks from the presiding judge. United States District Judge Benjamin Harrison called him a "hard-luck problem child," and blamed the Los Angeles melting pot for developing his illicit activities and disregard for local law enforcement.

On Wednesday, June 6, a bailiff restrained Mickey as he ran towards IRS agent Dan Goodykoontz shouting, "dirty double-crossing tramp." The near attack took place in the hallway during a recess. Goodykoontz was talking with Luke Smith, a Rochester, New York, betting commissioner.

Mickey yelled, "Who the hell do you think you are—trying to bulldoze this witness?"

Bailiff John Schiebe held on to Mickey as Goodykoontz hurried back to the courtroom.

Goodykoontz had tried to convince Smith to change his testimony, since he previously could not identify Mickey as the man who had received money for wagers. Smith kept to his story; he wasn't positive. He said that he had destroyed his records, and that his memory was failing him at age seventy. He did remember that Mickey still owed him $20,000.

During the recess, Mickey took time to autograph copies of Jim Vaus' book, *Why I Quit Syndicated Crime,* for which he had written the forward.[3] Missionary work in Asia would benefit from any proceeds.

John F. O'Rourke, from West Palm Beach, repeated his Kefauver committee testimony. Mrs. Una Taylor, from the telephone company, testified that Mickey had made 318 calls to West Palm Beach and 410 to Boston during 1948.

Judge Harrison was unexpectedly even more sympathetic in his remarks from the bench: "You're not as bad as you're pictured. Perhaps more of us would be gamblers if we'd been as lucky as you." He realized that "there was no serious effort to stop you on the part of law-enforcement officials. You operated here freely. If the officers had performed their duty, you would not be here today."

Most career judges and politicians were able to see Mickey's human side, as well as the mixed morality of government officials who allowed organized criminals to exist. However, the judge's admiration so disturbed United States Attorney Ernest A. Tolin that he interrupted the proceedings and said disdainfully, "This apparently has become a society for the admiration of the good qualities of Mickey Cohen… Undoubtedly he has been a good son to his mother. But he is here for the bad things he did." Tolin's perhaps inadvertently humorous moment did not prevent him from asking that Mickey serve consecutive sentences, which would have totaled ten years.

Judge Harrison defended Mickey: "This community has to take its share of the responsibility…permitted to operate as a betting commissioner…virtual agreement of law enforcement…you would have been in some other line of business."

Despite the accolades, Judge Harrison finalized Mickey's five-year concurrent sentence and four-count $40,000 fine, but added "…a very personable individual…" and repeated, "not as bad as some people had pictured him." Mickey was eligible for parole in twenty-two months.

After the tax trial, where writer Dean Jennings appeared as an adversarial witness, Mickey told Jennings, "No hard feelings," and invited the writer to dinner.

The conviction was a milestone. The nemesis of all mobsters, particularly the Capone brothers, finally impaled Mickey.

"Not one racketeer, hoodlum, or gangster of first-rank importance had ever been convicted of income tax fraud in California. In fact, not one had ever been prosecuted." Author Ed Reid knew its significance: it was more of a blow to a corrupt system than one to organized crime. The court of public opinion found the federal and local governments, FBI, and police guilty. However, it was Mickey's conviction.

Newsweek nailed the incriminating story on him: "Gambler Mickey Cohen learned last week that falsifying income tax returns was strictly a sucker's game. He learned it the hard way. The pudgy, pugnacious Los Angeles hoodlum, who in his 37 years had escaped gunmen's bullets, assassins' bombs, and criminal charges with equal ease, was convicted on four counts of tax evasion." Unlike so many of the Hearst newspapers, *Newsweek* was no friend to Mickey. The magazine chose an unflattering photograph of him, his head slightly bowed, with his fingers on his nose as if there was a stench in the room.

The state of California never prosecuted him, to the dismay of many politicians who saw an opportunity. Several appealed to Governor Earl Warren to ask the FBI for help in investigating if the State could collect some of Mickey's back taxes. Warren's Commission on Organized Crime still received little cooperation at the city level, despite attorney Warren Olney's attempts to trap Mickey on additional bookmaking charges. The conviction didn't stop the Mickey publicity machine, nor did it diminish his celebrity. He was a national figure, just like his Hollywood pals, and his exploits received day-to-day attention.[4]

On June 16, authorities sentenced Harold "Happy" Meltzer to five years in prison for his narcotics convictions. The national big brass had financed Meltzer's entire operation.

By July 1951, the FBI would only state that they had insufficient evidence regarding the kidnapping charges against Mickey. They were content with the investigative results of his income tax problems, and appeared ready to drop the Eddie Borden case.

17.

Extended Vacation by the Bay

The authorities incarcerated Mickey while he waited for his appeal on tax evasion charges. Attorneys filed the appeal on July 10, and sought his release pending his bond arrangements. He had told the papers that he didn't know if he could afford an appeal.

During his initial incarceration, Anthony Brancato and Anthony Joseph Trombino were victims of a hit on August 6, 1951, likely with Mickey's imprimatur. Brancato had initially worked for him after his older brother Norfia , who was on Mickey's payroll, asked the boss to give his younger brother a job. Joined later by Trombino from Kansas City, the two Tonys partnered to run their own operation after tiring of Mickey's work. Authorities suspected that both men had been in on the hits to kill him.

Mickey recalled his previous warning to the Two Tonys: "Tony lookit. I can't be in your corner like I could be at other times... So anyway, while I was in the can, the decision came down, not from here but elsewhere, and the two Tonys were going to get it."

He described Brancato in a way that sounded like a younger Mickey: "Then he started stepping out on his own. He was on the heavy and on the heist, but he was heisting people that were contrary to the rules of the people that he was supposed to have respected—not only me, but others. They were wild-haired young bloods that thought they were just going to run roughshod over everybody."

The Two Tonys had racked up tons of arrest records and a disappointing number of convictions. According to shooter Fratianno, Jack Dragna was in on the plan. The order came after the Tonys robbed the Flamingo Hotel cash room of $3,500, a cardinal mistake. Hy Goldbaum, who ran the local book operation, recognized the Tonys. They had robbed him before when he ran his own bookie operation in Beverly Hills. Brancato also lost his trademark straw hat at the Flamingo.

Fratianno had met with Jack Dragna and his brother Tom—who always refused to eat anywhere with Mickey present—at Nick Lacata's Five O'Clock Club, where Jack made the intentions clear: "…these guys are no good… The way I see it, we've got to clip them." Done deal. Licata supplied the alibi by hosting a party the night of the hit for all the barbarians, a complicated collection.

Fratianno rode with Charley "Bats" Battaglia and Angelo Polizzi (Rummel's assassin). Leo "Lips" Moceri drove a second protection car. Battaglia developed cold feet, a liability on a night like that; it was his inaugural hit. Fratianno had advised him, "Just don't shoot yourself in the balls." The Weasel then told him how he had actually known someone who had lost his balls in the war. When the car with the Two Tonys pulled up, Charley was so nervous he was unable to open the back door. Fratianno intervened; Charley slid into the back seat, followed by Fratianno, who sat directly behind Brancato.

Author Ovid Demaris described the gruesome process

> It happened so quickly that not a single word was spoken. Jimmy slipped the gun out of his waistband, shoved it against Brancato's head, and pulled the trigger twice, the slugs smashing the skull with tremendous force, jerking the body up on the seat, the head snapping forward—the way heads had snapped forward when Jimmy had struck them with a baseball bat on the picket lines—then snapping back, as if on a string, the body slumping sideways against the door, the bloody head flopping lifelessly against a shoulder. A mist of blood and brain tissue rose from the body like a fine pink stream.

Fratianno emptied the rest of his thirty-eight into Trombino. Bats was glued to his seat. Fratianno yelled, "Shoot, you motherfucker!" Charley would eventually fire one shot before fleeing.

Despite the police arresting Fratianno, his brother Warren, and restaurateur Nick Licata, the case remained unsolved. One of Licata's waitresses had supplied an alibi for the hit squad, testifying that detectives had strong-armed her into recanting her testimony.

Of course, Mickey never admitted that he was running his business from a jail cell, or had any connections on the outside. Nor would he turn in the shooter, Fratianno.

While the Kefauver activities rolled on, even Meyer Lansky received a local indictment on September 8, 1951, related to upstate New York gambling casinos in Saratoga Springs. Kefauver never called Lansky before the committee; he considered him unimportant, and not connected to the Flamingo, except as a guest.

Authorities released Mickey on November 27, 1951, to attend an appeal hearing. Trusting Chief Judge William Denman of the Ninth United States Circuit Court of Appeals allowed him to post only $5,000 bail.

An FBI report dated January 30, 1952, referenced that Mickey was running a regular gambling game in his cellblock. They knew that he received special treatment in the Los Angeles County jail, and visitors freely brought him packages containing all the comforts of home. A surprise visit from the Bureau of Prisons resulted in a hasty transfer for him. Chief Parker didn't fool around; he made sure Mickey went to a private lockup at a new jail in Lincoln Heights. There, he could only wash himself when he appeared dirty, and had to wait his turn for the shower. He begged for a transfer to Alcatraz to escape Parker. He endured five days before his notice for transfer arrived.

Black comedian Redd Foxx hosted a homemade gumbo dinner at his house the night before Mickey—briefly on the outside again—went back to prison on February 11, 1952. All appeals had failed.

He left behind sixty-five suits, thirty-five overcoats, fifty pairs of slacks, twenty-five sports jackets, and tons of sweaters, in the care of cleaning storeowner and friend Leon Metzger. Over time, Mickey's boys would help themselves to his belongings. He would not miss the duds; they were quickly out of style. Some writers claimed that he never wore a suit after a dry-cleaning had sullied it.

Mickey's new home was one of the worst prisons in the country. Alcatraz (McNeil Island) was the former home to Al Capone, George "Machine Gun" Kelly, and the Birdman, Robert Stroud.

As was the custom, Mickey's power extended inside the prison, and he controlled his own coterie of guards, who eagerly increased their payroll and benefits. The warden assigned him to the clothing department at the prison since he claimed haberdasher experience.

He had everything he needed, including extra towels to satisfy his compulsive hand washing, and six rolls of toilet paper per day. He was proud of his special treatment, and claimed that he introduced Kleenex and ice cream to the prison island, and even helped the warden secure a needed shipment of drugs. One guard supplied all the ice cream Mickey could eat. Another officer kept a roll of cash ready for him to buy whatever he needed. His cook from home, Mrs. Willa Haywood, sent cakes and cookies on a regular basis. He threw an elaborate four-grand party for the inmates, with all the sundries flown in from Los Angeles.

Warden Fred T. Wilkinson denied that Mickey received anything special, citing that any prisoner could buy ice cream. He confessed that he never measured Mickey's extensive shower time, and said, "These are invariably false reports that find some public acceptance, even though the facts are available." The public had always known that imprisoned celebrities received exceptional treatment.

Even with Mickey's incarceration, Dragna was unable to take over: he was too busy trying to stay out of jail himself. The local police enthusiastically pursued him, as if they were protecting the turf for Mickey.

During his prison stay, the Glasser brothers sued him on May 30, 1952, for Frankie Niccoli's unpaid bond. The bail bondsmen brothers had tried to collect the money since the Pearson trial, when Niccoli first disappeared. Louis and Irving Glasser wanted the court to foreclose on the trust deed to Mickey's Brentwood home. Since both he and LaVonne had signed the security arrangement, the Glassers even tried to take LaVonne's furniture.

Mickey's attorneys returned for the ninth time on August 6 to appeal his sentence. Counsel Morris Lavine, up for his own third try, asked the U.S. Court of Appeals in San Francisco to let Mickey out of McNeil Island Penitentiary until his appeals were completed. He argued that Mickey's testimony before the Kefauver Crime Investigation Committee should have entitled him to immunity from prosecution on income tax evasion.

Los Angeles Treasury Department Agent Ernest R. Mortenson answered that Kefauver already had the information on Mickey before arriving in Los Angeles. Lavine countered that the source of the material didn't matter, and the committee should not act against someone who testifies to incriminating facts. (Frank Costello walked out on the August 15, 1952, Kefauver hearings and received an eighteen-month prison sentence for contempt.)

Judge Homer T. Bone did not see it that way: "A smart gangster would make sure he was called before a committee and asked questions to gain immunity. I can't imagine a finer refuge for gangsters."

Mickey dug in. He had an older mentor at Rothschild's barbershop who had tutored him on the refinements of getting along in business, like remaining calm, dressing down, and being nice to the police. He had discussed his social and business problems freely with the retired businessman, and wrote a postcard from Alcatraz, sent directly to the Beverly Hills barbershop and sports book, which read, "Dear Sid. Okay. Now what do I do?"

Despite Mickey's sense of humor, prison life shocked him. Club Fed or white-collar environments did not exist at the time. Daily prison life rattled his sensibilities and any shred of naïveté quickly disappeared.

Awakened by screams one night, Mickey summoned one of the guards and the two men investigated the source of the shrieking. The unlikely duo traced the noise to a prisoner in a dark cell. The light switch wouldn't work, so the guard shined his flashlight on a pool of blood. Mickey's own words: "The screamer is lyin' in a pool o' blood two inches deep. When the guard investigates he discovers that this guy was tryin' to give himself some fun by stickin' an electric light globe up his behind. In the middle of his enjoyment the globe had busted." The warden reprimanded the prisoner for destroying government property.

Prison life did not prevent Mickey from pursuing his new love, show business. He corresponded with Ben Hecht, who wanted to write a biography of him and develop it into a movie. Nothing could have made him happier, nor better fueled his continued interest in the outside world, which for him had to include a role in entertainment.

While Mickey was in prison, authorities continued to focus on his associates. On December 27, 1952, Sam Farkas, described by the *Los Angeles Times* as "Mickey Cohen's bodyguard," beat the rap on a robbery charge. After his arrest, he supplied an alibi, even though sheriffs saw him on Christmas night near the Sunset Strip robbery location. His employer claimed that he had not left his job; both his employer and employment remained a mystery as police officials declined to comment.

Others took the opportunity to pursue their share of gambling interests. Mrs. Norma Rummel, lawyer Sam's widow, tried to gain control of Rummel's stake in the Gardena poker parlor. Owners settled in superior court on a one-time payment of $10,000, followed by payments of $2,000 per month, not to exceed a total of $34,230.

Other than Mickey, none of the top bosses received indictments for tax evasion. On May 2, 1953, Meyer Lansky began a three-month stay in a New York jail after settling his gambling indictment—his only conviction. He had agreed to plead guilty to five of the twenty-one counts, and paid a $2,500 fine. He received three years probation.

During Mickey's prison stay, Judge Tolin, who did his best to put the bookie away, ordered his federal court to watch strip movies of actress Sheree North. One reporter yawned while he watched the bra and panties show. Movie cast member Tempest Storm did a little shaking, but North was the star. Tolin decided that the movies were not lewd, but they stunk!

Homer E. Capehart, Chairman of the Senate Banking Committee, exposed Mickey's national interest in real estate in August 1954, and hoped to call him as a witness. Capehart traced prominent New York builder Ian Woodner's windfall $600,000 profit on twenty-four apartments. Marshals attempted to track down Mickey's brother under his alias Harry Cane. (Harry Cohen had his own long police record.) "The boys are in on the bonanza," bragged overzealous Capehart.

Mickey and LaVonne lost their treasured Brentwood home on September 11, 1954. U.S. Marshal R. W. Ware oversaw the sale of his residence to attorney Leon Cooper, who represented bail bondsmen Irving and Louis Glasser; they had persuaded the courts in their favor. The Glassers were remarkably able to secure a lien on the property and adjoining landscaped lot, ahead of the federal liens on Mickey's assets. The ultimate buyer got a great deal.

LaVonne moved temporarily to an apartment on Woodruff Avenue in West Los Angeles and used an assumed name while Mickey remained in prison. She performed office work for a Beverly Hills retail chain.

During the next two years, 1955 and 1956, the Italian Mafia opened up their membership. Difficulties with muscle, the growing Jewish syndicate, and attrition at the upper age range ushered in the dawn of a new Mafia. It was time to get back on the road, and enlist new brethren. The FBI watched as the Mafia held the equivalent of rallies around the country.

During Mickey's incarceration, his brother Harry was exceptionally vocal and had contacted Jewish leaders in Chicago to complain about Mickey's prison life. He wrote a letter to the editor of the *California Jewish Voice* on May 6, 1955. He had many concerns regarding the treatment of Jewish prisoners, and appealed to editor Sam Gach to write the new Alcatraz warden, David M. Heritage, and suggest changing Mickey's work detail to the farm or other improved environment. Harry mentioned that the new prison chaplain was Rabbi Wagner, someone who could help improve the treatment of Jewish prisoners.

Acting Warden L. P. Gollaher was sure to let the papers know that Mickey was a model worker. He started in the warehouse, according to Gollaher, and now did clerical tasks in the dental lab. He emphasized that Mickey "is working every day."

During Mickey's stay, William Randolph Hearst paid a well-publicized visit, and the Hearst newspapers told the story in detail.

Hearst proclaimed, "I know that Mickey has a deep desire to change his life."

Evangelist Billy Graham, a growing powerful political figure in America, was also instrumental in Mickey's eventual parole, and visited him just prior to a release hearing.

A newspaper story broke again, about how Mickey had refused Graham's offer of Christianity. Mickey later claimed that the awkward publicity fueled by the article had a negative effect on the parole hearing. He told Graham to refrain from mentioning his name, and that he didn't need that kind of publicity. But the strange bedfellows would make bigger news another day.

Mickey received regular letters from friends on the outside, including Harmon Fisher and Mrs. Ruth Benson, brother and sister acquaintances from his Irgun days, and who would play a role in his future.

After some negotiation, he agreed to sign a statement that detailed his role in two of Richard Nixon's elections—the run for the California House in 1946 and the Senate in 1950. Democrats had long sought this information about Mickey and Nixon, and this episode marked the beginning of an investigative effort that would span decades.

Mickey's relatives scurried all over town trying to come up with the balance of monies owed on his federal fine, approximately $10,000. Once the money was in the hands of John Maher, a clerk in the U.S. District Court, everyone anticipated his Sunday release.

Brother-in-law Jack Duitz dropped the money off and told reporters, "The money was made by a family pool...that's all there is to it. We got together and agreed to raise the money for the fine." (Mickey's sister Pauline and her husband Jack were wholesaler/infant-wear jobbers.) Duitz waited until the clerk wrote a letter to Warden Heritage on McNeil Island, indicating that Mickey was free and clear.

Technically, the fine did not have to be paid. Under Federal law, Mickey could have taken a pauper's oath, and avoided any exchange of money. Local police knew that he wasn't broke, and speculated that was why the fine was paid; he didn't want any legal documents that conflicted with his way of life. Moreover, he would have had to serve an additional thirty days if his relatives didn't pay the balance.

Folklore suggests that his three-year, eight-month, and sixteen-day prison stay ended with a conditional release after a phone call to actor-comedian-singer Jimmy Durante, who paid the balance of Mickey's fine.

He received significant time off for good behavior. The warden threw in the weekend release as a bonus. All reports said that he was a model prisoner.

When Mickey returned, Hollywood rolled out plenty of red carpets for the Czar of its still booming underworld.

Part Four

Mickey Redux

1955-1967

18.

Starting Over

The *Los Angeles Examiner* ran an anticipatory welcome home article for Mickey on October 5, 1955. He had announced plans to open a new bar and grill café in either Beverly Hills or the Miracle Mile district further east. Paul Davis, a local administrator, would remark that it would be tough for Mickey to get a license, and sealed it with "...not a chance." The *Examiner* journalist wrote that things had been quiet during his incarceration but recently bullets had begun flying again, some at Maxie Klieger, the boss of bay area gambling.

Many of Mickey's old gang had taken off for Vegas, where vertical business opportunities existed for career criminals. One of the few who remained was Sam (Nick) Farkas, who was friendly with the Los Angeles brothel operators, a group of women that ran high-class establishments in the Hollywood Hills.[1] Tuffy had died. His main driver was to be Irving "Ruffy" Goldberg, known to the police by his Damon Runyon description, "gambler, bookie, bank roll for other gamblers, and floating crap games." The FBI reports, apparently seduced by creative writings on Mickey, began to read more like the book for *Guys and Dolls* than investigatory files. They generously named the "top hoodlum coverage" in Los Angeles:

"Michael Cohen, James Aladena Fratianno, Nicholas Licata, Joe Sica," and blacked out two additional names.[2]

Newspapers around the country publicized rumors as to the location of Mickey's new digs, while gearing up his fan club for his hometown arrival. One mob haven in the Berkshires, Newton, was a prime possibility for his relocation. It was the rustic home away from home for members of the Cleveland and Detroit organizations, and a popular spot for Frank Costello's associates. Citizens and politicians lobbied Attorney General Kelly of Massachusetts to take action to prevent such a horrible scenario as to add Mickey to the list of country residents. Rumors had previously spread that Mickey was moving to Alaska.

More speculation cropped up regarding LaVonne traveling north to meet Mickey, but brother-in-law Jack Duitz said that she would wait for him in Los Angeles. She refused to speak to reporters: "I do not want to be rude, but I will not talk to anyone. I have no plans. I do not know what I am going to do."

Old reporter pal Jim Richardson sent Howard Hertel to get Mickey's story. LaVonne arranged through Richardson for Hertel to bring Mickey fresh clothing. She suggested that Mickey immediately go to the classy Olympic Hotel in Seattle for a bath, haircut, and manicure.

It was a rainy and foggy Sunday when officials escorted Mickey from the McNeil Island Federal Penitentiary and onto a boat that embarked at 4 a.m. When it was time to disembark at the Washington Steilacoom pier, he was upset that his brother Harry waited in a warm coffee shop while he had to walk down the gangplank in the freezing rain.

Mickey appeared ordinary, stripped bare of the material things that once defined him, and was twenty pounds lighter. He wore a single-breasted raincoat buttoned to the collar, and carried a small package under his left arm, probably some personal items. The walk back into society was a humbling experience for him.

A small melee ensued when the reporters spotted him. He ran the two blocks to the car, a 1952 dark blue Cadillac sedan.

When cornered by reporters Mickey said, "I'm glad to get out. I'm going back to Los Angeles as fast as I can get there." He also spoke about his new restaurant plans.

When Harry showed up with three other guys Mickey yelled, "Where-in-hell you guys been?"

The fancy Olympic Hotel, now a Fairmont, would not honor the reservations; the Seattle police had seen to it. He was not welcome so Harry drove toward Portland instead. On the way, the boys settled in for a T-bone steak, pancakes, and bourbon breakfast in a lesser, nondescript locale in Olympia. The shrimp bookie stuck to double orange juice, and left a twenty-dollar tip after the waitress appeared worried that the expensive tab wasn't going to be paid.

On Sunday October 9, 1955, Mickey checked into the Benson Hotel in Portland with some of his boys and Harry. The FBI secured records of his phone calls from the hotel. One of the people he called was a big slot machine operator who had an interest in the Sahara Hotel in Vegas. He didn't waste any time insuring his cash flow; Vegas was the biggest and immediate source of revenue.

He had time for a phone chat with a Seattle newsman and explained, "I didn't have the usual 'getting-out jitters.' Matter of fact, I slept so soundly that a guard had to waken me this morning."

That same day the local police ordered Mickey to take a plane out of town; the authorities told him that he wasn't welcome to stay the night in Portland, and escorted him to the airport. His notoriety and celebrity had its limitations in provincial areas of the country.

Los Angeles Times reporters noted that he flew Western Airlines. Slender Mickey arrived at 11 p.m., and three cars of LAPD officers greeted him at the airport. Observers said that he "sprinted" to LaVonne's car where she waited with her dog. He refused to speak with reporters. Television newsreel lights flooded the inside of the car. LaVonne eluded the caravan that followed and drove to the home of brother-in-law Jack Duitz, who lived in West Los Angeles, on Elkins Road.

The free man eventually broke his silence and invited in one reporter and one detective. He told them that his relatives "all look very good to me."

Mickey had left a lasting impression on the Alcatraz employees. At least one guard followed him to Los Angeles, where he helped him find work in the insurance business. "I couldn't see this good-looking young fellow wasting his life on that job and so I helped him the best I could."

While he was in prison, a federal grand jury had ordered him to testify in Seattle regarding the purchase of a vehicle for the police chief of a small southern California city. His memory loss protected the chief, and when Mickey hit town, the chief threw his arms around him, grateful to have avoided a prison sentence for tax fraud.

He was quickly in demand and back in the public eye. A reporter asked him at one of the first press conferences, "Mickey, is it true you're through with gambling, you wouldn't even wager maybe a deuce on the World Series?"

Mickey bowed his head, contrite as ever. "I'm washed up." He shook his head and brushed away the thought with his hands, like a croupier leaving his shift.

"I don't want no part of it," he added.

Another reporter asked him if he had heard that "there's a rumor around town that someone has posted a bounty on your head."

Mickey, nonplussed, smiled, after first suggesting that the remark might be a little delicate, and said, "No, I haven't... I don't see why it would be worth anything to anyone to do that."

When Mickey met with Cal Meador, the chief federal probation officer in Los Angeles, thirty-two photographers and twenty-one reporters witnessed his statement.

"I'm through with the rackets."

Meador liked Mickey; he believed in his reformation. To show his gratitude, Mickey spoke before organizations like the Volunteers of America. He also lectured scores of delinquent boys on how crime did not pay.

Probation required that the reformed gambler write a monthly report. He voluntarily visited Meador two to three times a month to inspire his confidence. Newspapers spoke of a legit job offer that resulted from his jailhouse correspondence with Mrs. Ruth Benson, coinciding with his new image as an educator.

Mickey surrounded himself with high-profile people, something Los Angeles locals now label "star fucking." Paul Caruso, his new celebrity attorney, also represented actor James Mason and Golden Boy boxer Art Aragon, and would represent Marlon Brando, Jackie Gleason, Sylvia Sidney, Ray Conniff, Audie Murphy, and baseball pitcher Bo Belinsky.

The famous gangster enjoyed the talents of custom tailor Al Pignola; wardrobe replenishment came before nightlife renewal. Mickey could still afford the best of everything. Most estimates indicate that he had stashed at least one million in cash before going to Alcatraz. He was quickly rolling in dough; he immediately provided himself with a tax-free income of over $200,000 per year, most of it coming from "loans." Nothing was off limits, not even places like a cleaning-and-dye establishment in South Central Los Angeles. Like most fearful and vulnerable businesses, they paid up; it was cheaper than incurring Mickey's wrath.[3]

Politically, things had changed. The Democrats regained control of the Senate, and Robert Kennedy took charge of the Senate Committee on Investigations. He wanted to make up for the time McCarthy wasted hunting Communists, and the lackadaisical national approach to the mob. He also wanted to make a name for himself, and didn't care who he alienated, even the unions. Some say he acted tough; others say he was tough. He could have picked easier targets. Mickey didn't know it, but he was one of them.

Gambling was still Mickey's largest and most consistent source of income. By 1956 Vegas was a vice-infested vacation spot that supplied unbelievable profits to the mob from both ordinary income and a steady flow of cash from the skim. It had become a man's world, a macho playground where greed, power, and women melded together in a strange way that was uniquely American.

Los Angeles' gambling should not be discounted, and the growing city was indeed crazed, too. The post-World War II mentality had made its way into the collective mindset, and gambling fever hit Southern California. Clubs like the Monterey sprang up in Gardena, where card playing had been legal since 1950, and Mickey's joints continued to operate. Gambling junkets flew "Flying Sportsmen" to tracks via chartered DC-3s, some with piano-playing stewardesses dressed as jockeys. Gamblers placed illegal bets on the races right outside Los Angeles city hall. Tip sheets and racing information were as readily available as daily newspapers.

Mickey wasn't back in the big money gambling loop. He had borrowed significant amounts to jump-start his life, and some suggest that he relied on his friends to support him while he eagerly plugged himself back into the business and social scene. He had national level support to continue his control over the gambling rackets, and maintain a piece of the action.

Years later, reflecting on his ability to lower the odds in his favor, he said, "… We need only one fixed fight or horse race a year in each territory. Ten or twelve of these a year around the country. The word goes out, and you get the big bets down."

He spent much of his free time at plush poker clubs like the Normandie in Gardena, when not visiting his other gaming operations. He ran a floating craps game and a private high rollers gambling club in the posh Ambassador Hotel, one of his favorites.[4] He sometimes holed up at the hotel for days, and acted as a host. A five-day junket once involved the "reformed" wiretap and recording genius Vaus, and since Mickey was still active in the extortion and blackmail business, he added to his growing tape collection, starring customers indulging in carnal relations.

He kept trying to establish a club in Chinatown, which concerned the FBI, since it was apparent it would be a front for his narcotics operations. The FBI mentions a previous narcotics conviction for the in-denial bookie, but it does not appear on its own arrest records.

Mickey held several meetings with the powerful criminal attorney and Chicago Capone consigliere George Bieber, of Bieber and Brodkin, defenders of over one thousand illegal gambling cases. The dynamic duo always drove the two hours from the Los Angeles airport to the eastern desert, and stayed at hotels including El Mirador and Desert Inn. On the return trip, they would check poker parlor interests in Cabazon.

On February 11, 1956, the police arrested Mickey in Palm Springs for neglecting to inform them of his arrival; he had a duty as an ex-con to register with the authorities. He was traveling with LaVonne and Bieber and had planned that trip to meet with coin machine venders who controlled sections of Oregon. Bieber, a two-hundred pound, six-footer, initially registered Mickey under the name "M. Weaver" when they checked into the Desert Inn Motel. He later corrected the register to read "Cohen."[5]

Mickey originally asked for a jury trial, but then changed his mind, pled guilty to the charge, and paid a slap-on-the-wrist fine of $75.00 after Judge Eugene Therleau reduced the amount. After he settled his fine with LaVonne's help, he promptly left for Chicago.

He went public with his experience, and told reporters that the Palm Springs chief of police was trying to make a name for himself at Mickey's expense, a patsy who accidentally fell into the chief's lap.

The Los Angeles papers, particularly the *Mirror,* covered Mickey's every move. On February 14, 1956, the paper ran an article outlining his Chicago connections. They rightly asked, "Is Cohen, through Bieber, making up with the group of Chicago gangsters, the remnants of the Al Capone syndicate? This meeting could mean Mickey Cohen is moving into the big time."

He had already achieved status on a national level, but his recent moves indicated he wanted more, including the imprimatur of the national syndicate. These events were more a natural expansion step rather than a sudden stab at a national hook-up. Critical journalists forgot that the connections that initially brought him to Los Angeles had come from the east decades earlier. The FBI also made note without comment that some of the people he had contacted were remnants of the old Capone mob.

Because of his desert meetings with Bieber, Mickey developed extensive interests in San Bernardino, Riverside, and Imperial Counties.

The business purist was ready to enhance his new public image. Flowers seemed to be a nice addition. The Biltmore Florists in Los Angeles were talking to Mickey about buying in. The local police told the FBI that they didn't understand how he would be of any benefit to an ongoing concern. The police were still naïve concerning his business interests, when they weren't looking the other way. He considered any opportunity for making money, and legitimate businesses proved a great distraction from his other activities.

Michael's Tropical Plants became a reality, and the blossoming dandy had new business cards printed: SALES RENTALS SERVICE; FIVE GREENHOUSES. The move into the flower and tree business baffled authorities. On February 15, 1956, the business registered as Michael's Greenhouse took off. It was located on South Vermont Avenue, close to the downtown skyscraper section of Los Angeles. Another location was 1402 Exposition Boulevard, a few miles south of Beverly Hills.

Mickey's business partners were Harmon Fisher and Mrs. Ruth Benson, who had befriended him because of his interest in Israel, and who had pitched the idea when he had left prison.

He boasted that he was now legitimate, all foliage, pleasant smelling flowers, and no longer needed the rackets for income. The police correctly assumed that the Greenhouse was the new Mickey headquarters. They watched the hangout regularly, and kept a list of license plates on autos parked outside the establishment.

Two police officers from the intelligence division interviewed him regarding the new business.

Mickey bragged to them like a proud parent: "…a tremendous racket…out of this world."

He hammered home his newfound love for the straight life, and lectured the homeless in the skid row section of town to prove his point. He wanted the public to accept that he had "chucked the rackets for tropical foliage." He also made it clear that he wasn't going to let anyone harass him, particularly now that he was a model citizen.

"I didn't know a camellia from a coat hanger when I came in to this, but I'm learning," said Mickey.

During this period, the East Coast mob evolved mainly due to attrition. For example, happy-go-lucky Jake "Greasy Thumb" Guzik, the financial mind behind Capone, died of natural causes on February 21, 1956. He had dined on his usual lamb chops and glass of Moselle, after making his regular payoffs, at St. Huberts Old English Grill and Chop House in Chicago. The cholesterol caught up with him, and he never left the table. Beats a bullet.

Mickey remained the consummate playboy; the girl-on-each-arm cliché was real. Ironically, and by Hollywood standards, his eighteen-year marriage was unusual. His pretty wife LaVonne maintained her cool charm, and successfully played a behind-the-scenes role that supported his social climbing.

Her marriage to Mickey followed the established pattern until she got another idea. On March 15, the newspapers had a field day when she sued Mickey for divorce. The Hollywood marriage was like that of movie stars in which one spouse is a civilian, always out of the public eye, until trouble hits.

The newspapers reported that his "pretty red haired" wife had charged him with mental cruelty. The Cohens had separated, and Mickey provided her with a couple hundred dollars a month in support, a number that satisfied reporters and minimized public knowledge of his enormous cash flow.

Thirty-eight-year-old LaVonne casually told the papers, "It's just one of those unfortunate things."

She added a teaser: "We haven't been able to make adjustments since he [Mickey] got back."

She was moving on. She was very polite to the reporters and waxed philosophical in a *Los Angeles Herald Express* article: "We've both changed since he's been gone; it's not any more Mickey's fault than mine."

The Cohen separation and divorce was not a battle scarred *War of the Roses*. According to LaVonne, Mickey had retrieved her over $60,000 worth of jewels, fur coats, and cars without incident.

She tried to paint a rosy picture for the public: "I'm sure there can't be a woman in a million who has had a marriage like mine. I've lived in a dream house furnished with every luxury a woman could desire. I've had mink coats and racks of wonderful clothes. I've been smothered in jewels and bought a new Cadillac every year. I could take all the money I wanted [out of Mickey's top dresser drawer] and had so many servants that it was unnecessary for me to lift a finger."

She lamented, "Now they are all gone—the money, the jewels, the clothes, the cars. The lot. And for the price I had to pay, I wouldn't have them back—not in a million years."

That was the most that LaVonne would ever say about the difficulties of being married to the mob. Mickey could have worn anyone down. Once he became such a popular target for hits, he insisted that they rarely go out as a couple, and if they did, he forced her to sit at a separate restaurant table. She accepted the tradeoff for many years, a business-type marriage not unlike those of many executives, politicians, or movie stars, where the benefits of being a silent partner outweigh the difficulties.

Mickey was not her friend; he was her provider, and she felt that he had never given her the love that she needed. She was sorry that they never had children. He had told her he was unable, and related it to a boxing injury. In spite of everything, LaVonne told journalist Florabel Muir that she never had any regrets about her marriage.

Naturally, Mickey described his marriage as "wonderful." If the circumstances of his pending divorce caused him any pain, he never spoke about it publicly.

Nobody was buying the floral approach to life. An outcry sprang up from conservative groups over his outlandish and defiant image. The pressure forced the L.A.P.D. to find something that would be incriminating enough to stand up in court. He had yet to have a single conviction within the jurisdiction of the city of Los Angeles.

John O'Mara, an L.A.P.D. detective in the special Organized Crime Unit, tailed Mickey as per his new assignment. "We couldn't get into his…where he had his meetings where he had his cohorts, and that was in a big, er, rumpus room, and that was where he had his television," complained O'Mara.

The police had a detective pose as a television repairman who returned several times to change the batteries on a James Bond bug that he had planted during his first visit. O'Mara reported that Mickey was a generous tipper each time the detective arrived to fix the television.

In May 1956, someone shot and killed gambling racketeer Elmer Perry. The police automatically suspected Mickey and Joe Sica. The authorities took no action after questioning Mickey.

The FBI still kept extensive tabs on him. They watched his charitable activities, and suspected that he had entered some kind of "religious racket," based on his continued association with Reverend Billy Graham. Every time he attended boxing matches, agents filed a report. They noted each time he bought a new car from Hillcrest Motors. He had traded up for one of his current new Cadillacs with an $1800 check, even though he only had $300 in his Tropical Plants account; not a problem for a good customer like Mickey. He used that car for the remainder of the year and traded up again for a new 1957. Basic sticker prices were as high as $7,000.

Mickey also traded his old bulletproof monster for a 1957, courtesy of Jerry Hellestoe, the manager of the local Beverly Hills dealership: "Mickey was always good for it and we had confidence he would pay. We took in his older car in trade and let him have the new one with a comparatively small down payment." The new model was a duplicate of hotel heiress Nicky Hilton's, and led to celebrity-spotting confusion around Beverly Hills.

The FBI maintained detailed pages of all Mickey's extensive business transactions. Agents traced every check written and every check cashed, including those out of state. If he bought an awning for his house, they investigated the transaction. In over a thousand pages, agents recorded his spending; knew the names of his vendors, the monthly payments, where he paid cash, and where he kept house accounts. He routinely spent two or three hundred dollars every night when he was out, and the FBI kept records of all his restaurant expenses. Despite political flaunting against licensing Mickey, he was still active in the restaurant business. On July 11, he opened the Cathey on Sepulveda Boulevard, west of Beverly Hills. Aquatic film star Esther Williams and Ben Gage had previously operated the location as the Trails.

LaVonne had reentered Mickey's life, and dismissed the divorce lawsuit. The papers said that he had won her back. Both he and LaVonne told reporters that the divorce was a mistake, and brought on by emotional problems related to his nearly four-year prison stay.

Mickey humbly confirmed to reporters, "LaVonne married a dashing, colorful, rough-tough hoodlum and when I came home she found me quite a bit different."

The happily married man now expressed confidence that the divorce would never go through, and said that he knew all along that his redhead wife would reconcile.

The reporters asked his probation officer Cal Meador what he thought of Mickey's new take on life. Meador was smitten by his charismatic charge: "I'm a little skeptical of all people. In 26 years I've handled the cases of about 50,000 men and women. But once in a while something outstanding comes along, a feeling so deep and sincere, that skepticism has to take a back seat. This, I think, is one of those cases. Mickey Cohen is becoming a very worthwhile individual."

When KFI radio falsely reported Mickey's untimely demise in a remote section of Griffith Park, he loved the publicity and his opportunity to prove the story wrong. Paul Caruso, still in the legal loop, filed one of Mickey's many frivolous lawsuits on July 23 in Santa Monica Superior Court. The $450,000 claim for the wrongful report of his death included the defendants Earle C. Anthony, Inc., the operator of KFI Radio; the City News Service (CNS); former public servant Fletcher Bowron, who had lost his mayoral bid in 1953 after a fifteen-year run; and Joseph M. Quinn, both executives at the news agency.

The story's dissemination, as detailed by the attorneys, had caused LaVonne severe physical and mental shock. Mickey suffered shame, humiliation, mortification, invasion of privacy, and the unauthorized use of his name.

By September 27, the story and case disappeared in the fuzzy legal world when Judge Stanley Mosk of the Santa Monica superior court sustained a demurrer. Judge Mosk, who went on to a thirty-seven year record run as a justice of the California Supreme Court, accepted the objection because Mickey's and LaVonne's complaint did not include a proper cause of action. Her mental shock had become a "collapse" that occurred before she was able to hear a retraction of the death report only eight minutes after it was announced.

Sometimes the media would mix up Mickey stories, confuse the public, FBI, and even Mickey himself. The newspapers ran articles questioning which businesses he actually owned. He denied that he owned the flower business, and claimed that he was helping the financially distressed owners, an explanation that he applied to all his legal enterprises.

Newspapers ran articles about Mickey's interest in plants, and loved to photograph him working in coveralls, not two $200 suits and monogrammed silk shirts. As if his destiny had finally arrived, reporters covered the startling before and after transformation, and speculated on the reality of his new life.

He played the role of the reformed: "I just got my bellyful of the life I used to live. It used to cost me two-three hundred bucks to walk out on the street with all the bites put on me. Dinner, every night, a couple of hundred bucks."

He even tried to convince his followers that he had really given up his flashy wardrobe: "Show you how crazy I was, I was going over my clothes after I got back and I found 600 pairs of socks, five bucks and seven-fifty a pair, all with the labels still on."

The sensible-living "former" gambler lamented about his money spent on Cadillacs: "I had a standing order with the Cadillac people. Every year when they got the new model they drove it out, put it in the garage, gave the keys to the maid and drove the old one away. And that was just for LaVonne. I had my own."

The florist lectured reporters about his troubled past coming back to haunt him: "I got a call from a fella high up in gambling circles. 'How's the flower business?' he asks. I tell him it's not flowers, it's plants, but he don't know the difference."

He continued, eager to convince the public that he could not be tempted. "'Look,' he says. 'Whatta ya fooling around with that stuff for?' Then he lays this proposition in front of me, but I tell him I'm not interested. 'Look,' he said. 'What's the score? You just doing this til your parole is up.'"

Mickey gestured to indicate his surprise and said, "That's what everybody thinks." It was the most logical conclusion.

He insisted that the large-scale botanical media blitz had nothing to do with his parole; he enjoyed the quiet life.

He became withdrawn during the rest of the year, and minimized his contact with reporters. That didn't stop the newspapers from reporting on anyone or anything remotely connected to him. While he camouflaged his emotional state to reporters—he proved once again to be a great actor—he was unhappy. Things were not that great at home.

During his sedate period, twenty-three-year-old Pauline L'Amoreaux recognized Mickey immediately when he strolled into now fabled Schwab's Drugstore at 8024 Sunset Boulevard, near Crescent Heights. Dapper Mickey wore a fancy sports car hat, noticeably flashy blazer, and rust-colored slacks. It appeared that he had innocently come for something to eat, and entered the popular dining area. Moments later, he charged out of the eatery, and began swinging and swearing at fountain manager Henry Maltman. Mickey had an ulterior motive to what normally would have been a friendly visit: Maltman has welshed on a $500 "loan" and Mickey was obviously unsatisfied with his take on the money and the likely vigorish. During the ensuing scuffle, he kicked Maltman and spit on him. Someone triggered the store's burglar alarm during the fracas.

Maltman yelled, "Mickey, you're crazy. Stop it. Calm down."

Mickey kept swinging.

With help, Maltman was able to control him, and someone called the police directly.

Mickey said defiantly, "Go ahead, I'll be back."

Intelligence officers Inspector Hugh Farnham and Captain James Hamilton arrived after Mickey had gone. The December 19 investigation found, "There was much use of vulgar words during the scuffle…"

Mickey's relationship with attorney Paul Caruso petered out when Caruso tried to collect his outstanding fees totaling about eight grand. Mickey allegedly pulled a gun and used his sister Lillian as a shield. He had his goons tell Caruso that *he* would have to pay up.

Caruso enlisted the police, but they ignored the situation even though he went public with information on Mickey's Model Linen Service, a strong-arm operation that forced restaurants to use their services. Later on, things died down.

The following week, on December 23, District Attorney William B. McKesson summoned Mickey and Golden Boy boxer Art Aragon regarding fight fixing. Mickey never showed for the meeting, and Caruso handled the matter for Aragon, who had temporarily lost his boxing license. Things soured for Aragon; he got one-to-five years for bribing boxer Dick Goldstein with $500.

LaVonne likely contributed to Mickey's caustic demeanor. Seymour Pellar, a convicted kidnapper, was one of her confidants. At dinner with Pellar on January 17, 1957, she told him that her husband was no longer mentally stable. The marriage was on the rocks again, after only six months of reconciliation and public bliss. She hired attorney William Herbert Hall to clean up the mess.

Probation officer Meador would eventually lose faith too: "I think he's sick in the head, and I doubt that he will make it." People like Meador found Mickey's sense of the world too far removed from their experiences. His suspicions were aroused when he learned that four local Italians had put up twenty-five percent of the front money to start Michael's Greenhouse, which was Mickey's major ticket to pulling the wool over Meador's eyes.

During this period, Mickey also spent time with well-known drug dealer and former Alcatraz pal Benson Wong (Ben Tue Wong), who fronted his own narcotics operations by working as a chef.

The Rat Pack grew in power and popularity.[6] Mickey's interests in nightclubs would open more doors for the Hollywood entertainers. His new favorite was Don Rickles, who regularly worked the Hollywood Boulevard clubs. Mickey thought Rickles' style matched that of straw-hatter Jack E. Leonard, and had originally promoted Rickles to the Slate Brothers, who owned a successful show biz hangout on Fairfax Avenue in West Hollywood.[7]

During 1957, Sinatra walked in on fledgling Don Rickles at the Slate club. The unknown comedian shouted, "Make yourself at home Frank…hit somebody."

Another night Mickey sat in the audience at the club. Rickles, becoming famous for his insult humor, assaulted Mickey. "Fine friend! I'm up in San Francisco and you don't even invite me over to visit you." Rickles had referenced Mickey's old Alcatraz address. Morals were loosening up for the advancing sixties; the nature of club entertainment had changed.

Both Sinatra and Mickey deserve credit for advancing Rickles' career and Rickles was on his way to becoming one of the darlings of the Rat Pack, courtesy of entry into the club scene, which Mickey and his cronies controlled.

The FBI remained baffled by Michael's Tropical Plant business. Why did he own and operate a mainstream business? During his interview with a popular television news commentator, the FBI concluded that he did not know that much about horticulture. Finally, agents assumed that the business had to be a front and Mickey was "right back in his old racket of shaking down bookmakers and probably any other illegal activity from which he can gain a dollar." No surprise here.

Police officers visited the plant store and weren't impressed by the inventory. They suspected that Mickey's strong-arms delivered imitation tropical plants to unsuspecting customers. Once the recipients saw whom it was from, they gladly paid the bill. Neither the police nor the FBI received any complaints from customers.

In March of 1957, Mickey faced a two-count indictment for disturbing the peace. The complaint described his behavior as acting "loud and boisterous" in front of women and had used the expression "son of a bitch" in an unflattering manner. Unfortunately for the prosecutors, the authorities had set Mickey up, and the argumentative women in question were two police officers, one a secretary to the chief. She admitted that she had heard the expression before, but never from the chief or his men. Mickey smartly, eager for the publicity, insisted on a jury trial.

His defense was simple: he had been harassed ever since his release from Alcatraz.

After acquittal, he shook the jury foreman's hand, and proclaimed, "I will try to live up to your verdict!"

The cautious jury foreman later told reporters that the jury was not convinced beyond a reasonable doubt that the peace had been disturbed.

Columnists and reporters frequently reported on him and his critical remarks against the police, and helped him insure the notion that the officers had violated his civil rights.

In less than two years, Mickey reestablished himself in Los Angeles, and was on the verge of increasing his national celebrity.

19.

Prime-Time Mickey

Mickey's flamboyant Rat Packing still attracted the most unlikely friends. During this period, he again met several times with Billy Graham, whom he called "Billy." Jim Richardson of the *Examiner* contacted Mickey to meet with William Randolph Hearst. Within moments, Hearst was on the line explaining the circumstances of his promoting Graham. Mickey was going to play a key role in the proposed publicity dynamic as a national Jewish personality who would support Graham and help him advance Christianity. Mickey saw an opportunity for a new racket, and Graham could always use a famous shill for theatrical purposes. To Mickey's chagrin, rumors quickly spread that he had again accepted Christianity.

Graham discussed the period years later: "I explained to Mickey, as simply and forthrightly as I could, the Gospel from A to Z."

The conversion publicity didn't stop Mickey from taking five grand from evangelist W. C. Jones, who was enamored with his interest in Christianity. Jones prayed regularly in Mickey's apartment, where he claimed that Mickey had agreed to accept Christ.

Jones said of his new pal, "I was very familiar with the kind of life he had been leading because I was once a bum myself, and I used to place bets with Mickey, and I was also a hopeless drunk until, with God's help, I licked the habit." It had to be comforting to Mickey that the showmen under Graham resembled his boys around the country.

Los Angeles investigative reporter Chuck Ashman, who later wrote about commercial evangelism in his book on Graham, knew that Vaus and Jones regularly slipped Mickey loan money. Ashman had a tape of two witnesses discussing the money exchanges, as well as the knowledge of former U.S. District Attorney Thomas Sheridan, who would become very familiar with Mickey's cash program.

Billy Graham went public regarding his relationship with Mickey, and told reporters that he regretted all the attention. He used the expression "deeply regrets" and said, "...a man ought to be able to seek spiritual counsel" privately. He admitted that his ties to Mickey had begun in 1949, and that he had suggested Mickey renounce his old life and accept Jesus Christ as his personal savior.

Graham was still cozier with him than he would have liked to acknowledge and told reporters, "Jim Vaus called me the other day and said that Cohen was going to be in New York and would I see him. I said certainly I would. I met him here yesterday [April 1, 1957]. We had lunch together. We had Bible reading together and prayer. I prayed for him..." Graham again mentioned his apologies for press involvement.

Mickey said, looking back, "I played them along for years." And milked them for cash.

Girlfriend Liz Renay hit on the underlying reality of the Graham relationship: "There was no way Mickey was going to become a Christian. He was proud of being Jewish. He even wore the Star of David on his trunks when he was a boxer."

Mickey's old flame Georgia from Cleveland sadly took her own life while he was palling around with Graham and Jones. "This turned my stomach... I was kind of stunned. I'd rather heard of anything else but that," said Mickey. He had never gotten over Georgia, and she had felt the same way about him. "She was the rightest girl in the world."

In April of 1957, the Chicago police questioned Mickey regarding the murders of banker Leon Marcus and former cop-turned-hit man Salvatore Moretti.[1] When the FBI read about these incidents only months later through a UPI report, agents circulated memos to find out who had rousted Mickey in the Windy City. The harassment incidents were never systematic. The city, state, and federal authorities barely cooperated with each other. The FBI still operated with strict limitations.[2]

(On May 2, Frank Costello, out of prison, survived an assassination attempt in the lobby of the Mayflower Hotel in New York City—the shooter was Vincent "The Chin" Gigante—and swore off mob work. Costello, the boss of all bosses, allowed Vito Genovese to take over, thus saving his own life.)[3]

Billy Graham asked Mickey to cooperate with a new request to be on television and his appearance marked a milestone in unrehearsed and uncensored broadcasting, and sent critics and right-leaning watchdogs reeling.

The remarkable show aired Sunday, May 19, 1957, at 10:00 p.m. The interviewer was a young Mike Wallace—now *60 Minutes* icon—who, after success on a local show in New York, received the go ahead to try his new style—no teleprompter—on a national scale. Previously, writers prepared scripts in advance, which amounted to what many critics felt was a confining mediocrity.

Through Wallace's persistence, Mickey had acquiesced to appear, although he felt the timing was wrong. The bookie television star wasn't certain if this was the right public relations move for someone with a recent prison record, but needed to jump-start his public image, which writer Anne W. Langman depicted as "waning notoriety."

Wallace knew that Mickey had problems with Chief Parker in Los Angeles and his plan was to goad him into making embarrassing remarks on the air. When Wallace pre-tested him with questions at the luxurious Hampshire House Hotel on Central Park South (Mickey had received a generous $2,000 in expense money), Mickey called Parker a "sadistic cocksucker." Wallace had his man.

Well before the show, Wallace encouraged Mickey to say whatever was on his mind, in any manner he felt comfortable. During the televised introductions, he described Mickey as colorful and notorious.

Wallace asked him why, after having "booked, bootlegged, and killed," he was going straight.

Mickey was always going straight, and said he had "his belly filled with the so-called rackets" and that he had the will to give up his life of crime.

He supplied his oft-repeated infamous quote: "I have killed no man in the first place that didn't deserve killing by the standards of our way of life...in all of these...what you would call killings... I had no alternative. It was either my life or their life. You couldn't call these cold-blooded killings."

Not surprisingly, Mickey did not want to confess to the actual number of people he had killed. He later repeated his firm stance that he never killed anyone who "by the standards of our society" didn't deserve it. All of his killings, he reaffirmed, were in self-defense.

Despite all the contrary tabloid publicity about his association with Billy Graham, Mickey made it clear that he was and would always remain a Jew. He did confess that Graham had a great influence on him, and his refusal to convert had not altered their unusual friendship.

Mickey told the national television audience that his "former" bookmaking business handled $250,000–$600,000 a day, and that it would be impossible to operate a business that size without the cooperation of the politicians. He refused to discuss any of his associates or anyone who might be involved in organized crime.

He also mentioned that Estes Kefauver and Frank Costello were both fine gentlemen and felt that politicians hindered Kefauver's successes, and that is why he was unable to dig deeper into organized crime.

On the air he changed his description of Chief Parker slightly: "I had a little bit more difficult time than probably somebody else would have because I have a police chief in Los Angeles, California, who happens to be a sadistic degenerate."

He further denigrated his adversary: "...this man has no decency...a known degenerate, in other words, a sadistic degenerate of the worst type...an alcoholic," and other adjectives, including "disgusting."

He added unkind remarks about Captain James Hamilton of the Police Intelligence Department in Los Angeles and had nothing nice to say about former mayor Fletcher Bowron and former police chief Clarence B. Horrall.[4]

When the show aired three hours later on the west coast, lawyers' telephones rang off the hook.

After the show, Mickey got into an altercation with police, who had tried to frisk him. They said that Mickey had attacked them.

Many viewers found Mickey engaging, while others found him laughable. An FBI theatrical critic handwrote on a report, "The whole performance was disgraceful."

Wallace rewarded non-smoking Mickey with an Italian red-leather engraved cigarette box, commemorating his appearance on the show.

That week federal agents in New York picked up Mickey and Fred Sica, the latter described as a bodyguard, to appear at a grand jury in Chicago. The FBI was trying to deport Paul Ricca on tax evasion grounds. He was a former Capone mob member, still considered the brains of the current outfit, and the FBI wanted Mickey to talk to the federal grand jury.

Mickey told the Chicago reporters that he was leading "an upright life as a Los Angeles florist under the spiritual guidance of Billy Graham, the evangelist."

The horticulturalist advised the local newsmen that Sica used the name McNamara for the trip because he didn't want to be bothered when he visited his eighty-six-year-old mother in New Jersey.

When reporters pressed Mickey about his rich New York connections, he said, "Nobody passed out any money. I'm here broke. Anybody who says so is blowing his Philadelphia."

He said that he had spoken with lawyers in town about making a movie on his life. He also predicted that no libel suit would result from his television remarks.

In another interview on WINS New York radio with Bill Stern, Mickey challenged Chief Parker to sue for libel so that he could prove the veracity of everything he had said to Mike Wallace. During the radio interview, which took place in Chicago, he spoke about his great friendship with Billy Graham, whom he had seen in New York. He begged everyone to file complaints against him. His taunting was extreme, and he remained confident that he would prevail.

He supplied a similar version of his favorite quote about murder and added, "I have killed no one that there hasn't been an acquittal on."

He eventually headed back to Los Angeles on Thursday, May 23. Once in town, he let the media know that he intended to pursue Ben Hecht to write his biography. Insider Walter Winchell made sure to remind his readers how amazed the mob was by Mickey's chutzpah.

Captain Hamilton was in New York, and complained bitterly about Mickey's reformed routine. Hamilton talked about all the Eldorado Cadillacs in Mickey's entourage, and described how he and his car mavens threw money all over town. Hamilton also mentioned that television should be more responsible.

After the television debacle had aired, Oliver Treyz, vice-president of ABC, tried to conduct his own damage control, which didn't include more gifts for Mickey. He read a retraction one week later before the start of Wallace's show at ten, with the cooperation of Democratic senator Wayne Morse of Oregon. Treyz, on behalf of network president Leonard Goldenson, made it clear that he and ABC "retracts and withdraws in full all statements" concerning the Los Angeles city government. The apology included the expression "something most unfortunate, unexpected, and profoundly regrettable." He denied that anyone had any advance knowledge of the contents of the show and finished his remarks with "deeply regrets the wholly unjustified statements made on this unrehearsed program and offers its most sincere apologies to" those beat up on the air by Mickey.

A contrite Mike Wallace followed, and agreed with the statement.

The news story, based on the apology, ran across the country Monday morning.

Mickey held his ground and sent a telegram to the papers: "Any retraction made by those spineless persons in regard to the television show I appeared on with Mike Wallace on ABC networks does not go for me."

He also let the ABC attorneys know that he had information about Parker's sexual escapades in Miami, which included one hostess on a private sailing junket who required medical care for her swollen derrière.

Chief Parker sued ABC and Mickey for two million dollars worth of libel and slander. In the suit his attorneys also targeted Wallace, the tobacco sponsor Phillip Morris and its advertising agency N. W. Ayer & Son, Inc. Against Mickey's wishes, counsel settled the matter out of court, and neither side discussed the settlement, which was $45,975 for Chief Parker and $22,987 for Captain Hamilton. The media also brought attention to Parker's childless marriage to Helen Schwartz, and his abusive reputation among coworkers.

Wallace suffered unmercifully under the gun of television critics. Langman, the *Nation*'s television columnist, defended the need for unrehearsed live interviews, but made it clear that Wallace had surrendered "to a sensational approach." Gloria Swanson, Eldon Edwards (Imperial Wizard of the K.K.K.), Earl Browder (former general secretary and chairman of the American Communist party), and Mickey made for lively shows, but "only because of the extremes to which each has gone in his own way."

Mickey certainly garnered national attention, but he had been only warming up. The Jewish community was outraged after Mickey attended a Billy Graham rally in Madison Square Garden only two days after the Wallace interview. Graham had promised Mickey $15,000 to attend, and he only collected ten. He always denied that he had made special telephone calls to coerce Mickey, or paid him. Mickey claimed that he had flown in on short notice, unaware of the promotional work done by the advance publicists at his expense. He posed for all the media, received wide coverage, and enhanced the publicity for Graham.

Big Jim Vaus would later quote Mickey, "They told me that Billy Graham's Crusade was in trouble and it needed some pizzazz. Jimmy asked me if I would become a Christian again, and I said, 'sure, why not?'"

Evangelist W. C. Jones, whom Mickey characterized as a gambler and alcoholic, continued to spread the rumor that he had converted to Christianity. Calls poured into Mickey's tropical plant store from all over the country, and he had to answer to his family, particularly his sister Lillian who was worried that Mickey was serious.

The newspapers described his escapades in New York as "soul-searching." Evangelist Graham had coerced him to play the role of celebrity Jew, and milked the one-way publicity relationship. Spectacle has always been part of the evangelist promotion and Mickey proved just another drawing card.[5]

He was unaware that Graham had duped him. He finally pulled the plug, after receiving multiple complaints from prominent Jewish leaders. He would remain friends with Graham, but would never convert to Christianity.

Evangelist Jones eventually turned on Mickey, telling Graham, "Wake up Billy. This man is a no-good bum."

Mickey still defended his escapade, and attacked writers who were critical of his relationship with Graham. He wrote columnist George E. Sokolsky, who criticized him for showing up at the crusade. The letter began with "My Dear Mockey" and he signed it "Michael Cohen":

> You little creep...get yourself knocked off of the pedestal... Did you do any checking with Billy Graham before you sat down to write your vicious crap? Did you ask Billy if I had not been an invited guest? ... Did you try to check out as to the facts...any decent writer would make it his business...you mockey shtunk... In my opinion a rotten two bit little mockey foul mouth Jew like yourself could drive more Jews to Christianity than could Billy Graham in a year of preaching.

Mickey had also let Sokolsky know that "...I was a pretty fair replica of the devil. But today I am Michael Cohen, and every day I have to wrestle with Mickey Cohen."

Chief Parker had been publicizing his thoughts regarding Mickey's sanity. True to form, Mickey countersued him, charging a violation of his civil rights. He told the superior court judge that what he had said about Chief Parker and everyone else was "correct and true...made in the public interest...fair comment on criticism of public officials...made in good faith without malice and without intent to harm." He corrected the complaints by Parker and Hamilton, since neither had used his proper name, Michael. The feud would naturally continue.

ABC vice president Treyz issued another apology to Chief Parker and Captain Hamilton on June 26 and again retracted all statements made on the air.

Newspapers made the most of the opportunity and carried stories about the lawsuits for months. Columnist Lee Mortimer, subbing for Walter Winchell, wrote how the favorable buzz of the underworld was wrong, and both Parker and Hamilton remained zealous in their attempts to collect damages. Mickey had been convinced that the sleazy record of one officer would prevent him from going public, but this time didn't say which one. Mortimer always went after Mickey: "this is a typical hood, and Cohen's pattern, to blacken by innuendo."

In August 1957, the gambling arborist sold Michael's Greenhouse to two Japanese investors—the Japanese had become the ubiquitous staple of the affluent gardening world in Los Angeles. Bank of America handled Mickey's sale transaction, although he also had accounts at the Union Bank and Trust, and the Pacific State Bank in Hawthorne. On the surface, despite what the police and FBI thought, the business transaction was likely legitimate. The Bank of America at 3191 Wilshire Boulevard was a dubious location for something fishy. Mickey had access to corrupt bank officers; however, his local business and its associated transactions would not have been worth the effort to conceal nefarious financial dealings through this bank.

He later rationalized the sale: "I didn't know a plant from a boxing glove, but I would have made a go of it if those cops had left me alone. We couldn't go into the greenhouse without their hot breath wilting the plants."

After he sold his plant and florist business he began a series of fresh interviews. Show business was still on his mind, and an emotionally drained Mickey told reporters that he would take several months off to visit Ben Hecht, who had a villa in Rome, Italy—and was no longer broke. Reporters naturally asked him if he would also visit Lucky Luciano, as if all criminals were vacation pals. Mickey bristled, and indicated that he had nothing to do with narcotics, or the likes of Luciano.

He told reporters, "The department of justice seems to think maybe I'm going over there for something other than the reason I'm really going."

The former flower lover explained that he had only worked as a manager in the nursery business, and had quit his job so that "...we could get away from telephones and interruptions...get the story done."

A passport was not easily forthcoming.

Instead, Mickey showed up at Hecht's place in Oceanside, California, on August 3. Once in town, he followed the proper protocol and registered with the Oceanside police as an ex-convict and stayed at a beach motel. His intentions with Hecht were clear: he desperately wanted to be in the movie business.

He brought a 150-page manuscript with him and told Hecht that he had dictated the material. Already on the road to becoming a producer, Mickey had borrowed $25,000 for the project.

"I found it exciting and unusual," Hecht said about the manuscript. "It was frank and startling and I thought it might be the basis for a good book."

Hecht knew that Mickey's life was the stuff of Hollywood, and he told reporters, "He must have done it himself. No one but Mickey uses words that way. It's a gold mine of facts—I haven't seen so many facts since I was a newspaper reporter. It has Mickey's indelible stamp. Mickey brought it to me and asked me to read it and tell him what I thought of it. I don't know of any plans he may have for it." Hecht was naïve regarding Mickey's quick business dealings.

Hecht soon publicized, "I interviewed Cohen for a month, in cars, cafes, bars, anyplace I could get him alone." That's all anyone had to hear; the movie hype was off and running.

Mickey and Hecht drew up a fifty-fifty split, and left the future money and contractual matters to lawyers. Suddenly, next July *The Mickey Cohen Story* would be in theaters, a bit of sensational publicity. This said despite rumors spread by Earl Wilson in his column "Ohioan On Broadway," that Hecht will not write a bio of Mickey.

Hecht never humored Mickey. The material must have been dramatic, since he contacted movie *machers* David Selznick, Darryl Zanuck, Harry Cohn, and Buddy Adler regarding the deal.

Hecht complained that Mickey was always on the phone during their creative sessions. The inspired duo wisely made plans to head off to La Paz, Mexico, unknowingly tailed by happy FBI agents who were likely looking forward to some fun in the sun for themselves.

The *Hollywood Citizen News* reported the travel plans. Mickey told the paper, "The Department of Justice seems to think maybe I'm going over there for something other than the reason I'm really going… We thought if we could get away from the telephones and interruptions, we could get the story finished." The article restated that he had given up the nursery business, and now had other creative interests.

When the IRS read about his travel exploits, it red-flagged his account, and tried to block his passport—to no avail. He still owed them close to one-half million dollars in back taxes, and they didn't like to hear about his extravagant vacations.

Mickey's position was, "Why should I give them what little money I have when they'll only throw it away on some foreign country."

Since he was trying to sell a movie about his life story, the IRS naturally had their eyes on any project that would bring money to their partner Mickey. Their agents actually employed people to sneak around town to see if they could get their hands on the actual Hecht-Mickey screenplay. The tax people felt entitled to sell the movie project, perhaps at an auction.

209

Movie *macher* Nick Schenck, perhaps the eighth richest man in the United States, and controller of MGM, had a nephew, Nicky Nayfack, who wanted to be the producer on Mickey's movie. A few phone calls later, and the interloper became part of the jaunt.

During the La Paz trip, Hecht would deepen his friendship with Mickey, and remained sympathetic to his harrowing experiences. The boys could speak freely, and were certain that the FBI or IRS did not bug the telephones at the new Los Cocas Hotel. Telephone service was abysmal anyway: it was difficult to call anyone, and the phones were only open for one hour in the afternoon.

The show biz entourage also consisted of comedian Billy Gray and George Bieber, the Chicago mob attorney and Mickey confidant. The vacationers had a good time with "tired clown face" Gray and his "joke-twinkling eyes" that "spell show business so vividly." Hecht also enjoyed Bieber, a tall man with disheveled hair, who laughed "like a man drunk with life."

Mickey's stories never stopped:

> I must have been a real crazy punk... For example, one night I'm fighting a pretty good man named Carpenter, and the fight was on the belly [the bout was fixed]. It's a very important fight for me because a lot of the people are at the ringside. And I'm eager to make a good impression. So from the first bell I climb all over my opponent and punch the hell out of him.... I finally got so upset by his not stayin' down that I jump in and start biting his ear off.

No wonder Mike Tyson liked Mickey.

When the boys went fishing in paradise, they spotted a whale.

"You want to go after him?" asked Bieber.

"No," answered Mickey. "He wouldn't fit in the boat."

Mickey discussed how easy it would be for the whale to tip the boat and end up with "cheesecake à la Bieber."

A Mexican sailor who worked on the vessel told Mickey that sometimes that happens, to which Mickey replied, "Killers all over the place."

The little angler did catch a marlin with Billy Gray. He kept the marlin photo in his bedroom.

Back from his trip, the Mickey Cohen story made the Hollywood rounds, yet no deal materialized. Mickey received his first taste of the difficulties involved with movie production.

He gladly testified for Joe Sica when the police accused him of conspiracy and assault to do great bodily harm. He rebutted the testimony of the defense witness, and Sica got off. He would remain tight with both Sica brothers, despite what sometimes appeared to be a cool but respectful relationship.

The authorities again accused Mickey of fixing fights, but no prosecution resulted.

He continued his public complaints regarding police harassment, and spoke bitterly in the press at every opportunity. He depicted one officer as a "bum" and challenged him to "have it out" with him. Every Los Angeles paper covered his daily escapades as front-page news. Future mobster John Gotti, the Teflon Don, must have taken cues from his predecessor, since both cherished their fancy suits, eagerly courted the glamorous life, and never shied away from a flashbulb.

On September 25, Police Chief Clinton Anderson had Mickey arrested in Beverly Hills for failing to register as an ex-convict. A minor scuffle broke out in Anderson's office, and he charged Mickey with disturbing the peace. Mickey challenged the city ordinance that said that an ex-con could only visit the city five times every thirty days. He filed a hardship case because Beverly Hills was between his residence and place of business.

Mickey's attorneys A. L. Wirin and Fred Okrand told the city that the law was ridiculous. Mickey, dressed in a dark suit, sat quietly in court on October 14.

Wirin said that Mickey was "a person who like many other Americans does not like to be pushed around." He had worked for the precursor to the American Civil Liberties Union, which made him a very unpopular "communist scumbag" to the conservatives.

The ACLU sided with Mickey and filed a separate brief. The City of Beverly Hills instead pursued Mickey for "disturbing the peace."

During the first week in October, former police chief C. B. Horrall jumped on the libel suit bandwagon and sued Mickey for two million dollars in connection with the Wallace interview. He included in the charges Mike Wallace and Paramount Theatres, which likely owned the broadcast building.

On October 25, 1957, a hit on Albert Anastasia took place at the Park Sheraton Hotel barbershop, making Carlo Gambino the undisputed boss in New York. Anastasia had tried to go it alone and set up gambling in Cuba, separate from Meyer Lansky and Frank Costello, not entirely retired.

The end of 1957 saw another reorganization of the Mafia. The small town Apalachin, New York, meeting included sixty of the top *made* leaders, all there to solidify the national syndicate. The FBI begrudgingly reconsidered the existence of the Mafia after reports of the meeting became common knowledge. Locally, Louie Dragna never accomplished much after Uncle Jack's death in 1957. Louie was ill-suited for the role. He deferred often to Fratianno, who answered to lawyer Frank DeSimone, and was now better acclimated to Mickey's presence.

ABC vice president John Daly suggested that Sammy Davis, Jr., substitute for Mike Wallace on an upcoming segment of *What's My Line?*, the popular panel show of the era. Wallace became the focus of a Hollywood boycott, and stars like Celeste Holm refused to appear on his show.

On January 17, 1958, former mayor Fletcher Bowron, now a superior court judge, sued Mickey for one million dollars in connection with the Wallace television show. He included two advertising agencies, ABC, and the Paramount Theatre Company.

So far, Mickey didn't contribute a nickel to any of the settlements.

A funny story circulated in the regional newspapers about how he was "bumped off." He had been sitting on a wicker chair in his driveway. A neighbor lost control of his car and shoved him twenty feet into a fence.

His shaky reply to reporters was, "You never know when fate is going to come around after you."

Fate never seemed to play a role in Mickey's life. Whenever he spoke publicly, his humor and cynicism masked his true feelings. Nobody had a real handle on the little mob boss. If he was afraid, he never showed it. He continued to carve out his own existence, treating Hollywood and its surroundings as his personal Garden of Eden.

20.

There's No Business Like Show Business

There was a lot of chatter in the Hollywood entertainment community about sultry sex kitten Kim Novak. The damsel in distress required Mickey's unique rescue skills. Hardly innocent, Kim had racked up two prior engagements before hitting town at age twenty. Her romantic links included Cary Grant, playboy Aly Khan, Sinatra, and British actor Peter Lawford.[1] This time it was Sammy Davis, Jr.

Harry Cohn, the boss at Columbia Pictures, became furious when the unkosher news leaked out about her interracial relationship; many Americans in the year of our Lord 1958 openly criticized her affair with Sammy. The country demonized him no matter what he did. Many people were upset that he even hung out with white entertainers, let alone having a relationship with a white movie star. The black press criticized Sammy too: IS SAMMY ASHAMED HE'S A NEGRO? One editorial demanded of him, "Look in the mirror, Sammy. You're still one of us."

Cohn was hell-bent on ruining Sammy and his fledgling career. Only six years had passed since he had become an overnight sensation. In early January 1958, comedian Jerry Lewis substituted for him in Las Vegas because Sammy was supposedly in Chicago with Kim. Some thought she and Sammy had planned to marry, and Cohn was now terrified that rumors of the relationship or elopement would ruin Kim's box-office draw. Her own agent advised her to dump him. Sinatra also spoke with her.[2]

Cohn contacted Frank Costello, who spoke to Mickey, now out of prison for three years and firmly reestablished in the Hollywood loop. According to Mickey, Costello told him to do whatever Cohn wanted. That meant eliminating Sammy. Mickey made plans to talk with Cohn directly.

He had previously been supportive of Sammy, and was in his corner to help perpetuate his club dates. Sammy nonetheless looks petrified of Mickey in a photograph they took together in his dressing room. The caption Mickey supplied was, "He called me in to have this picture taken." At home, Mickey always displayed a photo of Sammy.

At his meeting with Mickey, Cohn referred to Sammy as "that fucking nigger bastard." Mickey told Cohn off, and threatened his life if anything happened to Sammy.

Mickey despised Cohn for his racist sentiments, and didn't like a Jew testing another Jew for shared prejudice. His mixed morality surfaced again. He liked Sammy, was friends with his parents, and therefore Mickey felt that he had an obligation to protect him. Despite his support, a hit on Sammy was already in the making.

Someone informed Sammy about the hit. He recalled the messenger:

> He was shaking his head. "I'm not talking Chicago. I'm talking L.A. West Coast. Harry Cohn's mad. There's a contract out. To break your legs. But these guys have a habit of crushing kneecaps with a sledgehammer so they never mend... But don't you go back home unless you straighten out with Cohn."

Sammy biographer Burt Boyar depicted Mickey's role in the hit as somewhat more aggressive and less supportive. Mickey's men visited Sammy in Las Vegas before a Christmas run at Ciro's. The plug-uglies issued the usual threats of broken legs. The boys took him for a purported one-way ride, and later released him on his promise to stay away from Novak. Others report that the mob told him he might lose his good eye, and a few quote Mickey issuing similar warnings to Sammy's father.

The effect on Sammy was dramatic. Forced to give up his love Kim, he sulked backstage at Ciro's, and on at least one occasion considered suicide with a revolver. "Sammy was angry and crying in his dressing room during rehearsals," recalled Johnny Oldrate, the maître d' at Ciro's.

Sammy quickly married a black woman, twenty-three-year-old singer Loray White, with Harry Belafonte as the best man. Some report that Sammy paid her $25,000 to cooperate. The arranged marriage lasted six months.[3]

Sammy returned to Ciro's and the Vegas Sands with his famous eye patch, and solidified his—for the moment shaky—place in Hollywood lore and popularity.[4]

Mickey kept regular company during this period with Liz Renay (born Pearl Elizabeth Dobbins), though he sounded disappointed years later: "I really don't think that Liz Renay was ever in love with me." It's unlikely that any of Mickey's girls truly loved him.

Before becoming Liz Renay, she worked as a waitress in Phoenix and answered to the name Pearl McLain. Tough, good-natured Renay got around when she stopped giving the chef orders for "two over easy," and attained fame after winning a Marilyn Monroe look-alike contest.[5] Cecil B. DeMille spotted her in the Paramount commissary and promised her the role of Esther in an upcoming movie about the Bible. It didn't pan out, but DeMille wasn't alone in heaping attention upon the starlet-in-training.

She fit the bill perfectly for Mickey and Hollywood. She not only had hung around with syndicate regulars Champ Segal and Anastasia bodyguard Tony "Cappy" Coppola, but she had the pie-in-the-sky aspirations of so many young women who flocked to tinsel town to pursue acting.

Champ Segal arranged the initial phone call after a discussion with Cappy, and explained the circumstances. "Hey, Mickey, we've got somebody here we'd like you to look after. She's comin' out your way and she don't know nobody out there, see… Sure she's beautiful… She's Tony Coppola's girl. How should I know—maybe she wants to be a movie star—."

Renay recalled Mickey's response similarly with her movie dialogue recreation of Champ's introduction, "Look, honey, tell you what I'll do. I'll meet your plane and help you get settled in Hollywood, okay? Just give me a ring before you take off and let me know what time your plane lands in Hollywood. Here's my private number. Write it down."

Now that she had a sponsor, Renay left her two children with her mother and was off in a flash to seek fame and fortune in the core of popular culture.

At the Los Angeles airport, she looked to find her shorter version of George Raft, as described by Champ. When he didn't appear, the somewhat naïve new-kid-on-the-block had the celebrity gangster paged. Curious crowds gathered around her, waiting to get a glimpse of Mickey. He didn't show.

At the Knickerbocker Hotel, she was given an apology message from Mickey, who said that he would be there as soon as possible.

Renay claimed that she met Mickey under the popular unzipped circumstances as another girlfriend of his, blonde, green-eyed stripper Candy Barr. When Mickey arrived at Renay's hotel room, she had not yet completed dressing, and asked Mickey to help zip up the back of her dress.

"An immaculately dressed little man with dancing brown eyes stood smiling at me. His hair was black, faintly streaked with gray at the temples...," Renay wrote. She liked his soft touch, and marveled at his spotless polished nails. She remembered the pervasive scent of English lavender cologne; Mickey had a nice smile, like a little boy.

Renay liked the attention others offered when she was in Mickey's company. Everyone in the lobby stopped to ogle the local hero and the beautiful young woman.

Mickey took her to the Beverly Wilshire Hotel Coffee Shop, which was on the west corner of the legendary hotel of the same name, now the Regent Beverly Wilshire. On the drive over, she found a woman's high-heeled shoe in the back seat of his car. He had a logical explanation: a girl had thrown it at him, thus absolving himself of any culpability.

Renay joked, "I thought you might have put it here for effect."

Mickey had found someone who could offer repartee along with a striking figure. After a snack, they were off to Malibu beach. For the next few weeks, Renay was rarely seen without Mickey. They were out on the town for almost all her meals, and wound down the evenings at the clubs. She liked being part of his entourage, usually eight to ten guests, which fueled thoughts that her new friend disliked being alone.

Renay became aware of Mickey's talent for headlines when she discovered a collection of his clippings. He taught her a great deal about the manipulation of the media and staying in the spotlight, something she would continue to use to her advantage. She was just getting started. She would date George Raft, Frank Sinatra, Marlon Brando, Burt Lancaster, and Ray Danton. She would rub acting shoulders with Tab Hunter, James Garner, and Cliff Robertson, while garnering attention from Cecil B. DeMille

She also dated Mickey matchmaker Tony "Cappy" Coppola (who had proposed marriage to her), the pal and bodyguard of gangster Albert Anastasia. The grand jury summoned her for questioning when investigating Anastasia's murder. When police picked her up for questioning regarding her relationship with Coppola, they found over $5,000 in cancelled checks made out to Mickey. She testified to the total Mickey loan as $10,000.

She explained: "I loaned the money to Mickey because he was just a little short that day." Her biggest lament was, "I may be ruined in Hollywood after this." She added, "Mickey I can't control." Who could?

Thirty-one-year-old redhead Renay, also known as Liz McLain and Liz O'Ler, testified for over two hours on February 25, 1958, regarding her connections to Albert Anastasia. During the inquiry by Assistant D.A. Alexander Herman, she referred to Mickey as "a very dear friend of mine." She also testified on March 4 at a New York County grand jury.

On March 17, 1958, *Life* magazine ran a charming picture of Renay and "gambler" Mickey sitting behind two enormous sundaes, complete with a thick middle layer of syrup and globs of whipped cream.

She was unquestionably a knockout, and she knew it. During the Eisenhower years, *Life* stretched the boundaries of Ozzie-and-Harriet decency with an unfortunately black-and-white shot of Renay in a pink nightgown.

The layout looked like movie publicity stills from MGM. In the main shot, the photographer caught Mickey with a spoon of whipped cream halfway into his mouth.

Mickey reeked of money in his expensive suit and accessories, diamond pinky ring, solid gold watch with a powder blue dial, French cuffs, cufflinks, thin suspenders, and a conservative pocket square. He always wore a fancy diamond studded gold tie clasp engraved with his initials. Many photos show the gold chain dangling from his pocket watch. He sometimes wore both a Star of David and a Catholic religious emblem across his vest. It still took him hours to bathe and dress each day to achieve his look. He drove around town that year in a new two-door, two-toned Cadillac Brougham.

As a favor to Mickey, Renay once ran stark naked down two blocks of Hollywood Boulevard with him and television reporter George Putnam in creative pursuit.

Putnam shot the footage after the half-pint director had yelled, "Lights, camera, action!"

He had written a story that Mickey liked, so Mickey rewarded him by making him part of the cinematic entourage.

He once yelled to Putnam in a courtroom, "Did the kids get the dresses? Do they fit? I'm sending more! Give my best to your wife and the family!"

Putnam's relationship with him would deteriorate and he would eventually call Mickey "a horsefly on the rump of community decency."

Liz Renay wrote that Mickey was a Platonic friend. "Mickey was a strange, unpredictable little guy—but in my presence he was always a gentleman."

Gentleman Mickey casually pimped Renay off on a psychiatrist named Leonard S. Krause, who once testified regarding his obsessive-compulsive disorder. He claimed that Dr. Krause was also a rabbi, who really fell in love with Renay. Dr. Krause was also part of Mickey's show business aspirations.

On September 9, Renay met with Special Treasury Agent Harold E. Rassi of the Treasury Intelligence Division, regarding her connection to Tony "Cappy" Coppola. She said that no Mickey discussions surfaced at the September 9 inquiry.

Los Angeles Times reporters described the feminine witness: "Miss Renay appeared at the Treasury office in a tight-fitting royal blue jersey dress. Her red hair was set in a swirling pile. Her eyes which she said are green with brown polka dots were dramatized by long glossy lashes and blue-shadowed eyelids."

When she saw the enormity of the courtroom proceedings she remarked, "If I'd known you were all going to be here, I'd have worn my Capri pants."

Despite her wardrobe considerations, authorities also arrested Renay for perjury after her testimony about her financial involvements with Mickey. During the ensuing trial she stated that part of her cash income was won on Groucho Marx's television show *You Bet Your Life*, validating that she earned a living from show business, and not from being a pal of Mickey's or the Anastasia mob in New York. Groucho was afraid to release the show. His producer John Guedel shelved it, and it never aired in its original time slot. Renay had won only one thousand dollars.

When she was arrested for resorting (brothel association), Walter Winchell published her plea for help in his syndicated column: "I was arrested on a phony resorting charge…arrested me on grounds that I violated my probation. I was held for two weeks. They told me that if I don't tell them what I know about Mickey Cohen I go to prison for 5 years… They won't believe me… My children are alone and stranded and there's nothing I can do. Please help me."

Lawyer Norman Sugarman suggested that Renay plead guilty to the charges associated with Mickey, and she received three years. She wound up in local Terminal Island federal prison until July 1963 for protecting Mickey; she served twenty-seven months. When she left Los Angeles for good, the working actress stiffed the phone company for almost seven hundred dollars.[6]

Concomitant with Mickey's publicity surrounding Renay, on March 26, 1958, the country had learned about Mickey's fight with an agent named Howard Chappell, head of the Los Angeles Federal Narcotic Bureau.

Teenagers who hung around the Carousel ice cream parlor had warned Mickey about Chappell's snooping and tough talk. Mickey literally burst into Chappell's office at 5 p.m. while he was talking with two agents and hit him. The former bantamweight boxer tried to take on all three men, and claimed that Chappell had kicked him in the groin when he was down. Chappell maintained that the ice cream boys had misinformed Mickey regarding his, Chappell's, legal intentions. Agents brought Mickey to U.S. Attorney Bruce A. Bevan, who turned the case over to U.S. Attorney Laughlin E. Waters and Lloyd F. Dunn to prosecute the case.

Because of the arrest, Mickey spent the night in jail. He looked like he was the victim of the altercation; his left eye was closed from a blow, and he sustained a deep gash next to his eyebrow. The agents must have gotten in a few lucky shots; at least that was Mickey's interpretation as a former boxer.

He told the jury that he had only grabbed Chappell's feet to protect himself from the assault. At one point in the proceedings, Mickey became ill, which he attributed to taking medication on an empty stomach, and had to leave the courtroom. When he returned, defense attorney Samuel S. Brody had Mickey stand next to six-foot-two Chappell, eliciting a laugh from both men as well as the packed onlookers in the standing-room-only courtroom.

Federal judge Thurmond Clarke, unclear as to the events in Chappell's office, asked Mickey to sit for one of the early lie detector tests. Mickey attorney Jack Dahlstrum and the owner of Reid Lie Detector tried the new device on Mickey, whom the *Los Angeles Times* now called the "poor man's Don Quixote." Mickey's attorney asked the same for Chappell, but the judge would not allow it. By June 4, Judge Clarke had changed his mind and ruled out the results of the test. The jury deadlocked, and the judge dismissed all charges. Mickey would later boast that he was the first to beat the rap for striking an agent.

His action-adventure existence rolled on. Owner Frank Sinatra's Rat Pack hangout, Villa Capri Restaurant, with its smoke-filled red booths, requisite checkered table cloths, and hanging Chianti bottles, had organized an A-list party for Sammy Davis, Jr. During dinner, Mickey became embroiled with a waiter named Arthur Black. Mickey socked him, Black filed assault charges, and the legal wrangling and subsequent trials typified how the courts were ineffectual in dealing with Mickey. He wisely didn't show his face around Sinatra's joint again.

On April 4, 1958, Judge Gerald C. Kepple listened along with a jury of six men and six women. Mickey was the last witness called by attorney Cornell Ridley. Mickey was at his best in municipal court; he carried on as if it was his backyard.

He told a courtroom that the incident with Black "didn't amount to anything."

He described how he was chatting with Sammy Davis, Jr., who testified that Black jostled Mickey and spilt coffee on his hand. Robert Mitchum was also on hand as a character witness.

Mickey explained, "I thought it was a gag... I asked him, 'Don't you usually apologize when you bump into people?' and he said, 'Don't you stand in my way when I'm waiting on a table.' I was dumbfounded."

Mickey said that Black grabbed him; the two men scuffled, and rolled on the floor. Mickey's face sustained scratches. Singer Jane Powell's husband Geary Steffen, an insurance broker, pulled Mickey under the arms and lifted him off Black, who fled to the kitchen. Mickey left for the men's room to wash his wounds, and denied that he chased Black into the kitchen and yelled, "I'll kill the ——."

Prosecutor Don Bringgold listened as Mickey admitted that his memory was hazy when it came to measurements and distances. When he asked Mickey if Black had worn a cummerbund the night of the incident, Mickey asked back, "What's a cummerbund?"

The well-publicized incident made the rounds with comedians. Funnyman Marty Allen and his bushy "Jewfro" brought the house down with, "Ladies and gentlemen, Walter Winchell was supposed to introduce our act tonight. But he had an emergency. He's over at the Villa Capri, introducing Mickey Cohen to the new waiters."

21.

Who Dunnit?

One of the most famous Hollywood incidents involved Mickey's fondness for selling sex, and came at the expense of glamour movie queen Lana Turner, her daughter Cheryl Crane, and Johnny Stompanato.

Curly-haired Stompanato, often characterized erroneously as Mickey's bodyguard, was a handsome playboy who made the Hollywood rounds efficiently and easily. He had the profile of most Hollywood playboys: emotionally detached, good in the sack, and available. Before Lana Turner, Stompanato had dated Ava Gardner and Janet Leigh. He was briefly married for three months to Helen Gilbert and racked up three years with Helene Stanley. One of Stompanato's main pimping chores was to keep a constant stable of women on hand for Mickey's out-of-town guests. His supply chain stretched to Las Vegas, where demand for a steady flow of hot flesh ran high at the new hotels.

On the surface, Stompanato and Mickey were two over-the-top homophobic heterosexuals, hell bent on scoring as many women as possible. People close to the two men knew that the relationship ran deeper, even for two guys in the mob. Mickey's defense of Stompanato's sexuality was revealing of his own homophobia: "Johnny was a funny guy with girls. He took them when they came, like they were nothing. To my estimation, Johnny was the most handsome man that I've ever known that was all man. He was an athlete and a real man, without no queerness about him." Despite this, Stompanato on occasion was in the company of wealthy homosexuals. One informant stated that he would "go with either men or women for sexual purposes for a price." Gay life, even in progressive Hollywood, had to be conducted in secret; public exposure could ruin marriages and respected military service records. By acquiescing to blackmail, marks kept their private lives intact, and avoided arrest or even prison.

When Estes Kefauver had interviewed Mickey, he naturally asked about Stompanato.

Mickey said that Stompanato was "a nice fellow...a good boy."

Kefauver wanted to know how Stompanato made a living—why would a rich man loan him money.

Mickey was always amused when questioned about extortion, and answered, "That is a very funny question." Stompanato had blackmailed "Mr. Blank," to the tune of $65,000, and Kefauver demanded details.

Mickey applied his best logic: "He [Stompanato] just had dinner with the fellow three nights ago. I don't think he would have had dinner with the fellow three nights ago if he blackmailed him. It don't seem possible. On what grounds would Stompanato blackmail anybody?"

Johnny Stompanato had some voguish racket going around Hollywood, thanks to Mickey. As columnist Lee Mortimer wrote:

> The Stompanato-Mickey Cohen blackmail angles (first revealed here) will explode into a new and bigger page one story involving dozens of Hollywood, Broadway, and political figures who have been paying off in fear for years. The ring is operated out of Chicago by the Fischetti-Capone mob and the glamour boy and gal affiliates employ gigolos of the Stompanato type, babes and homos, while sleazy, slimy little hoods such as Cohen are the front men...a general stooge for Mickey Cohen, introducer of gals for visiting mobsters, and dancing escort to the star and would-be's.

Stompanato already had a kinky history with the Beverly Hills police. Estimates indicated that he had blackmailed women for close to $100,000. Beverly Hills police chief Clinton Anderson knew all about it: "We had considerable information on him. We know he had obtained large sums of money from individuals who were afraid to complain to the police, and we were aware that he had accepted money from a number of his women friends." Anderson also called Stompanato one of tinsel town's "wolves."

Stompanato certainly had his share of detractors in the police department. Fred Otash and his partner once beat Stompanato, left him naked in the Holly-wood Hills, and phoned in a report of a nude man roaming the foliage. Otash also liked to point his long barrel shotgun at Stompanato and yell, "Now you've had it, you motherfucker." He told the chief after Stompanato's car had gone over an embankment, "Hey, it was just a gag."

Another story supported how Stompanato's macho image was overrated. He often traveled with Turner, including a trip to England for the movie *Another Time, Another Place*. Mickey paid for his ticket. Stompanato hoped by hanging around the movie business that he too would become a producer, particularly after telling everyone that Turner was going to star in a Stompanato project. Nobody wanted him around the set at Pinewood Studios. He became jealous, forced his way onto the set, and flashed a gun at costar Sean Connery, who hardly supplied the milk toast response Stompanato expected; Connery knocked him on his ass with one punch.

Lana Turner and Stompanato had started "officially" dating in April 1957. Other reports say that he took up with her two years earlier, when Mickey was serving the last bit of his prison sentence.

Stompanato had first approached Turner as "Mr. John Steele," utilizing a tech-nique that today would be considered stalking. He called incessantly, sent obscene amounts of flowers, and waited outside her home. Despite using Ava Gardner as a reference, he was turned down flat. "And that's how the blackest period of my life began," wrote Lana Turner. By the time the relationship heated up, Stompanato thought nothing of entering her bedroom through an open window off the fire escape. During one episode, best described as asphyxiation sex with a pillow, Turner threatened to break off the relationship.

Because of syndicated columnists like Lee Mortimer, who wrote "New York Confidential," the entire country knew about Stompanato's activities. Johnny would take Lana Turner dancing at the in spot, Seville, when Chief Anderson wasn't escorting him out of Beverly Hills. The Seville was fifty feet outside of the chief's jurisdiction. Mortimer traced Johnny's changing roles from bodyguard to greenhouse manager to starlet escort.

Mickey was no stranger to Lana Turner and her former husband Steve Crane, second of four—he had married her twice due to a legal technicality. Mickey once hosted an extravagant champagne breakfast for Mr. and Mrs. Crane at Streets of Paris, one of his restaurants on Hollywood Boulevard.

Naturally, Turner, Stompanato, and Mickey made headlines. Mickey would see her frequently when she dated Stompanato. She kept an arm's-length relationship with him—at least that's what she stated in her book. He knew everything that transpired between her and Stompanato and he believed that Stompanato really loved her, and was fond of her daughter, Cheryl Crane. Mickey once gave Stompanato $900 to buy a horse for Cheryl.

Insiders knew the dark side of the relationship. Turner was an alcoholic who had a penchant for picking the wrong men; her romances and marriages came and went swiftly in the already fast-paced movie town. She would blame Mickey whenever Stompanato didn't show up for a date. Many strongly felt that he was a behind-the-scenes puppeteer, and deftly pulled the strings on the celebrated couple. Author John H. Davis revealed:

> One of Cohen's rackets was sexually compromising Hollywood stars for the purpose of blackmail. It had been Cohen who engineered the torrid affair between his accomplice, Johnny Stompanato, and Lana Turner, in the hope of getting pictures of the two in bed together.

Others have reported that he was successful in recording a tryst between Turner and Stompanato. Copies sold at fifty bucks a pop, and played to the delight of horny Friars Club members on both coasts.

Stompanato's relationship with Turner was no walk on the beach. One of his biggest mistakes was lying to her regarding his age. He had originally told her that he was forty-two, but was actually thirty-two. He was not alone in his birth date confusion; famous sweater girl Turner was clinging to a fading thirty-eight, one year behind comedian Jack Benny.

Most sources indicated that the two were a volatile match, both emotionally and physically. The front-page news often focused on Stompanato's alleged beatings. Journalist Peter Noyes knew that to be the reality: "She [Turner] is off to Acapulco with Johnny Stompanato, who beats the hell out of her and then they kiss and make up." The press wanted to make the most out of the situation, so painting Stompanato as a romantic thug fit the bill. People like police chief Anderson maintained the worst perspective on the lovebirds: "Stompanato threatened to disfigure her with a razor and cripple her if she ever tried to leave him."

Not everyone agreed. Jim Smith, a friend to both men, said:

Johnny Stompanato wasn't at all like what he was portrayed in the press. He wasn't Mickey Cohen's henchman or bodyguard. He wasn't anything like that. He was just a nice guy that Mickey happened to like. Johnny would never have beaten up on Lana Turner. He loved her too much. He even told me, "I really liked that broad."

Beverly Hills playboy Travis Kleefeld (the former singer Tony Travis) said that Stompanato was "one of the nicest guys you'd ever want to meet. You would have liked him."

The flamboyant and caustic fling came to a macabre halt at 9:40 p.m., April 4, 1958, Good Friday.

Turner wrote:

> …he grabbed me and spun me around, then shoved the door shut with his foot. I thought he was going to hit me, but instead he shook me hard by the shoulders… I heard the tinkle of the charm bracelet. "Cheryl! Get away from that door!"… I remember telling him to get out… Cheryl opened the door. What she saw was me sitting on the pink marble counter, and John coming toward me, his arm upraised, with something in his hand. She didn't grasp the fact that he was carrying clothing on hangers over his shoulder… I thought she punched him… "Oh my God, Cheryl," John gasped out. "What have you done?" I darted forward off the counter, afraid that John was going to punch Cheryl back… John took three little circling steps…then he fell backward… I stared at Cheryl as she dropped the knife…

"I didn't mean to do it. Johnny said he was going to hurt Mother," fourteen-year-old Cheryl Crane said in a variety of ways after Stompanato lay dead from stab wounds. (The week before the murder Turner had purchased the kitchen knife used to kill him at a hardware store in Beverly Hills.)

Everyone who arrived at the home heard the story from Turner, too. She even asked the police if she could take the blame. (Lieut. F. H. Colford said that Stompanato was dead when police had first arrived.)

According to Turner, this is what had happened after her daughter had stabbed Stompanato:

> Now I watched Dr. McDonald take out a syringe and lock an ampule of adrenaline into it. He plunged the needle into John's heart and pumped in the liquid. When he pulled out the needle he listened again for a beat through the

stethoscope. As he waited for the sound he waved me toward the phone. "Call Jerry Geisler," he said.[1]

Turner takes time to mention that one of the local lines around Beverly Hills was the expression "Get me Geisler," indicating that the person in need was in a legal conundrum. She further explained: "...Only now it wasn't a joke. It was something unspeakable, all too real."

Later, Cheryl was not entirely pleased with the course of action by all the high-powered celebrity-driven parties:

> Despite Geisler's efforts, Mother's wailings, my inarticulate testimony, and the chief's friendship with Dad—or maybe because of all of these—[Police Chief Clinton B.] Anderson was leaning toward a course that would be toughest on me and safest for the department. He favored my indictment for murder.

According to her, Mickey first rushed to the North Bedford Drive home after hearing about the incident on the radio.

Years before her remarks, Mickey revealed that his mother had asked him to stop by for a Jewish holiday dinner (Passover). He complained that he was in his pajamas and had to arise early the next morning.

Like a good Jewish mother she insisted. "Put some slacks on over your pajamas and eat, and ya can go home early."

Mickey dined at his mother's with his sisters and brothers, fell asleep on his her couch, and later headed over to the Carousel for ice cream. A call had already come in to the fountain boy Bob before Mickey had arrived. Inside, he took the call from a journalist pal at the *Journal-American* in New York.

"He says, 'Mickey, is Johnny dead, or is he alive?' I says, 'What the hell are ya talking about?' He says, 'What do ya mean? Don't ya know what happened? Johnny was stabbed.'"

Mickey first thought that it happened in New York, because Stompanato had told him he would spend the Jewish holiday there with Lana.

When Mickey arrived at the murder scene, Geisler told him that the body was already gone, and said,

> Mickey, do me a favor. If Lana sees you, she's gonna fall out all together. John's dead, the body's at the morgue. Don't blow your top about it. I want to

talk with you. I'd go over to the morgue with you, but I don't want to leave her right now. You wanna wait out here for me?

Mickey behaved properly, left promptly, and showed up in Chief Anderson's office.

Crane was already there and vividly remembered the moment: "The pudgy figure of Mickey Cohen tore up the stairs, taking the steps two at a time, yelling, 'Who done it? Who done it?"

He appeared stunned when Crane told him that she had killed Stompanato.

When told to go to the Hall of Justice, disoriented Mickey asked for directions, despite his familiarity with civil buildings; he had been to court earlier in the day for the ongoing Arthur Black trial.

At the morgue he said, "I can't take it."

He expressed interest in assuring that Stompanato had a decent burial and insisted that officials return the body to his Woodstock, Illinois, family. Johnny's brother Carmine , a barber and church elder, let Mickey handle everything; Mickey supervised Stompanato's burial in a tuxedo and linen shirt.

"Nothing but the best," said Mickey.

Steve Crane had discussed sharing the expenses with Mickey. However, money could not come directly from Lana Turner and Mickey never received any contributions.

Cheryl Crane had the dynamics right: "Mickey was able to jump into the drama as a principal player, taking the role of the grieving friend who was suspicious of police investigation methods." He was an expert at cover-ups and manipulation of the facts.

His name loomed large in all the accusatory morning editions of the papers. Turner's publicist fed reporters the perhaps unfounded suspicions that Mickey would come after Turner for revenge. Headlines included expressions like GANG VENGEANCE. Mickey called the publicist and insisted that the office stop sending out the revenge angles; they did.

That didn't stop Turner from dramatic public displays in restaurants. One night when Mickey arrived for dinner at chic La Scala, she and her dining companion made a beeline through the entire restaurant to leave through the back door. Owner Jean Léon had to endure the antics, including the upset maître d' who lamented over the warm dinners left on the table.

At his trendy south-seas-styled Luau restaurant, Steven Crane told reporters how he would like nothing better than to win custody of his daughter Cheryl. He added, "There's no excuse for not being a better father to my little girl in the past.

But I will make it up to her in the future.... I'm proud of Cheryl. She would have done the same thing for me in a similar situation." Crane also mentioned that Stompanato had been a regular customer at the Luau.

Mickey spoke to reporters about his role as a movie financier:

> Johnny and Lana needed money to tie up the story rights. They didn't have the ready cash so Johnny came to me for it. I didn't have the dough either, but I got somebody to loan it to them, and they locked up the rights to the script. What it amounts to, I was bankrolling the deal. Johnny was gonna be one of the producers and Lana was going to be the star.

He further described how his movie plans were on hold.

During the pretrial hearings for the murder, He called Al Aronowitz at the *New York Post* to make certain that Al had advance information on the trial, including planned testimony by Crane. He wanted to exclude his own omnipresent blackmail schemes from the press coverage, and felt by controlling certain reporters he could prevent the scandalous racket from taking a front seat at the trial.

Columnist and Mickey-hater George E. Sokolsky played up the ultraconservative perspective, how homewrecker Stompanato's advances were uninvited by fearful Turner, and portrayed Cheryl as someone denied a proper childhood, including dolls, by people like Stompanato.

The *Los Angeles Times* reported that when Mickey received a call to testify he said, "I refuse to identify him as Johnny Stompanato, Jr., on the grounds that I may be accused of the murder." Chief coroner's pathologist Dr. Frederick Nebarr revealed after the autopsy that Stompanato would have died in a few years from a kidney ailment.

The lackluster Friday, April 11, trial was more like a coroner's inquest. Mickey was the first witness called, and stood by his refusal to testify, citing that Chief Clinton Anderson would charge him with Stompanato's death. Anderson took the stand and identified the body.

Lana Turner, dressed in a gray suit, turned in a B-movie appearance on the stand: her lower jaw quivered, no sound emitted from her slowly moving lips, and she finally spoke. "It happened so fast... I thought she [Cheryl] had hit him in the stomach." She had removed her dark glasses, likely on Geisler's suggestion, so the jury could see her grieving expressions.

The jury heard the facts, including extensive details on Stompanato's abusive tactics, and arrived at only one conclusion: justifiable homicide.

Geisler had had Cheryl excused from the coroner's inquest because she was a juvenile; protective of her, he told the authorities that she had "gone through enough." She ended up a ward of the state, in the custody of her grandmother, Mildred Turner.

Mickey never believed that Crane killed Stompanato. "You know, Johnny was an athlete. He wasn't a guy that would go out and slug somebody or anything like that, but if someone came to challenge him, he could stand up for himself pretty well. They say that she stabbed him while he was standing." "Right-hand-man" Jim Smith corroborated that Mickey never accepted how former marine Stompanato allowed a fourteen-year-old girl to run across a room with a knife, and then stab him. He couldn't believe at the time that Turner killed Stompanato either, although Smith said that in later years Mickey had told him that he eventually thought it was Turner.

Not everyone shared Mickey's account of his thoughts, motives, and hidden agenda. Journalist Aronowitz suspected that Mickey fueled several theories in the media:

> Probably Mickey was behind accusations that Lana really stabbed Johnny. The rumor started flying that Cheryl, as a juvenile, wouldn't get much more than a slap on the wrist and so somebody was able to talk her into taking the rap for momma, or so the story went.

The popular salacious version of the circumstances involved the nickname Turner employed for Stompanato's penis. Named after the solid and more than foot-long Hollywood statue, Oscar must have been quite a sight at half the embellished version. Many people felt more comfortable picturing Turner interrupting a "show and tell" between Stompanato and daughter: Oscar was out in the open; Turner runs for the knife; Oscar survives unscathed; but she kills Stompanato.

Mickey never believed that Stompanato had eyes for the Lolita-ish Crane. However, she was no stranger to Hollywood pedophiles. Her stepfather, Tarzan actor Lex Barker, had sexually abused her at age ten. Her teenage world was a stormy one, and she briefly ran away from home at age thirteen.

At the end of the day, without a murder conviction, Mickey concluded: "This is the first time I've ever heard of a guy being convicted of his own murder."

The day after Stompanato's death, somebody had ransacked his apartment at the Del Capri Motel in Westwood, located at 10587 Wilshire Boulevard, and eliminated any further evidence, as well as Turner's love letters, written the prior year from Europe, to him. He had kept all the pale blue letters hidden in a shaving kit, not the best of clandestine files, and an easy mark for a burglar to grab. The burglar was a pro, entered easily from a bathroom window after cutting away the screen, and stole no valuables. Mickey also had an apartment at the Del Capri; he had invested over $5,000 on remodeling that included white leather furniture and a living room bar. With his knowledge of the residential venue, it would have been simple for him to have any apartment in the building searched. He likely had a key to the Stompanato apartment, and the cut screen could easily have been a ploy. He blamed the police for the break in.

Despite his denials that he had had the letters stolen, they ended up in his possession. He wouldn't identify who gave them to him. The FBI believed that he had met with Walter Winchell at the Mocambo, and it was there that he handed a brown envelope to Winchell—the love letters.

The Friday after the murder, the stolen love letters turned up on the front page of the *Herald Examiner,* followed by another batch in the *Herald-Express.* Some reports indicate that Mickey gave the letters to journalist friend Agnes Underwood, passed up five grand offered by a competitive New York paper, and insisted that Underwood scoop the entire nation. Eventually he admitted that he gave the letters to the newspapers.

The letters contradicted Turner's statements to the police. She had previously represented that she had little interest in Stompanato, that he had forced himself on her, and that his advances were not welcome.

The letters quoted her: "I miss you, want you, and ache for you," and other ditties like "I'm your woman and I need you MY MAN!" The lovebirds called each other Daddy and Honey-Pot, sprinkled with Pai, Papito, Gitano, and Janito. Hot stuff for those days.[2]

22.

I Want To Be in Pictures

Mickey had definitely caught the Hollywood virus; he would now list his occupation as "author's assistant." The Mickey Cohen book and movie deal was still in limbo, but he kept pitching. Acting independently, he paid a writer $400 per week to write a screenplay. He was unaware of how Hollywood worked, and the difficulties inherent in getting a green light for a project. Even with insiders Hecht and Schenck, two people who had been involved in movies, the deal fell flat.

Mickey focused on his usual antics of having people fork over money for his projects, a good trait for movie production. Worse, he sold shares in the book as a separate deal, while poor Ben Hecht was still trying to get his life down on paper based on continuous interviews, the original tome, and a voluminous list of prior notes. Before Hecht could finish chapter one, Mickey had sold off even more shares and new movie rights.

"I couldn't believe that anyone would be stupid enough to buy into a non-existent property," Hecht said retrospectively.

Mickey's continued antics with his movie could have been the inspiration for Mel Brooks' Max Bialystock from *The Producers*. Hecht had underestimated

Mickey's persuasive sales pitch, as well as the insanity that takes over people when they think that they're going to put on a show.

The *Los Angeles Herald Express* ran Walter Winchell's column on July 7, 1958. He wrote, partially incorrectly, regarding the manuscript: "Ben Hecht's book on Mickey Cohen is finished. A Los Angeles psychiatrist [Krause] angled it for $30,000. Mickey gave him stock in it."

Mickey would not give up on his show business aspirations.

He and LaVonne were back in divorce court on Tuesday, June 17. She never discussed Mickey's girlfriends, although the names of strippers Candy Barr and Arlene Stevens appeared in the divorce proceedings; Mickey had testified at a trial for Candy.

Forty-one-year-old LaVonne neglected to mention her own boyfriend Sam Farkas, who had stayed on when Mickey was in prison, obviously to look after his family for him.

She was no longer tight-lipped about her relationship with Mickey: "No matter what happened away from home, he was continually berating me—seemed to take pleasure in doing it—and humiliating me. I was under a doctor's care through most of the marriage."

Her younger sister, Doris Sachs, agreed: "I've seen him berate and belittle her and tell her how stupid she was in front of me and my husband and other guests. He made her nervous and highly emotional—in tears."

LaVonne accepted one dollar per year as part of the legal settlement. She must have had some confidence that Mickey would do as Dean Jennings wrote: "dole out to her." She complained duplicitously: "My lawyer said there's no use fooling myself. I can't get anything except what he wants to give. Of course, he does take care of me in a very small way. But I really have nothing and I almost have to beg for money." She also admitted to reporters that she was advised by her lawyers to accept Mickey's terms, since he didn't show any significant taxable income. Any wise divorce attorney did not want to poke around in his financial world.

Judge Bennett had questioned the dollar a month arrangement and no share in community property, but LaVonne convinced him that Mickey would support her. He ordered Mickey to pay the $250 in fees and $19 for the cost of the divorce.

Mickey would soon say, "The only one who could live with me was LaVonne, and even then we couldn't agree."

Columnist Lee Mortimer, substituting during August for vacationing Walter Winchell, warned Mickey in Winchell's syndicated "Along Broadway" column: "Top hoods telling Mickey (The Louse) Cohen that if he doesn't shut his trap and keep out of the papers, he'll get only one more story—on the obit page."

The *Saturday Evening Post* contracted with Mickey to publish a book on his life. The proposal for this Dean Jennings piece raised eyebrows all over the country; many mobsters had warned him against this sort of publicity.

Mickey foolishly granted publication rights to a series of interviews with Jennings, thereby killing his cinematic aspirations because the magazine told his life story in print prior to any movie production. The magazine had enormous exposure, and no movie producer would touch the subject after a large part of the audience already knew so much about his life. Since television movies were unheard of during this period, he had used the only other mass media venue available to him, a national magazine with a healthy paid circulation.

Dean Jennings wrote four magazine stories that played up Mickey as the dandy bachelor. Jennings called him the "Featherweight with the Dempsey Punch."

The jokes ran rampant about Mickey's new "clean life." Jennings spilled the cleanliness beans to the world: thirty bath towels per week, twenty-one Kleenex boxes, two large cans of Johnson's baby powder, one bottle of Lilac Vegetal, and one Yardley's after-shave lotion. Each Mickey shower required heating up his specially constructed ten-thousand-dollar, three-hundred-gallon hot water tank, similar to the one used in the Beverly Hills Hotel. Surprisingly, he needed only one bar of pink Cashmere Bouquet soap per washing. He was an unwitting pitchman for dozens of products.

Jennings unflatteringly described his first glimpse of Mickey at their Brown Derby meeting years before: "He looked like the Al Capone of thirty years ago."

He further depicted Mickey's physical attributes with unbecoming adjectives like "scowl, squashed, and paunchy."

What annoyed Mickey the most was a reference to "gargantuan characteristics." He needed a dictionary, and eventually confronted Jennings for an explanation, but Jennings stuck with his unflattering portrayal.

Mickey nemesis journalist George E. Sokolsky did not like the attention paid to Mickey. His syndicated column did its best to stir up detractors. He said that Mickey had no visible means of support and yet spent $200,000 a year without paying taxes, while his debt to the government was over $500,000.

He quoted Mickey: "Internal Revenue is making us a nation of cheats. Always snooping. You can't expect Mickey Cohen to go around like a three-dollar-a-day bum. Why should I give them what little money I have when they'll only throw it away on some foreign country?"

Sokolsky went on a tirade. The scathing article lambasted anyone who didn't pay taxes, but particularly Mickey, and equated him to wealthy citizens with foreign numbered bank accounts abroad. He virtually said that someone like Mickey who pays no taxes is useless to society and called him "privileged," "freeloader," and "elite."

During October, authorities arrested Mickey in Philadelphia—a new indictment had surfaced in Los Angeles. A grand jury would look into his tax records again, a summons materialized from a U.S. Senate committee, and he had an order to appear before the California Crime Commission.

Mickey found "The Private Life of a Hood" and its surrounding publicity difficult to digest. Jennings had let him down. Because of Mickey's new string of legal problems, he needed permission to fly to New York to seek what he felt was his just recompense. His attorney, Samuel Brody, convinced federal judge Ernest A. Tolin to let Mickey make the trip. In keeping with his quick libel suit style, Mickey sued the Curtis Publishing Company (Philadelphia) for $1,000,000 on October 24, 1958.

The major distractions did not interfere with Mickey's Hollywood efforts. On September 15, 1958, the new *Ben Hecht Show* had aired on WABC in New York. It was an offshoot of a February 1958 interview with Mike Wallace, who would produce the show for Hecht. The thirty-minute format brought in-depth, one-on-one interviews with controversial figures, everyone from eight Bowery bums to Jack Kerouac. The station's program manager developed cold feet and cancelled guests in November like Norman Mailer, and later Roy Cohn, followed by the entire show.

Yet, Mickey was booked and, according to Hecht biographer William MacAdams, "created a furor when he revealed that he'd never murdered anyone who didn't deserve it." The quote was one of Mickey's trademark favorites, and Wallace surely knew Mickey's act from their famous go 'round the prior year. Television was already cannibalizing itself.

On December 3, Gus Greenbaum, then an owner at the Sands, was found dead at his ranch home in Phoenix. An unwritten rule was not to kill anyone in town. He and his wife had had their throats slashed by a large carving knife; his head nearly severed, surrounded by pillows to soak up the blood.[1] He had gotten too greedy: he was skimming off the skim, the ultimate hubris, ignoring predecessors like Bugsy.

Mickey dropped his $1,000,000 libel suit against the Curtis Publishing Company on December 15. He cited a series of other harassments. Things were heating up again, and apparently he needed his attorneys to focus on other issues.

Despite the legal flourishes and televised controversies, Mickey never stopped fervently shopping the idea of a movie based on his life, contrasting the beliefs of celebrity-followers like Dorothy Kilgallen, who wrote in her "Around New York" column that Hecht and Mickey were having creative disagreements over the book version.[2] The *Los Angeles Times* would sometimes provide tongue-in-cheek coverage of Mickey utilizing expressions like "a risky job title," nonetheless fueling his efforts to keep his name in the papers, which could only help sell the screenplay.

He thought he should play the lead part, since no actor could capture his image. In a moment of casting weakness, he approached comedian Jerry Lewis, who invested $5,000, but respectfully turned down the opportunity to play him in a movie. Leading man Robert Mitchum was his and Jerry's new choice—again someone about the twice the size of pudgy jockey Mickey.

Following the plot of *The Producers*, by the end of 1958 Mickey had hustled like Bialystock and sold 200% of the movie rights, at $1,000 per share. He still had a contract with another group who had owned the story rights since 1951.

Max Fiegenbaum, a retired Beverly Hills manufacturer, put $25,000 in the deal.

Ruth Fisher of Los Angeles invested $7,500. She was proud to have Mickey as a friend: "I first heard of Mickey when I was on a trip in Israel. I'm one of the few people who can see his good side."

Aubrey V. Stemler, who was in the jukebox business, joined the party with a healthy fifteen grand. "I think Mickey has been pushed around a little bit, and I am interested in his movie and his book to help him out," said altruistic Stemler.

Appliance man David Krause bought an additional $25,000—part of a family investment that included his brother Dr. Leonard S. Krause (friend of Candy Barr) and sister, and Sadelle Bellows.

The extensive list also included gamblers like Phil Zahlout. Even Harold Brown, the former president of the West Hollywood State Bank, jumped into the act. He loaned $50,000 of his own money to the production.

Mickey took full advantage of the business amnesia that enveloped Hollywood locals when it came to the movies. The *Saturday Evening Post* had introduced one of its articles on him with the subheading, "Here is a revealing clinical study of a shameful American paradox." What once was paradoxical had become customary with Mickey, particularly when his associates knew that his efforts might result in a movie. He didn't need the P. T. Barnum sucker-born-every-minute types; his compatriots relished a role in the celebrity-driven Hollywood loop, and gladly plunked down cash. Producer Mickey also instilled an element of fear that pushed any shy investors to sign on the dotted line.

He boasted to the newspapers that he was producing another movie, aptly entitled *Flim Flam*. One investor forked over $18,000 for a piece of that enterprise.

The producers at Omecc, Inc., denied Mickey's participation in *Flim Flam*. The *Los Angeles Mirror* reported that he had promised the IRS 12½% of the deal. The IRS denied it when queried by FBI agents. He took this opportunity to try to settle his back taxes account for $200,000. The IRS did not bite, but kept a close watch on his movie dealings.

He was aware of the scrutiny and told associates, "We have to move slowly... Don't think the government isn't on top of the whole thing."

A "new" story surfaced: Mickey was going to star in a movie about his life. Now it was Carthay Studios and Hal Roach Studios. The budget was $100,000 and Mickey would put up fifty.

With his contacts, he was relentless in his efforts to stay involved with movies. Still, he never had much luck with the often-shadier producers and moneymen who surrounded the entertainment business. Erle Stanley Gardner wrote of the competitive environment, "The Stars of the screen rule Hollywood in regal splendor... In Hollywood you must be climbing or be crushed." Mickey tried his best to climb.

One story embodies the Hollywood sensibility best, and Mickey's hapless carousel ride in the entertainment business.

He was always a fan of comedian Lenny Bruce. "I tried to help Lenny... No one was able to get him off narcotics, of course, I did try... I helped him financially... I helped him get a job in Chicago when nobody else would use him."

Lenny was scurrying around town trying to raise money for an independent movie that was already in production, shooting on the streets of Los Angeles—something looked down upon by moguls as *facacta,* Yiddish for "little shitty." He would hang out in the legendary Canter's deli on Fairfax, "the Jewish deli that attracted more characters than Damon Runyon's Lindy's," as described by author Albert Goldman.[3]

Lenny's efforts struck a chord with Goldman. "He got so carried away with his vision of success that he even made an approach to one of the toughest guys in Hollywood, the notorious mobster Mickey Cohen."

Goldman described the meeting:

> There he is in Cohen's kitchen one afternoon, pitching, pleading, framing pictures with his nervous hands and selling his ass off for this new movie. All the while Lenny is shpritzing himself blind. Mickey Cohen is sitting there eating ice cream. He's got this big spoon in his hairy fist, and he's gouging the rock-solid ice cream out of a pint container.

Goldman paints a hilarious portrait of the famous comedian trying to make an investor out of Mickey: "Finally, Cohen has shoveled the carton clean. He burps, lays down his tool, and looks Lenny straight in the eye." Mickey turns Lenny down with only, "I don't have it!"

Mickey was actually making a small fortune, skimming as much as a half million each year from Vegas alone.[4]

The next day at Lenny's movie shoot, corner of Fairfax and Santa Monica, Mickey suddenly pulled up to the stoplight. Perhaps he had second thoughts about getting involved in Lenny's movie.

"Zug nisht, zug nisht, Mickey—we're making a movie," screamed Lenny.

Mickey was terrified to have disrupted the scene, and wanted to protect any chance of his Hollywood faux pas from surfacing in the papers. With a twisted expression on his face, his head jerked side to side as he looked to avoid the cameras. As soon as the light changed, embarrassed Mickey jammed his foot on the accelerator, barely missed running over Lenny, and disappeared quickly.

Like so many dreamers in Hollywood, Mickey's creative endeavors came up short. Many of his contacts dried up. King Cohn had died in early 1958.[5]

Despite no movie deals, Mickey continued the show business pretense as part of his daily life. In order to carry off the desired image, he surrounded himself with famous actors, and often tried to influence their careers.

The ensuing headlines spoke to his successful life, and it appeared he was coasting with ease. He was back, and some said bigger than ever before. The national syndicate established new municipalities and states as part of their dynasty, thereby dramatically increasing Mickey's opportunities for income outside of Los Angeles.

The country drew away from the Eisenhower years, Howdy Doody, and Wonder Bread. As the sixties approached, marijuana, the Beatles, free love, and flower power were on the horizon.

23.

Another Knockdown

The public devoured mob antics, and not just in the newspapers. Magazines, true crime publications, and pulp paperbacks sold thousands of copies with photographs and information on criminal exploits.

Cult hero Mickey's current band of Merry Men consisted of convicted felons Phillip H. Packer, Harold "Happy" Meltzer, Seymour Pellar, Max Tannenbaum, and William K. Howard, a pal from Alcatraz. Ralph Sills, a former rug dealer, and Ellis "Itchy" Mandel, who worked the Stagehands Union, were the only two with clean records.

Fred and Joe Sica were regulars at Mickey's new apartment; the days of the Brentwood home were long gone.

He lived in a small seven-hundred-square-foot, two-bath apartment on Barrington after vacating the even smaller apartment at the Del Capri on Wilshire Boulevard. He resided on the top floor, so he needed air conditioners added to the roof.

Julius Salkan, the architect-builder and owner, had warned Mickey when he contritely applied for one of the new apartments, "One bomb and you're out."

Mickey had a built-in soda fountain for root beer, cola, soda, and ice water. He kept a special ice-cream freezer for his addiction, which ran to one quart per day. He stocked an over abundant liquor cabinet that featured a blue-hue light for evenings. A gold sunburst clock hung over the mantle, just above the carved initials "M. C." in the hearth of the black satin, brick fireplace. He had six rainbow-colored telephones that matched the colorful eclectically shaped cushions on his sofa. In the living room, a console operated the electric drapes and a fancy $1500 hi-fi. One remote color television and two black-and-whites rounded out his luxuries. His security additions included multiple locks, a sliding bolt, alarms, and a one-way peephole.

He kept a color photo of LaVonne on display, inscribed, "For Ever, LaVonne." Other photos were of the now Reverend James Vaus (the surveillance specialist), Reverend Billy Graham, and Sammy Davis, Jr. The collection included a photo of sexy girlfriend Liz Renay with its inscription, "To my baby, Mickey, from Liz." He always displayed his favorite photograph of himself—seated, and surrounded by a collage of newspaper clippings. His art display included two expensive oils of his bulldog Mickey Jr.

A red leather scrapbook of all his escapades was available for guests. His library collection included the works of the Russian poet Pushkin, Boccaccio's medieval *Decameron, The Rise and Fall of the Roman Empire*, Plato's dialogues, Walt Whitman's *Leaves of Grass*, Renaissance writer Rabelais, all of Shakespeare, and Sir Walter Scott.

Florabel Muir's publicist husband Denny Morrison always gave Mickey a word or two to insert into his daily conversation, and made suggestions regarding literature. However, she insisted that the books were window dressing, part of a design by his interior decorator.

Mickey commented on the classics, "Why should I worry about Tolstoy's troubles?"

Naturally, the residence was spotless. "His asepsis, which has been a matter of objective interest to more than one psychiatrist, is as purposely visible as a blind man's tin cup," described unsympathetic writer Dean Jennings of his last visit to Mickey's digs.

Neighbors complained about scraping and shuffling noises from above, accompanied by wild laughter. They accustomed themselves to beautiful women showing up at all hours clad in mink coats. The block now attracted fancy cars and extra police patrols.

Mickey only identified himself as "Mr. Jones" to his neighbors. Residents wondered what Mr. Jones was doing traipsing around in his silk pajamas in the middle of the night. He rode around the block, and then "furtively crept back up the stairs."

When one Beverly Hills secretary found out that it was Mickey, she demanded that the owner cancel her lease. Mickey was very embarrassed and complained about the quality of the soundproofing in the building. He told the building owner that he had the thickest carpeting available and protected his public image, saying, "I never went near her."

The buddy-boy entourage took care of every detail for Mickey, including placing pillows in the back seat of cars for long trips. The full-time and loyal housekeeper and cook at his criminal hacienda was still Mrs. Willa Haywood. She resented the "moochers" who flitted by to drink the booze and smoke the imported cigars.

He granted lengthy interviews to reporters like James Bacon, who marveled at Mickey's cash flow, and mentioned his now sixty pairs of custom-designed shoes. Hundred-dollar tips at Mocambo were still part of the nightlife.

His response regarding his flashy lifestyle was always the same: "It's simple. I just have friends who have confidence in me. They loan me the money. They know they'll get it back some day."

The Los Angeles vice squad regularly tailed Mickey and his delinquents around town. During quiet dinners at the local haunts, the vice posse often stood at the bar eyeing his table. Mickey made sure to mention to reporters that he was "not a cop hater...nothing could be further from the truth. Some of my best friends are cops." That last line insured his cash flow. He had a soft spot for rookie cops: "...I don't want these new kids to have to make a report that they lost me. Many times I've turned around and started hunting for them." Mickey Jr., a new English bulldog, escorted him on regular jaunts to his barber. He patronized the Beverly Wilshire Health Club on South Beverly Drive, where lengthy treatments included shaving Mickey Sr.'s eyebrows. He gladly paid for anyone willing to escort him to the club. That usually meant "fitness" cronies Fred Sica, Max Tannenbaum, and Itchy Mandel.

Fred Sica's employment description included walking Mickey Jr. with his fancy red leather leash. The police visited the neighborhood just to catch a glimpse of a famous organized crime figure, a man with thick black eyebrows, reduced to dog sitting. Sica was also a resident chef, who served the meals on tables set with engraved sterling silver goblets and linen napkins. Mickey Jr. had his own set of pink-and-white plastic dishes, decorated with decals of other breeds. Sica did his own grocery shopping, cooking, and cleaning. He preferred to host dinner parties in his silk pajamas, protected of course by an apron. Ben Hecht described Sica as a handsome man, in the style of actor Victor Mature.

One night at Sica's residence, the gang watched dashing Errol Flynn in the movie *Robin Hood*. Mickey loved the scene in which Robin heists the Sheriff of Nottingham's rubies and diamonds. He wanted to find out if Flynn was a tough guy in real life, and was delighted to learn that he once kicked fighter-turned-director John Huston's ass. Mickey would soon strike up a relationship with Flynn, and spend nights with him at Rondelli's restaurant swapping stories for hours.[1] Flynn liked to spin sagas about his life as a seaman, sprinkled with his knowledge of smuggling gold and slaves, not unlike his movie life. One night private detective Fred Otash sat through a bull session and marveled at "two of the world's heavyweights, each in his own class."

During one of his regular daytime errands to buy cologne in a Beverly Hills drugstore, Mickey suddenly became cost-conscious; his personal expenditures were excessive. He thought that he was buying a few days' worth of his favorite cologne, and the almost twenty-dollar tab startled him. Before his incarceration, he had paid forty dollars for perhaps a week's supply of his favorite fragrance.

He remarked to the druggist, "They must have raised the price while I was in stir."

The druggist explained, "The price is the same, only you just didn't notice before."

By some accounts, Mickey owed the government over one million dollars, which may have explained his sudden frugal awareness. A steady supply of gifts from friends complimented his already overstocked cabinets in his bedroom, contradicting his concern. His personal apartment expenses were less than $500 per month at the Del Capri, making his cash flow needs easy to meet.

He continued his publicity campaign with the same fervor as in his younger days. He received fan mail from all over the country. FBI agents wrote that it was an irresponsible and immature act to make a hero out of a criminal. Thanks to the media, the public perceived Mickey as human, something the FBI missed in its cold analysis. Not unlike today, citizens were very forgiving, particularly if the subject suffered from universal frailties and appeared vulnerable, as he painted himself at the hands of bullying police and eager district attorneys.

The somewhat chubby former pugilist tried to redesign his new public image to resemble a head of state rather than a gangster with Robin Hood tendencies.

"Today you become more of a diplomat and you realize what life is and you're softer," he had told the readership of the *Saturday Evening Post*.

Mickey projected a congenial approach toward vengeance: "I think very differently about any enemy than I would have done maybe in other days."

The renewed good life was never without problems. He received a subpoena to appear at the McClellan Hearings in Washington, before the Senate Select Committee on Improper Activities in the Labor of Management Fields. He and other mobsters had no idea that Robert Kennedy, one of the lead counsels, was so concerned about their operations.

The mob had lived through these political interruptions before; the vast majority had survived unscathed. Hearings like this had historically included playing ball with politicians, a formality performed for the public and the growing media. The national syndicate perceived the youthful Kennedy as ineffectual and most high-level mob chiefs laughed him off. After all, his father Joe Kennedy was a notorious bootlegger. Some thought that the politicians in power chose Kennedy because of his ability to portray the concerns of the workingman, and was therefore a public relations shill. Nobody in the mob appeared the least bit scared.

Mickey stayed at the Washington Hilton, a short commute to the Senate building. The discounted government rate was an excessive $100 per day. The government "generously" gave each person $8.00 in spending money.[2]

Insiders say that the Mafia eliminated elder Longie Zwillman with a tad of compassion in late February 1959. After allowing him to become inebriated with a quality brandy, the hit squad hanged him with a plastic clothesline from a water pipe in the basement closet of his residence, his hands tied, garroted with wire. Newspapers reported the incident as a suicide, assuming Zwillman was despondent over jury-fix accusations in his income tax trial of the prior year.[3]

Locally, authorities were disappointed with their old failed tactics of arrest, interrogation, bail, and freedom for Mickey. Rumors swirled about his continued problems with the IRS. Chief Parker made headlines when he claimed that he had new information about Mickey's growing mob, many of whom came from the east and a few from the south. The March 14, 1959, headlines suggested that he and private detective Fred Otash were involved in the gambling rackets. Still, all these allegations were no surprise.

On March 24, Mickey appeared at the McClellan Hearings.[4] Counsel Robert Kennedy grilled Mickey while committee member Senator John F. Kennedy sat in attendance.[5]

Sam Dash, who began as a district attorney in Philadelphia and who later became involved in the Watergate hearings, protected Mickey's legal interests. He was a close friend of Mickey's sister Lillie.

Kennedy made sure that his position and the strength of his convictions was clear. He insisted that the mob members "have become so rich and so powerful that they have outgrown local authorities," a supposition that contradicted FBI and national policy. J. Edgar Hoover reliably dismissed the series of investigations as a "grandiose scheme," and continually thwarted RFK's efforts.

Carlos Marcello's long-standing friendship with Mickey dates back to these hearings. Politicians labeled Marcello "the Little Man" and the unchallenged giant of organized crime. Kennedy despised Marcello, who was an outspoken racist. Unfortunately, FBI director Hoover harbored similar prejudices. The mobster interviewees, including Carlos' brother Victor, sat close to each other as they squared off against RFK.

Mickey wore his usual dapper garb with a straight pocket square; Marcello wore movie-star sunglasses and a banker's pinstriped suit. They remained in the hot seat for a long time.

Marcello invoked the Fifth Amendment sixty-eight times, thirty-five times in only fifteen minutes, which irritated Kennedy and the rest of the committee. He refused to comment on his Louisiana operations.

Mickey was not pleased. "But Bobby Kennedy, this snotty little guy, questioned like an out-and-out punk, and I don't mean this with any animosity."

He also took the Fifth many times with an unhappy, grim face, although he prefaced his remarks with the word "respectfully." He chewed gum during most of the interview.

Kennedy pressed him and asked ludicrous things like, "What does it mean to have someone's lights put out?" He was referring to a $50,000 hit on a cigarette vendor.

Mickey would relax and respond, "Lookit, I dunno what you're talking about, I'm not an electrician... I got nuttin' to do with electricity."

During the hearings, he did his best to irritate Kennedy with his off-the-cuff quips and sarcasm. He riled him on several occasions, including one time when Chairman McClellan physically restrained Kennedy from attacking him.

Mickey refused to discuss his spiritual relationship with Billy Graham, took the Fifth when McClellan asked if he had ever earned an honest dollar in his life, and snubbed any questions regarding his personal wardrobe or flower business.

Mickey was still a showman, and had them rocking in the aisles with laughter. He brought the house down with, "I respectfully decline to answer on the grounds that it might tend to incrime me...and I don't remember."

Kennedy made Mickey laugh when he asked him if he had had only three fights and got knocked out in all three. Mickey said he couldn't answer that because it might be incriminating.

Some of his private conversations held in RFK's private office are also laughable.

Kennedy asked Mickey, "I have been given to understand that you are a gentleman."

Mickey was uncomfortable, but mustered an answer: "Well, I consider myself a gentleman, yeah. I sure would like to try to be one, or I break my back in every way to be one."

Like a disgruntled parent, Kennedy admonished Mickey with, "Well, you sure haven't been a gentleman before this committee."

RFK publicly pressed the issue of a threat made to George M. Seedman, who worked for the New Orleans Cigarette Service Corporation. Mickey grew serious when questioned about company president Thomas A. Vaughn, who had testified that Mickey had threatened Seedman, and that Mickey had received payoffs to stay out of the vending machine war. (Fred Sica also took the Fifth, particularly on his role in the vending machine battles.)

Mickey blamed old enemy Chief William Parker for the flak from Kennedy. A strong connection existed between Kennedy and Parker, who had Mickey followed as he made the evening rounds from the Mocambo to Chasen's. He provided Kennedy with dozens of pictures of Mickey out on the town and made certain that he knew about Mickey's high living, expensive cars, and properties. The committee ended up with a portfolio of shots including Mickey dining at Ciro's, hardly incriminating behavior, but enough to spike RFK's interest.

Kennedy made the most of the Parker leads:

A major vending company paid mobster Mickey Cohen $10,000 simply to remain "neutral," in a battle over location for machines in Los Angeles... Our investigation hearings show that Mickey Cohen spent $275 for his silk lounging pajamas, $25,000 for a specialty built bulletproof car and at one time had 300 different suits, 1,500 pairs of socks and 60 pairs of $60 shoes. His tax returns, however, showed a total income of $1200 in 1956 and $1500 in 1957. When asked where his money came from, Cohen said he borrowed it from his friends and thus it was not necessary to declare it.

The feuding vending machine companies were Rowe Cigarette Service and Coast Vending.

244

Private detective Fred Otash worked for Mike Carr, vice-president of Coast Vending. When Mickey was muscling in on the company, Otash and fifteen of his employees followed him, Sica, and the bruisers all over town. He claimed that Mickey's group threatened on-site owners and managers. He met with Mickey and attorney Sam Dash to settle the matter and suggested that Mickey relax his efforts. Mickey responded with a bribe. Otash had his own difficulties when subpoenaed by RFK, mostly related to his treatment by RFK and the committee. RFK backed down when confronted by Otash's attorney Art Crowley. (Otash subsequently had a showdown with Mickey over recordings that the local grand jury was after. Mickey paid off to hear the tapes.)

Kennedy also set his sights during this period on Nixon pal attorney Murray Chotiner, who had defended over two hundred members of Lansky's syndicate by 1952. Chotner's ties to the mob went back to Bugsy, Lansky, and Mickey.

Editorial pages around the country asked citizens to heed their warnings; if the country didn't take the Senate Rackets Committee seriously, no community would remain a safe haven from the mob. One Wisconsin editor suggested that everyone get "really mad" and insisted that authorities drag all the mobsters to court.

Kennedy had been doing his Mickey homework for years, and made his intentions clear during and after the hearings. He had a list of men he had to get rid of, including Mickey, Marcello, and Jimmy Hoffa.

Mickey appeared unshaken by his experiences with Kennedy and McClellan. To him, this was a little knockdown. He still felt that his ticket to success was his image, and on March 25, 1959, he bought a new Cadillac El Dorado Biarritz black convertible, for approximately ten grand.

In May, he traveled to Washington, D.C., and held court at the fancy Woodner Hotel, now rental apartments. The FBI wondered what he was doing there, why he would register for several days, and pay fifty bucks a night for the deluxe suite, albeit cheaper than the Hilton's government rate. He was undoubtedly expanding his business interests, while schmoozing with his political contacts in the Capitol, including *Washington Post* columnist Drew Pearson.

The war was on with Kennedy, but Mickey had a full plate at home.

24.

Mickey's World

Mickey's social life blossomed, and it became the subject of early supermarket tabloid journalism. To ensure convenient and luxurious trappings for the girls in town, Mickey kept a second apartment near the Hollywood nightclubs. The diminutive Casanova's regulars were Brandy Long, Tempest Storm (Annie Becker), Arlene Stevens, and statuesque Beverly Hills, a favorite through 1959 as a substantial fill-in for main squeeze Candy Barr. Popular Stevens' elaborate club act included an oyster shell, and little more. Many columnists, including Dorothy Kilgallen, followed Tempest Storms' exploits, also mentioning her romance with singer Herb Jeffries.

Said Mickey of Hills, "She's a real lady. Her morals and concept of life are really high."

Twenty-two-year-old Hills would tell reporters, "He's simply great."

Mickey's relationship with chocolate lover Candy Barr was no secret, and when he was older he confessed a certain friction. She had a talent for being able to ripple her muscles while standing still, which certainly didn't inhibit his original attraction. He spent much of his social time with Candy, and bought her lavish gifts such as new Cadillacs.[1]

His first introduction to Candy required bailing her out of a new jam, a few years after a grand jury had dismissed charges against her for shooting her drunken husband. Bing Crosby's son Gary had suggested that Mickey meet with her manager Joe DiCarlo because Texas authorities had sentenced her for possession of a single joint of marijuana.

Candy had always maintained that the Dallas police had framed her: "A girl-friend left marijuana in my house. I gave her permission to leave it there—but that was before I knew my phone was tapped, and that the police were laying for me."

Gary knew that Mickey's connections and affections could only be helpful to Candy. He appeared to speak from experience when he told Mickey, "One thing about that broad, she can make ya feel like a *real* man!"

Mickey-the-benevolent immediately contacted her attorney A. L. Wirin, someone already familiar to him. Mickey paid the legal fees, and fought the civil rights violations and the appeal for Candy's excessive fifteen-year sentence.

The sexless version of Mickey and Candy's first meeting involves Joe DiCarlo, who brought her to dinner at Chuck Landis' Largo to thank Mickey for his help.[2] The more salacious—and more often told—version took place at the Knickerbocker Hotel. Candy answered the door in a dress that required some final zipping—the trendy setup—and Mickey obliged. Candy worked as a stripper at Landis' Largo Club, adding a professional touch to her timing and movements.

Mickey began a steady relationship with Candy soon after he met her. When police arrested her in Los Angeles—authorities had vacated her appeal bond from Dallas—he accompanied her to jail. He waited for the fifteen thousand-dollar bond reinstatement that same day.

The public followed Mickey and Candy's torrid spring dating in 1959, with news of their exploits appearing in papers around the country and in Canada. Only a few weeks after their first meeting, he enjoyed teasing his fans with news of his marriage to Candy. (At one later trial, she would testify that she was engaged to Mickey. Many people thought they were, even though both were still married, and she was pregnant with another man's child. Mickey had bought her a four-carat diamond engagement ring, but most marked off the marriage plans as a publicity stunt.)

Reporters gladly hung out in Candy's dressing room at the Club Largo, where she replied to the marriage question: "He hasn't even asked me to marry him. I must say we are very happy when we're around each other. And I have a tender affection for him. But we are not even formally engaged."

The Largo's overweight emcee would wait in the wings while the band cranked out a barely recognizable version of Frankie Avalon's "Venus." After a few salacious guttural sounds and remarks by the fat host, the trained drummer provided the requisite rim-shot before the emcee wailed, "And now our lady of the evening, Miss Candy Barr."

Candy was built beyond the *Playboy* dreams of the most ardent breast men; her centerfold shots would become collectors' items. Followers in the audience couldn't take their eyes off the tiny spotlight that covered Candy's body as she slowly shed bits of her costume, eventually down to the popular nipple tassels of the day.

Mickey loved her sense of humor. Author Steve Stevens recalled how she described bullfighters as "little fags in sequined knickers," to Mickey's delight.

Mickey did not see her show every night. A typical date, like Sunday, May 4, began at three in the morning, after her last performance. While he waited at the stage door with reporters, he said that he was going to marry Candy just as soon as his divorce became official. Previously, he had been promoting the idea that he was going to marry stripper Beverly Hills. (When the Cohen divorce finalized on August 4, LaVonne and boyfriend Sam Farkas "eloped" to Las Vegas, where Farkas told interested parties that he had reformed and was now in the steel business. They officially married at the end of November.)

Despite the sexual connection, Mickey felt that Candy typified someone un-suitable for regular socializing. "Like even the exotic dancer Candy Barr, I couldn't take her." Mickey made a distinction between his regular social activities and more dignified venues: "There's a lot of girls I went with that I couldn't take to certain types of parties."

Candy obviously knew that Mickey had a high social opinion of himself, and the lopsided social arrangement created a strange relationship. He always preferred to describe his friendship with her as only superficially social—just a girl he knew.

Mickey overlooked her role in any of his political maneuvering, and minimized her contacts, which were extensive. As in most political thrillers, Candy was the shapely woman, and this one took her clothes off nightly on stage for $2,000 per week, when not performing sex acts in movies. Her most famous was *Smart Aleck*, a fifteen-minute black-and-white one-reel ménage. The plot involves a traveling businessman who meets well-endowed sixteen-year-old Candy at the motel swimming pool. The quick friendship leads to drinks and intercourse in his room. When he requests a little extra in the form of fellatio, she refuses, but secures the talents of her willing girlfriend.

The closest Mickey came to admitting any of Candy's nefarious connections was her command strip performance for Louis "Babe" Triscaro, a labor boss from Cleveland, and a room full of teamsters. JFK-assassin killer Jack Ruby, Candy

Barr, and Mickey maintained a perverse association. The fact that he shared Candy with Ruby is testimony enough for some to establish Ruby's deep connections to the L.A. mob.

Candy's legal troubles remained unresolved. Mickey enlisted attorneys Melvin Belli, A. L. Wirin multiple times, and Julius Echles. The trial was a huge sensation; the judge even snapped pictures of the voluptuous blonde while allowing photographers full access. Regardless of all the high-powered and specialized legal expertise, the court would deny the last writ. While she had waited for the results of her appeal, Candy and her almost completely nude line of chorus girls became the sensation of Las Vegas. The girls took it off to "A Pretty Girl Is Like a Melody" at the El Rancho Vegas, still a popular destination. Local authorities concerned with moral standards tried to get rid of her and female impersonator T. C. Jones. Hotel owner Beldon Katleman stuck up for his talent.

At a final press conference, Mickey and Candy announced that they would not marry.

"We have different standards of living, and different ways of life," said Mickey.

"He's nice, but we just weren't meant for each other," added Candy.

The newspapers were filled with expressions like "Cohen says Candy is dandy," and "Candy says Mick is a brick."

Judge Lloyd Davidson of the Texas Court of Criminal Appeals wrote a "blistering dissent" on Candy's case: "So the time has come…when peace officers can kick in the door of one's home and ransack it at will…then there is no due process of law."

While in prison, Candy would work in the clothing shop, clerk in the commissary, star in prison shows like "Goree Girls," and finish her high school education.[3]

In June of 1959, the FBI was aware of Mickey's "attempted badger game"[4] on Alfred Bloomingdale, heir to the famous department store fortune, and founder of the Dine and Sign (Diners Club) credit card. Mickey's sexual extortion racket appeared boundless, having infiltrated the highest levels of American business.[5]

He was one of the early Diners Club cardholders, and he "inadvertently" used stolen Diners Club cards, one of his consistent businesses. The authorities were unable to prosecute him on credit card fraud, despite the FBI's awareness of his lucrative side business.

Anywhere he went, the police hounded him. Chief Parker had made Mickey the number one enemy of Los Angeles. Parker's way of dealing with his "uneducated" man was harassment; he continued to have Mickey arrested for anything, including jaywalking.

Mickey became further involved with the American Civil Liberties Union because of the alleged harassment by Beverly Hills and Los Angeles police. He began a suit in federal court against the police department; it was never resolved. He still regularly screamed to the papers about the violation of his civil rights, which made him all the more sympathetic to his focused fans. He fought hard against his harassment, and used the available publicity to make himself appear clean.

When Mickey was in Chicago, the police insisted that he have two cops with him at all times. Even when he visited friend's homes for dinner, the two tails sat outside the front door. He should have known that the authorities weren't through with him, but he must have thought that he was invulnerable, because the police scrutiny didn't faze him.

Drew Pearson's syndicated column "The Washington Merry-Go-Round" featured a supportive half page on Mickey. The June 17, 1959, tribute referred to a visit from the "ex-ruler of the Los Angeles underworld." Pearson described how tough it must be for Mickey, trying to lead a straight life, surrounded by suspicious naysayers: "Mickey served time for his many sins… This isn't easy for an ex-convict, especially one as notorious as Mickey. Everything you do is likely to be suspect."

Pearson spoke about the former gang lord's altruistic approach to life, specifically how Mickey had enlisted him to help with Candy Barr's marijuana charge, which he deemed totally inappropriate and harsh. Pearson, raising attention to the existing racial divide in America, spoke about how two drug-dealing, dope-pushing Negroes received only six months to Candy's fifteen years. Pearson also detailed his past criticism of Mickey, and explained why now he had to be supportive of someone going straight. Anyone lecturing reformatory boys on the evils of criminal life needed accolades.

The Arthur Black trial (the waiter who sued for assault and battery) continued on July 22. The court records show that prosecutors and plaintiff's counsel grilled Mickey regarding his assets, in order to determine his "wealth and mode of living."

The now humorous exchanges included Black's attorney Arthur Strock, who was determined to pinpoint Mickey's socioeconomic strata: "As a matter of fact, it is an Eldorado, a brougham, that costs around $14,000—is that right?" Strock had not done his Cadillac homework.

Mickey corrected Strock: "It's an Eldorado, a convertible, not a brougham at all."

The lengthy exchanges established that Mickey did drive himself to the hearing in a fancy car.

Moments after conferring with his attorney Ridley, Mickey invoked the Fifth Amendment, a tactic that irritated the prosecutors and sent the trial into arguments involving legal semantics and protocol.

After the judge found him guilty, Mickey paid a five hundred-dollar fine. Still, the judge included a contempt charge that included five days jail time.

The Black trial attracted a contingency of Canoga Park High School students, who attended the court spectacle as part of their civics education. The teenage girls swarmed Mickey, demanding his autograph. The photo op made all the papers.

The Arthur Black jokes continued when sad-faced comedian Ben Blue opened a new restaurant on Wilshire Boulevard. Mickey chose his place as his new hangout. Blue knew just how to handle him when he called for a dinner reservation: "Mick, you can come out right now. I've got two waiters you can hit all you want." The new jokes only added to Mickey's popularity.

On August 13, Mickey's attorneys presented an action against the Superior Court of Los Angeles County, based on his treatment by the court during the Black trial. As usual, he received a suspended sentence for the contempt charges, this time reversed by the District Court of Appeal.

Attorney Melvin Belli and Mickey were real pals, socialized regularly, had many laughs together, and shared the same cynical world outlook. Belli, like so many friends, trusted the relationship enough to shell out three grand in cash at Mickey's request.

On August 24, Mickey gave a lecture on illegal tactics like tax evasion to the American Bar Association at the Fontainebleau Hotel in Miami Beach. Billed as "Professor O'Brien," he performed like a member of the future Saturday Night Live cast.

Straight man Melvin Belli provided a deadpan introduction: "Professor O'Brien from Harvard who's going to give you a talk on the tax laws."

"I probably got more courtroom experience than any of you guys," was Mickey's introduction as he stood at the podium in his wrinkle-proof three hundred-dollar suit.

"Mickey's put-ons epitomized a brand of in-your-face gutter humor shared by cops and crooks alike," recalled journalist Al Aronowitz.

It took the audience a while to catch on; perhaps thirty attorneys were in on the joke.

Finally Mickey made sure everyone knew it was a joke. "At the end of the talk I says, 'My advice to all of ya is to be sure to pay your goddamn taxes right to the letter,' and I walked off the stage. Well, the next day all hell broke loose. The governor of Florida got into the thing and, holy Jesus, they did threaten to disbar Mel."

He told the papers that he had gone to prison because "I didn't have the advice I gave out last night."

The American Bar Association chastised Belli and he issued a contrite statement: "I wish now he had never went here—and you can quote me on that...never again."

The episode prompted the FBI to further monitor Belli, whom they labeled "the king of torts." One of the negative FBI quotes from September 1, 1959: "Belli and Cohen have regarded this incident as humorous, but, of course this type of humor is in extremely poor taste."

Critics!

Belli wasn't afraid of attacking the FBI for harassing his clients. They viewed him as someone with "an extremely questionable record," and memos warned agents to "be alert for any violation of the law by Belli coming to your attention."[6]

Mickey pal Desi Arnaz had his own problems in 1959. He found himself in some deep trouble when he produced the hit television series *The Untouchables*, which depicted Treasury agent Eliot Ness and his efforts to crush the mob. The television show was particularly exasperating to Mae Capone and Sam Giancana, the latter rumored to have been Al Capone's real-life driver. The October 15, 1959, premiere was shown on Desilu Playhouse.[7]

Johnny Rosselli, who found the show's dialogue less than authentic, recruited L.A mobster Jimmy "The Weasel" Fratianno to solve the creative differences by shooting Desi Arnaz, who, of course, would survive to sing "Babaloo," but not without a lot of mob discussion.

Mickey still had his local enemies. Jack "The Enforcer" Whalen, also known as Jack O'Hara, was one of San Fernando Valley's biggest bookies. He was a classic mob bully; he thrived on extortion and the requisite leg breaking. He was the most unpopular mobster in the whole L.A. lot, and that's saying a great deal.

"He was the sort of thug who'd take money from somebody who wanted to buy a little justice, then split it with the intended victim—with whom he might even turn around and take a piece out of the guy who'd hired him in the first place," detailed author Levy.

When Whalen came out of the air force and began work at his chosen criminal profession, he initially told off boss Jack Dragna, "I'll make up my own mind whether I stay in business or not." He was as independent as Mickey, but without the charm or skill to efficiently run a mob.

Dragna tried to entice Whalen to run things with the promise that he would employ Mickey and Joe Sica as underlings. Whalen wanted no part of it; he was satisfied with his piece-of-the-action protocol, perhaps realizing his limitations. Juxtaposed to Whalen, author Reid characterizes Mickey as a bad syndicate manager with an inability to organize due to his greed. Reid insists that since Mickey didn't like to share; Whalen had to go.

Mickey naturally could not stand Whalen, who represented everything he wanted to leave behind in his quest to become Hollywood's gentleman mobster. He pulled no punches when he described Whalen: "This Jack Whalen was a big asshole that had a particular dislike for Italians...vicious, bullying, rotten bastard... He bullied everybody, even bullied cops—and particularly anybody that was smaller than him."

To make matters worse, Whalen once tried to rip Mickey's bankroll from inside his trousers to pay back someone who claimed that Mickey had shorted him. Detective Gary Wean supplied a one-sided, eyewitness account: "The gangster chief was torn loose from the booth like a giant sea turtle brutally ripped from its protective shell, and was being bashed off a wall like a basketball when O'Hara...crashed a fist into Mickey's forehead...taking the thick wad of bills he tossed the empty billfold on the quivering form and sauntered out the front door." Other folklore suggests that Whalen ripped the money from Frankie Niccoli's pocket, while Mickey waited in the car. After counting out his money, the story alleges that Whalen put the change back in Niccoli's pocket.

The local rumor was that Mickey had a contract out on Whalen. If the contract notion was true, Whalen was beyond brazen the night of December 2, when he walked into mob haven Rondelli's Restaurant to collect a payoff. His friend Jack Woods had warned him not to fuck with the little Jew.

Since Chief William Parker had taken charge, he was always hard at work trying to find ways to shut down Mickey's restaurants. Only a week before Mickey had testified at a hearing to secure an entertainment license for Rondelli's. He put on quite a show. He invoked the Fifth Amendment over fifty times and said, "I got no piece of that restaurant. I wouldn't take a piece of it on a silver platter." Mickey called the hearing a farce, and loudly demanded that attorneys and witnesses not mention his name in any derogatory fashion.

The entourage on December 2, 1959, at Rondelli's included Mickey's eighteen-year-old girlfriend Sandy Hagen (Claretta Hashagen), twenty-eight-year-old Georgie Bart Piscitelle (George Perry), Sam LoCigno (Sam Lombardo), Roger

Leonard (Kallman de Leonard), and sexy stripper Candy Barr's thirty-six-year-old manager Joe DiCarlo. Others at the restaurant were twenty-five-year-old singer Tony Reno (Anthony Amereno), Robert "Rocky" Lombardi, Harry Diamond, Michael and Toni Ross, Jack Gotch, Joe Friedman (Joe Mars), Jo Wyatt, Ona Rae Rogers, and Mickey's treasured bulldog Mickey Jr. Roger Leonard, doubled over with laughter, loved to tell how Mickey would drape the canine dinner guest in a proper napkin.

Host Mickey sat at table fifteen, midway between the east wall booths and the center of the room. Seated at his table were LoCigno, Georgie, Leonard, DiCarlo, Sandy, and Mickey.

When Whalen walked in, he pulled Tony Reno out of a phone booth and demanded, "Where are them friends of yours, them two Dagos? Where are those two Dago bastards? They're going to go. Are they in there?"

When Whalen approached Mickey's table he said, "Good evening, Mr. Cohen."

Whalen put his left hand on Georgie's shoulder and asked, "You want to see me?"

Georgie answered, "No. I don't have anything to talk to you about, Jack."

Whalen hit Georgie in the mouth, and he fell to the floor.

Near midnight, within minutes of entering the restaurant, forty-one-year-old Whalen took the first slug in the head, above his right eye, and another, moments later. Whalen was unarmed according to most reports when the five-shot Smith & Wesson .38 Special, a tiny two-inch barrel gun, was fired at him at point-blank range. The waiting men had pistols on their laps hidden under napkins. Mickey's was inside his bib.

Whalen slumped to floor and rolled over on his side. Purportedly, the killer calmly left the restaurant, while the twenty patrons watched.

The police arrived a casual forty-five minutes after the shooting. By the time they entered the dining room, the staff had cleared the dinner plates along with anything else that might have had fingerprints. The police found three guns wrapped in plastic inside trash bins behind the restaurant, but those weren't the murder weapons. Authorities later linked the guns to Mickey and the late Johnny Stompanato. No murder weapon materialized.

Inspector Ed Walker took the initial statements. None of the patrons was able to describe the killer, only that Whalen had punched Georgie in the face.

One early informant said that DiCarlo killed Whalen, although few theatrical agents enjoyed reputations as hit men. DiCarlo readily supplied a well-rehearsed explanation: "Whalen hit George Piscitelle and started around the table for Sam.

He was using foul language. I heard two shots fired. I was watching the man and didn't see who fired them. When I hear shots I run. That's what I did."

Mickey was booked at Van Nuys headquarters on December 3 and released on December 4. He originally told detectives that he was sitting across from Whalen when the gunfire erupted. "I just ducked... When I hear shots, I run." The popular response.

His later review of the circumstances: "With this killing of Jack 'the Enforcer' Whalen at Rondelli's restaurant in 1959, the first thing you got to understand is this: Sam LoCigno, who was accused of the hit, couldn't hit the wall of an auditorium." LoCigno, on a special diet, was still receiving treatment for injuries sustained in an automobile accident.

He arrived at the police station with attorneys Norman Sugarman and William Strong. Police escorted him to Chief Parker's office to record a statement.

After being asked to speak up, LoCigno repeated, "I'm the man that shot Jack O'Hara in self defense."

The grand jury heated up, and police insisted that the entire county jury be present for the proceedings. During the following grand jury interrogations and subsequent trial, not a single employee or patron would state that they saw the shooter.

Mickey told the grand jury that after Whalen struck Georgie, he said, "...Sam, you're next." Then Mickey heard the shots. After one hour with the grand jury, he told newsmen, "Honest, fellows. Sam's the last guy in the world I'd expect to be carrying a gun. I just can't believe he did it."

The courtroom came to life when judo expert George Sumption, a two hundred and forty-five-pound car salesman, explained how the little former boxer had grabbed him. The thirty-two-year-old victim explained, "He said, 'you're one of them, you dirty....' and backhanded me. Then he hit me with his open hand. All the time there was a couple big guys standing in back of him." When Mickey let Sumption leave the café, one of his boys, who tried to apologize, followed him.

Mickey told reporters, "I say I didn't do it, and I wouldn't do it again... I'm a lover, not a fighter. Ask Sandy."

New girlfriend Sandy, described as a blonde dancer, complained that after two weeks with Mickey she already had a police record, and lost her Vegas dance bookings.

Georgie explained to the grand jury that Whalen had come over to collect a disputed football wager that Georgie and LoCigno owed to bookie Al Levitt. Georgie and LoCigno had thought that they had won, and that Al had shorted *them* by two hundred and fifty dollars. Al threatened earlier the day of the

Rondelli's incident with the possibility of "J. O." visiting Georgie's and singer Tony Reno's apartment. Whalen (Jack O'Hara) called the boys and let them know that "he was going to come over and beat us up and probably wind up killing us if we did not pay up." Tony Reno, who would later incur Whalen's wrath at Rondelli's, took the phone from his roommate Georgie, and tried to calm Whalen down.

Roger Leonard explained that he was a writer and movie producer, and had come to dinner to discuss the Ben Hecht project entitled *The Life of Mickey Cohen*. He said that he had been in a phone booth at the time of the shooting, and had promptly left.

At the trial, Judge John C. Barnes presided while prosecutors Joseph Busch and James Ford never gave up on their theory that Mickey and his gunmen ambushed Whalen.

Mickey and the entire ensemble did a great acting job for the jury of six men and six women. Thirty-eight-year-old LoCigno agreed with the popular version of events and took the fall for the Whalen murder on December 8.

LoCigno told his pat story: "I shot twice. It didn't seem like I hit him. All I see was he put his hands to his stomach. I was scared to death."

Much discussion revolved around whether Mickey had said "Now, Sam, now" just before the shooting. Mickey testified that he did not know Whalen, and to the best of his recollection had never seen him before the night of the murder. Prosecutor Ford grilled him about meeting Whalen at the Garden of Allah Hotel and the Formosa Café.[8] Mickey denied leaving Rondelli's with LoCigno. The badgering prosecutors kept him in the forefront of the case. They reviewed his criminal record, back to 1934 Cleveland, and pressured him about alcoholic consumption. Mickey stood his ground, denied any criminal record, except his tax evasion case, and insisted that he never had a drink, no matter how many times asked by the prosecutors. The court record concluded that Mickey and Fred Sica enjoyed reputations as ex-mobsters and racketeers.

On another day, dark-haired Jo Wyatt, a friend of Whalen, told the court of Superior Judge Clement Nye how she rushed to Whalen's side. "I heard one shot, a pause, and then another shot."

Another witness, Joseph Friedman, had seen LoCigno holding a gun.

The jury, by a nine-to-three vote, returned their verdict in ten minutes. Cleveland-born LoCigno received a life sentence, while everyone else received acquittals. The court record states, "The case we are reviewing could truly be called "The trial of Mickey Cohen."

Mickey had exuded confidence with the authorities throughout the whole period. He knew that his acquittal was a done deal, despite reports that he had paid LoCigno $50,000 plus legal fees for the hit. He claimed that LoCigno might have collected half the amount. All that was required of liquor salesman, bartender, and asphalt employee LoCigno was to admit to self-defense.

Whalen's funeral was December 7, 1959. Rondelli's, with its cachet diminished, soon closed.

In San Quentin prison, LoCigno would later tell a priest about his collusion with Mickey. Word got out and a second investigation ensued. He also told police where to find a gun near make-out spot Mulholland and North Beverly Drive, overlooking the city. The rusted gun wasn't much help, but authorities traced it to a gun shop owned by Roger Leonard.

By now Las Vegas was a gold mine, and its success spilled over into the Bahamas and Caribbean. The Teamsters had so much money that leader Jimmy Hoffa splurged with the coffers, built hospitals, golf courses, mom-and-pop stores, and to perpetuate the obscene profits, even more hotels. The Fremont, Dunes, Stardust, and soon Caesars Palace—all had Teamster pension money flowing through their coffers. Casino owners expanded and refurbished at will, depending on the demand.

As early as 1959, fearless attorney Sidney Korshak, chief consigliere in Vegas and Hollywood, was a regular at the Desert Inn. Korshak, mouthpiece for the mob, a tall man with dark hair who never held a license to practice law in California, began as consigliere-in-training at age twenty-one for Al Capone. (One of the early bagmen was Bugsy Siegel.) He had Meyer Lansky's imprimatur to represent Mickey's interests.[9]

Despite all the political power centered in Las Vegas, none of it could help Mickey. While the entire country overlooked the mobs' role in Sin City's development, Robert Kennedy still had it in for him.

25.

Let's Get Mickey

Some new sort of heat was on. The FBI had evidence that Mickey ran many shady businesses, including a short-term note racket in Florida, but no action ensued. However, they watched his every move and traced all his telephone calls and numerous telegrams, many to famous people like Ben Hecht and columnist Drew Pearson. He frequently called all over the country—New York, Chicago, Las Vegas, Newport, San Francisco, Aurora (Colorado), Miami, Albuquerque, Cleveland, Santa Ana (California), Palm Springs, Corpus Christi, Oakland, Denver, Tarrytown (New York)—all within a few days. The FBI knew that his favorite airline was American. He now liked to stay at the flagship Statler Hilton in New York, directly across from Penn Station. He called friends at fancy hotels like the Navarre on Central Park South, the St. Regis on Fifth and Fifty-fifth, and the Essex on Central Park South.[1]

In one year, Mickey made 729 phone calls to his Boston and Palm Beach operations. His phone numbers in the GRanite exchange filled pages of reports. GRanite 6-1541, Mickey's home, and GRanite 3-9069, the Carousel ice cream parlor, were the two most popular.

The FBI proudly reported, "On 4/18/60 there was a 105-page list of persons who had been contacted by Cohen during the years 1958 and 1959 over the telephone."

The Los Angeles FBI office circulated copies of information about Mickey to agents in Cincinnati, Chicago, New York, Las Vegas, Boston, Pittsburgh, Philadelphia, Baltimore, New Orleans, Newark, Tampa, Cleveland, San Francisco, Miami, and Jacksonville.

Agents followed him all day, from the barber to a luncheon, made mention of every person he met, and kept records of all his women.

Someone had lit a fire under the FBI.

Robert Kennedy had never given up on his quest to get Mickey. For reasons that are unclear, he was a sitting duck, and had done little to protect himself. The social and political climate was changing, but Mickey wasn't.

The beginning of the sixties ushered in one of the most dramatic changes in pop culture the U.S. had seen in decades. Bellbottoms were in, while the sexual revolution, spearheaded by Playboy magazine, increased illegal drug usage, defining cult movies, and birth control, was starting to brew. Mickey wore thin white ties with his banker gray suits. All his white dress shirts had a blue-threaded "Mickey" embroidered near the pocket. His briefcase had a prominent gold engraved "Mickey." He still looked dapper, despite ballooning up to over one hundred sixty-five pounds, hardly his old fighting weight. He would consistently tell everyone he had gone straight. "Rehabilitated" was the key word.

It appeared that things had come to a grinding halt with another tax indictment on September 16, 1960. An arrest would follow. This time the IRS accused him of forgetting about $374,000 in taxes from 1956 through 1958, plus interest dating back to 1945. The thirteen-count indictment was almost a carbon copy of his previous trial and specifically named four additional counts, one for each unregistered Cadillac. Mickey claimed that the cars belonged to other people, like his sister. The *New York Times* now referred to him as a "former underworld figure."

Why didn't he pay his taxes this time around? Did he think he was immune after one prosecution? Either he was naïve, stupid, over-chutzpahed, or some strangely unique combination reserved for those empowered by our culture. People like Mickey actually believed that they could get away with anything, like their modern white-collar counterparts. Even after his first prison stay, he spent thousands in cash every month, and threw the money around publicly at night. He still liked to pick up the check, even if it meant borrowing money from people he spotted in the same restaurant or club. What motivated a man to buck an already angry government?

The exchanges between the FBI and the Department of Justice indicated how pleased everyone was with Mickey's new indictment. A lot of back patting ensued. The FBI tracked rumors that he had arrangements to leave the country by boat. They monitored commercial shipping firms and warned them about participating in escapes. Mickey's contacts were extensive, and it would have been relatively easy to leave by plane, particularly if he chose Mexico, where he occasionally had traveled. The FBI contacted police officials in Rome and London to see if they had any information on him or if anyone he knew had access to a ship. That could have been dozens of different suspects, and multiple shipping lines.

The aggressive IRS agents seized six cartons of jewelry, including a $25,000 ring, to serve as evidence and perhaps as repayment for back taxes.

Mickey was expressive:

> I just had a birthday September 4 and all those gifts were engraved and monogrammed. But no receipts! So they're in my apartment four hours and we go outside and they've got the street blocked off and there's a crowd out there. People standing there eating sandwiches and cokes and a guy drives up in a truck and starts sellin' coffee! Some secret indictment! You'd think it was one of those Hollywood premieres, with sirens blown' all over the place!

He likely made some calls to tip off the media while the agents were going through his apartment. An expert at drumming up a circus, he wanted to make the most of the opportunity. The story aired on the radio before the agents left with their booty.

As a crusader for public decency, he made a point of how painful it was to hear the children standing outside his residence shouting, "Hurray for you, Mickey!"

Then his self-effacing remarks hit home to his faithful public: "No matter we got a juvenile delinquency problem. They build up somebody as a hero who shouldn't be looked at as a hero."

Mickey blamed dishonest officials and the rigged carnivals for the rise in youth crime. "I'm 47 now, don't forget, and I got a different viewpoint," he added.

After his arrest, he posted $25,000 bail. He was in deep trouble, but he didn't act like it.

On September 27, 1960, Mickey flew with attorney Jack Dahlstrum on American Airlines to Washington National Airport. While in town, he wisely used public phones, but it was too late to worry about wiretaps.

The business trip would turn into a dog-and-pony show. First stop; check in at the Statler Hilton, the exquisite eighteenth-century Italian Renaissance structure, at Washington and Park Avenues. Mickey asked for a suite but instead received adjoining rooms 601 and 603. This confused the FBI, who reported that he was alone, yet he was with Dahlstrum, according to another of their memos. Then he was off for a brief visit to columnist Drew Pearson's house on Dunbarton Avenue. The FBI would eventually realize that whenever he was in town he regularly stopped by to see Pearson. This time he was lining up his defense team for the new tax evasion trial, and Pearson's column and connections could only have been helpful.

Mickey would end the first day calling for room service, and dining alone in his mock suite. Later that evening he mailed letters in the lobby, hardly the life of someone so famous, and opted to be alone.

The serenity vanished quickly. A local reporter named Tom Donnelly from Washington NBC affiliate WRC-TV featured Mickey in an interview on September 28, 1960, and followed up with a lengthy newspaper article. Many newspapers carried similar articles to Donnelly's, as often was the case.

Star-struck Donnelly was tickled to be in Mickey's presence, "at his invitation."

Mickey, seemingly unaware of media knowledge on his background, wondered how Donnelly located him since he registered in the hotel as "Meyer Cohen."

Donnelly's byline in the *Washington Daily News* was entitled "Shooting Down Memory Lane," and couldn't have been more appropriate for Mickey. He really did go down memory lane with him while the two men sat in a coffee shop and looked at old pictures of Mickey. Thorough Donnelly had shots of everyone from Candy Barr to Johnny Stompanato.

Despite the poor timing of the publicity, Mickey behaved like a true celebrity while Donnelly gobbled up his every word. He had adopted the popular theory that there was no Mafia; the media had created a Sicilian conspiracy to sell their product, and he dismissed the massive effort completely. Donnelly discussed Mickey's friendship with Drew Pearson, who was worried about the country's future. He confessed that his visit to the nation's capital wasn't all social: he had attorneys in town to help with his case.

Donnelly made sure to mention that Mickey lived an honest and decent life.

While in Washington, Mickey openly sat for interviews with any journalist who was interested. Myra MacPherson, of the *Evening Star*, ran with MICKEY COHEN IN TOWN LOOKING FOR LAWYER. He had plans to meet with former assistant attorney general Thurman Arnold, who was then in private practice.

MacPherson met Mickey at the Statler Hilton in Washington. She took notice of her dapper subject: "For a man up to his thinning black hair in back taxes, he looked expensively dressed in a sharply creased suit and gleaming, black shoes he stopped to polish twice. He was clean shaven and smelled as sweet as the roses in the flower shop he once owned."

Mickey cut the meeting short with her, since he was on the way to see Arnold. Then he was off to New York to locate witnesses for his case. He needed to be back in Los Angeles by October 4. MacPherson noticed that he tipped the bellman twenty dollars for helping him with his briefcase. Her article included Mickey's recalcitrant description of his financial life, insisting that he lived on loans from people whom he had helped when he was at the top, and there was no money to tax. His persecution story had worn thin.

While in New York looking for more legal muscle, Mickey posted $1,000 bail after his arrest on a Thursday night for hanging around with known criminals Anthony and Joseph Stassi, aged fifty and fifty-four, respectively. The pinch took place outside the Warwick Hotel, built by Mickey's friend William Randolph Hearst for Marion Davies. Newspapers around the country mentioned his $300 suit and his custom-made shoes. Police said that he carried $2300 in cash.

From the time of his prison release, until his new indictment, punch-drunk Mickey had carried on in exactly the same manner that had ruined him in the first place. He had too much undeclared cash to appear legitimate, even to the most liberal investigator, and this time the national mood had shifted against organized crime.

26.

Time Out for Politics

Despite all his cumulative troubles and his dreadful relationship with the Kennedys, Mickey still played his role as an honorary member of the developing Rat Pack. Whether it was social or politics, his efforts never ceased, not even while he waited for his pending new tax trial.

During his tenure, all of his well-known contacts may have helped his business and publicity, but in later years, those same associations led many to place him at the core of the worst-case conspiracy theories, a voyeuristic peek between the sheets of celebrities and politicians.[1]

Insinuations and direct accusations exist regarding Mickey's specific connections to both Kennedy assassinations, the suspicious death of Marilyn Monroe, and the extensive efforts to cover up the horrific events.

Like Woody Allen's Zelig, Mickey pops up in a series of unlikely historic episodes, alternatively disguised as a Machiavellian politician, two-faced lover, or confidant. Beyond accusers' sometimes-amusing agenda-motivated claims, including anti-Semitic overtones, are theories based on his unusual liaisons, connecting him to nefarious national and international activities.

Theorists blame Mickey and Meyer Lansky, because of their extensive Israeli interests, for a variety of American tragedies. National Jewish organizations were continually fundraising for Israel, and the Jewish mob was no exception, protecting the larger community from anti-Semites, as they had done locally for generations. Charitable and political connections to Israel provided the Jewish syndicate recognition, legitimacy, and the approval of their established mainstream brethren. Fundraising was the proper entry to upscale synagogues, country clubs, and Jewish-sponsored events.

Mickey certainly enjoyed hobnobbing with the Jewish elite, but he instinctively wanted to protect the Jewish state. Israel remained the central political issue for him during the 1960 presidential election.

Clearly, Menachem Begin, an Israeli acquaintance of his, or any politician, was not befriending Mickey for Las Vegas comps or the female companionship he supplied. However, it would have benefited Begin or any Israeli operative to have inside information about John Kennedy. Was JFK a friend to Israel? Could the Jews count on Kennedy? If elected, the fate of Israel would be in his hands, and Mickey knew that as well as anyone.[2]

He had abstained from helping JFK: "Frank [Sinatra] didn't particularly ask me to do anything for the Kennedy campaign." Not that Mickey avidly volunteered, or the Kennedys wanted anything to do with him. Despite his friendship with Nixon, Mickey did acknowledge that he thought Kennedy was the best of the bunch seeking the presidency.

Nixon's defeat by Kennedy in 1960 was no help to Mickey's cause. Not only was the fate of Israeli support unknown, but his own Washington connections were dramatically diminished—the Kennedys would never help him, particularly with his tax dilemma. Author John Davis referred to him as one of the Kennedys' "most determined enemies."[3]

Mickey said that the Democrats stole the election in Chicago, and Republicans had ample reason to believe him. Mobster Sam Giancana would boast about how he put JFK in the White House. Mickey confessed the mob's political realities: "I know that certain people in the Chicago organization knew that they had to get John Kennedy in. There was no thought that they were going to get the best of it with John Kennedy. See, there may be different guys running for an office, and none of them may be the solution to what's best for a combination…"

The Giancanas in writing their book were privy to some of the details:

> To assure the election's outcome, guys either trucked people from precinct to precinct and poll to poll so they could vote numerous times or stood

menacingly alongside voting booths, where they made it clear to prospective voters that all ballots were to be cast for Kennedy.

Mobsters like Giancana and Rosselli expected special treatment in return. Mickey knew that Sinatra spoke to all the Kennedys, including Joe, requesting a soft touch from the new regime. Robert Kennedy left Sinatra cold, and Giancana lost confidence in Sinatra's Kennedy connection.

Many also reported cheating by the Republicans, but obviously not at the skill level of the Democrats, whose own mob machine out-foxed Nixon's mobsters.

While Mickey had a polarized association with the Kennedys, he had a perverse one with Marilyn Monroe, whom he does not mention in his memoir. Former investigator Gary Wean had observed Mickey's handsome boys Sam LoCigno and Georgie Piscitelle, escorting Marilyn all over town, including Barney Ruditsky's Plymouth House and a motel on Van Nuys Boulevard in the Valley. On one occasion Wean heard a bedroom recording of Marilyn, part of Mickey's extortion racquets. Mickey had tapes of her having sex with both Georgie and Sam. He thought that his attractive professional pimp Piscitelle could persuade her to talk about her dalliances with JFK. He believed that he could leverage Kennedy once he started having sex with Marilyn. Blackmail was no stranger to Mickey; it was part of the business.

The hazy source for the above material is a party girl named Mary Mercadante, who also worked for Georgie, and became eager to turn against Mickey since Georgie found Marilyn more attractive. According to Wean, Mercadante also told him, "Cohen got mad and told Georgie to stick with Marilyn and pour drinks or pills down her, whatever it takes and find out what John Kennedy intended to do about financing Israel."

Mickey definitely wanted a closer connection to JFK, and it was through Monroe that he got that link. He was the king when it came to manipulation. While some credit Sinatra with making the Monroe connection to the White House—Sinatra introduced Marilyn to JFK at Peter Lawford's Malibu beach house, a popular show biz hangout—there is evidence that it was really Mickey. The Lawford compound was renamed "High Anus Port," likely by Rat Pack wordsmith Sammy Cahn. Everyone but Kennedy sister Pat Lawford seemed aware that the locale was the "in" place for wild sex. Commented Marilyn Monroe, who had taken to hair dye jobs below the waist, "Poor Pat's so out of touch... She probably thinks we're playing football" (the popular Kennedy pastime).

The shared credit goes to Mickey pal comedian and Rat Pack regular Joey Bishop for making the *shidech*—Yiddish for "match." According to Wean, Bishop was personally responsible for setting up JFK with Marilyn during the presidential campaign in 1960. "It was Joey Bishop that came up with the idea of a wild party for JFK. He talked Lawford into it." Wean persists based on ethnic bonds: "Bishop was a Jew and real tight with Cohen"; and further makes his case: "Bishop knew Kennedy would be taken by the Monroe sex appeal."

When it came to women, Mickey and the Rat Pack passed them around like dispensable commodities. The mob and show business crowds mingled in a very small community, where any attractive starlet-in-training would be introduced around as part of an unspoken courtesy. Mickey, JFK, and Sinatra dated some of the same women. On occasion, Mickey told Sinatra to stop sending the shared women to Washington—some brought to the White House under cover of night. Mickey claimed that JFK needed two to three women per day. Marilyn would confide the details to Sinatra's assistant George Jacobs, outlining JFK's obsession with sex. The locations included fancy suites at the Plaza in New York, as well as broom closets at the Vegas Sands. "That guy [JFK] would say *anything* to score!" Gossipy Monroe blabbed that he suffered from premature ejaculation, something she preferred to attribute to her irresistible charms, and his preoccupation with the presidency. She preferred Sinatra in bed. "He's the best... And *I* should know." Sinatra would never forgive the boys for arranging a Monroe tryst with Robert Kennedy.[4] It was likely during RFK's Hollywood romp with screenwriter Budd Schulberg and movie macher Jerry Wald for production of the younger Kennedy's anticrime book, *The Enemy Within*. Former Monroe husband Joe DiMaggio did his best to bar the entire Rat Pack from Marilyn's funeral.

"Frank [Sinatra] got him [JFK] all the broads he could ever have used... I guess they preferred to go to bed with John Kennedy instead of Mickey Cohen, you know—Frank Sinatra instead of Mickey Cohen," Mickey surmised in later years.

Not all the political ladies declined Mickey's company, and he made of point of emphasizing the quality of his philandering: "And these girls were not unknowns. They were all starlets."

The Kennedy list featured Judith Exner Campbell,[5] Angie Dickinson, Jayne Mansfield, Kim Novak, and the aforementioned Marilyn Monroe. Lesser famous names included Mary Meyer,[6] and the unknown blondes from the White House secretarial pool whom JFK codenamed "Fiddle and Faddle." Jackie Kennedy preferred the term "White House dogs." The White House was not off limits for JFK's guests.

Many linked Exner to Mickey, particularly since she was close to clothier and Mickey associate Sy Devore, who dressed the Rat Pack, and had run Slapsy Maxie's.

Exner, who first met Dean Martin at age seventeen, would eventually work her way up to JFK after an introduction by Sinatra, but not before a dalliance with papa Joe Kennedy, who loved his stays at the Sinatra-Lawford-Giancana Lake Tahoe Cal-Neva Lodge and Casino. When visiting Sinatra in Palm Springs, Joe Kennedy insisted that Sinatra cover his expenses for his "date" with the then Judy Campbell. She once told a press conference that she gave up sex with Sinatra because he was too kinky. Sinatra's public answer: "Hell hath no fury like a hustler with a literary agent."

Sinatra maintained an apartment, complete with private pool, at the Sands Hotel in Vegas. At this poolside lair, Exner had her first of many dinners with JFK, with whom she would carry on an affair until 1962. Sinatra also introduced her to Sam Giancana in Florida. She dated Kennedy and martini-drinker Giancana at the same time and in her book mentions that Kennedy was fond of the occasional ménage a trois. Both he and Giancana spoke on the telephone with Exner's impressionable mother, who was pleased that her daughter was dating such important men.[7]

Thin-built Robert Blakely, former chief counsel and staff director of the House Select Committee on Assassinations, links Exner's promiscuity to JFK's demise: "From the mob's point of view, Kennedy had been compromised. He had crossed the line. In the Greek sense, the liaison with Judith Campbell was, we came to believe, Kennedy's fatal flaw, the error in judgment for which the gods would demand their due." The mob viewed Kennedy as vulnerable, perhaps too much like them.

For the Exner introduction and likely many other reasons, Jackie Kennedy couldn't stomach Sinatra.[8] She was happy when he fell out of favor with the entire Kennedy circle, and they refused to stay at his Palm Springs residence, opting instead for Bing Crosby's house. This followed a visit from FBI Director Hoover to President Kennedy identifying the Exner-Giancana connection. Peter Lawford, Rat Packer and husband of Kennedy's sister Pat, who himself had been initially rejected by patriarch Joseph P. Kennedy, would take the blame. Longtime friend Sam Giancana would hold Sinatra accountable for his own political downfall.[9]

After JFK's election, there were always problems with Sinatra's Rat Pack associations. Columnists Dorothy Kilgallen and Ruth Montgomery, who worked for Hearst, needled the White House about its relationship with the fabled entertainers who had ties to Mickey and other nationally connected mobsters. Kilgallen wrote during the election: "The situation was becoming especially delicate in Massachusetts, where important church figures don't quite understand the Sinatra-Kennedy connection."

Writer Joe Hyams, Mickey's friend and a Hollywood mainstay, published articles that were also critical of the Rat Pack for their seedy associations. Sinatra tried to push the accusations aside: "The various guilds that are part of my professional life are the only organized groups to which I belong."

Peter Lawford did his share of public spin:

> Now look—that Clan business—I mean that's hokey. I mean it makes us sound like children—like we all wore sweat shirts that said "The Clan" and Frank with a whistle around his neck. They make us sound so unsavory. We're just a lot of people on the same wavelength. We like each other. What's wrong with that?

Comedian Joey Bishop milked the subject with "Clan, Clan, Clan. I'm sick and tired of hearing things about the Clan—just because a few of us guys get together once a week with sheets over our heads!"

When Sinatra and hard-drinking cocaine user Lawford first opened Puccini, at fancy 224 South Beverly Drive, Mickey was one of its famous regular customers. He remained a recalcitrant Sinatra friend, something that Lawford despised. Lawford did not like Sinatra's mob associations. When Puccini first opened, "Mr. Television" Milton Berle quipped, "If Kennedy is elected, will Puccini's be the summer White House?" (Puccini had four other partners whose names never appeared in the papers.)

On February 12, 1961, at twelve-fifteen in the morning, an angry Mickey stormed inside Puccini and headed for comedian Red Skelton's manager, who was dining with actor George Raft.

The eight customers and the bartender froze to watch him zoom in on his target. Like a well-scripted B-movie, two goons took their places inside the front door to stand guard. Red's manager was having an affair with Red's wife—or so Mickey thought. He actually jumped up on the booth's table and started kicking Red's manager.

Raft tried to intercede but Mickey was firm. "You shut up, Raft, or you know what you're gonna get."

Mickey slapped the manager around yelling, "This is for you, you no good S.O.B." He put him in the hospital.

Outside the restaurant, the Lilliputian fighter and his *shtarkers* met a third party, who upon hearing what had happened walked inside and informed Red's ailing manager, "You should consider yourself lucky, you're supposed to be dead now."

Red's manager denied to Beverly Hills police that any physical attack took place. He also insisted that he was dining alone that night, but did say that Mickey had given him some sound advice concerning Red Skelton.

The story mushroomed through the media. The police regularly sent eager undercover cops to feast at chichi Puccini. The restaurant now had a national reputation as a Mafia hangout for Sinatra's friends. When business slacked off Lawford blamed Mickey, and overlooked the larger picture of Sinatra's need to associate with unsavory characters.

On May 4, 1961, forty-nine-year-old Max Tannenbaum was the victim of a hit outside a bar owned by Max Lerner. Mickey's crony Tannenbaum survived, nearly lost an eye, and faced misdemeanor charges for having burglar's tools in his car.

Despite all the publicity over the discovery of organized crime in America, on May 5, 1961, the FBI closed all its extensive Anti-Racketeering files on Mickey. It appeared that the IRS had nailed him again, and the FBI felt confident in the case.

27.

Down for the Count

Like celebrities in trouble multiple times today, Mickey could not bring himself to accept that he could be prosecuted a second time for the same crime.

The indictment had moved ahead efficiently. He faced a maximum sentence of thirty-two years and a $65,000 fine. If the judge and jury imposed the worst-case scenario, his life would be over. The *New York Times* noted that he was forty-seven.

When it was time to face the music, unlike today, there were no trial experts to coach Mickey. He always walked into court with the same story. His plan was to convince the judge and jury of the silly notion that appeared in the papers; he lived on loans. He must have sounded like a child caught in a lie, while thoroughly prepared prosecutors listened to the fable. What could his attorneys have been thinking? Did his defense team roll over after pressure from federal authorities and high-ranking politicians? His attorneys had many prior opportunities to prepare him with better records and functioning shell companies that shifted untraceable cash. Tax attorneys had already done the same for much of the syndicate, but not for Mickey, who left himself vulnerable.

At the request of lead IRS agent Donald F. Bowler, seventeen tax districts had reported to the IRS to help nail Mickey on the new tax evasion rap. The under $400,000 sum appeared paltry compared to the huge amounts of cash generated by his and other mobsters' action.

The *Los Angeles Times* described Mickey as five foot three, with thin black hair and elevator shoes. He audaciously showed up at his trial with lists of people who had lent him money, including his own mother, Fanny Cohen (Fanny Friedman—she was married to Charles Friedman), Sarah Cohen (Mrs. Sammy Cohen, his brother Sammy's widow), and comedian Jimmy Durante, who purportedly paid part of Mickey's fines the first time around. He behaved as if his life was going to continue without interruption.

The trial covered everything the agents could dig up. Not all parties invited by the well-armed prosecutors were located, and several said that they had never heard of Mickey. The prosecution called a monstrous 194 witnesses. The process generated 8,000 pages of reporter's transcript, 947 government exhibits, and 27 defense exhibits. The witness list at the trial read like a who's who of Hollywood. Ben Hecht, Jerry Lewis, Red Skelton, and welterweight Don Jordan all testified. Stripper Candy Barr and "dancer" Beverly Hills added the surreal air that had become part of all Hollywood-related trials. (Mickey felt that Hills' testimony didn't help his case.)

Mickey's own nephew Allan Weiner testified regarding almost $23,000 in checks that he had issued or endorsed for him. Weiner said that he didn't remember any of the checks, although the signatures looked like his. He maintained that his handwriting was evolving, related to year-long psychiatric meetings. He had worked for Mickey attorney Paul Caruso at Mickey's flower shop and the Carousel ice-cream parlor that Mickey's mother officially owned. He didn't remember storing fifty grand in his personal account by age nineteen, with some of the money originally earmarked for his uncle.

U.S. Attorney Sheridan grilled Mickey's gray-haired sister Lillian Weiner. She had been the owner and president of Michael's Greenhouse, but had no recollection of $30,000 in cash deposits made to the business during Mickey's tenure as its super salesman. She acknowledged that monthly deposits usually ran between $300 and $7,000, with only one $800 amount paid regularly by a chain of restaurants. Mickey's sister remained firm, and said that she did not recall the reason for several deposits in the thousands. She was also unable to recognize any signatures, with one exception, "that one could be my signature." Her credo became, "I don't remember right now."

Estranged attorney Paul Caruso took the stand and discussed his fee dispute with Mickey. He said that Mickey told him, "Don't worry about it—you'll get paid." Caruso said that he was still out $7,900.

Mickey's attorney Jack Dahlstrum approached the bench, and after a three-minute conference, Judge Boldt dismissed Caruso, but said that he should make himself available for furthering questioning.

Aubrey V. Stemler, the vending machine manufacturer, agreed that he had given Mickey loans totaling $15,000 in exchange for a healthy ten percent of Mickey's life story. Stemler's contract called for a repayment of the money at six percent if no motion picture materialized.

Joseph E. Bishop, manager to Ben Blue and the entertainer's Santa Monica club, only received two percent of the movie venture for $7,500.

Despite Mickey's hapless first meeting with Jackie Gleason, the unlikely and chubby duo developed a decent relationship down the road. Former fight promoter Barney Peller testified that he had loaned Mickey $1,000 since Mickey promised Gleason the lead in a movie called *Gus the Great*. Peller had owned the rights to a novel that was the basis for the screenplay. At the trial, he said that Gleason had agreed to do the movie, but later backed out when he lost the rights. He also paid bills for Mickey when he stayed at the Terrace Hilton in Cincinnati, and on one occasion sent him $1,500 in money orders.

Publisher and evangelist W. C. Jones had sent attorney Rexford Eagan, who worked with Jerry Geisler, a $1,000 check to pay for Mickey's legal fees. Jones also testified that he had forked over $5,000 to Mickey during his alleged conversion to Christianity.

As mentioned earlier, the Krause family had given Mickey $25,000 for an interest in his book and movie. With a straight face, Dr. Krause told the prosecutor that he had expected Mickey to commit himself for psychiatric study in return for the loan. His interest in Mickey's theatrical venture was worth a huge ten percent, according to the contract. His sister had sent Mickey an additional $10,000, through Chicago mob lawyer George Bieber. The psychiatrist had halfheartedly asked Mickey to refund his money.

Dr. Krause told the crowded courtroom, "…greatly interested in Mr. Cohen when I first met him…gentle nice man." He told the jury that his own movie aspirations were minimal and that he was more interested in Mickey's "past history, present behavior, present symptomology, the way he behaves and what motivates his behavior."

More of the doctor's own personality profile materialized when oil lease dealer Nate Suess took the stand and said that Krause was a "big speculator." The Hollywood Boulevard oilman had introduced Krause to Mickey.

Theatrical agent Lou Irwin had given Mickey a grand to invest in the movie on his life. Irwin took the Hollywood high road; a thousand bucks was nothing to hand out: he always handed out cash at the end of the week for actors to survive the weekend.

Phil Packer, the greeter at Rondelli's, home of the Whalen shooting, had loaned Mickey $9,500. Mickey had given him a diamond watch and fancy ring for security.

When asked about his association with bank president Harold Brown, Mickey answered, "I helped him make money and so naturally he thought kindly of me."

One of Mickey's interior decorators, William K. Howard, tried to come to his defense even though Mickey still owed him about $8,000. Howard had designed a stainless steel kitchen, remote controlled draperies, stocked the dining area cabinets with china and silver service, and installed a typewriter and adding machine in the business section of the apartment.

He overstated his case when he said that Mickey "always paid the tabs wherever he went." He made a huge mistake when he said that Mickey sometimes carried thirty grand in cash. He, and many others who testified, were either ignorant of, or didn't care about, the tax laws. Howard, upon further questioning and perhaps a few dirty looks from the defense team, recanted and said that he hadn't really see the money, perhaps only a $100 bill.

The IRS contributed many unreported Mickey money exchanges as evidence. The twenty-three grand front money for Michael's Greenhouse had come from colorful attorney George Bieber. After prison, Mickey had received welcome home money from Thomas Vaughn, a New Orleans businessman. Babe McCoy, a famous boxing impresario, who occasionally suffered from his friendship with Mickey—Chief Parker was convinced that McCoy fixed fights—had also chipped in $6,000. Restaurateur Morris Orloff, who once won a suit against the Los Angeles Turf Club for denying him entry based on his unsavory reputation, gladly added his ten grand to the "restore Mickey foundation."

Mickey could not provide any evidence of a consistent form of legitimate income, and didn't try. He was a victim of his own sloppy accounting, dinosaur record keeping, and blinding stubbornness.

The convoluted messy list of non-reported income had one fairy tale ending. Mickey had taken over two grand from Cincinnati tree surgeon Charles Schneider; Barney Peller had introduced the two men in Cincinnati. Schneider wanted his twelve-year-old daughter Janet to get into show business—who better to ask than impresario Mickey? Mickey first introduced her to Red Skelton and Frank Sinatra. The Schneiders met everyone, from Danny Thomas to Bobby Darin, and Edward G. Robinson to Don Rickles. Janet appeared on television with Louis Armstrong and Jerry Lewis. Schneider also gave Mickey another $2,500 for his life story. He told authorities that he had no complaints about Mickey.

Jerry Lewis, on Wednesday, May 24, told the packed courtroom how he had loaned Mickey $5,000 in cash without any security or written contract "because he needed help." He also spoke about how he had helped further the career of young Janet Schneider, arranged a guest appearance for her on his television show, but despite her talent could not hire her for the entire 1957–1958 season because of skittish sponsors who preferred big name acts.

Jerry explained seriously how he had entered into discussions as a movie producer for Mickey's life story, citing Robert Mitchum as a better casting choice. He said that any production utilizing his skill "should deal with levity—for some strange reason that's what people expect. It would be difficult for me to apply myself to this [the Mickey Cohen story] concept."

When Jerry was ready to leave the courtroom Red Skelton took his turn in the hot-seat-turned-P.R. chair.

He taunted Red. "Let's see how funny you are going to be. Let's see you get a laugh."

Red did. The standing room only crowd got its "money's worth."

Skelton typified Hollywood's cynical wink-wink attitude toward the mob. He had met Mickey in early 1957 at Los Angeles International Airport when they were seeing off mutual friends. Mickey kept up the relationship, often sending greeting cards and gifts for the Skelton children.

Mickey was a close enough friend to ask Skelton for five grand at a time—his regular quick-cash routine at dinner. Red always paid.

When Assistant U.S. Attorney Thomas Sheridan asked Red if he had any financial dealings with Mickey, Red replied, "None whatsoever—except paying for this trial, as a taxpayer, I mean."

He pressed Red and asked, "You pay your taxes do you, Mr. Skelton?"

Red did not feel he had to succumb to the prosecutor's style. "You know I do. I'm allergic to that bay up there."

He explained that Mickey was welcome at rehearsals for his television show and often brought friends. He could not remember much about singer Janet.

"She couldn't have sung because of the facilities in our house. We have a Hammond organ and nobody can play the thing," Red told the judge.

Judge Boldt jumped into the act. "Can't you play it yourself?"

"Yes," answered Red, his head bowed. "But just by the numbers on the book."

The judge jumped at the opportunity to illustrate his show business acumen and said, "You're not a bad straight man."

Red discussed the $15,000 that Billy Graham had promised Mickey to attend the revival meeting in Madison Square Garden. He also said that Graham had promised Mickey an additional $25,000 if he converted to Christianity.

During his eclectic casting call, Mickey had also asked the lean six-foot comedian to consider the lead in his movie. Red had politely declined the role, and Mickey later confessed to him that he was just fishing for a star name: "Well, it was just a shot in the dark."

When asked by the prosecutor about appearing in Mickey's movie, Red stated the obvious. "I couldn't see myself—or I should say, Mickey—as a tall redheaded fellow." It drew big laughs.

During the hearing, Mickey brazenly admitted that he had run a gambling operation in the Ambassador Hotel during the late forties with the imprimatur of hotel operators Myer and David Schine, of Schine Enterprises. Perhaps he thought that the admission might distract his prosecutors, and he would end up pleading to a lesser crime.

He bragged to his interrogators about the high-roller entourage that floated in and out of the luxurious hotel. "…I've seen $30,000 to $50,000 exchange hands in one roll." (The *Los Angeles Times* ran a quote from the hotel management on June 21, 1961: "Mickey Cohen did not operate any gambling concerns in this hotel to our knowledge. If he did, he did it surreptitiously.")

Mickey also owned seven gaming operations throughout the United States and three within Los Angeles. Each one brought in over $80,000 per month. The big casinos were at Dincara, San Bernardino, Lake Arrowhead, and Watts.

Judge Boldt had made sure that the jurors, seven men and five women, had the thirty-nine page index to all the material introduced at the eight-week trial. The federal judge lectured the jury for nearly three hours. The agents had compiled a strong case against Mickey by overloading the evidence on an already tainted dossier.

The jury heard final arguments on June 27. The forty days in court ended on June 30. Reporters speculated that Mickey might get forty years, one for each day of the trial. The jury took only twenty-two and one-half hours to put Mickey away; they convicted him on eight counts, while acquitting him on five others. The inevitable had become a reality, and attorney Bieber could not save him.

Before sentencing, Judge Boldt made his position clear regarding Mickey's obvious business style: "...he has followed a fantastically extravagant way of living without paying any income tax...without productive employment or visible means of self-support..." The sometimes-affable judge sentenced Mickey to fifteen years and $30,000 in fines on Monday, July 1, 1961.

Mickey clasped his hands and bowed his head when he heard the verdict.

He took time later outside the courtroom to make his feelings known. "They convicted me because I am Mickey Cohen. They thought they had to." He may not have realized how close the statement was to the truth.

Mickey was the victim of multiple vendettas. In addition to his criminal activities, his punishment was as much for being a long-term pain in the ass and consistent wise guy to his enemies. His public notoriety had come back to haunt him. Because of his celebrity, authorities insisted on the most severe approach.

Mechanisms existed for early release, with some based on good behavior and many mobsters bought early parole through political channels. Authorities offered Mickey an opportunity to escape any incarceration by ratting on Paul Ricca and Tony Accardo. He declined, and remained a *stand-up guy*.

To add insult to the injury of a repeat trial, the Los Angeles police confiscated his remaining custom-built Cadillac.

Mickey said goodbye to his regular routine: the Beverly Hills Health Club, Gaiety Deli, Largo Night Club, Cloisters, Crescendo, Carousel Ice Cream Parlor, Coconut Grove, La Rue, Top's On The Strip, the Moulin Rouge, and Slate Brothers.

On July 28, he flew in a Border Patrol plane to take him back to the hellhole Alcatraz. When he began his fifteen-year sentence, the prison population consisted of only sixty-four inmates; it could house between 260 and 275. The dismal structure was in disrepair; not that it was ever the darling of the penal system.

"It was a crumbling dungeon. At the time I was in Alcatraz it was only for personal enemies of Bobby Kennedy," he said retrospectively.

RFK, appointed attorney general in 1961, announced that Mickey would continue to be a priority target, and initiated a new full investigation. It was as much a vendetta for the hot exchanges during the McClellan hearings as it was a need to clean up organized crime.[1]

Mickey was taken by surprise.

But nobody in my line of work had an idea that he [JFK] was going to name Bobby Kennedy attorney general. That was the last thing anyone

276

thought. In fact, he had just openly promised in his campaign that he wouldn't name Bobby as attorney general.

From the mob's perspective, this was hardly a small double-cross.

While he was in prison, microphone surveillance continued in many of his businesses and associations, including the Dunes Hotel in Vegas. Robert Kennedy had started the new wiretaps and eavesdropping, and the system would continue through 1965 and beyond, under Attorney General Katzenbach.

The convoluted legal process made appeals difficult. After much legal wrangling, authorities begrudgingly released Mickey on October 17, 1961, having served eighty-two days of his long sentence.[2]

The *New York Times* mentioned that Mickey, now reported to be fifty years old, was unhappy because his now twenty-year-old blonde girlfriend Sandy Hagen did not meet him when authorities released him on bail.

He told reporters when he got off the prison launch at Fort Mason, "I expect to marry her as soon as I get permission... It depends on the advice of my attorneys and what the law permits."

The national attention to his plight forced FBI boss Hoover to answer letters from the public. Some constituents complained about Mickey's release.

Mickey lived up to the naysayers. He beat up a Teamsters Union picket, and stole his sign. The negative publicity complicated the ongoing appeals process for his attorneys.

Mickey was out on bail only two weeks when police arrested him. A grand jury had geared up to reopen the murder case of Jack "The Enforcer" Whalen, with new information about the missing murder weapon. Superior Judge Evelle J. Younger initially denied bail for Mickey. Multiple attorneys appealed the decision, including A. L. Wirin, Paul Augustine, Jr., Ward Sullivan, and Al Mathews.

Mickey told reporters, "What can I say? It's a complete roust."

The new Whalen indictment followed three days of closed-door sessions, pushed forward by persistent Deputy District Attorneys James Ford and Joseph Busch. Mickey voluntarily arrived for his booking with attorney Wirin, and bail bondsman Abe Phillips, the usual arrest entourage. Phillips always brought an old set of clothes for Mickey, since he dressed to the nines for the photographers, and then changed before entering his cell. He was soon out on bail.

Police also arrested handsome Georgie Piscitelle, now thirty, at his home on 8214 Sunset Boulevard, and listed his occupation as a liquor salesman. They arrested Joe DiCarlo, no longer Candy Barr's manager, at a café in Santa Monica.

Movie producer Roger Leonard was arrested as he arrived at University of Pennsylvania Hospital to visit his wife who had gall bladder problems. Leonard told police that he was working on filming scenes for his brother Herbert, the producer of the immensely popular television series *Route 66*.

David Marcus and Paul Augustine stood by their client Lo Cigno's earlier trial and issued a statement, "two years ago this was a classic self-defense case involving only LoCigno and Whalen and it still is."

At an appeal to reduce his prison sentence for tax evasion, Mickey played a television interview in which he appeared contrite, and appeared confident that he might get off.

At holiday time 1961, he was the focus of a feature story by Ron Rieder of the *Valley News*. Forty-eight-year-old Mickey included his twenty-year-old girlfriend Sandy Hagen in the piece told to Rieder, with both subjects benefiting differently from Mickey's revisionist aging. He lived in a rented house in Van Nuys, a less expensive neighborhood in the San Fernando Valley.[3]

"As long as he is quiet and doesn't cause any trouble around here, he is as good as any other neighbor," said a local.

"It's better than a bunch of drunks and rowdies," added another citizen.

From his lawn chair near the swimming pool, Mickey was soft-spoken and candid about his life. He wore a white sweater with his initials monogrammed over his heart. The doormat also had the initials "M C" carved in the center. Under the sunny California sun, Mickey reveled in telling the details of his home expenses, only two hundred a month, and "They even pay for gas and electric and a gardener takes care of the place." He complained about the lack of closet space; his clothes lacked organization, more were still in boxes. The hot water tank, of course, was not big enough to accommodate his unusual shower usage.

Rieder noted that aside from Mickey's pending tax appeal, he would go to trial on March 5 for the reopened Whalen case. A District Court of Appeal had set aside the original murder conviction in the murder, allowing the judge to order a second trial for LoCigno.

Mickey rehearsed the Whalen details again. "I've been shot at so many times, when I heard those shots, I just ducked. It was pretty dark in there anyway. I didn't even see the gun fired."

He and Sandy displayed the rings they had exchanged with her parents' blessing. The government forbade a marriage until the outcome of the tax case.

Another article in the *Nation* mentioned that Mickey's silk pajamas now cost $275.

Writer Joe Hyams, who also lived in the Valley, had replaced Hecht as the author of Mickey's life story. Mickey continued to shop the movie rights to any suckers who were impressed by the newspaper articles outlining his venture. The working title for Hyams' book was the unfortunate *The Poison Has Left Me.*

On January 12, 1962, the United States Court of Appeals affirmed Mickey's conviction and declined bail. U.S. Supreme Court Justice Douglas agreed with Mickey's interpretation; the IRS had convicted him twice for the same offense.

Sandy-the-girlfriend saw Mickey off as he again prepared for prison. He wore a cream-colored jacket and light slacks, brown and white shoes, and Hollywood sunglasses for the prison cruise.

Sandy lamented, "I'll wait for Mickey…and I'm going to try and lead a normal life despite the publicity."

After what appeared to be one last holiday season on the outside, Mickey headed back to Alcatraz on January 12. When he boarded the heavily guarded launch that would take him across the bay, he paused on the gangplank for photographs with his hands already cuffed.

On January 30, Justice Douglas issued a second release order, pending Supreme Court action and $100,000 bail. On February 17, Mickey was free on bail again.[4]

The second Whalen trial began. An actress named Ann Root testified against all the diners at the Italian dinner at Rondelli's. A USC psychology student with a penchant for dating people in the fast lane, she had hung around with Mickey and Joe DiCarlo.

Joey Bishop was dragged into the mix by DiCarlo's lawyer Harvey Byron, and somewhat came to Mickey's and DiCarlo's rescue. Author Shawn Levy spotted the irony in the moment. "All the creeps that Frank liked to run with, all the thugs whom Dean and Sammy worked for, all the awful shit Peter was in on—guess who was the only one ever to testify at a murder trial: Joey."

Bishop told the new jury that stripper Candy Barr's theatrical agent and four-year friend Joseph DiCarlo had invited him to dinner, but true to form, Bishop had cancelled. His own character assassination was his best defense for removing himself from the scene of the crime: "I have a reputation for not keeping dinner engagements. So, how could I have been there?"

Bishop spoke of his lengthy golf day; he claimed that he had played forty-five holes. He was too tired to drive to Rondelli's, but not tired enough to stay home. Bishop had invited DiCarlo to catch his act at the Cloister Club on the Strip later that evening.

Mickey's defense was simple: "It was the hottest place in town. So when the move was made to knock Whalen in, would I blow up my own joint?"

DiCarlo's was similar—why would he have invited Joey Bishop to dinner at Rondelli's the night of a planned hit?

The jury of eleven women and one man was deadlocked nine to three on April 10 after five days of deliberation. Superior Court Judge Lewis Drucker declared a mistrial without clarifying the disposition of the nine jurors.

Mickey waited for the final appeals process to run its course, and was back in custody on May 8, 1962. His attorneys had exhausted all avenues of appeal.

No dice.

Mickey told reporters when he surrendered on a Tuesday, "I don't feel too good about it."

Sandy Hagen stood by and cried in her handkerchief.

Mickey offered up his philosophy: "If the Supreme Court thinks this is the kind of sentence I should have, that's the way it's going to be."

Over two hundred people watched him as he held his own court outside the Civic Center Federal Building in Los Angeles. He wore a tan silk suit with a gold monogram on the pocket and dabbed cologne behind his ears as he spoke.

Attorney A. L. Wirin and bondsman Abe Phillips stood by him as he told reporters how he had visited his aged mother the night before.

Autograph seekers blocked Mickey's entry to the courtroom. He obliged his fans until Wirin called him away.

When the formalities ended, he made a final statement: "I always been decent and right."

He then kissed Sandy and said, "I followed the concept of life man should— except for that gambling operation."

Later, when it was time to leave the courtroom, Mickey picked up two brown paper bags that held his clean underwear and socks. The unflattering AP wire described the two towering marshals who sandwiched the "short, balding, plump little man" as he left for prison.

He returned to Alcatraz to resume his original sentence on May 14, 1962. His full term release date was December 13, 1976. His first parole eligibility date would be December 1966. The understanding of the FBI was that his Mandatory Release date was January 1972.

The changing political climate had influenced Mickey's harsh sentencing, had hurt his chances of successful appeal, and would likewise complicate early parole.

Ironically, 1962 was the year J. Edgar Hoover came out of the closet, not about his rumored sexual preferences, but about recognizing organized crime. The

FBI announced the astonishing turnaround, including the discovery of a ten-million-dollar white slave trade (a popular government and FBI term for prostitution) that catered to mob-controlled casinos and nightclubs.

The FBI bragged publicly that it had recovered over 17,000 stolen cars the previous year, an all-time record. The stagnant organization still clung to past victories, operated as a federal fat cat, and was afraid to risk its reputation by tackling the highest level of organized crime. While it appeared to have altered its political agenda with regard to Mickey's syndicate life, his prison life became the target of an unexpected full-scale intensive investigation.

By September 1962 the FBI employed 6,000 federal agents, and had the available work force and inclination to make Mickey's prison life a hardship. Alcatraz was already one of the worst examples of the penal system in the United States.

28.

Stripes But No Stars

Mickey and Al Capone were the only tax evaders ever sent to Alcatraz. Some said that it was cruel and unusual punishment for Mickey. Alcatraz was no Club Fed; the grim decrepit Rock was the worst example of malignant neglect.

Mickey was unable to come to terms with his fate and the substandard prison conditions that he thought he could improve. According to him, there were no playing cards, magazines, newspapers, televisions, or radios. The library was antiquated and filled with crumbling, yellowed pages. He was unable to get any candy, except perhaps during holidays.

He maintained his own protective clique: some very well-known criminals like Frankie Carbo, Freddie Stein, likeable Harlem boss Bumpy Johnson, and public enemy number one Alvin Karpis, who had worked the Barker-Karpis gang. Between all of their contacts, there must have been an occasional piece of candy to share.[1]

Mickey did confess that San Francisco's Paoli's restaurant was able to keep him stocked with prime steaks and fresh Italian peppers, which were smuggled into the prison inside loaves of bread. The prison guards ate regularly at Paoli's, courtesy of Mickey.

The truth of the matter concerning cuisine was that the prison chef would cook whatever the big boys in the house wanted, including Kosher corned beef on Mickey Cohen Day. Alcatraz had had a history of prison riots because of the substandard food. But during Mickey's stay, the cuisine included salads, fruit, multiple entrees, and desserts. That was the only good news.

JFK and RFK knew that Mickey needed politicians to support his early release. The Kennedys thought that he would cooperate if they dangled opportunities to leave. In October 1962, the brothers pressured him to spill whatever else he knew about Nixon, whose association with Mickey the Democrats naturally loved. Others like Adlai Stevenson had tried to get more of the Nixon story years earlier, but Mickey initially stood by his mixed morals: it would have been ratting on Nixon. Overall, he maintained a pragmatic rationale; he couldn't have given a damn about Nixon or any politician, and described him years later, "like the newspapers stigmatized him…a used-car salesman or a three-card monte dealer…a hustler." All he ever needed from any politician was "the best of what you've got going."

Democratic liberal politician Governor Pat Brown, who had been campaigning early for the 1962 election, contacted Mickey in prison. Brown was up for re-election in California against recently defeated presidential candidate Nixon. JFK personally sent Chief Deputy Attorney General Richard R. Rogan to take Mickey's statement, as Brown's emissary.

The politicians had Mickey in a tight spot; he told them more of what they wanted to hear, that he and many others like him had supported Nixon for years. He sent word to his brother Harry in Las Vegas to help Brown, whose chances looked good, with the election. The behind-bars lobbyist appeared to be lining up an early release, and through, of all people, the Kennedy Democratic machine.

It certainly didn't hurt Brown when Drew Pearson received Mickey's support to write articles on Nixon's mob connections, particularly the fundraiser at the Knickerbocker Hotel.[2] Pearson's "Washington Merry-Go-Round" column stayed with the Cohen-Nixon story for years, despite Nixon's purported friendship with Mickey. Pearson was a consistent Nixon basher, not only because of the conservative views expressed in "Washington Merry-Go-Round," but also because of Nixon's egregious and corrupt leanings.[3]

The IRS followed through and sued Mickey on December 26. U.S. Attorney Francis C. Whelan pursued the uncollected taxes dating back to 1945—$374,476.38, including interest.

Mickey moved from decayed Alcatraz[4] to Atlanta on February 27, 1963, where his predecessor by four years was Mafia family boss Vito Genovese (Don Vito).

Vito had had a job in the electric shop; it would become Mickey's. He also gave some of his personal belongings to Mickey, including a hot plate and a radio. Mickey was proud to take over for Vito, who ran his mob from his cell in Atlanta and who saw to it that Mickey received special attention, including access to a private shower. Mickey bought all the comforts possible with extra cash and cigarettes.

Attorney General Robert F. Kennedy was not satisfied with Mickey's assistance, and decided to make the most of his incarceration before his first parole date. He wanted extensive information about syndicated crime, and hoped to make Mickey an informant. Early in Mickey's Atlanta stay, Kennedy personally traveled to the prison to intimidate him, unexpectedly cornering him when he was about to shower.

With five reporters all holding cameras, Kennedy confronted nude Mickey and asked, "How the hell are ya gonna live fifteen years in this goddamn chicken coop?"

Mickey replied, "...Don't worry about me."

Kennedy all but told him he was a free man, if only he would "be a little cooperative."

Mickey declined to cooperate, covered himself with a towel, and moved toward the shower, again a *stand-up guy*. He was not a stoolie and did not regard Kennedy as a trustworthy confidant, but as an enemy.

RFK had made many enemies, and some like Jimmy Hoffa and Carlos Marcello plotted his demise. Marcello had also discussed the idea to murder JFK, in order to neutralize RFK's activities against organized crime.[5]

After rebuffing Kennedy, Mickey dug in for a long haul. Unlike Marcello on the outside, Mickey never publicly swore vengeance against RFK, who relentlessly pursued Marcello through deportation attempts and more McClellan hearings.

On Wednesday, August 14, 1963, a dramatic event changed fifty-year-plus Mickey's life forever. While he was watching the midday news, unstable fellow convict Berl Estes McDonald hit Mickey on the head with a three-foot, lead conduit pipe. McDonald would have had to scale a twelve-foot wall in the yard, an obvious breach of prison security, to reach Mickey.

The medical report included a left homonymous hemangioma field defect, triplegia involving left arms and legs, a compound comminuted depressed skull fracture with a three-centimeter depression, and brain damage that required the removal of thirty grams of macerated tissue from the right superior parietal region.

The neurosurgeon who relieved the pressure on Mickey's brain reported that his survival was in limbo for forty-eight hours. His blood pressure and pulse soon stabilized, and his respiration returned to normal. He could have easily died. He was unconscious for six hours after the beating, and thereafter mentally alert. The injury was serious enough to warrant surgery to implant a steel plate, which doctors initially held in abeyance pending his recuperation, but subsequently placed.

A week after the incident, medical officer Dr. Richard Yocum told Mickey's girlfriend Sandy Hagen, "It's a little bit early to assess any permanent damage. He's doing well, considering the damage that was done." He said that Mickey had weakness in the left arm, and some leg paralysis, but none of the symptoms were indicators of permanent damage. Although not reported by the doctor, Mickey had limited use of his right hand.

Investigators represented that McDonald acted independently, and charged him with assault with intent to murder. He had a history of violent acts against prisoners, and yet authorities cut his now fifty-year sentence down to twenty-five years at the time of the incident, resulting in little reprisal for his actions.[6]

Warden David M. Heritage tried to minimize Mickey's condition by publicly stating that he had only a compound depressed fracture. He stated that Mickey provoked McDonald during an argument in the prison shop, adding that the mob was not connected.

Heritage told reporters, "It was a personal disagreement between two prisoners."

McDonald later apologized for his actions and made sure that Mickey received the message. Mickey remained puzzled as to why inmates like McDonald had access to the general prison population instead of being isolated in special sections for the mentally unstable. He was not buying the authority's explanation that McDonald had gone to great lengths to reach his section of the prison.

On October 2, 1963, Mickey left for a federal medical prison in Springfield, Missouri, where he would undergo more extensive brain surgery. After the operation, he was unable to walk and lost the use of one arm. Doctors suspected he would never regain total use of his legs. His recuperation was slow, and began with daily four-hour physical therapy sessions at General Hospital in Los Angeles, where he had a twenty-four hour guard. When he returned to Springfield medical prison, he spent his first eleven months in deadlock—completely isolated from the prison population. The director of the clinic, Dr. De Armond Moore wanted to be certain that no further harm came to him. Mickey didn't agree with the recommendation, but had little choice in the matter.

When he was feeling better, he engaged Melvin Belli to initiate a lawsuit against the government over the beating incident, which Mickey insisted was preventable. This marked the beginning of his long-standing interest in prison reform.[7]

Many conspiracy theorists have linked Mickey and the mob to the Kennedy assassination of November 22, 1963, despite the timing of the McDonald attack and his recuperation. Money to help the mob cause was supposedly pouring in from unlikely sources, like California, where wealthy ranchers were angry with JFK for helping the farm workers. Even Robert Kennedy, without labeling the mob's role, later told Arthur Schlesinger, Jr., in New York's famous hamburger joint P. J. Clarke's, that the Warren Report "was a poor job." Gerald Posner wrote in his book *Case Closed*, as many believe today, that the JFK assassination has only one conclusion: one shooter, one bullet, no conspiracy.

Nevertheless, a few roads led to Mickey. Jim Garrison's investigation, Frank Mankiewicz's connecting JFK assassin Lee Harvey Oswald to David Ferrie/Ferret Man, and Ferrie's connection to Jack Ruby, Carlos Marcello, and Mickey all raised eyebrows. Author Michael Collins Piper cites Ferrie's employment from Carlos Marcello in New Orleans, down the hall from Jim Braden. Dallas, the city where the assassination took place, was a Marcello stronghold, controlled by boss Joseph Civello.[8] Author Piper, no friend to the Anti-Defamation League, loves to involve the Jewish mob, Israeli lobby, and even the Mossad in his theories on JFK's assassination.

Mickey's relationship to Marcello looms large on the list of guilt by association. He had become a player on the national scene, partly through Marcello, who had connections all the way up to the CIA; they asked his advice on how to assassinate Castro.

After Jack Ruby shot Lee Harvey Oswald, many Americans felt that he had done the right thing; he was a great citizen; he got the SOB who killed our president. They could not have been more wrong about Ruby's character, and were in the dark about his mob background, relationship to Mickey, and abusive style.[9] FBI agents interviewed Mickey and Ruby's girlfriend Candy Barr twelve hours after Ruby shot Oswald.

The level of Mickey's involvement is a connect-the-dots insinuation. Some conspiracy mavens, like author and former detective Gary Wean, can't get enough of the fact that Ruby and Mickey were both Jewish. Wean had access to all the information that the local police and prosecutors knew about old friends Mickey and Ruby.

Conspiracy theorists also thrive when they review the fact that famous defense attorney and Mickey buddy Melvin Belli jumped in so fast to represent Ruby after he had killed assassin Oswald. To defend him, Belli accepted a paltry $25,000 fee, and hoped to make up the difference on the book rights.

He likened Ruby to Mickey. "If you had to pick Cohen up to drive him to the court at 8:30, he would have to start getting himself ready at 5:30. Ruby was the same type."

Belli also referred to Ruby as "a junior version of Mickey Cohen." Ruby loved to name drop Mickey.

Throw in Menachem Begin again, and the Jewish plot thickens. The fact that Belli, Mickey, and Begin met occasionally to discuss how to cope with the Kennedy administration's foreign policy makes for lively speculation and further connections. Gary Wean, whose writing about Mickey sounded anti-Semitic, wrote, "[My partner] and I'd been watching Mickey Cohen from a distance. We knew he was up to something out of the ordinary. He spent a lot of time with a weird-looking little guy at the Beverly Wilshire Hotel lunch counter and drug store area." The little guy turned out to be Menachem Begin. Wean employed a Yiddish-speaking spy to find out what the two had discussed. Much of it had to do with Cuba, military operations, and the Kennedys. Both men despised JFK's appro-priations for the "crazy Peace Corps." After the meeting, the two men adjourned to the home of Melvin Belli.

Utilizing an objective approach, even Jonathan Mark, associate editor of the *Jewish Week,* wrote, "Yes, Jack Ruby did kill JFK's assassin, Lee Harvey Oswald, and as far back as Lenny Bruce Jews have wondered whether Ruby's Jewishness had anything to do with it. It may have been a motive, after all." The Ruby photo caption raises the old question, "Jack Ruby: Did he have a 'Jewish reason' for killing Lee Harvey Oswald?" At the simplest level, some questioned if Ruby's motivation was to get even for the loss of JFK, whom, he felt, had done a great deal for Israel.

Mark mentions that Hugh Aynesworth of the *Washington Times* saw Ruby only five minutes before the assassination. Ruby was doing his schmooze act at the *Dallas Morning News*, and complained about an unsigned, black-bordered ad that attacked Kennedy: JFK—WANTED FOR TREASON. Ruby called the ad "dirty."

He later surmised that authorities could connect him to the assassination since Bernard Weissman, an associate of his, had placed the ad. Ruby told his sister that he had to leave Dallas because he could "never live this down." Aynesworth said that Ruby "connected [the unfolding events] to the fact that he and Weissman both were Jews." All media coverage dropped the name "Rubenstein" after the first go 'round surrounding Oswald's death, the opposite of standard reporting procedures. Instead of his proper name, Jack Rubenstein would become only "Ruby."

Author David Scheim expounded on the Ruby links: "It turned out that 'Jim Braden' was a changed name... Eugene Hale Brading had in fact used four other aliases...was checked through the California Department of Motor Vehicles." Brading was loitering around Dealey Plaza in Dallas when authorities took him into custody the day of the JFK assassination. He had stayed at the mob hangout Cabana Motel in Dallas the day before the assassination. Ruby had stopped at the hotel around midnight. Both of them visited the H. L. Hunt Oil Company in Dallas at approximately the same time the afternoon before the assassination. Brading worked as a courier for Meyer Lansky, and was an original member of the Lansky-financed La Costa Country Club.

Brading's connections in the California underworld led to Mickey. He was close to Jimmy Fratianno, Harold "Happy" Meltzer, and Joe Sica, all with strong ties to Mickey. Another link is Al Gruber, also a Mickey associate. Ruby contacted Gruber right after the JFK assassination.

The conspiracy books cite multiple connections between Lansky's people, Carlos Marcello, and Mickey's circle. Mickey was undoubtedly Lansky's West Coast representative. Lansky biographer Hank Messick described Mickey as Lansky's "eyes and ears," and after Bugsy's death continued to rely on him directly for information, utilizing couriers like Brading. While Ruby knew Mickey and Lansky, Mickey's day-to-day knowledge of Ruby's activities surrounding JFK is pure speculation, but possible. Some of Ruby's own comments confused observers, making his motives and connections impossible to nail down. In his memoir, Mickey wisely avoided mentioning Ruby. Michael Collins Piper in *Final Judgment* felt that Mickey's role was more significant: "Cohen—who was one of Jack Ruby's idols—apparently had a direct hand in the assassination conspiracy and the subsequent cover-up." Further, he suggested an alternative motive for the alleged murder of Marilyn Monroe: if she had publicly revealed how Mickey had used her to get information on JFK's Israeli foreign policy, the exposure of Israel's uneasiness with JFK would have caused catastrophic political consequences here and abroad.

Local attention did not diminish while Mickey was in prison. The IRS arranged to sell his jewelry that agents had confiscated against his back taxes. Newspapers advertised the public auction, set for December 18, 1963. Jeweler Jack Fuerst, 222 W. 5th St., authenticated the unique forty-three-piece collection, and handled the sale. LaVonne's nearly thirteen-carat diamond ring was the cornerstone of the collection. Mickey's solid gold key chain, diamond-studded and sapphire cuff links, tie tack made of two gold dice with diamonds and rubies for the spots, gold his-and-her pen set, and a gold house key were all part of the expensive and gaudy jewels. Mickey had a collection of watches to match every color suit. Even the face of the watch coordinated with each ornate wristband. The IRS expected that the auction would fetch a minimum of $50,000. Fuerst mentioned to reporters that only one fake diamond existed. Mickey had given the kitschy bauble to stripper girlfriend Candy Barr in 1959. After sealed bids, IRS agents recorded sales of $20,000.

Paul Coates offered one of the best newspaper assessments of Mickey's complex life and morality in a piece for the *Los Angeles Times* on December 27, 1963. The KTTV Channel 11 television reporter spoke in detail about Mickey's generosity, wry humor, and interest in love.

He recalled the Pearson beating episode: "It was an incredible scene beyond, even, the imagination of Damon Runyon."

A letter to a nurse that Mickey knew in Los Angeles revealed yet another side of his multifaceted makeup. He wrote her because he was unable to keep a Christmas package that she had sent him during his prison stay.

> I received your always most appreciated letter… I was very pleased that you spoke with my sis…. You know it is not easy enough to tell one not to become bitter or not to become hateful. But the thing is, how to tell one how to avoid becoming that way… it is a terrible thing when you read about some young fellows who just got released from a place like I'm in, and soon after they're out, they kill a police officer. If you could witness, as I have, the embittered frame of minds of some of these persons just before they are released to live in the free world… You would be shocked and disturbed at some of the statements made to me by some of these soon-to-be-released prisoners…many just mouth off to make an impression on me…

About six weeks into 1964, Jack Dahlstrum of Los Angeles, Melvin Belli of San Francisco (still working on Jack Ruby's case), J. Victor Candy, Jr., of Nashville, and William B. Paul of Atlanta had filed a suit against the federal government for $10,000,000. The more than twenty-page civil action filing was extensive and very clear: the government had failed to keep Mickey safe in prison. The lawyers had done their homework; they knew every inch of the penitentiary and utilized schematics to make their case. The landmark complaint accused the penitentiary of operating "in a negligent and careless manner," resulting in Mickey's leg paralysis and brain damage. Attorneys asked for loss of income damages, a difficult figure to estimate, particularly based on Mickey's tax trial statistics.

On March 12, Mickey requested a medical parole. He wrote the document himself, and attorney A. L. Wirin delivered the biographical twelve-page hand-written plea to the court, supported by signatures of 305 respected citizens.

Mickey excused his chosen profession in the request: "…in those days was looked upon as being a normal process for an unschooled and uneducated young boy who had to earn money to eat, and to help feed his loved ones."

Wirin sent copies of the documents to pardon attorney Reed Cozart, who worked for the Department of Justice and who would recommend and forward the material to Attorney General Robert F. Kennedy with copies to President Lyndon Johnson.

This go 'round would prove futile. Mickey's first scheduled parole date was still December 1966.

Ben Hecht died April 19, 1964, but not before the British vilified him for his Irgun activities. Sidney Zion spoke of the irony: "Thus Ben Hecht became the first blacklisted Hollywood writer. And by the goddamn English, at that."[10]

Mickey added another lawsuit for $1,000,000 against the government of Atlanta, Georgia, under the Federal Tort Claim Act.

Less than a year later, he would receive a break from prison life. He returned to Los Angeles on a Friday in late February 1965. Federal Judge Gus Solomon, brought in from Portland as a substitute, had signed a court order to allow Mickey to attend the government trial for the more than two-year-old tax case. Attorney Jack Dahlstrum insisted that Mickey be present as a witness at the March 15 court battle.

His method of travel and subsequent treatment in Los Angeles indicated that his power had not substantially diminished. His twin-engine Beechcraft plane touched down at a private landing pad owned by AiResearch Corporation, within the confines of Los Angeles International Airport. The *Los Angeles Times* remarked that the scene resembled a "secret mission" of "a high government official."

An officer of the corporation had ordered the plane for Mickey, and the company provided an extensive number of security guards, who had instructions to keep the press onslaught away from him. He shuffled to the waiting station wagon with the aid of a cane.

He had a "hotel reservation" at the prison ward in General Hospital, including around the clock guards. Only attorneys and family could visit.

Dahlstrum arranged a press conference on March 2 to drum up sympathy for broken-man Mickey. He discussed Mickey's memory loss, which attorneys attributed to his attack. Reporters questioned the extent of his impairment, and naturally wondered about the accuracy of his answers during any trial.

Two days before the tax trial, a new three-column Paul Coates piece on Mickey appeared in the sympathetic *Los Angeles Times.*

Coates began with, "Mickey Cohen, the banty rooster who once strutted the walks of the Sunset Strip…"

Dahlstrum had told Coates about the shoddy prison conditions and treatment and described the hospital as a place filled with "dangerous psychotics." Mickey never fully recovered from the savage beating and was in pitiful condition. He, who avoided the television room, still wondered if he had ever seen McDonald before the beating, while authorities refused to show him his assailant's picture. He was at one time totally paralyzed, permanently lost his left field of vision in both eyes, lost the use of one arm, still had paralysis in both legs, and had a "silver" plate in his skull.

Dahlstrum complained: "Until they brought him here for this tax suit, he hadn't been out in the open air for 18 months. They're afraid to let him out in the yard. He hasn't been allowed to attend a movie or religious service in that time."

The reporter pleaded the obvious. "I wouldn't argue that he should not do his time…as a simple matter of humanity, I do not think he should be made to do it in a prison where it might cost him his life." Mickey had received the rawest of deals. Officials refused a transfer to Terminal Island at the ship dock in San Pedro closer to his family. The medical staff at the Springfield penitentiary could no longer improve his condition.

He arrived for his IRS tax trial in a neat suit, and walked with the aid of a black twisted cane. In order to protect his relatives, who had a controlling interest in his greenhouse, he had signed a waiver under duress in 1956 upon advice of attorney Paul Caruso and pressure from IRS agent Peter R. Bertoglio, who threatened foreclosure on several properties.

After a visit by a U.S. attorney, Caruso denied that he had planned to support Dahlstrum's case. Angry Judge Solomon challenged Dahlsturm's perjury implications regarding Caruso, denying his move for dismissal because of Caruso's flip-flop.

Assistant U.S. Attorney James S. Bay continued with the case against Mickey, despite acknowledging that he held no assets. That was the end of the witness list.

Mickey waited at the prison hospital until March 24 for Judge Solomon's reserved decision. The judge ruled against him, allowed him a minuscule credit for $15,000 worth of seized property, and sent him back to Springfield.

Mickey idol Owney Madden died on April 24, 1965, in a Hot Springs, Arkansas, hospital. Chief Parker finally retired in 1965, and died the next year.

The FBI continued to keep a close watch on Mickey, despite his debilitating episode. Agents were convinced that he was still running his operations on the outside, and they were desperate to incriminate him. FBI guru Hoover had reported only sixty-five gambling and racketeering convictions, with few leaders. Many government officials, politicians, police, and agents represented then and now that Mickey was not a significant national player. The resultant FBI effort became one of the most costly and ludicrous reportages in the history of the federal agency.

Brother Harry became the focus of the FBI for the next two years. He confessed to smuggling contraband to Mickey—all necessities to keep his life civil.

Mickey's big drug score in prison was twenty Dristan inhalers. The FBI raided the prison on July 12, 1965, but recovered only ten of the inhalers, one can of vegetable beef soup, one two-ounce jar of Brilliantine (hair tonic), a jar of antipasto, a jar of Aqua Velva, and six slices of rye bread.

The FBI continued to watch his every move, despite acknowledging that he did not take drugs. His treatment smacked of personal vendettas; he had alienated himself from so many high-ranking officials that his political power had substantially diminished; the FBI harassed him unmercifully.

They discovered that Harry had bribed a nurse with $100 to provide additional food and toilet articles for his brother.

The prison nurse cracked under pressure from FBI agents: "...I was contacted by Mickey Cohen...to get him some tea that had lemon and sugar in it. I told him he could get tea here but said it did not have lemon in it. He kept asking me... I brought him a couple of packages of tea." Then all hell broke loose. "Cohen thanked me for it and he asked me for something else, probably salami, mustard or something to eat... I continued bringing him pretty much the same items including herring and Jewish salami."

The nurse confessed to other atrocities like mailing letters for Mickey, and making phone calls to Harry.

The FBI contraband investigation spread to New York; Patterson, New Jersey; and Springfield, Missouri. Five nurses and three senior officers at the prison got into the act. A whopping two hundred bucks were involved. The livid FBI interviewed banks and traced money orders.

Mickey's attorneys told him not to talk to the FBI, who advised him of his rights in accordance with new policy: "...any statements he did make could be used against him in a court of law." During a second brief, illogical meeting,

292

Mickey told the agents that he would be stupid to eat food that he found in his room.

This slapstick epidemic of prison violations produced more non-commissary items on January 14, 1966. The new list of niceties included a six-ounce jar of Mr. Mustard. Five new packages of Nestea ice tea mix. A jar of Lipton ice tea mix. A twelve-ounce jar of Torrido brand chili peppers. A Fanci-Food three-ounce jar of hot mustard. Two glass jars of relish, and horseradish.

The FBI found a small bottle of yellow Sominex pills. Unlike the commercial, there would be no "Take Sominex tonight, and sleep, sleep, sleep" for Mickey. Somebody tipped off the agents about a roll of meat and two non-government-issue rolls of pepperoni in the dark room.

They assigned a fulltime undercover agent to keep an eye on him. On January 27, 1966, the warden cooperated in a crackdown on the entire prison population. The only confessions were chewing gum. An interviewee ratted Mickey out. The prison-striped clotheshorse had four or five pairs of fancy pajamas. He liked Czech broadcloth, which the FBI mentioned was very hard to get—they meant in general, not in prison.

The big casino closer: the Cohen brothers were after fresh linens and shower-related items. Case closed! For the moment.

While many show-business people stuck by Mickey during this prison stay, the majority of people, including the throngs of politicians and police who missed the payroll money, slowly wrote him off. The celebrity mail trickled in. Journalists had less to say about him since he was no longer in the public eye. Many smaller articles focused on anything remotely related to him or his associates.

The FBI still watched his mail with interest. Agents labeled one love letter "obscene." Very likely, Sandy Hagen sent these excerpts. Agents blacked out the affectionate terms, greeting, and signature:

> ...I keep thinking of you constantly—what do you look like—I'm so afraid I won't even recognize you...am I dreaming or being hopeful—at times I start thinking—asking myself how many weeks—days—then I get a cold chill—I'm so afraid—everyone tells me to think positive—I'm...praying-begging God—for this one favor-a chance to bring you home to make you well...the few years that we have left—will we enjoy them somewhat... I'm so sick at heart—not having been able to visit you—see you—..."

Mickey received extensive letters from friends and relatives, some from comedian Joey Bishop. People supplied narratives about life on the outside, and allowed

Mickey to envision the ordinary things that might help a prisoner look toward the future.

Mickey's devoted sister, likely Pauline or Lillian, wrote descriptive and dramatic letters:

> ...I must take my hat off to you for what you once told me about how to handle all people and supposed to be friends when you do anyone a favor, to make them pay for it thru the nose and have no mercy for anyone, money wise when they come to you for a favor...guys who were former pals and I grew up with, who completely play the cold shoulder...

Sister Rose, an FBI creation, perhaps Mickey's sister-in-law, ran a children's apparel store, although they blackened the signature on the letter. The lengthy letters cover extensive details of his sister's business relationship with him, plus discussions with attorneys, and how generally to help him.

On January 25, 1966, authorities released Mickey to travel to Atlanta regarding his $10,000,000 suit against the government. On trips like this, he would have to pay off between fifteen and twenty-five hundred dollars to support the extra prison guard entourage.

U.S. District Judge Sidney O. Smith, Jr., listened to juryless arguments over a two-day period, January 31 and February 1.

In court, when federal marshals tried to assist a hobbled Mickey, he told them, "I'm OK, leave me alone."

Attorneys for the government kept him on the stand for over one hour.

Mickey told Judge Sidney Smith, "I would be willing to do anything to be able to walk again."

The government still tried to establish that the prison had reasonable security measures, and that guards had control over the inmates. Attorneys conceded that Mickey's assailant McDonald was not of sound mind. Testimony revealed that he had escaped into the exercise yard from a separate maximum-security area, traveled over 500 feet, and then clubbed Mickey. He was incapable of standing trial.

Judge Smith had no problem chastising the penitentiary staff. The judge deemed Mickey permanently disabled, lame, and crippled for life. However, the judge deferred his verdict.

When Mickey returned to prison, the FBI did not let up. They traced money from cities all over the country to the prison.

The pulled Mickey's brother Harry in for further questioning about letter writing, money orders, and telephone calls.

Toward the end of March, Mickey ultimately received a judgment against the government for only $110,000, due upon his release.

Despite government objections, Russian-born Allen Smiley, who had shown Bugsy to his last seat, received his United States citizenship in July. West Hollywood resident Smiley said that he was in the oil business, and proud of his recent honor.

The persistent FBI had to take a breather in July, since an airline strike halted their peripatetic trips to interview witnesses.

They suffered a rare glimpse into reality during September 1966: "Within the prison Mickey Cohen is well regarded and respected by many of the inmate populace... As the Bureau is aware he is paralyzed from the waist down and incapable of physical harm to anyone in his present condition..." The same report discussed the work-release program, and stated that no one previously released under the program had fled.

Mickey was outliving many of his enemies. After a one-year illness, fifty-seven-year-old Captain James Hamilton, who had collected a judgment in the libel and slander suit against Mickey and ABC, died on November 7. On November 30, 1966, the Federal Parole Board denied his current request for release. It offered no reason for the decision, and refusal to offer him work programs. Fans followed the two-weak media coverage.

Harry Cohen's only recourse was to publicize Mickey's predicament. On December 9, Los Angeles KLAC radio interviewed him. He candidly told Mickey's public about prison homosexuality, harassment, horrible medical care, and brutality.

On January 31, 1967, Mattie Capone died. Few attended the service in which two reporters covering the funeral filled in as pallbearers.

Prison authorities allowed Mickey to visit the Kaiser Foundation Hospital to see his eighty-two-year-old mother Fanny, who had suffered a heart attack. Mickey returned to prison on February 5.

On May 21, he attended his mother's funeral. He needed assistance to stand, and used a cane to steady himself. He was tired, but refused his wheelchair. He buried Mrs. Fanny Friedman at Hillside Memorial Park cemetery, known as the resting place of the stars.

Despite his poor health, he could not ascertain a release based on his medical condition.

On May 31, the FBI still wondered: should they prosecute the nurse or only Mickey?

Finally! Wonderful news for taxpayers. January 5, 1968, Assistant United States Attorney Anthony P. Nugent, Jr., confirmed: "…reported that in view of the age of the proposed case against Mickey Cohen as well as other problems….decline prosecution."

Nevertheless, Mickey was in terrible physical condition, and still in prison. In 1968, his brother Harry[11] appealed to Attorney General Ramsey Clark:

> …My brother's "life" is in grave danger…attempt to murder him by "poisoning him." …capsules prescribed by the U.S. Medical Center… We his family are mighty worried… My brother was sentenced as a healthy perfect physical specimen…today is a hopeless cripple.

Harry's list of Mickey's ailments included asthma and ulcers. He asserted that Mickey's punishment was cruel and unusual, and that maybe Robert Kennedy had been behind his extensive and inflexible sentence. He asked for leniency, and pointed out that Mickey had already served half of his sentence. His request for Mickey's medical parole had a legitimate basis. Success would have come more easily to a less celebrated and notorious inmate.

The FBI stated that Harry had offered to "buy" Mickey's release, and also noted, "He [Harry] claims that the inmates are treated like animals, that he is in the process of preparing a book concerning the alleged cruel, inhuman care, violation of human dignity and civil rights."

In a separate letter to Director Hoover, Harry pleaded, "…even you would be shocked and amazed at some of the goings on…inhumane, sadistic, etc… His large family never condoned his escapades, and past life and activities, however, he is my baby brother and I am concerned." He made it clear to Hoover that many less deserving inmates had received parole through payoffs and fixes. He got nowhere with the FBI or anyone else.

During 1968, Nick Licata took the reigns of the Italian mob, and did not fair much better than his predecessors Frank DeSimone and Jack Dragna.

When Sirhan Sirhan assassinated Robert Kennedy on June 5, 1968, conspiracy theories related to Mickey immediately sprung up. The shooting occurred in the Ambassador Hotel—always a Mickey stronghold. The existing theories on the RFK assassination are detailed and widespread, and even suggest that Los Angeles was the target city because Mickey could more easily order and control the set-up.

The simplest conspiracy theory makes Sirhan the fall guy, and identifies a security officer—not Sirhan—firing and hitting Kennedy, since the fatal bullets came from close range, closer than the two to three feet some people reported as Sirhan's position.

RFK conspiracy theorists mention Mickey's name frequently because his motive was obvious and simple: if Kennedy became president, Mickey could kiss the rest of his own life goodbye. He had always been an RFK priority, years before his brother's assassination. After JFK's death, Robert Kennedy did somewhat reduce his focus on Mickey.

According to author John Davis, it is impossible not to consider the obvious: Hoffa, Marcello, and Mickey all would benefit from a "plot to murder the man who, while serving as attorney general, had ordered J. Edgar Hoover to go after Jimmy Hoffa, Carlos Marcello, and Mickey Cohen." Even prison did not stop Hoffa from hatching a plan to kill RFK with the help of Marcello and Carmine Galante, underboss of the New York Bonanno crime family.

Kennedy was particularly disturbed by Mickey's history of extortion and pimping; it was no secret that he controlled movie stars through blackmail. As president, Kennedy would have had the familiar Department of Justice at his disposal; it could have had a field day with Mickey, and blocked his release.

Conspiracy mavens vigorously stir the pot when it comes to assassin Sirhan's connections to Mickey, the mob, and Hollywood. He worked at the Santa Anita racetrack, where Mickey's organization had pervasive influence. Sirhan, who attended Pasadena's John Muir High School and Pasadena City College, was never the extreme Arab activist as painted by the media. He mistook our pop-culture to be the real America, as did many foreigners implanted in Hollywood. His acquaintances described him as very much American; he loved to make a buck, and shunned anything Arab—cuisine, garb, etc. He performed grooming and exercise work around the stables, but like other track bums, his salary was hardly enough to pay his gambling debts, making him beholden to the mob. An impressionable Arab-Palestinian exercise boy would have been a likely choice by someone interested in igniting the smoldering differences surrounding the political struggle for Israeli survival. Nevertheless, Sirhan was schooled on the Arab warrior Saladin, who expelled unwanted crusaders from Jerusalem, and weaned on typical anti-American, anti-Semitic, and pro Palestinian sentiments.

The conspiracy theory rolls on with the *I Love Lucy* connection. Sirhan was friends with well-known horse trainer Frank Donneroumas, who introduced him to Desi Arnaz, who had a fancy horse-breeding ranch in Corona, where Sirhan worked. Arnaz was always on good terms with Mickey, as well as with Sinatra, despite the embellished public confrontation over *The Untouchables* television show. Donneroumas was former criminal Henry Ramistella, a middle management racketeer from New Jersey who disappeared west after being banned from the East Coast tracks. FBI investigations linked Ramistella, Sirhan, and Arnaz to Mickey.

Another conspiracy angle involves Richard Nixon. Carlos Marcello and Mickey were always supporters of Nixon, despite Mickey playing both sides of the fence in the 1962 California gubernatorial election. Marcello had donated $500,000 to Nixon's 1960 loss to JFK. Senate investigator Walter Sheridan understood the Jewish mob's likewise interest in Nixon: "If you were Meyer, who would you invest your money in? Some politician named Clams Linguini? Or a nice Protestant boy from Whittier, California?" With RFK gone, Nixon would likely win the presidency, assuring mobsters access to the White House.[12]

Murray Chotiner, who was still one of Nixon's closest allies, tried to distance himself from Mickey. He had always stayed on good terms with Mickey since he represented the interests of East Coast syndicate bosses like Costello and Meyer Lansky.[13]

Chotiner threatened to sue columnist Pearson if he continued to play up Mickey's relationship with him and Nixon. He called Mickey to intervene. Mickey did call Pearson and asked him to focus on other stories. Chotiner dropped all charges against Pearson.

Mickey's failed attempts for release, his prison treatment, and the silly FBI scrutiny had more to do with his political enemies than any public outcry to see justice served. Since his power and influence had reached the highest levels, many people associated him with high crime against America, things that went way beyond the scope of his local operations. If any of the implied conspiracy allegations were true, then his extensive punishment may have been appropriate, but his trial and subsequent incarceration had been solely for a tax law violation.

His role in American politics was that of a businessman in a national company that needed a lobby in Washington, but his heart really wasn't in his political success and its trappings. His passion was with Hollywood, and his deeply personal need to tell his own story, rather than someone else's. Watching others rise on the national scene did not appeal to him as much as his own celebrity needs.

Mickey still smiling at his income tax trial, June 7, 1951.

Senator Estes Kefauver.

Desi Arnaz, the "Mambo King."

Mickey checking in with his probation officer after his first prison stay, Oct. 12, 1955.

Mickey after his arrest in the Pearson case.

Ben Hecht.

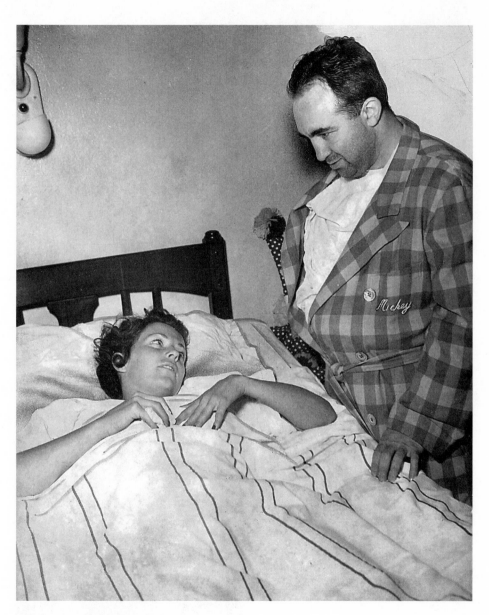

With Dee David after Sherry's shooting.

Sheriff Biscailuz at the Old Spanish Day
Fiesta in Santa Barbara.

Albert Anastasia in 1956,
the year before his execution.

Mickey leaving court,
February 10, 1958.

Carlo Gambino.

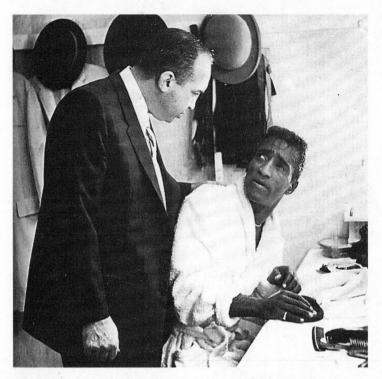

With Sammy Davis, Jr., in his dressing room backstage during a movie shoot, 1950. Sammy called Mickey in to have this picture taken.

Richard M. Nixon *(right)*, J. Edgar Hoover *(center)* and Charles "Bebe" Rebozo.

Hedda Hopper *(in hat)* with Eddie Fisher and Debbie Reynolds.

Tempest Storm, January 6, 1957, at the
New Follies Theater.

Kim Novak.

Dean Martin and Jerry Lewis in their heyday.

Marilyn Monroe, August 1958.

Frank Sinatra in the late 1950s.

Liz Renay. Inscribed to Mickey, February 27, 1958.

Billy Graham and
Martin Luther King.

Mickey and girlfriend Sandy Hagen after
Jack Whalen's murder, March 8, 1960.

Mickey and Sandy Hagen,
July 2, 1961.

Unshaven Mickey leaving jail during his tax incarceration, November 29, 1961.

The confrontation between Jimmy Hoffa *(right)* and Robert Kennedy *(left)*.

Jack Ruby, after shooting
Lee Harvey Oswald in Dallas,
1963.

Patty Hearst mug shot,
1975.

John Gotti.

Mickey Cohen in 1975, the year before his death.

Part Five

The Survivor

1967–1976

29.

Things Change

For many years, the police in Beverly Hills, Hollywood, and greater Los Angeles had denied the existence of the Mafia or any Mafia-like organization that operated within shopping distance of trendy Rodeo Drive or Sunset Boulevard. In June 1967, Attorney General Thomas C. Lynch of California broke the "startling" news. "Our state has become the favorite investment area of the veiled finance committee of organized crime." Author Ed Reid listed the discoveries:

> ...hidden interests on state licenses: the intrusion of criminal cartelists into our sensitive world of finance; the layoff of huge sports bets into the Los Angeles area; loan sharking and the reported moves of the remnants of the old Mickey Cohen mob to control it.

The same year that Lynch started his late war on crime, contrarians like U.S. Deputy Attorney General Warren M. Christopher, who later became secretary of state under President Bill Clinton, made statements about the lack of organized crime in California. Organized crime did not exist "because of the quality, honesty, and integrity" of our law enforcement agencies. He did not believe that anyone involved with crime in California had anything to do with national or secret organizations. Reid was critical of the blanket appraisal: "But perhaps Christopher was the victim of ignorance." More realistically, Christopher had followed the pattern established years earlier by FBI deity J. Edgar Hoover.

The *New York Observer* writer Ron Rosenbaum's recent description of Hollywood may account for its having fallen easy prey to Mickey and the mob for so many years: "Hollywood is our nation's head injury, the source of our spiritual retardation."

The export of pop-culture from Mickey's neighborhood always took a front seat to any serious anti-crime activity. The country was regularly infused with news of Hollywood, and on its way to becoming a celebrity-driven society. More than one American pop icon, television guru, or minimally skilled actor would publicize their felonies that ranged from narcotics violations to stock swindles, and from sex offenses to murder, while most of their careers continued to soar.

Thanks to the inadvertent activities of peripatetic Mickey and his boys, the actual city of Hollywood would change dramatically. Mob-controlled illegal and posh conventional activities shifted west, to the newer and safer West Hollywood and Beverly Hills. It was no longer possible to see a movie star strolling along famous Hollywood and Vine; there was a much greater chance to see one on chichi Rodeo Drive. Regular Hollywood destinations of the prior decades eva-porated. The last big Broadway department store had seen better days, and the posh Pig and Whistle restaurant, along with many other famous eateries, even-tually lost its movie star-driven clientele. The local movie theaters had all but given up on Hollywood premieres, except the famous Grauman's Chinese, today the Mann and still a tourist trap.

The money shift west produced unmanageable crime in the vacated sections. The Hollywood vice squad had its hands full with pimps and drug addicts who had infiltrated the once innocent sightseers' haven, ironically no longer protected by more upscale organized crime. The corruption in the police department was still widespread; official cooperation ensured the success of criminals like Mickey in the volatile landscape.

Even while incarcerated in the late sixties and early seventies, Mickey main-tained the dubious distinction of being the reigning king of rackets. His crews pro-longed his hold on the business and warded off interlopers while he served the last few years of his second prison term. Police designed special units to help exclude organized crime from the more fashionable neighborhoods. That was fine with Mickey, who was more than willing to cooperate with the police to assist in keeping out the competitive undesirables. This perverse symbiotic relationship even allowed people like Mickey to help appoint police officials. The business-as-usual philosophy had perpetuated his operations, notwithstanding multiple public crusades by politicians seeking election to rid Hollywood and its bordering communities of organized crime.

While Mickey was in prison, *Life* profiled the success of Carlos Marcello in Louisiana, one of many examples of mobsters who avoided Kefauver, McClellan, RFK, and Hoover (who by then had completely turned his back on pursuing the bosses).[1]

During his absence, a reclusive gambling boss named Harry Gross tried to infiltrate Mickey's bookie operations. New Yorker Gross, convicted of bookmaking in 1950, had moved west and seized the opportunity created by Mickey's misfortune.

Al "Slick" Snyder, who suffered injuries in the Hooky Rothman slaying, became embroiled in the famous Friars Club card-cheating case. He refused to tell authorities anything about the installation of electronic cheating devices in the fabled Friars card room, peepholes in the ceiling and radio transmitters. Steven Crane's popular restaurant partner Al Mathes, who drove a white Rolls-Royce, was in on the take from the droves of Friars' pigeons.

When Nixon beat Humphrey in the 1968 presidential election, Mickey's hopes of early release diminished.[2] He had again agreed to let columnist Drew Pearson use the information about his relationship to Nixon in the hope that it would help elect Humphrey. Mickey's assessment of Nixon never changed over the years, and he told Pearson (who some say toppled Nixon), "...let's hope he isn't the same guy I knew as a rough hustler... I never had no idea that this guy Nixon could go anywhere..." He received no assistance from President Nixon, because this time Pearson published Mickey's entire statement.[3] He had been working directly with Pearson, who had the ear of then president Lyndon Johnson, whom Mickey swore double-crossed him on the parole issue. Governor Pat Brown in California likewise had stiffed Mickey on his medical parole

Florabel Muir died of a heart attack on April 27, 1970, at age eighty. Every obit mentioned the time that she was "shot in the hip" by a fusillade of bullets meant for Mickey, or some similar embellishment.

Mickey would not give up on early parole. The wounded warrior appeared before U.S. District Judge William H. Becker during July 1970. Listed as fifty-six, Mickey hobbled to the witness chair during his hearing for a writ of habeas corpus.

He described his life before McDonald hit him on the head. "...I was in charge of the tool room in the electric shop. It was a responsible position...my immediate supervisor said I was doing a good job... I was eligible... for meritorious good time." He had not received any time off for good behavior.

His attorneys asked for thirty-six days of credit for his first year of service at the penitentiary. Each additional year would bring sixty more days.

Mickey was pleased that his right hand had improved; he was now able to write, and told the judge that he was willing to work. He made certain to say that his sentence was "cruel and unusual punishment." He found the prison population difficult to bear because of his homophobia. He had frequent run-ins with prisoners whom he considered gay, and constantly complained to the guards and wardens. He was very vocal and called the prison "a male whorehouse," and refused to work with any man he suspected of being gay.

"I don't mix with no fags, no queers, no fruits," he said during interviews for good behavior sentence reduction.

Sexually panicked Mickey had had talks with Springfield Warden Dr. Pasquale J. Ciccone about the complications of his day-to-day existence, brought on by his response to many of the inmates whom he found repellent. The warden had encouraged him to be more accepting of sexual diversity, at least intellectually—something Mickey insisted was impossible. (Of course, there are no records of his sex life in prison. If anyone had girls smuggled in at night by prison guards, it was Mickey. Although, based on reports by friends, he probably appreciated his contraband steaks just as much as any outside companionship.)

He referenced his doctors, who said that release from prison tensions would improve his health.

The worried judge had his assurance that no harm would come to him on the outside. "No, I have no fears... My heyday is long past," said Mickey.

Judge Becker found Mickey's detention lawful, and he remained in prison. His raw deal continued.

In 1971, Meyer Lansky faced skimming charges involving the now older Flamingo Hotel. He would utilize Israel's law of return, and eventually retire to the Tel Aviv Dan Hotel, which he had built.

That same year Mickey's brother Harry appealed to Attorney General John Mitchell. In a pathetic and sad letter, he mentioned that someone had robbed Mickey on a Friday night when he had tried to attend a Sabbath service. Harry called the attacker "sadistic and bigoted." He asked Mitchell to use his influence to help Mickey retrieve his glasses from the thieves. Mickey claimed that it was a shakedown by a staff member, and not an inmate.

Harry contacted the American Civil Liberties Union for relief. He reiterated how the prison system had destroyed Mickey rather than rehabilitate him; he had never received the proper medical care, including physical therapy.

The matter was dumped in Hoover's lap, and he responded for everyone: "The copy of your letter to the Attorney General was received … While I readily understand the concern…there does not appear to be a violation of Federal law within the investigative jurisdiction of the FBI." He forwarded Harry's complaints to the Bureau of Prisons. No action resulted from any of Harry's efforts.

Donald F. Bowler, the IRS agent who had headed the team that put Mickey away, retired from government service on March 26, 1971. He went to work for Intertel (International Intelligence), a company designed to keep the mob away from its clients, including mogul Howard Hughes.

The occasional story about Mickey's old gang made news. One example was on December 17: Seven-Dwarf Eli Lubin was indicted on mail fraud, related to a 1962 bond theft of twenty-eight $1,000 Series E savings bonds.

While Mickey's brother and others did their best to ascertain his release, he could do little more than wait. His Mandatory Release date was coming up soon.

30.

Mickey's Back in Town

After years of requests, authorities announced that Mickey would be coming home on January 9, 1972, the Mandatory Release date, and the year FBI chief Hoover died. Only two months earlier, Riverside County sheriff's deputies had arrested fifty-eight-year-old interloper bookmaker Harry Gross, either ironically or conveniently for Mickey.

Mickey felt that his release should have come sooner, and prison authorities, who now wanted to appear sympathetic, publicly exaggerated the good behavior reports. Springfield Prison director Dr. Pasquale Ciccone claimed that Mickey had received the five years off his sentence for good behavior, although he would always adamantly deny it. Warden Ciccone released a statement that Mickey had been a "reasonably cooperative prisoner." Many reports claimed that he had been a favorite of wardens, guards, and inmates, despite his personal denials. Mickey insisted that no officials had gone out of their way to see that he received credit for good behavior. Authorities had denied him early release benefits while other prisoners consistently racked up reduced time. That bothered him more than any other element of prison life. Prisoners who were incarcerated for cold-blooded murder left quicker than he did.

Despite Mickey's model reputation and debilitated condition, countless FBI reports still ended with a warning to agents: he is likely armed and dangerous and he has killed in the past. Prison officials had ignored the FBI advice and had treated the celebrity gangster with a level of respect reserved for famous public figures.

Newspapers prepared the waiting public with a history of Mickey's career, including details about his varied business operations. Expressions like "bookie's bookie" and "successor to Benjamin 'Bugsy' Siegel" filled the papers across the country. Reporters reviewed Mickey's prison life, the bizarre attack, and subsequent rehabilitation. Ironically, just before his release, stripper Tempest Storm, admitting to age forty-three, received a one-year probation for not paying her taxes. (Folklore never ceased to remind us that the fiery redhead had her 44DD bosom insured with Lloyd's of London for $1,000,000.)

Harry arrived this time in a new 1972 white Cadillac El Dorado with Ohio license plates; some things never change. Mrs. Harry Cohen and associate Jim Smith were also in the car. Harry told reporters before Mickey appeared, "Mickey could leave earlier but he's taking three hours to get dressed. He's the same goof he's always been."

Authorities released Mickey from prison between nine-thirty and ten in the morning on January 6, 1972. He had received an early weekend release, as was the custom. He sometimes needed a three-footed cane for stability, and today he took advantage of its support. He held a supply of paper towels, so his hand would never touch the germy cane handle.

When interviewed for a filmed biography of Mickey, journalist Peter Noyes, choked with emotion, said "It was really sad to see him [Mickey] on camera… It was the end of the brash, cocky, little man, who cut such a path through Los Angeles."

Mickey left prison wearing a white T-shirt, an ill-fitting pair of pants rolled to the ankles, and a windbreaker. He looked rather ordinary, but not totally destroyed by his beating and prison stay.

He spat on the ground and said, "Pass my family." He explained later that as a child he would spit whenever he saw a dead cat or dog and invoke "pass my family," meaning "Death, pass my family."

He hobbled to the El Dorado and said, "To hell with this rotten joint," struggled into the car, sat quietly in the front seat, and stared straight ahead as Harry drove through the front gate of the U.S. Medical Center for Federal Prisoners. Newsmen from around the country congregated outside the gate, and packed the perimeter.

Mickey told reporters, one of whom was his nephew David Cohen, "I wanted to throw away the cane and start walking."

Harry told him that they would stop at a local motel in Springfield. Mickey remembered a little café called Hamby's across from the Springfield Federal Building nearby; he had eaten there during his appeal in July 1970. His later version recalls having Jim Smith bring the food to the marshal's office during court recess. Harry agreed to drive him to Hamby's so he could have a piece of the chocolate pie he remembered and now craved.

Reporters surrounded the boys at the local café.

Within an hour, Mickey was on the telephone with friends. One call was to Sandy Hagen, in San Diego.

"Why are you crying?" he asked.

After the call, a reporter asked him if he intended to see her.

"It's my intention to see her if she would care to see me—you know." He would soon encourage his girlfriend Sandy to marry. She would take his advice, and eventually had two children.

Mickey declared, "It's good to be free, that's all," and refused to reveal any detailed vacation plans, although he mentioned Hot Springs, Arkansas, "to wash the stink and stench of prison off me." He had remained friends with Owney Madden's family, who resided in Hot Springs.

He said that he planned to live in West Hollywood.

More relaxed, Mickey responded to questions about Bugsy. "I knew Bugs and I loved him. He was one of the best human beings I ever met in my life."

He devoured his piece of chocolate pie plus a large orange juice, ham, fried potatoes, and three fried eggs smothered in catsup.

The satiated free man referred to an $800,000 lien by the IRS and made it clear that the government wouldn't see a nickel. "Any money I can beg, borrow, or steal will have to go to correcting my physical condition."

He asserted, "I'm not a vicious man. I haven't been involved in any vicious incidents…even the days when I was considered a tough hoodlum. I had a strong sense of ethics."

Mickey now acknowledged that he had received eight hours of physical therapy each day, including weight lifting for his upper body, but had to return to substandard cell conditions—"unbelievably bad" solitary—most of his nights. He was convinced that McDonald had clubbed him because of his underworld connections.

His overall take on the medical facility was dismal, a "place where they sent the best-known Mafia types to die just like one of those elephant burial grounds

I've read about," mentioning victims Vito Genovese and Jimmy "The Monk" Alegretti. Don Vito, as he liked to be called, died of a heart attack in prison, following a ten-year stay.

Los Angeles Times reporter Bryce Nelson observed, "He is still a quick conversationalist whose dark eyes flash and whose bushy gray eyebrows bristle when he describes the 'rotten, sadistic conditions in prison.'"

Mickey commented on his employment possibilities: "I've had my belly full of it [gambling]—I'm not that strong any more…in my day it was different. People look at those kinds of things different nowadays. What I want to do for the rest of my years is live them out as easily as I can."

After a manicure and haircut, fifty-eight-year-old Mickey hosted a party that night in Springfield, Missouri, at the aptly named Shady Inn. Another gala awaited him on his return to Los Angeles, where he would find that his world had changed substantially. Much of the old mob was gone. Sam LoCigno—who went to prison for the Whalen shooting—had died of a heart attack in Cleveland the previous year.

The movie hit of the year was *The Godfather*, an epic based on the Mario Puzo book, starring Marlon Brando, Al Pacino, and James Caan. Some New Yorkers said that the book was derivative of the actual lives of the Profaci crime syndicate, while others had different favorites. Surely, the singer Johnny Fontaine could be no one but Sinatra, and Jack Woltz, who found his thoroughbred horse's head in his bed, Harry Cohn.[1]

Las Vegas had survived multiple scandals and tough times.[2] The operation was extensive, and local and state politicians cooperated. Jewish Americans built most of the hotels.[3] Some of the early hotel names would survive, such as the Golden Nugget. Others, like the Apache, Pioneer Club, and Last Frontier would disappear into history. Reno had begun to fulfill its role as a mini-Las Vegas. Harrah's Reno advertised headliner singer Bobby Darin and comedian Larry Storch during Mickey's first month of freedom.

Mickey had minimal juice in the big Vegas loop. That didn't stop him from using his influence to catch up. He still ran most of the gambling in Los Angeles, and kept his nefarious influence at the Santa Anita and Del Mar racetracks. There was still a little boxing action at the Hollywood Legion Stadium, between Vine and Gower. True to form, he resumed his regular role, in the company of beautiful actresses, and appeared down front at the local bouts, now considered secondary to venues like Las Vegas. His dates were impressed when Frank Sinatra stopped by to kiss his friend "Michael" on the cheek. Other times it was Sammy Davis or Redd Foxx who dazzled Mickey's escorts.

On January 25, 1972, Mickey, accompanied by his associate Jim Smith, visited his parole officer at the U.S. Courthouse in Los Angeles.

"I don't want nothing—no notoriety, no publicity," Mickey told reporters waiting for him at the courthouse.

Deputy U.S. Probation Officer Stuart Makagon told him to return once a month, and explained that the parole supervision would last five years—the remainder of his term.

Despite all his contrite speeches, Mickey pursued his old line of work, being the boss, now somewhat of a pretense. He sent messages around the country, trying to rekindle his old relationships. They read, "Tell —— I said hello, if you ever see him around." He would tell anyone within earshot that he lived on loans and couldn't afford a car. The size of his operation had diminished, but that didn't stop him from living well: the skim arrangements with the slick organized national network provided immediate cash flow. Reliable friends keep him living in luxury; Frank Sinatra supplied a quick $25,000, and a promise of more. Not everyone was happy to see Mickey out of prison. Joe DiCarlo, who was now making tons of money as Sonny and Cher's manager, never paid him back any of the money he had shelled out for legal fees during the Whalen matter.

The IRS still watched Mickey, and forced him to live without reporting any income—not that he suddenly had decided to become a law-abiding taxpayer. If he did, they would collect a chunk of it. He found it impossible to get a court order to collect the money that attorney Belli had won for him from the government, the only known bulk income possibility.

"Criminally rehabilitated" Mickey moved to a smallish apartment at 1014 Westgate in West Los Angeles. Times had changed, and many places initially refused the celebrity tenant's request for occupancy.

After eleven years in prison, he naturally found the adjustment to civilian life a slow process. He arranged physical therapy appointments at UCLA Medical Center through a Dr. Rubenstein, where he complained about the high cost of health care.[4]

Despite his ordeal, he never sounded bitter. He was more interested in reporting on his exploits than on how it had affected him, but remained critical of prison conditions. It was hard for him to accept that the society he loved—and loved to pillage—could take such a subhuman approach to prisoners. He continued to seek the limelight, and made a public case for prison reform.

Mickey traveled around the country talking to the old crowd, and lectured his fans. He visited with Owney Madden's widow Agnes in Hot Springs, Arkansas;

Carlos Marcello in New Orleans; the remaining Cleveland mob; and those who had flocked to Vegas.

Separating himself from his origins, he adopted the stance that the crime world was full of Young Turks and "freaks," the latter a new breed of criminal that didn't share his mixed morality. The old rules were gone.

The bad-guy-turned-good-guy told reporters, "That's the whole problem, nobody has any shame, or respect, or pride anymore." Mickey lamented the days when a handshake sealed the deal, when friendship and a man's word meant everything.

He keenly observed the change in business: "Today, well, you couldn't even trust a signed contract—if you had one."

He admonished the past and told all reporters that he did not intend to resume his decadent life, repeating often, "I've had my belly full of it." He denied any illicit activity. "I live like I lived before, but I'm not into what you would call any action. I don't know if I'm living on my reputation or what, but very seldom can I go to any kind of affair where I'm not asked for my autograph."

Mickey-the-celebrity appeared on the Merv Griffin television variety show in 1972, his first year out of prison. Prime-time Mickey made the most of his spot, and offered his trademark statement that he never killed a man who didn't deserve it.

His fan mail rivaled that of any movie star. Some of the letters asked for his help, but a few wanted to give him gifts. Strangers offered him houses in Glasgow (Scotland), Florida, and Wyoming. A letter in French asked if he was interested in a gambling business near the Alps.

On January 16, 1973, Mickey lost his brother. Seventy-year-old Harry Marvin Cohen was the victim of a hit-and-run driver. He was in front of his Oxford Avenue home at seven in the evening when a foreign car, possibly a Renault, struck him. A second car traveling in the opposite direction also struck him. The first driver sped away. Police did not hold the second driver, only sixteen-years-old. Harry died at Hollywood Presbyterian Hospital. The police all-points bulletin for a black foreign car with a white top did not provide any leads.

On March 9 longtime Mickey pal Eli Lubin died of a heart attack at age fifty-two. Lubin was in the furniture business, but his obit naturally mentioned his Mickey associations, particularly the Pearson beating, and his own $10,000 tax evasion fine.

Four days later, Mickey opened a restaurant called Sonny's on La Cienega Boulevard, the fashionable restaurant row area of eastern Beverly Hills. Another Mickey acquisition was Paoli's in San Francisco, his steak and occasional cash source while he was in prison. He had hopes of opening another Paoli's at the Century Plaza Hotel, the favorite of Ronald Reagan and George Bush. He also made plans to open a restaurant in Beverly Hills called La Famiglia, which would become home to many Rat Packers, including nightly regular Dean Martin.[5] He also opened Gatsby's in Brentwood, not far from his apartment. The FBI was certain that Gatsby's was a front for gambling. By the end of 1973, he was back to bookmaking, business as usual.

Mickey spent his nights at popular Chasen's, Scandia, Gatsby's, Perino's, Matteo's, the Playboy Club, and in bars like the West Side Room. He liked to have a drink in the evening, although he didn't want his public to think that he ever imbibed.

One of the most popular Beverly Hills hangouts was the Luau restaurant, complete with indoor lagoon, celebrities, and high-priced hookers. He avoided it, despite its action-every-night reputation, because Lana's former husband Steve Crane owned it. Mickey did not want to relive the Turner-Stompanato episode or the old revenge accusations by her.

His name was on the publicity sheets for premieres and new clubs. He was proud of his opening night tickets for venues like the modern Shubert Theater in newly constructed Century City, adjacent to Beverly Hills, and built on the old 20th Century Fox back lot.

The Italian mob, whose pejorative nickname the "Mickey Mouse Mafia" seemed to fit more over time, didn't improve its chances for dominance when Dominic Brooklier took over in 1974. He is most remembered for ordering a hit on "The Bomp."

Long-time Mickey and Nixon pal Murray Chotiner died under suspicious circumstances that fueled conspiracy theories related to Henry Kissinger and General Al Haig. On January 23, 1974, Chotiner was in an automobile accident with a government truck in McLean, Virginia. Rumors suggested that the driver of the truck was a naval officer. First reports indicated that he had suffered only a broken leg; he died a week later in a hospital. Some relate his death to a decision by Kissinger to have General Haig issue a report on President Nixon's organized crime connections, which included Chotiner's shady history. Kissinger and Haig hoped that Nixon would resign. Chotiner's widow had no legal recourse since President Gerald Ford had pardoned Nixon.

The L.A. Press Club invited Mickey to speak in 1974. He sat at the dais next to associate Jim Smith. He kept a box of tissues within reach: his OCD never dissipated; he had his housekeeper alcohol everything in his home. Even after she

312

cleaned the bathroom, Mickey felt it was necessary to give the sink the once over before using it.

For multiple reasons, including his own personality traits of self-doubt and low self-esteem, Mickey was still disappointed in himself. He lamented, "I was just a plain vulgar heist man. I hadn't been around with a lot of good decent people… Even right now, I'm not too sure of myself, although I have gained some confidence."

He craved the type of fame and universal acceptance that surrounded the Rat Pack. The lengthy prison sentence didn't help his reputation. He was unable to achieve the social status afforded most celebrities, and could not mingle in all elements of society. Even though he had become a celebrity in his own right, he knew that he was not welcome in certain social, political, and business circles. Mickey despised performing what he called "dirty work" for many prized citizens because hours later the same people would ignore him in public. Yet, one of the country's most prominent citizens would soon call upon him for help.

31.

Mickey, the Elder Statesman

Fate thrust Mickey back into the national spotlight. The anti-capitalist Symbionese Liberation Army kidnapped Patricia Hearst from her Berkeley apartment on February 4, 1974. She subsequently appeared in a videotape robbing a bank with her kidnappers. Her father Randolph Hearst contacted Mickey. Likely Ed Montgomery, a crime reporter for the *San Francisco Examiner*, suggested the aging bookie since he was an old Hearst family friend and someone well versed in the criminal arts. Mickey "begrudgingly" agreed to assist, out of respect for Randolph's father William Randolph, who had always befriended Mickey and had regularly suggested that he enter legitimate business.

He seized the opportunity to act the role of the elder statesman and dealmaker, a matured stance he thoroughly enjoyed, and looked forward to the public lapping up his participation. As Ben Hecht once predicted of criminals, "And he will become as full of nonsense as a Secretary of State." Mickey had aged and slipped graciously "into the tame ways of the voting population." In a videotaped interview in which he spoke about the Hearsts, he looked haggard but well fed. He appeared in a neat short-sleeved sport shirt, and by this time he looked like everyone's Jewish grandfather from Encino, with thinning hair and whitish bushy eyebrows.

When the Hearsts first planned their visit with Mickey, the most difficult element of the arrangements involved the restaurant selection. The Hearsts naturally wanted to go to popular Chasen's, home of movie stars, high-ranking politicians, and the moneyed crowd. It was closed every Monday, the day of the meeting. They mentioned their other preferences, Scandia and Matteo's,[1] but those were also closed. The Hearsts finally settled on Gatsby's for the Monday, October 7 meeting. They flew in from Hillsborough after Hearst attorney James M. MacInnis finalized the details.

Mickey said of the legal counsel, "I know Jim very well, and have for some time...he's been a visitor in my home and I see him whenever I go to San Francisco."

Thirty-six-year-old Jim Smith picked up the Hearsts and MacInnis at Los Angeles International Airport around six-thirty. He told reporters, "I drove them to the restaurant for dinner... But I didn't take part in the conversation. That was between them and Mickey."

Gatsby's "owner" Bill Rosen warned Mickey that the local police intelligence squad was at the restaurant before the Hearsts arrived.

Mickey recalled that after a few drinks, Patty's mother Catherine Hearst revealed that they didn't think rescuing Patty from her kidnappers was prudent because she would face a prison term immediately upon her return. He was disappointed with the present understanding between the Hearsts and the authorities. He was surprised that the Hearsts hadn't negotiated a better arrangement before bringing him into the loop. He didn't like the deal, accustomed as he was to brokering deals that were clear between all parties, often well in advance. He refused to locate anyone that might serve twenty or thirty years in prison.

Mickey described his dismay: "When I learned that, it was a shock to me because I thought they knew what they were doin'. When I learned that they didn't have it in that kind of a shape I says, 'lookit, I won't bring nobody in to go to prison.'"

He watched as "Randy" Hearst and his attorney tried to chastise Catherine for misrepresenting the legal aspects of the dilemma.

Smith told reporters that after a two-hour meeting he drove the Hearsts and their attorney back to the airport around ten-thirty.

At the airport, the FBI watched as local police stopped them, MacInnis, and Mickey. Two detectives ordered the three men to put their hands up against the wall. One detective asked Catherine Hearst for identification. When she was unable to produce any proper documents the eager detective said, "We'll have to place you under arrest for consorting with a known criminal."

Moments later the other detective calmed the overzealous one when all the authorities realized whom the police had rousted.

Mickey was clearly upset and did his best to apologize to the Hearsts "for the hassle."

It was more likely that he had actually heard about the long prison term facing Patty Hearst while at the airport, but he preferred to erase the airport incident from his memory. However, he did mention that "the intelligence squad" had stopped the Hearsts.

Mickey did express his concerns for Patty soon after the roust at the airport. "Hell, all this time I thought it was all fixed up—that the kid wouldn't have to go to jail... I've been there—I can't walk, only shuffle like a duck 'cause I was there."

The FBI had monitored the entire meeting, but refused to comment. Assistant Director William A. Sullivan from Los Angeles said that they were in close contact with the Hearsts.

Hearst did not deny the meeting. "It was no big deal... I'd rather not discuss it, frankly, but we did have dinner and we did talk about the situation... Mr. Cohen thought maybe he could be of some help, and he offered to do what he could. We don't know if we can help or not, but we thought it worthwhile to talk to him... He didn't ask for anything, certainly not for himself... He was trying to help and I don't want to say anything that would cause a problem." His rationale for contacting Mickey had more to do with Mickey's reputation in the black underworld.

"I was involved in gambling in other days in the black community. I have a lot of friends there that love me and that I love dearly," said Mickey.

He told *Los Angeles Times* reporter Bill Hazlett, "I offered to help in any way I could, and I've already laid out some of my own money—not much, $250 here, $300 there—for some meetings and a couple of plane tickets."

The dapper Sherlock Holmes made the most of the expanded publicity routes and appeared on Los Angeles television Thursday night, October 24, to discuss the entire Hearst saga.

Mickey had tried to contact SLA leader Donald DeFreeze after multiple meetings with others. (DeFreeze was killed soon thereafter.) He was able to reach three people who were either SLA members or close associates; one was in Soledad Prison. Reporter Ed Montgomery had suggested that Mickey try the prison. He ended up with two solid leads, supplied by a white woman and a black man known to a numbers operator. Some reports suggested that Mickey met with

Emily and Bill Harris, also wanted by the FBI. He refused to reveal the location of the meeting. The nature of his rendezvous surprised him. "You know, it was really sort of weird—like one of those cloak and dagger things you see on TV. Go here, then go there…"

Mickey said in many interviews, "You know. I speak their language. The cops don't—the FBI don't. But I do. So it took a little time. But finally I got a lead that was good."

By October 25, rumors had cropped up that he had located Patty Hearst in a city near the U.S.-Canadian border. He immediately denied the story. "I have never seen Patricia Hearst and I have never talked to her. The information I got about her came second, third, fourth, and fifth hand." The new facts had originated with San Francisco television reporter Marilyn Baker, and then became a widely disseminated UPI story.

Reporters checked with Catherine Hearst, who told them, "Mr. Cohen offered to use his underworld connections in an effort to find Patty. He never told us he had seen her and he didn't say anything about her being in one town or another or anything about the Canadian border." Catherine Hearst was critical of reporter Marilyn Baker, whom Catherine felt was fueling the story to "…keep herself in the public eye."

Based on what Mickey represented as a clairvoyant hunch, he somehow pinpointed Patty Hearst's previously unknown location as Cleveland; more likely, Montgomery had directed Mickey there and then rescinded the suggestion. The current speculation on Patty's whereabouts included the West Coast, Canada, Panama, and Guatemala.

The day after the Baker-UPI story broke, Mickey washed his hands of the whole matter: "I've done the best I could, but it just didn't work out… I thought I could help and I hoped to be successful in getting her back… I didn't—I failed, and it's all over."

Mickey actually had had all the details in place before his October 7 meeting with the Hearsts. He initially had flown in several of his Cleveland contacts for advice. Once he had planted the word, he waited for the results to materialize. He explained the plan: "I was supposed to have gone to Cleveland myself if arrangements could have been made to speak to Patty Hearst and relay to her a message from her parents: all her parents were interested in was her well-being and safety. If she would come back and clear herself of all these charges, and if they were assured of her welfare, then if she chose to go back to the radical way of life and— to use the words of the Hearsts—'to live a life like Jane Fonda,' it would be OK with them."

317

When the SLA threatened a shootout, Mickey backed off on pressuring a meeting with Patty. "I'm on parole, and that's all I needed for a goddamned shootout to happen and somebody getting killed," he said. Furthermore, consorting with the wrong people was enough to raise a parole officer's eyebrows.

He explained, "I couldn't go where she was at. The people I got involved with, they thought I was going to where she was at." Mickey told the *New York Times* that if he could have traveled to Cleveland, he would have delivered Patty back unharmed.

He said, "...that I would have to use force to bring her in." The feisty sleuth also admitted that he was afraid for his own safety: "...a little scared to talk with them SLA members... Hell, they're wild kids, those kinds. You know, jittery, shaky. You don't ever know what they're going to do."

To make matters worse, Patty wasn't ready to leave the SLA, and nothing Mickey or anyone else could do would influence that decision.

Randolph Hearst, rightly fearful of harm coming to his daughter, told reporters that it was unlikely that Mickey had located her. The Hearsts always maintained that they had rejected Mickey's offer. MacInnis, attorney for the Hearsts, later confirmed to reporters that Mickey did locate Patty in Cleveland through black radicals and people connected to the numbers racket.

He said, "It was a definite thing, and it was a definite thing she was coming back to San Francisco."

Gentleman Mickey uttered his original final word on the juxtaposed stories and politicking: "I don't want to be rude, but I got to beg off this thing."

Mickey's elder statesman adventures would continue, again putting him in the spotlight.

32.

The Last Round

News regarding the original possibility of Mickey's presidential pardon hit the papers again on October 27, 1972. Jack Anderson, who took over for Drew Pearson at the *Washington Post*, said that the pardon angle from President Johnson had been possible. He explained that Pearson had visited Mickey in prison several times. Pearson, who spoke often with Mickey, also had President Johnson's ear, and Anderson concluded that a compassionate friend like Pearson could easily have asked Johnson about a pardon for Mickey.

Mickey's voice displayed his anger and disappointment whenever he spoke about Johnson. "Drew Pearson had it right when he wrote about it. Johnson promised me a full medical pardon through Pearson. Pearson was a friend of mine. He visited me in jail regularly."

He said that Pearson wrote this memo to him: "I got a definite promise from LBJ that one way or another, if Humphrey wins or loses, you're going to get a parole or a medical parole at least."

Many articles contained his laments regarding the pardon. "I know he [Drew Pearson] didn't lie to me. I was to get that pardon after the 1968 campaign no matter what. Everybody thought Humphrey would win. But I was to get that pardon… So sure, I was involved in the 1968 race between Nixon and Humphrey. But how can you do much from the pen? … So what happens? Nixon beats Humphrey, and that S.O.B. Johnson died… [As did Drew, of course. And Mickey's still in jail until they give him a parole]. I should have had that pardon." (Johnson died the year after Mickey left prison.)

With Pearson and LBJ gone, there was little chance to prove the promise, not that either party would have jumped at the opportunity. Anderson had none of secretive Pearson's files, so it was impossible to check his letters.

Mickey felt strongly that all the politicians had double-crossed him. He was also quick to speak to the media concerning his dealings with Murray Chotiner and Nixon, and the story circulated once again.

Word was out that Mickey was writing a book about his life. John Peer Nugent had received a $7,500 advance to start work on the autobiography. Mickey told reporters on October 26, "I tell it all…all that I know…like it was." Mickey wasn't sure if the book would be published. "These lawyers are worried about lawsuits and statutes of limitation and things like that. I'm not. It's the truth—and that's more than I can say for some of those books everybody reads."

On November 13, 1974, John Hall elaborated in the *Los Angeles Times* about his evening out with Mickey at Gatsby's. Journalist Hall still found him a man with flare. Mickey enjoyed his veal plate while he reminisced about his youth, his prison stay record, his speech and writing tutor from twenty years ago, his dislike for Muhammad Ali—"Cassius Clay is a rotten example for kids"—and his upcoming biography. He liked fighter Bobby Chacon, but said that he had quit and didn't give it his all against Ruben Olivares.

Balding Mickey kept his cane nearby, complained about his legs, and popped antacids for an ulcer. He dressed in a "neat, conservative, expensive" suit with a perfectly knotted tie. Waiters watched his every move, tried to anticipate his needs, and could not do enough for him. He handed out tips to the waiter, cocktail girl, maître d', and busboy. He washed his hands with lemon water, and dried them with a large white napkin.

He made it clear that he lived on loans and had no money for luxury items. His book was in limbo until the IRS agreed on profit-sharing terms. He said that he did collect the government award for his Atlanta prison experience, this time adding that the money went to the IRS. He excused himself from dinner to check a tape of his recent talk show interview.

Mickey continued his regular publicity campaign, and during the first week of March 1975, his extensive AP interview with Linda Deutsch circled the globe. He was looking forward to the end of his parole in eighteen months and explained how his life had changed: "I live practically the same life I lived before. The only difference is that I'm not involved with gambling or any illegal activities... Not that I've lost all my friends or contacts... Everyone comes to see me. And I'm out to all my old haunts... I just don't have the strength or stomach to get involved in anything."

He spent part of each day doing his physical therapy exercises. He enjoyed going to the movies, and remarked that both *Godfather* movies were accurate depictions of mob life.

He made sure to plug his book, which was still in the works. "A lot of my friends are prejudiced. They think this is gonna be bigger than the *Godfather*. I really wrote the truth."

The new author spoke about his disappointment with the Hearsts: "It was a heartrending thing anyway. My sisters kept bothering me about it."

He said that Al Capone was one of his favorite people, explaining that he only showed love and respect, although Mickey commented that he had never seen Capone angry.

Mickey had become critical of Las Vegas:

> I remember when there were only two roads to Vegas. It was a little frontier town. My place was the first one in town... The environment is so different now. The color seems to be lacking... It's become an assembly line. They used to cater to a more gambling element. Now you see women and children running up to the slot machines... It takes a lot of glamour out of gambling.

The fastidious dandy still tried to cut a dapper image, and was meticulous about his clothing. His social life hadn't diminished, and he dated actress Lita Baron, who was divorced from actor Rory Calhoun. He also spoke fondly of Gail Fisher, who worked on the hit television series *Mannix*.

Mickey lamented about his physical difficulties. "...if I never came out of that coma I just wouldn't have known what hit me. Sometimes walking is so painful... There were times when I could do things with a snap of my finger. It's not quite like that anymore."

He also looked on the bright side: "...it's good to be with a pretty girl or with company I enjoy, at a prizefight or a restaurant I enjoy."

The criminal pundit was rarely out of the media spotlight. Newspapers published his speculations on the disappearance of Jimmy Hoffa through July of that year. He called the Hoffa matter a "setup"; the whole Hoffa meeting was a ruse.

Mickey spoke with reporter Bill Hazlett. "I think Jim fell into a trap that somebody set for him because of an internal squabble in the union... I've got my own ideas about that but I certainly can't talk about that on the telephone."

He begged off on giving the information to the Hoffa family. "I didn't want to take away any of the hopes that Jimmy, Jr., Barbara, or his wife, Josephine, might have. It just wouldn't be right."

During August, he still spoke to reporters about Hoffa. He explained that people in Detroit had asked him to use his contacts to help locate Hoffa. He said, "I'm trying in every way to find out what the score is." A few more Hoffa and Mickey stories circulated around the country. He finally said by telephone: "I feel Jim is gone... I know what I know from my own connections." He was correct regarding Hoffa's execution.

Whenever possible, he appeared on television. On Friday, September 19, 1975, Mickey joined former attorney general and political activist Ramsey Clark (currently Saddam Hussein's attorney) on a ninety-minute show, part of the Wide World of Entertainment, entitled "The Underworld: A Portrait in Power." Actor Robert Stack hosted the television show, and the two guests discussed "the power of organized crime."

Just ten days later, Mickey entered UCLA Medical Center for a suspected abdominal tumor, and doctors performed immediate exploratory surgery.

On October 1, doctors removed most of his stomach at UCLA. He had been suffering from cancer, not simply an ulcer, although doctors referred to his tumor as a malignant ulcer. Dr. Herbert Machleder presided over a team of surgeons during the three-hour procedure.

Old companion Liz Renay visited Mickey the day before and the day after his operation. She told reporters, "He told me that he had cancer and was on the way out. He said he knew it was a down approach to take, but that he knew he was dying."

She offered Mickey's long-standing quote, but changed it to read that he had killed "no one who didn't deserve it."

Two days later doctors offered a good prognosis for Mickey, and his condition was now listed as satisfactory.

He "wrote" his book, complete with the misspelled names of his legal associates, employees, acquaintances, and even his barber "Gelbar[t]." Naturally, the movie buzz was back in Mickey's life.

He wanted to set the record straight, and clear up misrepresentations by critical author Ed Reid, and others. Yet, his book did little to outline a linear history, or shed light on unsettled events. He was still in denial about his past, which accounts for some of his omissions. Many people also had high stakes in what he was willing to spill in his book. His rambling dialogue supplied the censorship, edited from years of retelling the stories. Diplomat Mickey was not looking for any more trouble; he was more interested in cultivating his image as one of the first talking head pundits.

Even his unique autobiography, one of the few memoirs having to do with organized crime, has become the subject of a cover-up since it appears censored. He was one of the stronger links between the unholy alliance of the entertainment business and organized crime, a relationship he cherished. Since some of the rich and powerful allowed Mickey into their lives, he was in a position of great influence and, as mentioned, often resorted to blackmail in order to solidify his control of celebrities. He wasn't talking, despite knowing where many of the Hollywood skeletons were buried, and does not give up much in his book, certainly none of the salacious celebrity stories that people crave. His mixed morality and revisionist view of his life prevented him from revealing the backroom politics either.

Author Michael Collins Piper suggests that John Peer Nugent, the writer who penned the autobiography from Mickey's long-winded stories, was subject to CIA editing: "Interesting enough, Nugent himself once participated in a debate with JFK assassination investigator, A. J. Weberman, co-author of *Coup d'Etat in America*, where he—Nugent—sought to refute CIA complicity in the assassination."[1]

By the time his autobiography hit the shelves during late 1975, the country was still in the midst of severe a cocaine epidemic. The illicit coffers overflowed with the success of the international drug trade. The white powder was everywhere, a staple to many in the entertainment business, as it was on the set of the new late night television comedy hit *Saturday Night Live*.[2]

Resilient Mickey didn't give in easily to the cancer. The old boxer walked with a limp, his right leg almost useless. By the end of November 1975, he was on his feet and in Manhattan to promote his book. He sat for interviews in his elegant suite at the Pierre Hotel, across from Central Park. One interview was with journalist Ira Berkow. Mickey, wisely not trusting the cleanliness of hotel housekeeping, sat on a clean white bed sheet, draped over a chair. Berkow noted the star sapphire pinkie ring, platinum watch, and half-dollar sized golf cuff links, all on loan or gifts from friends. He wore a three-piece glen-plaid suit that fit nicely on his "solid frame."

Mickey reflected on his past, surrounded by oak walls and Degas reproductions. "He [Nixon] was a big help to me in my operations in Orange County...but if you ever told me that he'd be president I would have died laughing."

The showman went down memory lane, and spoke about Al Capone, who would always "lay a couple of hundred dollar bills in my pocket."

Regarding Mickey's murder record, he admitted to six, "but every one of 'em needed killing."

Frank Sinatra was "A stand-up guy, and if you call his hole card, he's going to answer."[3]

The crime philosopher added that Jimmy Hoffa was buried in a lime pit, and that should serve as a deterrent to the youth of America who pursue criminal careers.

Berkow sensed the frailty of the elder criminal: "...one looked at him and his tissues and wondered if in some subconsciously humanitarian way, he was, in the end, not so much fearful of being contaminated as he was concerned with contaminating."

In another interview, Mickey told *New York News* writer Anthony Burton that the assassination attempts on his life numbered twelve. He again spoke of his love for Al Capone.

He lamented the bombing death of an old Cleveland associate Alex "Shondor" Birns. He found out about the death after a reporter had mailed him the press clippings. To show his gratitude, he sent the reporter a cashmere sweater.

Burton liked his subject. "That too, for Mickey Cohen, was class."

Toward Christmas 1975, UPI circulated a story about Mickey. The article spoke about his flamboyant life, how his world appeared modeled on the movie life of James Cagney, George Raft, and Edward G. Robinson. The story mentioned his lavish wardrobe, his association with strippers who wore fur coats and diamonds, how he hobnobbed with movie stars, and unfortunately his five-foot-three stature and elevator shoes.

The same year, producers released an offbeat documentary about the Kennedy assassinations entitled *I Due Kennedy* (The Two Kennedys). The piece, originally released in Italy in 1969, featured Mickey footage along with Fidel Castro, Ramsey Clark, Al Capone, Carlos Marcello, Hubert H. Humphrey, Barbara Hutton, Lyndon Johnson, Ted Kennedy, Phyllis McGuire, and Benito Mussolini. *The Two Kennedys* had all the voices dubbed except Lauren Bacall, Marilyn Monroe, and Hitler.

In summer 1976, the *compares* buried long-time mobster Johnny Rosselli in a fifty-five gallon oil drum, but not before sawing off his legs. After tossing the drum in the ocean, they renamed him Deep-Six Johnny.[4]

Mickey's book did not make a big splash. It never became the hit to bring him back to the forefront of Hollywood; he had been out of the limelight too long.

Hollywood's memory was always a short one. The public had new idols; bad boys of rock took center stage and grabbed the headlines. The public relegated him to history, but he was as much a part of the nation's fixation with Hollywood as any matinee idol or actor turned politician.

On July 6, 1976, he returned to UCLA hospital, complaining of fatigue. Further diagnosis revealed that he was suffering from jaundice. He remained in the hospital until July 20.

Mickey died quietly in his sleep on Thursday, July 29, just weeks before the end of his parole. Some references cite a coronary as the cause of death, likely secondary to his deteriorating bout with cancer.

Ironically, he held the record for surviving unsuccessful murder attempts, and none of his adversaries ever dreamed he would still be around that year.

When he died, Mickey's net worth, including his cash, was $3,000. His will, filed for probate on August 5, indicated a twenty-five percent share for "right-hand-man" Jim Smith, and fifteen percent shares for Smith's children, James and Tina. Sisters Pauline Duitz and Lillian Weiner each received fifteen percent. The U.S. Attorney in Los Angeles was suing Mickey for back taxes totaling $496,535.23. The debt was over ten years old.

About 150 people attended Mickey's funeral. Only one shoving match started during the services; it involved a photographer. Funeral officials would not reveal the names of the guests at the private service.

Meyer Harris Cohen lies in a crypt at Hillside Cemetery in Culver City, final resting place of the stars. He would have been pleased with the view, an endless list of Hollywood luminaries and their monuments. His neighbors run the gamut from comedian Jack Benny to singer Dinah Shore and from Stooge Moe Howard to immortal makeup czar Max Factor.

He lies in the mausoleum's second drawer from the bottom, the Alcove of Love, A-217. The plaque reads, "Our Beloved Brother, Meyer H. Cohen, Mickey, 1914–1976."

Obits around the country quoted Mickey on his sense of ethics and repeated his trademark lines. Estimates on his mansion reverted to the quarter of a million-dollar range.

The *Los Angeles Times* obituary stated that he was "the undisputed boss of Los Angeles gangdom and lived in a mansion surrounded with an electronically equipped fence and spotlights and containing closets filled with expensive suits and shoes...traveled in a Cadillac followed by another car carrying his armed "helpers." The *New York Times* called him "the tough little former professional boxer who rose to become a leader of the West Coast gambling rackets in the 1950s and 1960s…"

Melvin Belli recalled Mickey less than two months after his death: "Mickey Cohen was a very sweet, gentle guy."

Actor Harvey Keitel, who played Mickey in the movie *Bugsy,* knew his character well. "A guy like that could have been anything in life—had he had the right guidance he could have gone anywhere in life because his drive, his intellect…it was all there."

Mickey's former wife LaVonne had experienced the multilayered personality firsthand: "…behind all the excitement and violence that surrounds his life is a guy who is very easy to like. There is nothing mean about Mickey. He is generous and kind in his own way, but he would rather die than admit it."

Ben Hecht had once summarized Mickey's positive side:

He paid off on the dot and to the nickel. He fixed fights and let his pals in on the take. He operated hideaway gambling rendezvous where the dice, wheels and cards were as on the level as any operator could afford to have them. On the side he beat up Nazi propagandists, staked bums to binges, never overlooked the birthday of a policeman's kid, paid medical bills for all wounded supporters and was good for a touch from anybody who smiled and said, "Hello, Mickey."

Crime historian James Johnston was likewise enamored but reminds us that "Mickey was one of the nicest killers you'd ever want to meet."

Peter Noyes recognized Mickey's influence: "Mickey Cohen was a big name in this town. You didn't get any bigger than the Mick." He was larger than life, larger than Hollywood life. He was the underdog who defied everyone in town, and became an international celebrity because of his criminal notoriety.

Life magazine wove him into the social fabric of the nation. "In the Rat Pack Era, the guys and dolls were having a time; Sinatra swingin', Vegas sizzlin', and one brazen gangster struttin' his stuff."

Hecht may have said it best: "The Republic's most colorful, and, for a long time, most successful criminal, Mr. Cohen."

That was Mickey.

Epilogue

For the next three decades, mobsters floated through the Sunset Strip and Beverly Hills oasis, while the commercial and social transition from Hollywood continued west.

The fashionable "Bomp" was one of the most visible Italian figures. In 1977, Chicago associate Tony Spilotro likely gave the orders to have The Bomp, who was blabbing extensively to the FBI, shot and killed. Four bullets in the head from a silenced automatic pistol felled the spiffy assassin. The local goomba Mickey Mouse Mafia continued to decline due to failed leadership.

The Two Tonys gruesome murder case would have remained unsolved, but Jimmy "The Weasel" Fratianno spilled this and more—he killed five times for Jack Dragna—when he had entered the Federal Witness Protection program two years after Mickey died.

Mickey's journalist friend seventy-eight-year-old Agnes Underwood sued Fratianno in 1981 over the false claim that she wrote the story about the fake ship destroyed on its way to deliver Israeli armaments, suggesting that she was in on the fundraising fraud. Fratianno's statements had resulted in years of published false accusations against Mickey. The $110,000,000 defamation suit stated that Underwood first heard about the much-bandied Fratianno quote from her grandson after television's *60 Minutes* ran the story. Underwood's attorney Caryl Warner insisted that no such *Herald-Express* article ever existed, and that Underwood didn't meet Mickey until 1948. Fratianno claimed that he *never made* the statement, and had no idea how his biographer Ovid Demaris got that idea. He said that it was Demaris' responsibility to fact check. Also named in the suit were Mike Wallace, still of *60 Minutes*, the *New York Times Book Co.*, radio station KMPC, and KMPC's Billy Rose.

Underwood said, "I never took 5 cents from anyone, and now they are accusing me of stealing a million."

CBS and KMPC refused to retract their statements.

In January 1982, *Playboy*'s Hugh Hefner ran into problems with Mickey's old pal Joe DiCarlo after helping him set up Pips, a fancy and exclusive private club in Los Angeles that featured backgammon. Hefner said he was aware of DiCarlo's past, but never considered it a problem, and had resigned from Pips over a control dispute. When Hefner sought a gaming license in New Jersey, authorities brought up Mickey's name.

Mickey's exquisite custom-built car ended up in the hands of Negri's Antique and Classics on Mt. Baldy Circle in Fountain Valley, California. Owner Frank Negri advertised the car for his 1982 Memorial Day Collector Car Auctions and Show, but it was not part of the auction; it went on display with *Waltons'* John Boy Model A Ford Coup and vehicles from the *CHiPS* police series. Negri explained: "The younger generation will probably not remember Mickey Cohen, but he was a colorful character…and we will have his bullet-proof Caddie at the show."

Through the eighties, the Los Angeles Strike Force identified brothers Peter and Carmen Milano, sons of Cleveland mobster Anthony Milano, as the local bosses. Informant brothers Craig and Lawrence Fiato wore FBI wires for six years right under the Milanos' noses. In May 1987, the last remnants of organized crime supposedly disappeared with the conviction of the Milano brothers. The eighteen-count indictment alleged, among other things, that they had plotted the murder of Louie Dragna (Jack's nephew) with Cleveland boss Jack Licavoli. Peter Milano received six years on federal racketeering statutes. Mike Rizzitello, the next in command, was sentenced to thirty-three years for conspiracy to murder topless bar boss William Carroll. Carmen Milano received his sentence in July 2000. "I'm in the twilight years of my life, and I'll never be in this situation again," said disbarred attorney Milano. "I'm here to retire."

When the survivors of Mickey's organized clique went their separate ways, a new breed of independent, grandiose, and brazen criminals developed. Supposedly, and many wrote, when "Fat" Herbie Blitzstein was iced on January 6, 1997, it marked the end of any link to Mickey and the Mickey Mouse boys.[1]

The announcement echoed one from ten years before, when authorities had gotten the Milanos. Thirty years back, U.S. Deputy Attorney General Christopher had said that all crime around town was a local phenomenon. The FBI currently knew of at least 1,700 *made* mafia members.

Epilogue

Residents like to view potential crime as they do their movies, Hollywoodized—a more glamorous approach to white-collar crime and capers. Retired FBI agent William J. Rehder wrote, "Capers...are...crimes in which cunning and intelligence and careful planning trump weapons and violence...payoff is big, the methods stealthy, and nobody gets hurt... When a jewel thief in a tuxedo slips out of the masked ball and steals the duchess's diamond tiara from the safe hidden behind the cognac in the liquor cabinet, that's a caper..." Rehder knows the harsher reality as well as he does the Hollywood version: "...when an ex-con gang-banger puts a cap into a Beverly Hills jewelry store owner and does a smash-and-grab on the Rolexes under the glass counter, that's not a caper."

With the exception of Larry Flynt's Hustler club in Beverly Hills, Tiffany, Wolfgang Puck, The Gap, and banks have replaced the gambling joints, nightclubs, and movie theaters. Comedy clubs, dance clubs, and upscale restaurants and shops fill the Sunset Strip.

Crime goes on, but in ways that would be unfamiliar to Mickey. A local business, Beverly Hills Estates Funding, recently pulled off a $140,000,000 mortgage swindle. In the process, the investment firm Lehman Brothers took a hit for $60,000,000 in bad loans. Two Beverly Hills residents utilized the Internet for manipulating stock prices by posting false information on message boards. One local received a six-year sentence and had to pay $6,000,000 in restitution for a more complex money laundering conspiracy. He had operated for ten years, manipulating over thirty different stocks. The press release read, "...Beverly Hills businessman, real estate investor, and film producer, sentenced to six years in prison for money laundering and securities fraud." After a three-year investigation, the FBI nailed a dentist for health care fraud. Can you believe that she audaciously bilked insurance carriers by submitting false claims? A bogus Beverly Hills modeling school paid $50,000 in fines. Did you hear the one about the illegal prescription-writing doctor who sold millions in narcotics?

Despite the availability of computers and the worldwide Internet, criminals continued to make money the old-fashioned way, with the oldest profession. The LAPD announced the culmination of a two-year investigation dubbed "Operation White Lace." One of the largest prostitution rings in the history of Los Angeles and Beverly Hills was the focus of indictments issued in December 2002. Some of the fanciest hotels supplied the backdrop for escorts to make the most of their efforts. To save time, the Organized Crime Division of the district attorney's office should have checked the Beverly Hills yellow pages that had advertised Exclusive Girls Escort, European Blondes, and European Delight Escorts—the ones used by the targeted group—or the current Bad Girls, Fun Girls, and Play-mates, with "Naughty" and "Escorts" in oversized type.

In January 2003, the Beverly Hills police answered a call from the famous Osbournes, who reported that an ICM agent had robbed them! The Osbournes had conducted a raffle that included a necklace worth fifteen grand. The agent won the raffle but the forever-play-by-the-rules first family of reality television claimed that the winner had to be an invited guest, and the ICM agent had been a party crasher.

The United States District Court grand jury filed a 110-count sixty-page federal racketeering indictment against sleuth-to-the-stars Anthony Pellicano. The February 2006 indictment sounds like a carbon copy of Mickey's extortion and wiretapping operation. The suit alleges that Pellicano used confidential police and law enforcement records, including the National Crime Information Center, to access information on actors Sylvester Stallone, Garry Shandling, Kevin Nealon, and Keith Carradine; journalists Anita Busch and Bernard Weintraub; powerhouse agents Bryan Lourd and Kevin Huvane; and former professional tennis player Lisa Bonder Kerkorian, who was married to three-times-her-age billionaire entertainment mogul Kirk Kerkorian. The wiretapping scheme, efforts to dig up dirt of any kind—"responsible for securing clients who were willing and able to pay large sums for the purpose of obtaining personal information of a confidential, embarrassing, or incriminating nature"—included an LAPD officer, phone company employees, and Pellicano's own software bugging engineer. The *New York Times* indicated that the "noir clichés" of Mickey's world survive: "…the scandal's tentacles have extended beyond show-business figures to reach people prominent in the rarefied worlds of fine art and classical music." Witnesses included hedge-fund manager and art collector Adam D. Sender, who needed Pellicano's services regarding a sour movie deal with producer Aaron Russo, and Jacqueline A. Colburn, the former ninth wife of arts patron Richard D. Colburn; she used Pellicano to wiretap her husband. Lawyer and art collector Alan S. Hergott had pointed Sender to entertainment lawyer Bert Fields (his wife is art consultant Barbara Guggenheim), who had suggested Pellicano.

Crime is here to stay, organized or not. *Zai nisht narish*—"Don't be a fool."

Mickey Cohen Headlines

Mickey chose these early front-page headlines when he posed for one of his favorite photos:

COHEN SHOOTING SUSPECTS FREED
INDICTMENTS SLATED FOR 5
HOLLYWOOD SEX ORGIES DESCRIBED
HOWSER GIVES MICKEY "GUARD"
HORRALL REED INDICTED, OTHERS ALSO NAMED
MOB GUNS MICKEY, COHEN, 3 PALS SHOT
COHEN MOBSTER DIES
INDICT 5 TOP COPS
AMBUSHED COHEN PAL NEAR DEATH
EX-NY COP MAY HOLD MOB CLUE
COHEN GANG KILLER TRAILED IN MEXICO
PLOT TO BOMB MICKEY BARED
COHEN SECRETS REVEALED IN HIDDEN MICROPHONE
WITNESS MISSING IN COHEN INQUIRY
HIDDEN "BUG" RIPS VEIL OFF COHEN SETUP
D.A. WORTON IN BITTER FEUD ON COHEN MESS
JIMMIE TARANTINO NABBED IN S.F. COHEN SHOOTING
DYNAMITE PLOT ON COHEN REVEALED
PRETTY REDHEAD HUNTED IN COHEN QUIZ
COHEN MOB MUSCLING INTO LABOR ROWS
U.S. VICE LORDS TO HUDDLE WITH COHEN
NEW SIEGEL KILLING IDEA CLEARS COHEN
STATE TO MOVE IN L.A. CRIME MESS
DELAY VICE INDICTMENTS
JURY PROBE SEEN IN STRIP SHOOTING
D.A. PROBES COP IN COHEN MESS
BLAME DOPE RING IN COHEN SHOOTING
D.A. PROBES BOWRON INTO COHEN ACTION
WOUND MICKEY COHEN IN GUN TRAP, 3 NEAR DEATH
COHEN EXPOSE MAY LEAD TO SIEGEL SLAYING CLUB
BISCAILUZ NET SNARES FEW SUSPECTS IN COHEN AMBUSH
HOWSER GIVEN NAMES OF 3 IN SHOOTING OF COHEN
COHEN KNOWS ASSASSINS WILL TAKE CARE OF THIS

Jewish Mob Deaths

He eats well, sleeps well, lives well, and his only disadvantage is that he may die ahead of his time from an enemy bullet, the gas chamber, or electric chair

— Ben Hecht.

IRVING "WAXEY" GORDON would die in Alcatraz.

ARNOLD ROTHSTEIN, forty-six, shot outside New York's Park Central Hotel in 1928, over a card game gambling debt. Rothstein made his way to the service entrance of the hotel, holding his stomach to prevent the gushing blood from escaping. Rothstein never revealed the shooter.

DUTCH SCHULTZ (Arthur Flegenheimer), who came from a kosher home, was too cold-blooded, even for the killers. Shot at the popular Palace Chophouse in Newark, New Jersey. Twenty-nine-year-old Dutch lay on the floor of the washroom while his body oozed blood, courtesy of several thirty-eight slugs. Even a five-hundred cc transfusion could not save him at the hospital, where he lay dying and raving after receiving last rites from a priest.

ABRAHAM "KID TWIST" RELES, thirty-four, flew out of his sixth floor window at the Half Moon Hotel in Coney Island, Brooklyn, and his splattered bottom found twenty feet from the hotel. The great-grandson of the Half Moon builder unveiled the Lower East Side kosher Blue Moon Hotel on Orchard Street in 2004.

The first "Bugsy," MARTIN (MEYER) "BUGSY" GOLDSTEIN worked for Murder Inc. He got the chair at Sing-Sing.

LOUIS "LOUIS COHEN" KERZNER died at thirty-five. Shot on a Manhattan street—Lepke's orders.

ABRAHAM LANDAU, member of Shultz's gang, made it to forty, shot while dining at the Palace Chophouse Bar in Newark, New Jersey.

IRVING and MEYER SHAPIRO shot; WILLIE SHAPIRO, buried alive.

AUGIE "LITTLE AUGIE" ORGEN, twenty-six; he and KID DROPPER (Nathan Kaplan) were running the rackets.

JACOB "GURRAH" SHAPIRO, forty-seven, ended his career in a gun battle on a Manhattan street; died inside Sing-Sing. He or his victims shouted, "Gurra adhere," and accounted for his nickname.

HERMAN "HYMAN" AMBERG shot himself in the Tombs jail in Manhattan.

ABE RELES and Murder Inc. killed JOSEPH and LOUIS "PRETTY" AMBERG," two of Brooklyn's most feared gangsters. Louis "Pretty" Amberg, was reportedly so ugly that Ringling Brothers wanted to feature him in the circus as the missing link. Damon Runyon immortalized Amberg's killing style—stuffing victims in laundry bags, and letting them strangle themselves trying to get out.

LOUIS LEPKE, forty-seven, died defiantly in the Sing-Sing electric chair, seven years after becoming an informant. "...wheeled about sharply and fairly threw himself into it. The muscles of his jaw worked slightly and his eyes rolled up to see the head electrode descend upon him"—Jay Robert Nash.

LOUIS COHEN shot NATHAN KAPLAN (KID DROPPER), while he was standing outside the Essex Market Courthouse in lower Manhattan.

MONK EASTMAN, forty-seven, shot to death outside the Fourteenth Street subway.

Queens cemeteries Mount Carmel in Ridgewood, Montefiore in Saint Albans, and Mount Hebron in Flushing house most of the bodies.

Many of their Italian competitors and successors are only a short drive away, mostly in Queens and Brooklyn.

Bibliography

Books

Adler, Bill. *Sinatra: The Man and the Myth*. New York, Signet, 1987.

Anderson, Clinton. *Beverly Hills is My Beat*. New York, Popular Library, 1960.

Balsamo, William and Carpozi, George Jr. *Crime Incorporated*. New Jersey, New Horizon Press, 1991.

Bass, Warren. *Support Any Friend: Kennedy's Middle East and the Making of the U.S.-Israel Alliance*. Oxford University Press, 2003.

Berle, William and Lewis, Brad. *My Father, Uncle Miltie*. New York, Barricade Books, 1999.

Blakey, Robert G. and Billings, Richard M. *The Plot to Kill the President*. New York, NYT Books, 1981.

Block, Alan A. *Space, Time & Organized Crime*. New Brunswick, Transaction, 1994.

Bluestein, Gene. *Anglish/Yinglish*. University of Nebraska Press, 1998.

Bodner, Allen. *When Boxing was a Jewish Sport*. Connecticut, Praeger, 1997.

Boller, Paul F. Jr. *Presidential Wives*. New York, Oxford University Press, 1988.

Boller, Paul F. Jr. and Davis, Ronald L. *Hollywood Anecdotes*. New York, William Morrow, 1987.

Breines, Paul. *Tough Jews*. Basic Books, 1990.

Bynum, Lindley and Jones, Idwal. *Biscailuz—Sheriff of the New West*. New York, William Morrow and Company, 1950.

Cantor, Norman F. *The Sacred Chain*. New York, HarperPerennial, 1995.

Capeci, Jerry. *The Complete Idiot's Guide to the Mafia*. Indianapolis, Alpha, 2002.

Carpozi, George Jr. *Bugsy*. New York, SPI Books, 1992.

Cobb, Sally Wright and Willems, Mark. *A Hollywood Legend: The Brown Derby Restaurant*. New York, Rizzoli, 1996.

Cohen, Mickey. As told to John Peer Nugent. *Mickey Cohen: In My Own Words*. Englewood Cliffs, New Jersey, Prentice-Hall, 1975.

Cohen, Rich. *Tough Jews*. New York, Simon and Shuster, 1998.

Cohn, Art. *The Joker is Wild*, New York, Bantam, 1955.

Crane, Cheryl. *Detour*. New York, Morrow, 1988.

Davis, John H. *Mafia Kingfish*. New York, Signet, 1989.

Davis, Sammy, Jr., and Boyar, Jane and Burt. *Yes I Can*. New York, Farrar, Straus, and Giroux, 1966.

——. *Why Me?* New York, Farrar, Straus, and Giroux, 1989.

Demaris, Ovid. *The Last Mafioso*. New York, NYT Books, 1981.

Eisenhower, Julie Nixon. *Pat Nixon*. New York, Zebra, 1987.

Exner, Judith. As told to Ovid Demaris. *My Story*. New York, Grove Press, 1977.

Evans, Jr. Rowland and Novak, Robert D. *Nixon in the White House*. New York, Vintage Books, 1972.

Feder, Sid and Joesten, Joachim. *The Luciano Story*. New York, Da Capo Press, 1994.

Fried, Albert. *The Rise and Fall of the Jewish Gangster in America*. New York, Holt, Rinehart and Winston, 1980.

Gabler, Neal. *An Empire Of Their Own*. New York, Anchor Books, 1988.

Gentry, Curt. *J. Edgar Hoover: The Man and the Secrets*. New York, Plume Books, 1992.

Giancana, Sam and Chuck. *Double Cross*. New York, Warner Books, 1992.

Geisler, Jerry. As told to Pete Martin. *The Jerry Geisler Story*. New York, Simon and Schuster, 1960.

Goldman, Albert, from the journalism of Lawrence Schiller. *Ladies and Gentlemen Lenny Bruce!!* New York, Penguin Books. 1971.

Bibliography

Goren, Arthur A. *New York Jews and the Quest for Community.* New York, Columbia University Press, 1970.

Hammer, Richard. *Playboy's Illustrated History of Organized Crime.* Chicago, Playboy Press, 1975.

Harris, Warren G. *Clark Gable.* New York, Harmony Books, 2002.

Hecht, Ben. *Child of the Century.* New York, Signet, 1955.

Howe, Irving. *World of Our Fathers.* New York and London, Harcourt Brace Jovanovich, 1976.

Israel, Lee. *Kilgallen.* New York, Dell, 1980.

Jacobs, George and Stadiem, William. *Mr. S.* New York, Harper Entertainment, 2003.

Joselit, Jenna Weissman. *Our Gang.* Bloomington, Indiana University Press, 1983.

Kantor, Seth. *The Ruby Cover-Up.* New York, Zebra Books, Kensington Publishing Corp., 1978.

Karpis, Alvin, with Trent, Bill. *The Alvin Karpis Story.* New York, Berkley, 1971.

Kefauver, Estes. *Crime in America.* Garden City, New York, Doubleday & Company, 1951.

Kennedy, Robert F. *The Enemy Within.* New York, Da Capo Press, 1994.

Kelley, Kitty. *His Way.* New York, Bantam, 1986.

Krassner, Paul. *Murder at the Conspiracy Convention.* Fort Lee, Barricade Books, 2002.

Krefetz, Gerald. *Jews and Money.* New Haven and New York, Ticknor & Fields, 1982.

Lacey, Robert. *Little Man: Meyer Lansky and the Gangster Life.* Boston, Little Brown, 1991.

Lait, Jack and Mortimer, Lee. *USA Confidential.* New York, Crown, 1952.

Lawford, Christopher Kennedy. *Symptoms of Withdrawal.* New York, William Morrow, 2005.

Lawford, Patricia Seaton, with Ted Schwarz. *The Peter Lawford Story.* New York, Carroll & Graff Publishers, 1988.

Levy, Shawn. *Rat Pack Confidential.* New York, Broadway, 1998.

Lewis, Jerry and Kaplan, James. *Dean and Me.* New York, Doubleday, 2005.

MacAdams, William. *Ben Hecht.* New York, Barricade Books, 1990.

Mankiewicz, Frank. *U.S. v. Richard M. Nixon.* New York, Ballantine, 1975.

Marrs, Jim. *Crossfire.* New York, Carroll & Graff, 1989.

McDougal, Dennis. *The Last Mogul.* Da Capo Press, 2001.

Messick, Hank. *Lansky.* New York, Berkley Medallion, 1971.

Messick, Hank and Goldblath, Burt. *The Mobs and the Mafia.* New York, Ballantine Books, 1972.

Messick, Hank. *The Beauties and the Beast.* New York, David McKay Company, 1973.

Morton, James. *Gangland International.* London, Warner, Little, Brown and Company, 2001.

Muir, Florabel. *Headline Happy.* New York, Henry Holt, 1950.

Nash, Jay Robert. *Look for the Woman.* M. Evans and Company, 1981.

——. *Bloodletters and Badmen.* New York, M. Evans and Company, 1995.

Otash, Fred. *Investigation Hollywood.* Chicago, Henry Regnery Company, 1976.

Otfinoski, Steve. *Bugsy Siegel.* Woodbridge, Conn., Blackbirch Press, 2000.

Peterson, Virgil W. *The Mob.* Ottawa, Green Hill, 1983.

Piper, Michael Collins. *Final Judgment.* Washington, D.C., The Wolfe Press, 1993.

Posner, Gerald. *Case Closed.* New York, Anchor Books, 2003.

Pritchett, Wendell. *Brownsville, Brooklyn.* Chicago, The University of Chicago Press, 2002.

Ragano, Frank, and Raab, Selwyn. *Mob Lawyer: Including the Inside Account of Who Killed Jimmy Hoffa and JFK.* New York, Scribner, 1994.

Rappleye, Charles and Becker, Ed. *All American Mafioso: The Johnny Rosselli Story,* New York, Doubleday, 1991.

Reeves, Richard. *President Nixon.* New York, Touchstone, 2002.

Rehder, William J. *Where the Money Is.* New York, W. W. Norton & Company, 2003.

Reid Ed, and Demaris, Ovid. *The Green Felt Jungle.* New York, Pocket Books, 1964.

Reid, Ed. *Mafia*. New York, Signet, 1964.

———. *The Grim Reapers*. New York, Bantam, 1970.

———. *Mickey Cohen: Mobster*. New York, Pinnacle Books, 1973.

Renay, Liz. *My Face for the World to See*. New York, Bantam, 1971.

Rockaway, Robert A. *But He Was Good To His Mother*. Jerusalem, Gefen, 1993.

Rubin, Rachel. *Jewish Gangsters of Modern Literature*. Urbana and Chicago, University of Illinois Press, 2000.

Russo, Gus. *Supermob*. New York, Bloomsbury, 2006.

Samish, Arthur H. and Thomas, Bob. *The Secret Boss of California*. New York, Crown, 1971.

Scheim, David E. *Contract on America*. New York, Zebra Books, Kensington Publishing Corp., 1988.

Schoell, William. *Martini Man*. Dallas, Taylor Publishing, 1999.

Server, Lee. *Robert Mitchum*. New York, St. Martin's Griffin, 2001.

Shales, Tom and Miller, James Andrew. *Live From New York*. New York, Little Brown and Company, 2002.

Sidorenko, *Konstantin*. Robert F. Kennedy. New York, Crossroad, 2000.

Sifakis, Carl. *The Mafia Encyclopedia*. New York, Checkmark, 1999.

Spada, James. *Peter Lawford: The Man Who Kept the Secrets*, New York, Bantam, 1992.

Stevens, Steve and Lockwood, Craig. *King of the Sunset Strip*. Nashville, Cumberland House, 2006.

Summers, Anthony. *Conspiracy*. New York, McGraw-Hill, 1980.

———. *Goddess: The Secret Lives of Marilyn Monroe*. Macmillan, 1985.

———. *The Kennedy Conspiracy*. New York, Warner Books, 1998.

———. *The Arrogance of Power*. New York, Penguin, 2000.

Summers, Anthony and Swan, Robbyn. *Sinatra: The Life*. New York, Knopf, 2005.

Tosches, Nick. *Dino: Living High in the Dirty Business of Dreams*. New York, Dell, 1992.

Turkus, Burton B. and Feder, Sid. *Murder, Inc*. New York, Da Capo Press, 1951.

Turner, Lana. *Lana*. New York, E. P. Dutton, 1982.

Waldron, Lamar with Hartman, Thom. *Ultimate Sacrifice: John and Robert Kennedy, the Plan for a Coup in Cuba, and the Murder of JFK*. New York, Carroll & Graf, 2005.

Wean, G. L. *There's a Fish in the Courthouse*. Castitas Books, 1987.

Webb, Jack. *The Badge*. New York, Thunder's Mouth Press, 2005. Introduction by James Ellroy. Originally published in 1958.

Weberman, Alan J. and Canfield, Michael. *Coup d'État in America*. San Francisco, Quick America Archives, 1992.

Weller, Sheila. *Dancing at Ciro's*. New York, St. Martin's Press, 2003.

Wilkerson, W. R., III. *The Man Who Invented Las Vegas*. Beverly Hills, Ciro's Books, 2000.

Wilson, Earl. *Sinatra*. New York, Macmillan, 1976.

Wolfe, Donald H. *The Last Days of Marilyn Monroe*. New York, William Morrow, 1998.

Wolf, George with DiMona, Joseph. *Frank Costello: Prime Minister of the Underworld*. New York, Bantam, 1974.

Yablonsky, Lewis. *George Raft*. New York, McGraw-Hill, 1974.

Film, Radio, Television

"Hoodlum with a Heart, Mickey Cohen," True Crime Stories: Rogue's Gallery, Andrew Solt Productions, 2002.

Simon, Scott, host. Mann, Iris, reporter. "Weekend Edition," National Public Radio, September 6, 2003.
Due Kennedy, I, Gianni Bisiach, Writer/Director, 1969.

FBI Files

FBI FOI/PAS. Subject: Michael Mickey Cohen, File #62-HG-89947; File #7-HQ-5908; File #58-HQ-6129; File #92-HQ-3156.
FBI FILES. 183-HQ-912; 183-SD-57; 62-HQ-29632; 62-81518.

Legal Case

Meyer Harris COHEN, aka Michael 'Mickey' Cohen, Appellant, v. *UNITED STATES of America,* Appellee. 297 F.2d 760; 62-1 USTC P 9202; No. 17503; United States Court of Appeals Ninth Circuit; Jan. 12, 1962.

Magazines and Journals

Greenberg, David. "Shocked, Shocked," *Forward,* October 10, 2003.
Greenberg, Eric J. "JFK's Mideast Legacy," *Jewish Week,* November 21, 2003; "Graham Endorses 'Passion,'" December 5, 2003.
Hecht, Ben. "The Incomplete Life of Mickey Cohen," *Scanlan's Monthly,* Vol. 1, No. 1, 1970.
Hollander E, Tracy KA, Swann AC, Coccaro EF, McElroy SL, Wozniak P, Sommerville KW, Nemeroff CB. "Divalproex in the treatment of impulsive aggression: efficacy in cluster B personality disorders." *Neuropsychopharmacology.* 2003 Jun; 28(6):1186-97. Epub 2003 Apr 02.
Johnson JG, Cohen P, Smailes E, Kasen S, Oldham JM, Skodol AE, Brook JS. "Adolescent personality disorders associated with violence and criminal behavior during adolescence and early adulthood." *Am J Psychiatry.* 2000 Sep; 157(9):1406–12.
Langman, Anne W. "Television," *Nation.* June 15, 1957.
Life, "Mobsters and Gangsters" Time Life Books, 2002.
——, January 16, 1950; March 17, 1958; February 1, 1960; April 10, 1970; March 10, 1972.
Longato-Stadler E., Klinteberg B., Garpenstrand H., Oreland L., Hallman J. "Personality traits and platelet monoamine oxidase activity in a Swedish male criminal population." *Neuropsychobiology.* 2002;46(4):202–8.
Los Angeles Business Journal, "The Newsmaker," February 21, 2000.
McWilliams, Carey. "Machines, Political and Slot." *Nation.* May 17, 1949.
——. "The Big Fix in Los Angeles." *Nation.* August 20, 1949.
Newsweek, November 27, 1950; May 28, 1951; July 2, 1951.
Nation, Editorial, November 18, 1950.
Saturday Evening Post, August 20, 1958; August 28, 1958; October 4, 1958; October 11, 1958.
Time, July 5, 1948; November 27, 1950.
Turner, William W. "Crime Is Too Big for the FBI," *Nation.* November 8, 1965.
Warnock J. K., Kestenbaum T. "Obsessive-compulsive disorder." Dermatol Clin. 1996 Jul; 14(3):465–72.
Wieseltier, Leon. "Against the Ethnic Panic of American Jews: Hitler is Dead," *New Republic,* May 27, 2002.

Zullino D. F., Quinche P, Hafliger T, Stigler M. "Olanzapine improves social dysfunction in cluster B personality disorder." Hum Psychopharmacol. 2002 Jul; 17(5):247-51.

Newspapers

Berkshire County Eagle, October 19, 1949.

Black, Edwin. "Hitler's American Enablers." *Jewish Week*, New York, September 12, 2003.

California Jewish Voice, May 6, 1955.

Canby, Vincent. "Once Upon a Time in America," *New York Times*, June 1, 1984.

Coates, Paul. "Mickey Cohen Letter Gives Still Another Side to Complex Moods," *Los Angeles Times*, December 24, 1963; "Even 'The Mick' Rates a Break," *Los Angeles Times*, March 14, 1965.

Edelman, Rob. "Boxing Writer Learned His Love of the Gloves as a Child," *Forward*, May 23, 2003.

Editorials, "Kristallnacht Lessons Too Real," *Jewish Week*, November 7, 2003.

Evening Herald and Express, July 11, 1949; July 20, 1949.

Evening Star, September 29, 1960.

Gray, Geoffrey. "Tyson's Last Match," *New York Observer*, December 22–29, 2003.

Gumbel, Andrew. "LA Stories," *Independent on Sunday*, November 11, 2001.

Hall, John. "The Old Fighter," *Los Angeles Times*, November 13, 1974.

Harvey, Steve. "Only In LA," *Los Angeles Times,* Beverlyhillsbarbers.com.

Hazlett, Bill. "Ex-Mobster Mickey Cohen Aids Hearsts in Search for Daughter," *Los Angeles Times*, October 24, 1974; "Cohen Backs Out of Hearst Case," October 26, 1974; "Patricia Hearst, Harrises Were Hiding in Cleveland, Cohen Says," October 27, 1974; and Paegel, Tom. "Cohen Denies Knowing Miss Hearst's Location, October 25, 1974.

Herald Examiner, October 10, 1955.

Herald-Express, March 23, 1949.

"HBO Depicts Meyer Lansky Through A Very Jewish Filter," *Telegraphic Agency*, February 23, 1999.

Hoberman, J. "A Co-Production of Sinatra and J.F.K.," *New York Times*, September 14, 2003.

Hollywood Citizen News, August 27, 1957.

Independent Press-Telegram, June 14, 1959; January 1, 1972; March 17, 1963.

Indiana Evening Gazette, August 19, 1948; September 23, 1949; January 24, 1950; May 17, 1950; April 11, 1958; May 26, 1961.

Ironwood Daily Globe, March 20, 1958.

Johnson, Ian. "Conspiracy Theories About Sept. 11 Get Hearing in Germany," *Wall Street Journal*, September 29, 2003.

Lincoln Sunday Journal and Star, May 4, 1968; October 11, 1959.

Lipman, Steve. "A Legend Down Under," *Jewish Week*, September 26, 2003.

——. "A Hotel for the Old Hood," *Jewish Week*, December 12, 2003.

Long Beach Press Telegram, November 17, 1950.

Los Angeles Times, Dec. 11, 1930; Aug. 13, 1942; May 19, 1945; May 20, 1945; Nov. 21, 1945; May 3, 1946; Jan. 31, 1946; Jan. 15, 1947; Aug. 19, 1948; Aug. 21, 1948; Sept. 2, 1948; Sept. 17, 1948; Nov. 2, 1948; Mar. 16, 1949; Mar. 23, 1949; May 31, 1949; June 16, 1949; June 30, 1949; July 28, 1948; July 30, 1949; July 31, 1949; Aug. 10, 1949; Sept. 1, 1949; Sept. 29, 1949; Oct. 7, 1949; Nov. 22, 1949; Dec. 1, 1949; Jan. 5, 1950; Jan. 19, 1950; Feb. 9, 1950; Feb. 11, 1950; Feb. 16, 1950; July 16, 1950; Aug. 5, 1950; Aug. 8, 1950; Sept. 28, 1950; Nov. 26, 1950; Nov. 30, 1950; Mar. 22, 1951; May 25, 1949; Apr. 1, 1951; Aug. 7, 1952; Dec. 27, 1952; May 30, 1952; Aug. 6, 1952; Mar. 3, 1953; Aug. 4, 1954; Aug. 5, 1954; Aug. 21, 1963; Sept. 11, 1954; Oct. 4, 1955; Oct. 11, 1955; Feb. 4, 1956; Mar. 16, 1956; July 15, 1956; July 24, 1956; Sept. 27, 1965; Dec. 19, 1956; Dec. 24, 1956;

Apr. 3, 1957; May 22, 1957; May 28, 1957; Aug. 4, 1957; Sept. 26, 1957; Nov. 8, 1957; Dec 1, 1957; Apr. 4, 1958; Apr. 12, 1958; Aug. 15, 1958; June 4, 1958; June 5, 1958; June 18, 1958; Sept. 10, 1958; Dec. 15, 1958; Feb. 21, 1961; May 9, 1961; May 10, 1961; May 11, 1961; May 26, 1961; Oct. 17, 1961; Feb. 17, 1962; May 27, 1962; Dec. 27, 1962; Aug. 16, 1963; Dec. 9, 1963; Dec. 19, 1963; Dec. 27, 1963; Feb. 18, 1964; Mar. 12, 1964; Feb. 27, 1965; Mar. 3, 1965; Mar. 14, 1965; Mar. 16, 1965; Mar. 25, 1965; Feb. 2, 1966; May 22, 1966; July 7, 1966; Dec. 9, 1966; Feb. 5, 1967; July 31, 1968; July 11, 1970; Mar. 25, 1971; Jan. 6, 1972; Jan. 7, 1972; Jan. 8, 1972; July 3, 1972; Nov. 5, 1972; Jan. 17, 1973; Oct. 24, 1974; Nov. 14, 1974; Aug. 14, 1975; Sept. 30, 1975; Nov. 25, 1981; Jan. 13, 1982; May 8, 1982; Oct. 14, 1984; Jan 3, 2006; Mar. 21, 2006.

Mark, Jonathan. "The Missing Peace," *Jewish Week*, November 28, 2003.

Maslin, Janet. "The Dark Underbelly of a Sunny Town," *New York Times*, Sept. 19, 1997.

Mirror, July 20, 1949; July 21, 1949; February 14, 1956; April 8, 1958; April 29, 1958.

Nelson, Bryce. "Mickey Cohen Says Farewell to U.S. Prison," *Los Angeles Times*, January 8, 1972.

New York Mirror, "Walter Winchell of New York," April 28, 1961.

Nevada State Journal, November 28, 1939; June 22, 1947; November 16, 1947; March 27, 1949; June 5, 1951; June 7, 1951; December 23, 1956; May 23, 1957; March 25, 1959; September 15, 1961; November 2, 1961; August 15, 1963.

News Journal, Mansfield, O., October 8, 1958; July 30, 1976.

Oakland Tribune, October 25, 1937; November 24, 1939; November 25, 1940; October 15, 1944; July 4, 1947; July 20, 1949; July 21, 1949; August 23, 1949; November 17, 1950; April 5, 1950; April 10, 1958; April 11, 1958; August 5, 1959; October 1, 1959; September 1, 1976.

Overend, William. "When The Sun Set On The Strip," *Los Angeles Times*, November 27, 1981.

Pasadena Independent, October 10, 1955.

Portland Press Herald, Portland, Maine, July 21, 1949; July 29, 1949.

Post Standard, September 1, 1950.

Prager, Dennis. "How Jews, Christians See Gibson's New Film," *Jewish Journal of Greater Los Angeles*, November 7–13, 2003.

Reno Evening Gazette, August 23, 1949; February 8, 1950; November 16, 1950; February 13, 1954; August 24, 1957; October 16, 1958; May 10, 1962; January 7, 1972; August 5, 1975.

Rieder, Ron. *Valley News*, December 31, 1961.

Rosenbaum, Ron. "Can Wieseltier, D.C.'s Big Mullah, Have It Both Ways?," *New York Observer*, September 27, 2003; "Re Laci and Kobe—Celebrity Concussion and Sensational Truths," *New York Observer*, October 24, 2003.

San Mateo Times, August 19, 1948; August 24, 1948.

Stevens Point (Wisconsin) *Daily Journal*, February 2, 1959.

Sunday Gazette-Mail, Charleston, West Virginia, May 4, 1958.

Sunday Post-Crescent, Appleton-Neenah-Menasha, Wis., March 2, 1975,

Sullivan, Andrew. "Evangelist to the World," *New York Times*, July 6, 1997.

Syracuse Herald-Journal, November 15, 1950; July 15, 1957; August 12, 1975; July 21, 1976.

The Berkshire Evening Eagle, October 27, 1950.

The Bridgeport Telegram, February 21, 1951.

The Chronicle-Telegram, Elyria, O., October 1, 1958; October 25, 1975; October 26, 1974; November 20, 1975; July 30, 1976; August 6, 1976; September 9, 1977.

The Constitution Tribune Chillicothe, Mo., June 17, 1959.

The Coshocton (Ohio) *Tribune*, July 26, 1949; February 26, 1958; April 24, 1958; April 17, 1960; December 22, 1975.

The Daily Courier, Connellsville, Pa., January 8, 1972.

Bibliography

The Dothan Eagle, July 24, 1976.

The Daily Times-News, May 30, 1957; July 29, 1957.

The Gettysburg Times, August 17, 1963.

The Hammond Times, July 2, 1961.

The Herald-Press, St. Joseph, Mich., October 11, 1955; September 30, 1960.

The Holland Michigan Evening Sentinel, June 18, 1958; July 30, 1976.

The Independent, Long Beach, Calif., November 18, 1950.

The Kerrville Times, November 29, 1959.

The Lethbridge Herald, May 24, 1957; May 4, 1959; March 29, 1951; October 25, 1974.

The Lima News, June 6, 1951; August 29, 1957; January 7, 1972.

The Marville Daily Forum, February 6, 1950.

The Modesto Bee, March 17, 1954.

The Morgantown Post, March 7, 1958.

The New York Times, July 21, 1949; July 24, 1949; July 26, 1949; July 28, 1949; July 31, 1949; Aug. 18, 1949; Apr. 22, 1950; May 31, 1950; June 7, 1950; July 2, 1950; July 4, 1950; July 14, 1950; Sept. 29, 1950; Nov. 7, 1950; Nov. 17, 1950; Nov. 18, 1950; Nov. 19, 1950; Dec. 12, 1950; Mar 6, 1951; Apr. 7, 1951; Apr. 8, 1951; Apr. 2, 1941; Jan 3, 1951; Apr. 3, 1951; Apr. 4, 1951; Apr. 25, 1951; June 1, 1951; June 5, 1951; June 14, 1951; June 16, 1951; July 10, 1951; July 11, 1951; Nov. 28, 1951; Oct. 10, 1955; Oct. 6, 1957; May 23, 1957; May 27, 1957; July 9, 1957; Jan. 3, 1958; Jan. 18, 1958; Feb. 26, 1958; Mar. 5, 1958; Apr. 5, 1958; June 14, 1958; Oct. 25, 1958; Mar. 25, 1959; Aug. 14, 1959; Aug. 25, 1959; Dec. 4, 1959; Dec. 5, 1959; Dec. 8, 1959; Dec. 9, 1959; Sept. 17, 1960; Oct. 1, 1960; June 5, 1961; June 27, 1961; June 31, 1961; July 1, 1961; July 2, 1961; Oct. 13, 1961; Oct. 16, 1961; Oct. 18, 1961; Jan. 31, 1962; Apr. 11, 1962; May 15, 1962; Jan. 31, 1962; Oct. 19, 1962; Feb. 28, 1963; Aug. 15, 1963; Feb. 18, 1964; May 21, 1967; Feb. 25, 1970; Apr. 28, 1970; Jan. 25, 1972; Jan. 17, 1973; Mar. 9, 1973; Oct. 24, 1974; Oct. 30, 1974; July 29, 1976; Nov. 21, 1976; Mar. 20, 1980; Feb. 15, 1981; July 6, 1997; Oct. 19, 2005; Jan. 4, 2006; June 26, 2006.

The Newark Advocate, April 7, 1958; November 24, 1959; December 3, 1959.

The News, Newport, R.I., February 21, 1951; October 4, 1955; October 10, 1955.

The News, Port Arthur, Texas, October 2, 1975.

The News, Van Nuys (Calif.), August 4, 1949; October 15, 1957; December 11, 1959; December 13, 1959; March 20, 1960; November 17, 1961; January 14, 1966; December 17, 1971; October 3, 1975.

The Post-Standard, July 24, 1949; February 24, 1951; March 11, 1962; February 19, 1970.

The Sheboygan (Wisconsin) *Press*, October 2, 1949; June 9, 1951; March 27, 1959; October 31, 1968; December 29, 1975.

The Sunday Chronicle-Telegram, Elyria, O,, October 27, 1974.

The Vidette-Messenger, September 24, 1949.

The Zanesville Signal, August 8, 1958

Tolkin, Michael, "Unacceptable," *Jewish Journal of Greater Los Angeles*, October 24–30, 2003.

Traverse City Record-Eagle, Michigan, July 28, 1949; February 6, 1950; March 29, 1956.

Tri-City Herald, May 27, 1957; May 19, 1959.

Union-Bulletin, September 4, 1949.

Washington Daily News, September 29, 1960.

Washington Star, August 24, 1949.

Waterloo Daily Courier, January 3, 1951.

Waukesha Daily Freeman, July 21, 1949.

Weinraub, Bernard, "A Sidekick Gets a Chance to Take Center Stage," *New York Times*, February 17, 2004.

Websites & Internet Sources

American Studies International, February 2000, Vol. XXXVIII, No. 1,
www.gwu.edu/~asi/articles/38-1-6.pdf.

Appraisalintelligence.com. "Phantom buyers, bogus documents alleged in Beverly Hills fraud."

Aronowitz, Al. The Blacklisted Journalist, March 1, 1996,
www.theblacklistedjournalist.com/.

The Big Bands Database Plus, "The Night Club Era."

Bowen, Kit. "News Roundup: Spielberg Finally Gets His Own Star," Hollywood.com. January 7, 2003.

BoxRec.com.

Brennan, Sandra. All Movie Guide, www.allmovie.com.

Brin, Herb. davidbrin.com/herbbrin.

The Canadian Press. September 26, 1999, cp.org.

Cubbage, Robert. "L. A. Confidential," *Notre Dame Magazine*, Spring, 2003.

Crimemagazine.com.

Deltadentalca.org. "Beverly Hills dentist pleads guilty to five counts of fraud," August 18, 1998.

Detnews.com. "Michigan Casino Guide," The Detroit News.

Geer, Carri. "Mob underboss gets 21 months," Reviewjournal.com, Las Vegas Review-Journal, July 7, 2000.

Gribben, Mark. "Mickey Cohen." Court TV Crimelibrary.com.

Hyman, Gretchen. "Two Beverly Hills Men Sentenced for Securities Fraud," siliconvalley.internet.com, January 24, 2001.

Ipsn.org. Illinois Police and Sheriff's News, June 4, 1997; July 16, 1997.

Jewishaz.com. "Jewish News of Greater Phoenix," February, 2000.

jewsinsports.org.

Jewishtribalreview.org.

Jfkresearch.com/morningstar/killgallen.htm

La2you.com. "Ambassador Hotel & Coconut Grove."

Lapdonline.org. "Operation White Lace," December 5, 2002.

Lindberg, Richard C. "The Mafia in America: Traditional Organized Crime in Transition," search-international.com./Articles/crime/mafiaamerica.

Los Angeles Business Journal.

Marshallmcluhan.com

May, Allan. "The Two Tonys," americanmafia.com, May 24, 1999.

——. "Frank Bompensiero," americanmafia.com, May 5, 2000.

Newspaperarchive.com

Online.ceb.com/calcases/CA2/193CA2d360.htm.

Putnam, George. "One Reporter's Opinion: The Don is Gone," NewsMax.com, June 14, 2002.

Rhino.com.

Risling, Greg. "Feds Say Pellicano Taped Client Talks," washingtonpost.com, February 16, 2006.

Seeing-stars.com/Dine2/Formosa.shtml.

Suite101.com.

Bibliography

Thompson, Scott. "The Witches of Whitewater," *The Executive Intelligence Review*, February 6, 1998, american_almanac.tripod.com/witches.htm.

Thesmokinggun.com/archive/0206061pell1.html.

Torro, Kenny. Mafiainternational.com. glasgowcrew.tripod.com.

Travers, Peter. "Bugsy," RollingStone.com, 1991.

Tuohy, John William. "Televised Gangsters," AmericanMafia.com, November 2001.

Ukrweekly.com. "Facts and Places," *The Ukrainian Weekly*, May, 2001.

Usdoj.gov. June 24, 2002.

Notes

Prologue

1. "Jews were…involved in many of the most visible and spectacular frauds of the post-Civil War period"—Benjamin Ginsberg. Franklin Moses, the Jewish governor of South Carolina, watched as the state bilked its people in a $6,000,000 stock swindle, and the public servant pocketed hundreds of thousands of dollars. Some credit the "Black Friday" stock crash of 1869 to German-born pushcart-peddler Joseph Seligman, who rose to become a prestigious investment banker. Jacob Schiff, who married investment banker Solomon Loeb's daughter, once pushed the price of Northern Pacific Railroad so low that the market dove, and contributed to Teddy Roosevelt enacting stricter anti-trust legislation. During the first decade after the turn of the twentieth century, the population of Jews in New York City was over one million, and approximately half of all prison inmates were Jewish. The U.S. Immigration Commission reported that in 1909 approximately three-quarters of the prostitution cases brought before the New York City Magistrates Court were Jewish women. During 1909, approximately three thousand Jewish children appeared in juvenile court in the New York area. Wealthy Jewish leaders, alarmed by the situation and fearful that Jewish gangs promoted anti-Semitism, started organizations like the National Council of Jewish Women. To combat the rise in Jewish criminals, Judah I. Magnes established the New York Kehillah to promote education, philanthropy, labor, and morals. The organization maintained a Bureau of Social Morals, which discovered that Jews had developed an extensive cocaine industry. During prohibition (1920–1933) Jewish gangs dominated illegal bootlegging activities, and operated strongholds in Cleveland, Newark, New York, Detroit, and Minneapolis. Gambling, extortion, and drugs were the other moneymakers.

2. Monk was the son of a legit restaurant owner who established his offspring as a pet shop owner. "Monk began life with a bullet-shaped head and a short bull neck…he acquired a broken nose, a pair of cauliflower ears and heavily veined, sagging jowls. His face was pocked with battle scars and he seemed always to need a haircut"—Robert Rockaway. He never wore a shirt, collar, or coat; he carried a baseball bat notched with a tally of his victims. At the height of his nefarious escapades, he controlled over 1200 men who could materialize from the scummy bars and pool halls at a moment's notice.

3. Arnold Rothstein lived in the posh Upper East Side of Manhattan. His father was chairman of the board of New York's Beth Israel Hospital; his brother became a rabbi. While young men, Rothstein and Phillip "Dandy Phil" Kastel started investment bucketshops that defrauded investors out of millions. Kastel survived for the next four decades, later running the Beverly Club in New Orleans' French Quarter for Lansky. Rothstein rubbed elbows with Governor Al Smith and Judge Louis Brandeis. A gambler at heart, his world would give rise to killers like Albert Anastasia, Joe Adonis, Red Levine, and Ben "Bugsy" Siegel. He fixed the 1919 World Series between the Chicago White Sox and Cincinnati. Rothstein, a theater impresario, invested in *Abies's Irish Rose*.

4. "No one understands what it's like to kill. The power you possess when you kill someone, it's like being God. Do I want this guy to continue living, or should I kill him? No one can understand it unless you do it"—Roy DeMeo, Gambino crime family member.
5. Popularized first in nineteenth-century Chicago, the thirty-eight became the staple of many police officers and criminals.
6. Mickey's sociopathic personality, if as extreme as depicted by some, could be improved, or eliminated, today with drugs like clomipramine (Anafranil), fluoxetine (Luvox), fluvoxamine (Prozac), sertraline (Zoloft), or paroxetine (Paxil).
7. Mickey's OCD (obsessive-compulsive disorder), was likely neurobiological. It would one day save his life.

Chapter 1 - Once Upon a Time in Boyle Heights

1. "Brooklyn's Jewish gangsters were a cut above out-and-out sadism, but they were tough and didn't mind getting their hands dirty to do a "hit job" under contract for Anastasia, Lord High Executioner for just about every mob in the country"—Ed Reid. "It was the Jews, by and large, not the Italians, who created what was later called the Mafia. In the 1920s the Italians began to replace the Jews in the New York organized crime industry, but as late as 1940 if you wanted a spectacular hit you were looking for a representative of the Lepke Buchalter Gang, also known as Murder Inc."—Norman Cantor. "Now, in the operation of an industry of such magnitude and character, murder was necessary, at times, to prevent interference with business. That is where the Brooklyn branch came in"—Burton Turkus. Turkus, nicknamed "Mr. Arsenic" by the mob, worked at the D.A.'s office in Kings County, Brooklyn, New York, while co-author Sid Feder was a popular writer for *True, Collier's,* and the *Saturday Evening Post.* Brooklyn was the hub of the nationwide syndicate, and its graduates supplied hit men and weapons. The Brownsville boys included Abe "Kid Twist" Reles, Harry "Pittsburgh Phil" Strauss, Abraham "Pretty" Levine, and Martin "Bugsy" Goldstein. Authorities indicted Strauss and Goldstein for the murder-by-fire and strangulation of twenty-nine-year-old Irving "Puggy" Feinstein. The Italians had Harry "Happy"—he never smiled—Maione and Frank "Dasher" Abbandando. Harry Feeny dubbed this core group Murder, Inc.—200 unsolved murders in a fifteen-year period. The one office, called "Midnight Roses" after the owner, was a dilapidated candy store located under the noisy elevated train at the corner of Saratoga and Livonia avenues. The area spawned Mendy Weiss, Phillip and Vincent Mangano, Joe Adonis, Seymour "Blue Jaw" Magoon, Dukey Maffetore, Pretty Amberg, Albert Anastasia, Moe Dalitz, Waxey Gordon, Meyer Lansky, Doc Stacher, Louis Lepke, Dutch Schultz, and Bugsy Siegel. Many attended P.S. 34, not far from Grand and Delancey streets, on the Lower East Side of Manhattan. "Anyone who knew Siegel took his threats seriously—or was wise enough to"—Greg Bautzer. The boys, including close friend and mentor Lansky, called Bugsy a *chaye* (a wild animal). The gang included the requisite fat boy, Doc. By age fourteen, Bugsy and Lansky had the Bug and Meyer Mob—bootleggers. By age twenty-one, Bugsy's rap sheet included everything from rape to murder.
2. Both Ben Hecht and Al Aronowitz thought that Mickey's father's name was Sam. Mickey's revisionist memoir refers to Max.
3. Unglamorous Brownsville remained the same through the depression. Years of loan sharking, slots, dice, and extorting shopkeepers took their toll.
4. "The neighborhood (Brownsville and East New York) was a launching pad from which the sons and daughters (American-born, unaccented, regular Yankee Doodle Dandies) of immigrants from the shtetls and ghettos of Europe were expected to shoot like rockets from the shoulders of their peddler, tailor, and shopkeeper fathers and pierce the professional stratosphere"—Sheila Weller.

5. Dave Lewis, from Pitkin Avenue in Brownsville, was one of the major importers of cocaine, and controlled ten wholesalers and 173 retailers. Al Lampre, "Nigger" Hyman, Eddie Friedman, Sammy Cohen, Mike Goodman, Abe Kutner, and Abie Cohen ran the drug trade, and collaborated with the Irish and Italian mobsters. "Cocaine was imported, wholesaled, franchised, and retailed; it moved from South America to New Orleans, Canada, Buffalo, Philadelphia, West New York, New Jersey, and so on. It traveled back and forth from Broadway and the Forties to the Lower East Side, Harlem, Brooklyn, back to Philadelphia, and also to Boston. It slid up and down the Bowery and Second Avenue and Third Avenue, across 14th Street where it circled Tammany Hall, then slipping down toward Mott and Mulberry Streets…"—Alan A. Block. Cocaine was color blind and non-sectarian; a dark void that lurked beneath the bright lights and bustling metropolis that pretended to have a moral psyche. No socioeconomic group was untouched by its popularity and pervasive usage. "It was traded in movies, theaters, restaurants, cafes, cabarets, pool parlors, saloons, parks, and on innumerable street corners… It was sold many times over…to show people, the military, newsboys, prostitutes, Jews, Italians, blacks, and so on"—Block. Irving "Waxey" Gordon (Irving Wexler), who bankrolled comedian Jimmy Durante in a movie, participated in five different cocaine groups. He started as a rumrunner for Arnold Rothstein. At age twenty, he had a full resume: labor goon, burglar, dope dealer, strikebreaker, and extortionist. By the end of the twenties, he had made millions and operated out of fancy suites at Forty-second and Broadway. He invested in a "Joisey" brewery and an upstate New York distillery. His profits bought an apartment on Central Park West, many luxury automobiles, and a summer home on the Jersey shore. Waxey, another theater maven, produced Broadway musicals like *Strike Me Pink*.

6. Years later Ben Hecht would label Mickey "The Bookie Emperor of California."

7. Sam remained honest. When Mickey established his nefarious career in Los Angeles, Sam lost his clothing business to creditors. He insisted on paying off over $300,000 rather than file bankruptcy. He died soon thereafter.

8. "The dispersion of the immigrant Jews began the very day they started shaping themselves into a community. In the act of creating their own subculture lay the certainty of sharing a later dispersion. This did not even mean ceasing to be a Jew or to identify with Jewish interests, it did not even mean ceasing to live among Jews. It meant, simply, moving away… Moving away from immigrant neighborhoods in which Yiddish prevailed… Moving away from parents whose will to success could unnerve the most successful sons and daughters…and moving towards new social arrangements; the calm of a suburb, the comfort of affluence, the novelty of bohemia"—Irving Howe.

Chapter 2 – Not-So-Famous Jewish Boxers

1. "My father passed this on to me . . . Jews were largely barred from the corridors of upscale America; the sport was as much an outlet for ambitious Jews as the movie industry itself. The boxing world, he said, had less overt anti-Semitism than did other sports"—Budd Schulberg. "…Jews entered the ranks of American boxing in large numbers and in 1928 were the dominant nationality in professional prizefighting… By 1950, there were virtually no Jewish boxers"—Allen Bodner. "I must confess we had a special *qvell* for the exploits of our Jewish boxers"—Schulberg. "Mushy Callahan (Morris Scheer), Jackie Fields, Newsboy Brown, and Maxie Rosenbloom were not only sports heroes but personal friends"—Schulberg.

2. By the 1930s, Mushy Callahan's career was over and he entered the movie business as a boxing instructor for studio stars. He worked on *Rebel Without a Cause*, *Somebody Up There Likes Me*, and *The Great White Hope* (in the latter teaching James Earl Jones). Jackie Fields won an impressive seventy-two fights with twenty-nine knockouts. Taylor, the "Blond Terror of Terre Haute," sent two of his opponents to an early grave.

3. Young Mike Tyson resided in Brownsville, Brooklyn. "Even though they were Jewish, they were very tribal, and there were all different kinds. Jewish fighters from Russia, the Balkans, Lithuania; they had different styles and different basic ways to even study their religion. They wanted to be classy, they wanted to be accepted by society—and people looked at them as being Uncle Toms, but really it was evolution, just ethnic groups evolving"—Mike Tyson.

4. Dalitz started in Detroit as part of the notorious Purple Gang. Known to the FBI in his early days as Moe Davis, he became the early visible leader of the Cleveland Syndicate gang along with partner Morris Kleinman, the largest bootlegger in the United States. He also stayed close to Louis Lepke. Dog tracks were popular in the early days, and Dalitz controlled all the gambling. On June 1, 1939, the FBI recognized Dalitz as "a shrewd and careful leader, who usually remains in the background of all his operations." Dalitz owned the Liberty Ice Cream Company, Pioneer Linen Supply Company, an interest in the Ohio Villa and Thomas Club, and the Frolics Club in Miami. He sold the Stardust Hotel for $15,000,000 in a fast deal by powerful attorney Sidney Korshak, who made a half a million finder's fee. Jimmy Hoffa once called him "a respected citizen." Californian Dalitz lived to be ninety, the owner of the popular La Costa Hotel and Spa, as well as golf courses and casinos. When the Watergate scandal broke in 1973, President Nixon, Murray Chotiner, and Sam Ehrlichman were guests at La Costa, allegedly to work on the damage control. The FBI listed the La Costa founders as Allard Roen (protégé of Meyer Lansky), Mervin Adelson, Irwin McClasky (convicted stock manipulator), and Dalitz, considered the second in command of the "Jewish Mob" under Lansky.

5. Lou "Rody" Rothkopf had a share of the Desert Inn in Las Vegas. He bragged that the government was missing over $24,000,000 in taxable income during the first year alone. Known for his ice cream, he also headed up all the major dairies in Cleveland, including the Midwest Dairy. He committed suicide in 1956, suspiciously attributed to carbon monoxide poisoning. His wife Blanche sadly followed one year later after a bout with depression.

6. FBI interviews with Mickey indicate a 1930 embezzlement conviction that resulted in a two-year stay in the Mansfield, Ohio, reformatory, although the arrest record escaped the FBI. Once he was out, it was business as usual until a February 2, 1933, indictment for income tax evasion. He paid a huge fine of $15,000 and was sentenced to four years, but didn't serve any time, and again no FBI record. FBI files have only one arrest for him, dated July 18, 1933, for robbery, and no record of the court's disposition. The FBI concentrated mainly on its public enemy list, and after apprehending someone on the lam, rested on their past laurels for decades.

7. An FBI report from April 1933 spoke about the early scheming during a meeting at the San Carlos Hotel in Tucson, Arizona. The Yiddish-only discussions hatched a plot to assassinate Hitler. The FBI investigated and found nothing concrete, not a trace of information materialized regarding the mobsters present at the meeting since the hotel staff wisely remained silent.

8. Madden controlled bootleg liquor, nightclubs, taxicabs, laundries, and club concessions. He had a significant piece of the popular Cotton Club in Harlem and heavyweight boxing champion Primo Carnera. Actor George Raft began his career as a dancer at one of Madden's cabarets.

9. Bugsy insisted that his friends call him Ben or Benny like Mickey did, and the pejorative "Bugsy" existed only behind his back. Everyone else called him Mr. Siegel. Bugsy had a certain charm, which helped catapult him to the center of show business social life. He was articulate, and always wore silk shirts and $200 suits, a combination that went a long way in Hollywood.

10. Detroit mobsters managed to commit or arrange 500 assassinations. The Jews cooperated with Sicilian Joseph Zerilli, an immigrant at age seventeen. He worked his way up from a day laborer to $150,000,000 per year, mostly extortion and narcotics. Abe Bernstein of the Purple Gang organized the St. Valentine's Day Massacre, a Capone hit on the Moran gang. On September 16, 1931, Jewish gangsters from Chicago, Herman Hymie, Paul Joseph, "Nigger" Joe Lebovitz, and Joseph "Izzy" Sutker murdered Irving Milberg, Harry Kewell, Ray Bernstein, and Harry

345

Fleisher, all with the Purple Gang, in cold blood—the Collingwood Massacre took its name from the street on which it took place. On November 27, 1933, Detroit Public Enemies Nos. 1 and 2, Abe Waxler and Eddie Fletcher of the Purple Gang, were also murdered.

Chapter 3 – Tinsel Town

1. Two hundred years earlier the Los Angeles Basin was a plain filled by swamps. Long occupied by the Gabrieleno Indians, the Spanish took over easily; later, the Mexicans ruled. Sunset Boulevard was part of homesteads that stretched for miles. In 1850, the city consisted of twenty-eight square miles. The rich families, Mulhollands and Dohenys, owned most of the sprawling property in the early part of the twentieth century. The entire area known as Hollywood was mostly citrus orchards planted by migrant workers. When the movie business took over, studios sprang up, some by luminaries like D. W. Griffith.

2. Bully Luft, who started as an agent, picked a fight with CBS Harvard attorney Charles Straus in Romanoff's. That night Straus was with a current beauty queen from Sweden. He politely asked Luft not to approach the table. Luft started a fistfight with Straus, who tore Luft's suit jacket down around his arms. Straus sought first aid for his bloody nose in the middle of the night by ringing his brother's doorbell, and asked for ice. "One night Sid Luft, Judy Garland's husband, got so drunk that he brushed a row of books off Bogart's bookcase, climbed into the empty shelf, and passed out. The next morning Bogie called me at home and said, 'What the hell am I going to do with Luft? He is still in that bookcase!' I told him, 'Let him sleep it off, he's a frustrated bookend, I guess'"—James Bacon. "He once tried to punch Don Rickles for insulting him during his nightclub act. Rickles taunted, 'Laugh it up, Sid! Judy has written you out of the will!'"—Bacon. An enraged Luft stormed the stage, but security guards hauled him back to his seat. One night Luft tried to beat up a nosy reporter who spotted him washing away his grief.

3. Mickey incorrectly cites the Boyle Heights timeline, which encouraged crime historians to link the sheriff and Mickey as children. They likely never crossed paths until years later. Biscailuz was born on March 12, 1883, about thirty years before Mickey. He started life in a home with a huge garden and indigenous California eucalyptus and pepper trees. The neighborhood houses looked more like New England than Southern California, with big bay windows, verandas, colored fanlights, and tall iron fences. The two men could not have had origins that are more different; they shared the ability to control large groups of men, while manufacturing a public image that would serve their business and political interests. Biscailuz rose from bookseller to the most famous sheriff of Los Angeles County, with a record fifty-one consecutive years of service. He became an on-camera consultant to television shows like Jack Webb's *Dragnet*. (Webb cut Mickey anecdotes from his book, just prior to publication.) The sheriff liked to ride palominos in the Pasadena Rose Parade, and dressed to the nines in an authentic costume on a horse laden with silver. "Eugene Biscailuz is an institution in Southern California and the citizens are as proud of him as of any of the landmarks in this fabulous country. Eugene Biscailuz, an aristocrat to his fingertips, a competent executive, a courageous law enforcement officer, knows every inch of his empire, Los Angeles County, and is the connecting link between the picturesque pueblo of the past and the great, sprawling industrial center of the present. He is one of the best loved men Southern California has ever known"—Erle Stanley Gardner. Biscailuz once accepted a $5,000 gift from oil man Edward L. Doheny in order to help prisoners who were released from custody—by giving them tobacco and candy. He was quick to point out that all the money went into the project.

4. Until 1937, when he left for Reno, John Harrah, and his son Bill, famous for their casino empire, operated several of the seemingly legal bingo and modified gambling operations in popular Venice Beach.

5. When Mickey set up shop in Los Angeles, Dragna (Anthony Rizzoti), was already a well-known figure and had the police and local officials in his pocket. Stocky, with thick lips and a wide nose, Dragna had received orders through Joe Adonis, a New York hood who became one of the national powers in organized crime, to watch Bugsy, and rightly so. Dragna felt secure in his belief that he had the full imprimatur of Tony Accardo from Chicago, who took over when Al Capone went to prison. Nemesis Dragna enjoyed a mixed reputation as he spiraled upward through the Sicilian ranks after 1914, only six years following his arrival in California with his brother Tom. A 1915 conviction for extortion and three years in San Quentin secured his position as a leader. He embraced the Unione Siciliano, a Black Hand variety, small-town, old-fashioned organization. His business umbrella embraced a variety of illegal activities, protected by a front called the Italian Protective League, organized during Prohibition. He was a member of the Grand Council, the Sicilian insider's club. The Board of Directors begrudgingly accepted Bugsy, a position relegated to non-Sicilians. The outwardly friendly gesture never fooled Mickey. Joe "Iron Man" Ardizonne was originally second in command, and succeeded in running the local Cosa Nostra. He disappeared on October 15, 1931, likely a hit designed by Dragna, who already had the backing of the local Sicilians. With his position solidified, Dragna built the Los Angeles operation through his connections with the entertainment business. He held the dubious distinction of being the only mob boss in town to serve on a national advisory commission to the fledgling industry. Gambling and loan sharking were the underlying backbone of Dragna's operation, and provided a steady cash flow. He ran a rough business, threatened smalltime operators for a piece of the action, and like all Mafiosi had plenty of legitimate business interests: a ranch, a nearly 600-acre vineyard in Puente, California, a banana business, a winery, and a fleet of tankers. Al Guasti, of the Los Angeles County Sheriff's Department, supported Dragna's efforts.

6. Lucky Luciano dressed impeccably, had a shock of wavy hair, and preferred silk underwear like Mickey. He was a constant gambler who enjoyed big odds, big stakes, and the ladies. Nevertheless, he mostly managed to operate and travel under the radar of authorities and journalists. He was a member of the original "Big Seven" bootlegging monopoly, which included the forceful Bugsy-Meyer Lansky connection, Longie Zwillman, King Solomon, Danny Walsh, and Cy Nathanson. His close friends were Joey Adonis, Lansky, Jimmy Hines, Frank Costello, and Lepke. He died of a massive heart attack on January 26, 1962, at the Naples airport moments after greeting his biographer. Luciano, sixty-five, had lived a peaceful life in Naples since his deportation sixteen years earlier. He had always harbored hopes for a return from exile.

7. Dragna and Johnny Rosselli had previously operated the Monfalcone, a luxurious floating casino with entertainment and a sports book. Water taxis took the well-heeled patrons out to the ship, until it burned down in 1930. Rosselli would move on to be the point man in Vegas for Sam "Momo" Giancana, and an associate of Mickey's.

8. "I knew half the movie people in this town on a first-name basis. Jack Warner, Harry Cohn, Sam Goldwyn, Joe Schenck, Clark Gable, George Raft, Jean Harlow, Gary Cooper. Shit, I even knew Charlie Chaplin. I knew them all and enjoyed their company"—Jimmy Aladena "The Weasel/Doctor Schwartz" Fratianno.

9. Louis B. Mayer, like many moguls, relied on California State dealmaker Artie Samish. "I have known Arthur Samish for some twenty years. During this time I have always found his two outstanding characteristics to be loyalty and truthfulness"—Louis B. Mayer.

10. "Prince" Mike Romanoff—he claimed to be royalty from Russia—and wife Gloria held court at their palatial restaurant. Humphrey Bogart was one of their famous regulars. Sinatra was a close pal. Bogart had invested in Romanoff's, and would joke to Sinatra that nobody had ever bought him a drink. Mike was a former pants-presser from New York named Harry Gerguson. "Mike went to Hollywood where fake royalty is as good as any other... An amusing imposter with an

Oxford accent"—Jack Lait. Romanoff ended his restaurant career in a failed Palm Springs venture ironically called "Romanoff's on the Rocks."

11. "Los Angeles is a metropolitan country. There are suave, steely-eyed individuals who would like to prey upon the wealth of Hollywood"—Erle Stanley Gardner.

12. American theater included the names Fanny Brice, Al Jolson, Sophie Tucker, Milton Berle, Ben Blue, Jack Benny, Eddie Cantor, George Burns, Ted Lewis, and Bennie Fields. "How are we to explain this explosion of popular talent among the immigrant Jews? The immediate Yiddish past offered some models—the badkhn, the jester, the fiddler, the stage comedian—but while providing sources of material, these figures were not nearly so consequential in old-country Jewish life as the entertainers were to become in America"—Irving Howe. The Jewish theater chains included, Klaw and Erlanger, Balaban, Orpheum, Schenck, Loew, and Zukor—all engulfed by the growing movie business.

13. Billie Gray's Bandbox was a hot spot; comedian Buddy Hackett honed his Chinese waiter routine there.

14. Bugsy also had a need for recognition and social popularity, and sought out international social contacts. He swiftly became a local celebrity under the tutelage of the café society Countess Dorothy DiFrasso (his hostess in Italy), daughter of Bertrand Taylor, a New Jersey millionaire. New York hotelier James McKinley had introduced him to the Countess. With a million-dollar trust fund, the fun-loving Countess-by-marriage gave lavish Hollywood parties attended by Gary Cooper and Cary Grant. Bugsy and Countess di Frasso once sailed for two months aboard the *Metha Nelson*, the 150-foot ship used in the movie *Mutiny on the Bounty*, captained by Marino Bello, actress Jean Harlow's stepfather. Other social links to Bugsy during his marriage included Wendy Barrie and Marie "The Body" MacDonald. He took up with old Williamsburg pal and established gangster actor George Raft, who employed his own full-time bodyguard, and at one point was the manager of Meyer Lansky's Hotel Capri in Havana. The other big movie stars of the day, Clark Gable, Jean Harlow, Marlene Dietrich, Charles Boyer, Fred Astaire, and Cary Grant all knew Bugsy.

15. "Has history ever toyed so wantonly with a people as history toyed with the Jews in the 1940s? It was a decade of ashes and honey; a decade so battering and so emboldening that it tested the capacity of those who experienced it to hold a stable view of the world, to hold a belief in the world"—Leon Wieseltier. The Carnegie Institution established a research laboratory on Long Island to study eugenics, to justify the elimination of blacks, Indians, the poor, and the sickly. The Rockefeller Foundation and the Harriman railroad fortune also helped finance projects that "sought to legitimize his [Hitler's] innate race hatred and anti-Semitism by medicalizing it, wrapping it in a pseudoscientific façade"—Edwin Black. "The Rockefeller Foundation financed the Kaiser Wilhelm Institute and the work of its central racial scientists. Once WWII began, Nazi eugenics turned from mass sterilization and euthanasia to genocidal murder. One of the Kaiser Wilhelm Institute doctors in the program financed by the Rockefeller Foundation was Josef Mengele, who continued his research in Auschwitz, making daily eugenic reports on twins. After the world recoiled from Nazi atrocities, the American eugenics movement—its institutions and leading scientists—renamed and regrouped under the banner of an enlightened science called *human genetics*"—Black.

Chapter 4 - Setting Up Shop

1. Because of events like the Rosselli robbery, Mickey's callous indifference to other criminal families in Los Angeles, and the archaic Dragna-run mob, the locals likely nicknamed the Hollywood boys the Mickey Mouse Mafia. Many people thought it had something to do with Walt Disney, particularly when his famous black rodent became the talk of the town, or the later proximity to Disneyland, or Mickey's own first name and diminutive stature. (Some later

credit Los Angeles police chief Daryl Gates' 1984 Operation Lightweight for coining the phrase Mickey Mouse Mafia.) When Dragna was in power, the West Coast operation utilized an unorganized methodology that was perhaps three decades behind the rest of the country, and Mickey Mouse Mafia remains a convenient term to excuse decades of sloppy mob-controlled activities.

2. Geisler was born in Iowa, and relocated in California to attend USC Law School. He once chaired the California Horse Racing Board. He defended Robert Mitchum on marijuana charges; represented Shelley Winters when she sued Vittorio Gassman for divorce; Zsa Zsa Gabor against husband George Sanders; Marilyn Monroe when she dumped Joltin' Joe; Barbara Hutton against Cary Grant; Busby Berkeley; Edward G. Robinson; Charlie Chaplin on morals charges; the stripper Lili St. Cyr; Greta Garbo; and Errol Flynn. "...in every one of them [cases] he knew in advance what the prosecutors knew and a lot of other things they had never heard about. I have never seen him taken by surprise"—Florabel Muir. Mickey always remained close with Geisler and his wife Ruth, whom Mickey described as a heavy drinker. "I have long been aware of the fact that 'Get me Geisler' has become a gag used by a husband when he is in the doghouse for some minor domestic offense which has riled his wife. I suppose that an attorney can't take part in as many trials of national interest as I've been involved in without becoming a household word, but this fact really hit me for the first time when Ingrid Bergman's divorce from Dr. Lindstrom was racing the stork"—Jerry Geisler. Geisler died in 1962 after two prior heart attacks in 1959 and 1960.

3. Bugsy muscled in on the Agua Caliente racetrack in Tijuana, a welcome sign of good times to come for the Hollywood crowd and its forever wannabe followers. He christened a greyhound track with dapper don Johnny Rosselli. When his relationship with Rosselli and the movie moguls solidified, Bugsy, together with Mickey, controlled the International Alliance of Theatrical Stage Employees. Simple extortion schemes regularly bilked the studios, who were afraid of wildcat strikes, easily orchestrated by Mickey. Bugsy also made legitimate investments in hotels, restaurants, and real estate with money he garnered by muscling in on existing businesses. Some of the financing for his operation came from making loans to movie stars. He wisely also made political donations, including a hundred grand to politician John Dockweiler, who was running for district attorney. Many enterprising politicians benefited from systematic payments that helped pave the way for Bugsy and Mickey. Bugsy eventually moved with his wife Esther, two daughters, and a nasty German shepherd into a thirty-room mansion owned by famous opera baritone Lawrence Tibbett. The Holmby Hills mansion had a swimming pool and a marble bath. He would later build his own $125,000 house on a $29,000 three-acre lot in the same area. He shelled out an additional $25,000 for the furnishings, with monthly expenses at $1,000. Add to that his two daughters' private schooling, their riding lessons, his wardrobe, including riding habits, and his wife's everyday expenditures. His daughters always remained enrolled in the best private schools, where he mingled with the wealthy, famous, and powerful. He knew how to play the crowd, but he didn't know how to control his character flaws. "A thoroughly arrogant, uninhibited hoodlum, the Bug had an ego that was incredible. The Mob had pinned the Bugsy label on him as a complimentary token for his indifference under fire"—Sid Feder. The fabled Hillcrest Country Club board claimed they didn't know that new applicant Benjamin Siegel was the notorious criminal, even though he was recommended by two major film executives. When club members got wind of the new member, the board voted to have the oldest member of the club visit Bugsy and tell him the bad news: he could no longer attend Hillcrest. The rationale was simple: Bugsy wouldn't take it out on the elderly Jewish gentleman. He didn't, and resigned from the club, with a full refund. According to Bugsy, "No one asked me to get out. I didn't wait for that. I wanted to avoid being embarrassed or embarrassing anyone else. I sold my membership for three hundred dollars, which was less than it cost me. I missed the golfing."

4. Frankie Carbo was a former hit man for Lepke, arrested five times for murder without a single conviction, and later served as boxing czar. Despite two convictions, one for managing fighters without a license, and conspiracy/extortion, Carbo would live the good life in Miami Beach, and die of natural causes at age seventy-two.

5. Billy Wilkerson, who founded the *Hollywood Reporter* and was a big influence in the club scene, eventually developed a less-than-desirable relationship with Bugsy. A degenerate gambler, Wilkerson would control Vendome, Café Trocadero, Sunset House, La Rue, and L'Aiglon, and personally influenced what the movie stars ate. Joe Pasternak, one of Hollywood's popular directors, said that he "…brought Paris to Hollywood." Wilkerson, the son of a gambler who had won Coca-Cola distribution rights in a poker game, tried the priesthood and a medical career before discovering the world of trade papers. He drank Cokes nonstop throughout his caffeine-driven gambling days. Irresponsible Wilkerson once borrowed $75,000 from friend and wealthy movie mogul Joe Schenck in order to buy property near Monte Carlo. After a two-day binge, Wilkerson was broke.

6. Longie Zwillman had a long history with the Hollywood movie business; a best friend was Harry Cohn of Columbia Pictures. He had his own bungalow at the Garden of Allah on Sunset Boulevard, where Mickey, Bugsy, Meyer Lansky, Moe Dalitz, Frank Costello, and a host of other Hollywood luminaries entertained in twenty-four private bungalows.

7. Sinatra was close with Mickey, Sam "Momo" Giancana, Rosselli, Anthony "Big Tuna" Accardo, Santos Trafficante, Jr., and Carlos Marcello—the top racketeers in the country. He was quick to throw a punch in any venue. "I've heard Sam [Giancana] say on many occasions that Frank was a frustrated gangster"—Antoinette Giancana, Sam's daughter. Ciro's Herman Hover had to ignore his imagined "three strikes and you're out" rule for brawlers when it came to Sinatra. He had previously gone after Peter Lawford and Ciro's publicist Jim Byron. Sinatra and bullies also beat up columnist Lee Mortimer in Ciro's, who was no fan of the underworld. Mortimer publicly admitted that he disliked Sinatra's singing, and dug into his mob connections, referring to him as "Lucky." Sinatra claimed that Mortimer called him a "little dago bastard." Mortimer recalled hearing Sinatra mouth "fucking homosexual and degenerate" during the beating. Sinatra paid a $9,000 fine. One raucous night after too many drinks at Jilly Rizzo's, the singer had Jilly and Brad Dexter drive him out to Mortimer's grave so that he could piss on it. Sinatra had continuous problems with columnists Robert Ruark, Dorothy Kilgallen, Louella Parsons, Hedda Hopper, and Westbrook Pegler. He also beat Hunt executive Fred Weisman senseless with a telephone, inside the Beverly Hills Hotel's chichi Polo Lounge. Weisman suffered a fractured skull. Witness Dean Martin denied that the incident took place. The fight was over too much noise emanating from Sinatra's table. Casino manager and executive vice president Carl Cohen knocked out Sinatra's front teeth after the crooner spilt hot coffee on him. Sinatra was purported to have told Kirk Douglas later, "Never fight a Jew in the desert." He likely gave the word to beat up comedian Jackie Mason, whose act featured Sinatra in an unfavorable light. His break up with Lana Turner was complicated, and involved all kinds of ménage a trois possibilities, including wife Ava Gardner. Frank threw everyone out, while the police acted as referees. When he got wind of a Peter Lawford sighting with Ava Gardner, Lawford received this earful personally from Frank: "What's this about you and Ava? Listen, creep. You wanna stay healthy? I'll have your legs broken, you bum…." Singer Andy Williams once successfully joked that when Sinatra opened at Caesars Palace in Vegas "A lot of the audience put their hats over their faces. There was 500 years off for good behavior in the first row."

8. Joseph "Doc" Stacher further organized the Jewish Mafia in 1931 at a meeting in his hotel room. The eight men present included Bugsy Siegel, Louis Buchalter, and Harry "Big Greenie" Greenberg, the core of the fledgling organization. The idea of a national syndicate became a reality. Stacher, a tried and true member of Lansky's operation, ended up in Israel under that country's law of return. He fled the U.S. in 1965 because he faced a jail term for income-tax

evasion. The expressive and comical term "Kosher Nostra" involves Stacher. The cynical Israeli press always referred to Stacher as a member of the Kosher Nostra after a meek rabbi swindled Stacher out of $100,000. The rabbi invested in a kosher hotel rather than the promised educational institutions.

9. Dragna may not have been the patsy that many reported. The California Crime Study Commission wrote that when race wire maven James Ragen lay dying, his last words included, "Dragna is the Capone of Los Angeles." Ragen's death was unquestionably an asset for Bugsy and Mickey to set up and run their wire shop; he naturally lost his race wire business. Author Sid Feder also supported the idea that Dragna was the Capone of the West, hardly in need of advice for running illegal activities. Authorities and crime reporters took up the Capone crack, but it was only an embellishment probably meant to sell newspapers. "Dragna was a man who thought small. The limits of his successful capers involved such matters as providing protection to certain illegal operations and then sending in a confederate to shake them down"—Carl Sifakis. He and at least two of his relatives, a brother and nephew, survived a long time despite the difficulties. "Dragna rose to the top among the 'home-grown' California mobsters only because he was the best of the poor lot—although practiced murderers, they simply lacked the abilities of their eastern-compatriots"—Carl Sifakis.

10. The competing news services were fronts for the race wire. The news services sold racing guides and scratch sheets to bookies around the nation. The initial main interest of the wire service was horseracing, and a bookie who handled a significant illegal cash flow needed up-to-the-minute changing track odds, in order to take advantage of fluctuations. The technology developed by the news services was the best available and sometimes exceeded what Ma Bell was able to offer classified government agencies. Regional bookies had multiple phone lines and switchboards. The largest operations had a ticker (a device similar to those used in the stock market) capable of printing out race-related information on a narrow band of paper. The news services were able to keep an arms-length relationship with the bookies by claiming that they only sold race information to distributors. The wire company owners claimed that what the regional distributors did with the information had nothing to do with the news services. The distributors were dummy corporations, often owned by news service principals or their relatives.

11. "In covering the clubs I found myself enmeshed in the underworld, without quite realizing what was taking place"—Earl Wilson.

12. Joan Crawford made the rounds at Ciro's and the Mocambo with dapper socialite attorney Greg Bautzer. "...[he] was such a good lover that, after one performance in bed with him, Joan Crawford bought him a Cadillac"—Jim Bacon. Bautzer supposedly had seduced knockout blonde virgin Lana Turner. "Easily one of the most handsome..."—Peggy Lee. Bautzer dated Ava Gardner, Dorothy Lamour, was engaged to Barbara Payton, and married Dana Wynter. Porn flicks discovered in Roman Polanski's loft after the Manson murder investigations included Bautzer. Author Sheila Weller referred to Bautzer as Bugsy Siegel's lawyer. He was more a legend, and represented Sinatra, Howard Hughes, and Kirk Kerkorian. He also knew how to keep Meyer Lansky happy, and that included lending his expertise to help organize in Los Angeles.

13. Renowned Ciro's occupied prime Strip real estate. "Billy Wilkerson's stand-alone Ciro's was a creature of his own—and architect George Vernon Russell's—fantasy. The exterior was pure early Southern California sophistication...bearing dozens of appliquéd squares in bas-relief: the scripted logo (with its piquantly tiled, comically triple-oversized C) sitting on a swirling-edged white slab overhang, propped up by an elegant screen of white slats rising from planters bursting with tropical flora"—Sheila Weller. The interior of Ciro's: "dreamy apple" color with ribbed thick silk walls, bronze columns, glass dance floor, fish pool, an American Beauty Red ceiling that matched the plush banquettes and urns that hid the lighting. "...celebrating clever

people's ability to restyle themselves to their passions"—Weller. The vice squad closed Ciro's the year Mickey arrived; it reopened, more grandiose, in 1940. Sinatra, Piaf, Holiday, Cole, Dietrich, Martin and Lewis, Horne, and West all worked the room. Backward-style striptease star Lily St. Cyr caused a temporary closing: "She emerged onstage wearing pasties and a G-string and proceeded to clothe herself, caressing every part of her body in the process…more Dada than burlesque"—Weller. Manager/owner Herman Hover, former Earl Carroll chorus boy from New York, hired decorator Jamie Ballard to build a special marble bathtub for a courtroom stage. "The bathtub was transparent; it was illuminated from the inside and through it Miss St. Cyr's seductive curves and undulations could be glimpsed"—Jerry Geisler. In defense of St. Cyr, Geisler had Hover stand before the jury and scientifically show the subtle differences between a lawful bump and the dreaded illegal grind. The all-male jury gladly finished observing the testimony at Ciro's. Florabel Muir, journalist and Mickey pal, testified that she had an unobstructed view, and was not offended. She insisted that the deputy D.A. call her "Madam"; it got one of the biggest laughs at the trial. "It was the most daring thing on the Strip. It was startling for those days"—Army Archerd. After banishment from the dance floor for salacious dancing, actress Paulette Goddard crawled under the table at Ciro's and more privately and orally continued her attention toward director Anatole Litvak. Some reversed the action. "Litvak crouched, and—unmistakably to the diners nearby—performed cunnilingus on her"— Weller. "Part of the building is on city property and part on the county. While the two outfits were trying to decide who had jurisdiction, Ciro's practically burnt down"—Wilkerson. It would close after the fire in 1957.

14. Fred and Joe Sica were two thugs who handled the rough stuff for Mickey and Bugsy. Mike Howard—no relation to Bill—would hang himself years later in New York, after surviving years around Mickey without a scratch, including the Battle of the Sunset Strip.

15. Dr. Sanford Zevon, Stumpy's nephew, recalled Mickey as a pleasant, affable man, who was always polite at the family home in Brooklyn. Crystal Zevon, Stumpy's daughter-in-law and former wife of Warren Zevon, spoke similarly of Stumpy, but recognized that there were times to stay clear.

16. Bogart and Bacall liked to hang out at the Mocambo, where Sinatra made his first club appearance. Charlie Morrison, a former usher from the fabled Palace Theater in New York, ran the club designed by Tony Duquette. Sinatra frequently engaged Morrison and Dave Chasen in conversation about their spaghetti and clam sauce. Clark Gable, Carole Lombard, Lucille Ball, and Desi Arnaz were also Mocambo regulars. Gable loved the track, and didn't mind rubbing elbows with the bad boys in town. The famous radio personality and columnist Walter Winchell, King of Broadway, dined regularly with Marilyn Monroe. His sometimes inaccurate column appeared in over 1,000 newspapers.

17. Massachusetts-born Fred Otash became an FBI informant. The FBI dropped him when he publicized his working relationship with the government agency. Otash moved to New York in 1965, after the State License Board revoked his private investigator's license.

18. Drucker's morphed into Rothschild's on Beverly Drive. This famous tonsorial hangout became home to a major sports book where regular gambling clients, occasional newcomer locals, and out-of-town guests could bet on an array of games that rivaled current sophisticated Vegas parlors. Mickey's autobiography displays a picture of Harry Gelbart giving his balding client a haircut. Harry's Hollywood contacts would help find work for his son, comedy writer Larry. Harry even introduced his nephew, now fashionable Brentwood dentist Dr. Michael Eilenberg, to Mickey. Whenever the intimating George Raft appeared for a shave at busy Drucker's, he needed only to move toward any occupied chair, and the patron, particularly if mob connected, would relinquish the seat.

19. Samuel Bronfman was the patriarch of the wealthy Canadian-Jewish family that traded its stake in the Seagram's liquor business for the Universal entertainment conglomerate and the music

business. Bronfman's original fortune came from peddling Canadian booze to American bootleggers for fourteen years. That meant doing business with Rothstein, Lansky, Luciano, Dalitz, and the Purple Gang in Detroit. Lake Erie, nicknamed the "Jewish" lake, was the entry point for Dalitz' bootlegging operations. The Canadian Parliament had restricted the sale of alcohol in 1919, labeled it a drug, and sold it only in pharmacies. The Canada Pure Drug Company was the source of booze for millions of Americans. "We loaded a carload of goods, got our cash, and shipped it. We shipped a lot of goods. I never went to the other side of the border to count the empty Seagram's bottles"—Samuel Bronfman. Paul Matoff, Bronfman's brother-in-law, would lose his life in a gun battle with rival bootleggers. Some of the family relocated in New York and made the business and cultural assimilation that was common for second and third generation Jewish families with criminal backgrounds. "...they invested in real estate, commodities, stocks, and bonds... They supported the arts, attended synagogue, raised racehorses, and made generous contributions to charities, especially those that championed the Jewish state of Israel"—Dennis McDougal.

20. Moses Annenberg, another super rich patriarch, who once hired Luciano and Lansky as circulation monitors for the *Mirror*, would build his empire on gambling. "Moses Annenberg had fought his way up from Chicago newsboy to high executive positions in William Randolph Hearst's empire on the strength of his performance in the interminable 'circulation wars' between competing newspapers and magazines. Then, step by step, he brought out the first daily racing journals, and, soon after, the wire service company that had been supplying the results to those journals...seizing control of a service on which every bookie depended with the help of the gang/syndicates"—Albert Fried. Each wire service provider had thousands of customers. By using a special telephone line, the bookie had continual access to the fluctuating odds, race results, and payoffs from tracks throughout the country. Annenberg could never have set up the Nationwide wire service without Al Capone. "That Annenberg and the Prohibition and gambling mobs had interests in common is indisputable... Annenberg was allowed to reap inordinate profits and become one of the richest men in the land..."—Albert Fried.

Chapter 5 - The Jews Return to the Desert

1. One of Charlie and Mickey's fighters was lightweight Jimmy Joyce, brother of nationally celebrated Willie, whom Mickey had managed. Willie was one of the top four lightweights; he beat Ike Williams three times in seven months.
2. The Jim Dandy and Food Basket labels are today part of the Albertson's chain.
3. Stanley Adams would do jail time for killing Davidian. He was friendly with actress Barbara Payton and actor/drug dealer Don Cougar. Payton, Mickey, and tough-guy actor John Ireland made the social rounds together. Payton, once engaged to attorney Greg Bautzer, also had a fling with actor George Raft.
4. During the forties and fifties Los Angeles was the prostitution wholesaler for the state of California and, later, Nevada. Farmers and miners demanded companionship. So did fancy hotel guests in San Francisco. Truck drivers supplied the transportation for delivering ten bucks worth of fun on the cuff. Sex establishments advertised afternoon nude modeling sessions. For two bucks, a patron could buy the phone numbers of fifty models, including nude photos.
5. Sedway was a lifer with Meyer Lansky, and helped set up the Trans America wire service, by supplying national muscle that competed with Continental. The Trans America Publishing and News Service would become the cornerstone needed to pave the way for the move into Las Vegas. Anti-Semitic FBI files on Moe Sedway were direct: "...a dwarf Jewish boy with all the worst traits of his nationality over-emphasized... Prone to be a snappy dresser...obsessions are monogrammed silk shirts and silk underwear as well as manicured nails."

6. When Thomas Hull opened the El Rancho Vegas in 1941, the idea of a complex with gaming, lodging, dining, entertainment, and retail facilities did not exist. The Hotel El Rancho was the first full-scale hotel and casino resort on Highway 91 south of Las Vegas, a roadway that would become the Las Vegas Strip. The El Rancho Vegas changed hands a few times before Beldon Katleman, who inherited a share from his uncle, took over. He renovated the hotel and it became a Vegas cornerstone throughout the 1950s. He knew the value of entertainment and sexy girls; El Rancho was one of the first hotels to feature a risqué revue, a Vegas staple. Jimmy Fratianno and comedy star Chico Marx partnered in the El Rancho race book.

7. Uneducated Sinatra shared many of Mickey's habits and self-esteem problems. He was meticulous when it came to cleanliness, and was obsessed with his appearance. His germ phobia required no less than four showers every day. His baldness troubled him, so he used spray-on hair coloring, endless toupees, and hats. He always wore makeup applied with a powder puff before leaving home, designed to cover the deformities on the left side of his face and ear caused by a forceps birth. He was jealous of Peter Lawford's smoother delivery and social acceptance. His publicist Warren Cowan, formerly of Rogers and Cowan, once said that with a client like Sinatra there was little need to generate publicity. The biggest Zionist of all Mickey's friends was Sinatra. He loved to travel to Israel and donate to supportive organizations.

8. Tarantino would find himself in San Quentin after prosecution for using his Hollywood rag for blackmail purposes. Mickey claimed that he had warned him that the police were bugging his phone. After Tarantino's parole, he moved to New Jersey.

9. Myford was the son of James Irvine, and one of the most successful southern California ranchers. On Saturday, January 11, 1959, police found his body in the basement of his home. He had been shot twice in the abdomen with a sixteen-gauge shotgun and once in the right temple with a twenty-two-caliber revolver. The coroner ruled the death a suicide. Mickey commented, "But not over this," referring to the Nixon campaigns. The case remains unsolved.

10. When Raft was having tax problems, Neddie Herbert asked Mickey to return the favor by giving Raft the necessary short funds; he did. A reporter once asked an elder Raft what had happened to all his millions. His answer: "Part of the loot when for gambling, part for horses, and part for women. The rest I spent foolishly."

11. Dave Chasen, who started at Mocambo, remained friends with Sinatra. When he first opened his restaurant, it served spareribs for thirty-four cents and chili for twenty-five. Director Frank Capra called the hangout Chasen's Southern Barbecue Pit. Chasen's, by then serving its signature Hobo Steak and iced seafood tower, would become a second home to the Rat Pack, the Reagans, and countless executives.

12. Mickey relied on lifelong friend Artie Samish for protective state connections. Samish, a politician-fixer-lobbyist, did not know Mickey from the neighborhood, as many true-crime writers have claimed. Los Angeles-born Samish spent most of his youth in San Francisco, and was approximately fifteen years older than Mickey. "A meaty individual of some three hundred pounds, Samish has an interesting political credo himself, which he once expressed as, 'To hell with the governor of the state; I am the governor of the legislature'"—Burton Turkus and Sid Feder. Samish once posed with a dummy to illustrate how he controlled the puppet California government. The California State Brewers Institute paid the chubby Samish $30,000 a year, with a slush fund of $150,000 more. He received another $36,000 from Schenley Distillers in New York. He made close to $1,000,000 in only six years. The IRS and Senator Estes Kefauver relied on telephone company records to establish that Samish was a crook. "Next to Hollywood and oranges, Samish is California's biggest crop for export"—Jack Lait and nephew Lee Mortimer. He acted as the inside contact for real estate moguls. When Kefauver investigated him, he told the committee that he threw away all his canceled checks. For Treasury agents, he added, "and the waste-basket is in my safe." "He is a combination of Falstaff, Little Boy Blue, and Machiavelli, crossed with an eel"—Estes Kefauver. Samish, who liked to wear bright-banded

straw hats, would do time in prison for tax evasion. His case went to the U.S. Supreme Court, where Chief Justice Earl Warren removed himself from the hearing.

13. The Burbank land was originally part of two large Spanish grants, one in 1798 and the other in 1821. Dr. David Burbank, a dentist, purchased portions of both ranches totaling 4,000 acres. Lockheed moved in, and later produced 19,000 planes during World War II. First National Pictures purchased a seventy-acre site and later sold it to the four Warner brothers. Columbia Pictures followed, as did Walt Disney.

14. Arthur "Mickey" McBride, who had worked for wire-founder Annenberg, took the reins of the Continental Press Service in 1939. McBride, the first owner of the Cleveland Browns football team, would tell the Kefauver committee in 1951 that he started the business "on a modest bankroll of $20,000 purely out of sentiment and goodwill to provide a job for my brother-in-law, [Tom] Kelly," whom Kefauver made a point of calling "bald and seemingly disingenuous." "I didn't buy anything from Nation Wide, not so much as a toothpick... I started a new business," confirmed McBride. Kefauver illustrated that the investment paid off several hundred fold in a matter of months. The Chicago mob naturally had wanted to cut itself in on the operation.

15. Most critics ignored the historical inaccuracy of the movie, a story line taken from the then twenty-five-year-old Dean Jennings' anecdotal biography of Bugsy.

16. Del Webb would become involved in several casino ventures, including the Sahara Hotel. He helped build many of the city's municipal facilities and retirement communities.

17. Los Angeles flooring contractor John Biren had meetings with Tony Cornero, who had started the Stardust Company. Cornero would only meet at odd hours. Biren and his partner, with carpet samples in hand for the hotel, went to Cornero's residence at one in the morning. Cornero argued with his mother over the samples, finally yelling to her, "Who the fuck asked you?" Then he turned to Biren and calmly stated, "You will take stock." Biren logically and bravely explained that he couldn't afford to wait for payment, and left unscathed. When assassins shot Cornero outside his Beverly Hills home, the police questioned Mickey, who told them that Tony was an upstanding citizen in the Mexican meat business. When the Stardust officially opened in 1955, the guests of honor were future president LBJ and protégé political secretary Bobby Baker.

Chapter 6 – Goodbye Bugsy

1. In 1963 builders demolished the luxurious late nineteenth century Hollenden Hotel to make way for a box-like modern structure.

2. Well-built Hill, also known as Ginny, was the daughter of a cocktail-friendly Alabama marble polisher of Slovak descent. She lived a tomboy existence with her grandmother on a Georgia cotton farm, learning to ride horses and swim naked. She quit school at fourteen, and three years later made a showing as a young woman on the Midway at the Chicago World's Fair, in a show called "Elephants and Fleas." Before she met Bugsy, she had been married four times in sixteen years. One of these spouses was Chicago betting commissioner Joe Epstein. He wasn't rich enough for her, although he received a cut from every bookie in town. Epstein, a protégé of Greasy Thumb Guzik, ran the mob's wire service. Through unattractive Mr. Magoo-ish Epstein, Hill met mobsters Frank Nitti, Tony Accardo, the Fischetti brothers, Joe Adonis, Frank Costello, and Lucky Luciano. Her mating ran the gamut from Mexican rumba dancers to Austrian skiers. Known for her flamboyant tendencies, she often dropped ten grand a night for parties, and she once convinced Bugsy to invest in a poppy-growing business. The FBI coldly referred to Hill as a thrice-married obscene dope addict. Many considered her only a mob courier, her duties no more sophisticated than a bagman's. She sometimes carried sums in the millions. When she talked Sam Goldwyn into a part in *Ball of Fire*, directed by Howard Hawks,

she had hit the big time. In the company of stars Gary Cooper, Barbara Stanwyck, Oscar Homolka, Henry Travers, S. Z. Sakall, Dan Duryea, Elisha Cook, Jr., and Dana Andrews at the Grauman's Chinese premier, Hill strolled up with her escort Bugsy Siegel. Bugsy's wife Esther headed back to Brooklyn with the Siegel daughters, and soon agreed to a Reno divorce, netting $32,000 per year. Bugsy and Hill had a rocky relationship. She abused sleeping pills, and often ended up in emergency rooms, followed by oodles of bad publicity. She starved herself to remain thin. "He's [Bugsy] very overbearing. He always wants his own way. I'm used to having my own way, too, and we're apt to have lots of battles"—Virginia Hill. She appeared before the Kefauver hearings on March 15, 1951, and overdosed on sleeping pills in 1966.

3. The house belonged to Juan Romero, Rudolph Valentino's manager.
4. Mickey's routine included a minimum of one Cadillac in front and one behind his vehicle. When he went out at night, the caravan would circle his restaurant destination. One vehicle would peel off at a time, and his boys would check out the inside of the restaurant while the rest of the vehicles continued around the block. The circling repeated, with Mickey's car pulling in to the parking lot last. Los Angeles folklore maintains that he would use the same method for returning to the Boyle Heights Cornwall Street Synagogue, where he would say Kaddish for his father. The Cadillac was the chosen vehicle for the mob. The sons of mobsters, who sometimes were able to take the cars on dates, referred to the sleek machines as Dadillacs, and dressed to the nines with pinky rings to impress their hot dates.
5. Costello began in the mid 1920s as a sub-capo in the Manhattan Joe Maseria family. His brethren included Lucky Luciano, Vito Genovese, Albert Anastasia, Joe Adonis, Anthony Anastasia, Carlo Gambino, and Willie Moretti. Those mobsters avoided the public eye, while Arnold Rothstein, Dutch Schultz, Legs Diamond, Owney Madden, and Bill Dwyer made headlines. Costello's mentor was Rothstein. In 1929, playground Atlantic City played host to Costello, Luciano, Lepke (who controlled the garment center), Adonis, Johnny Torrio, Lou Rothkopf, Moe Dalitz, King Solomon, John Lazia, Joe Bernstein, Sam Lazar, and kingpin Al Capone. The Traymore Hotel hosted the cigar-chomping organizers, who took time out to scan the white beaches for girls sporting the new fashion—bathing suits above the knee. During the Kefauver Hearings, Costello refused to be televised, allowing only his moving hands to be photographed, suggesting what some called a "hand ballet." He would eventually retire, and commute from his Long Island mansion to his New York apartment.

Chapter 7 – Hello Mickey

1. Under the guidance of East Coast interests, the Flamingo showed a $4,000,000 profit at the end of the year, after skimming $15,000,000 (according to the authors Giancana). The Flamingo and later the Desert Inn would easily outdo the El Rancho, and attract national attention to redrawing the landscape of Las Vegas. The city moved along, and ten neon-lit casinos soon spotted the desert, increasing in short order to thirteen. Jake Katleman, Tutor Scherer, Guy McAfee, Farmer Page, Bill Curland, Chuck Addison, and other high-profile gamblers migrated to Vegas from L.A., while New York's Frank Costello, the Chicago Fischettis, the Detroit Liccavolis, Brooklyn's Joe Adonis, and New Jersey's Longie Zwillman watched their investment in the Flamingo soar.
2. Since 1946, Governor Warren had been working on an Organized Crime Commission; he received final approval in 1947. Squeaky-clean Warren continued his commission. He smelled something fishy about Howser's campaign compatriots. Howser had sent John Riggs and Wiley "Buck" Caddel to investigate bookmaking. Riggs doctored his reports and the courts convicted Caddel and retired Los Angeles police officer James M. "Chinese" Mulligan for bribery and conspiracy to violate gambling laws. Caddel was part of the $2,000,000,000 slot business, with $400,000,000 allocated for protection.

3. The *Nation* was founded in 1865, and declared it would not be the "organ of any party, sect, or body." It remains a left-leaning, liberal periodical.
4. An odd example of Mickey's creative interests involves an author of children's stories who had met him. When he learned that she was traveling to Boston, he arranged for her to meet Rocky Paladino, who escorted her around town. The Damon Runyon character inspired her, and she subsequently wrote a series of children's stories about him and his stable of horses.
5. Hecht had been an acrobat, magician, newspaperman, playwright, author, and screenwriter before meeting Mickey. Some of his many screenplays were *Gunga Din, Wuthering Heights, Scarface, Notorious, Spellbound,* and *The Front Page*; perhaps half of all the great Hollywood movies, according to critic Pauline Kael. He was also famous on the literary scene: he authored books, plays, and an extensive number of short stories.
6. The Irgun, a derivative of the kibbutz-based Haganah, was a Jewish defense organization that began with the imprimatur of the British to help with Arab rebellions in the late thirties. By the forties, British policy toward Jews changed dramatically, and the British forced Jewish refugees to live in Australian internment camps behind barbed wire. One year after the start of WW II, the British government arrested 75,000 Jews, citing them as "enemy aliens." Survivors of the HMT *Dunera*, a ship that brought about 2,000 Jews to Australia, still meet each year near the dock in Sydney where the ship had arrived. Two years after *Dunera*, the British reversed their position and publicly admitted that they had made a "deplorable mistake." The Haganah developed its attack corps, the Palmach, and the main revisionist group, the Irgun Zvai Leumi; the two operated under similar charters. The major distinction was the Irgun's policy of openly condoning terrorist attacks against the British, including killing officials and hostages. "…initially the Israelis were poorly armed, inadequately trained, and disorganized, but the officers of their liberation army, drawn almost entirely from the kibbutzim, in the end prevailed"—Norman Cantor. The Irgun made international headlines after blowing up the British military headquarters at the King David Hotel in Jerusalem. The Irgun fighters had entered the basement of the hotel disguised as employees and the explosives were hidden in milk cans. A warning phone call informed the British: either get out or be blown up. Sir John Shaw answered, "I am here to give orders to the Jews, not to receive orders from them." He eventually left with a few of his top officers. The Irgun destroyed the British headquarters and archives.
7. Preminger more likely sought expert advice from Mickey during the preproduction period of one of his earlier film noir movies like *Where The Sidewalk Ends*, about a cop killing a murder suspect, or *Whirlpool*, about a shoplifter married to a psychiatrist, perhaps even *Angel Face*, about a woman who kills her lover.

Chapter 8 – The Fundraiser

1. Hecht was comfortable with his Jewish origins but did not become an activist until 1939. He had "turned into a Jew…some 45 years after his bris."—Sidney Zion.
2. "The more guns, the better chance for game, so overseas solicitors are frequently brought in for the attack."—Gerald Krefetz.
3. "The techniques range from appealing to the most profound Jewish instinct of charity by using the most flagrant and cynical panhandling techniques of the schnorer. It pulls out all the stops, from pathos to bathos, and cashes in on every emotion."—Gerald Krefetz. "There are rules to this game as in any other. When out for big trophies, a safari is the preferred hunting method. It is an accepted principle that one man should never go alone to solicit a major gift. It is too easy to say no to one man, especially if he is a friend or neighbor. When two or more go, it is no longer one Jew asking another for a gift—it is the entire community, it is the Jewish people."—Paul Zuckerman.

4. The *Altalena* carried 900 people, including Menachem Begin, 5,000 rifles, 450 machine guns, and enough ammunition to fuel a significant battle, according to author Rockaway. While other sources report different numbers, the fact remains that the ship was loaded for war, heavily assisted by the Jewish mob. The Irgun was intent on docking the vessel, despite warnings from the Israeli government and the United Nations. *Time* magazine reported on the June 25, 1948, altercation: "Bitterest Blow. On the beach at Kfar Vitkin, 20 miles north of Tel Aviv, waited slight, sharp-eyed Menachim Beigin [Menachem Begin] and a force of his bully boys, to help unload." The Haganah, now Israel's official army, was waiting with orders to stop them. The result was a short, sharp civil war of Jew against Jew, which Prime Minister David Ben-Gurion described as "the bitterest blow." Some historians wrote that the argument had more to do with how to distribute the materials. Ben-Gurion insisted that the Irgun be part of the one nation-one army theory, with no special privileges, everything divided equally. He was afraid that a civil war would erupt, but started one anyway. The terrorists partially unloaded the cargo at Kfar Vitkin, and lost six, twenty wounded, while the Haganah suffered fewer losses. Begin boarded the ship, and ordered it southward. At midnight, the *Altalena* rammed the beach at Tel Aviv. At noon, an assault boat with a few armed Irgunists headed for the beach and set up a mini-beachhead amidst small-arms fire. On orders from Prime Minister Ben-Gurion, the army shelled the ship and it caught fire. Correspondents and U.N. observers had been watching from the balcony of the Kaete Dan Hotel. By morning, the soldiers had destroyed the ship, and forty died.

5. Russian journalist Jabotinsky was the father of the Revisionist (New) Zionist Movement and the associated Betar youth camps. He died of a heart attack during a trip to a Betar summer camp in upstate New York in 1940. He had fought for the formation of a Jewish state on both sides of the Jordan River and was against any partition plans for the new nation. He was one of the greatest proponents of the Hebrew language. Denied reentry into Palestine by the British in 1929, his remains were ultimately returned to Jerusalem in 1965.

6. The soldiers fought alongside the British as the Zion Mule Corps at the battle of Gallipoli and in North Africa directly against the Nazis.

7. Actor Walter Matthau told this story to movie producer Eliot Kastner at the Beverly Hills Tennis Club. "A lot of things were being stolen at a shtetl in Israel. There was one suspect, but the residents decided the best thing to do was have the rabbi settle the dilemma. The rabbi confronted the thief and made a suggestion, 'If you want a new life I can arrange for you to move over the hill to the shtetl on the east side, and you can start a new life there. I've talked with their rabbi, and it can be arranged.' The young man was very grateful and agreed to move. About one year later, the rabbi received a message from the east side rabbi, 'We are continually losing our silver and gold. Please take him back.' The young man returned to the original shtetl, and stood before his old rabbi, head bowed, ashamed. The rabbi spoke in a deep, solemn voice, 'How can you have done this after the opportunity I have provided for you?' The man thought for a moment and answered as if he had made a brilliant discovery, 'I guess I'm just a thief, rabbi.'"

8. The structure of many charities lends itself to the kind of creative accounting commonplace in Mickey's business. Charities have been notorious for expenses associated with operations. It is conceivable for someone like Mickey to skim some of the proceeds, but unlikely in this case since it was a national mob venture. In addition, the Jewish fundraising machine was as powerful and as well organized as Mickey's mob. They would never have stood by and watched the money disappear. In addition, Mickey's exaggerated payroll was now a whopping $500,000 a day, with his take estimated as high as $250,000 after expenses. A ton of cash floated around the country, and although skimming wasn't the worst crime, particularly amongst criminals, Mickey and the Jewish mob did not need to defraud the Zionist organizations.

9. Irish Vernon Ferguson was tall with white hair, and was an imposing presence in the courtroom. He would head up the Los Angeles County grand jury for three decades.

Chapter 9 – The Virtuoso

1. Sinatra continually relied on the mob. His lifelong gangster friendships intertwined his social life with Hollywood mob life. He didn't take his legendary breakups well. When he split with Lauren Bacall (Betty Perske), he chose the telephone to deliver the bad news. He had difficulty facing former girlfriends, and developed a solid "Hit the road, Jack!" attitude, isolating himself from most. If any of the women persisted in pursuing him, he would ask attorney Mickey Rudin to step in and Rudin hammered home the stay-away message with cold legal letters. Sinatra was not fond of "spoiled Jew brats," and dated none of the locals. When Bacall fell out of favor, she became "the Jew bitch." He wasn't shy about describing her lack of talent in the fellatio arena: "All she does is whistle." Aside from Bacall, his only other Jewish love was Jill St. John (Jill Oppenheim), who after indoctrination with George Raft proved a perfect mob match for Sinatra, who loved gangster dialogue. Sinatra didn't date black women, although he was no stranger to black call girls, a steady stream of which was readily available. He would quip, "Trade you two vanillas for one chocolate." One night he tried to entice Judith Exner into a ménage a trois with a naked black guest who appeared unexpectedly and began performing fellatio on him in front of her.

2. D'Amato never graduated from elementary school, and started out with a small gambling operation. His 500 Club was renowned for its headliners and mobsters, and he for his gambling and pimping skills. He was no stranger to Giancana and Lucky Luciano, maintained a lifelong friendship with Sinatra (helped him when his career was flailing), and promoted Jack Kennedy to win the primary in West Virginia.

3. Throughout his life, Sinatra referred to Dean as "the wop." Jerry Lewis was always "the Jew," Laurence Harvey was "Ladyboy," Cary Grant was "Sheenie," and Johnny Mathis was "the African Queen." Sinatra's private plane was *El Dago*. Comedian Jan Murray, who occasionally appeared first at Sinatra's concerts, was only greeted by "Hey, Clyde." George Jacobs, Sinatra's African-American assistant, tolerated "spook." Between the mafia-speak and "ring-a-ding-dings," only insiders knew the entire code. When Sinatra felt it was appropriate, he could turn on the charm and the altar boy sensibilities.

4. Egoless Dean Martin, always friendly with Mickey, was born in mob-tolerant Steubenville, Ohio (population 20,000), where casinos, speakeasies, and brothels operated freely. He had dealt cards and boxed (Kid Crochet), but preferred his singing waiter jobs at mob-run clubs. "I had a great time growing up in Steubenville. There was everything a boy could want. Women. Music. Nightclubs. Liquor. And to think I had all that when I was only thirteen"—Dean Martin. "...he was a good guy, very easy to get along with...he was rough, uncouth, not educated—I don't think he ever read a book"—Herman Zlotchover (Hover). Hover also took credit for Martin and Lewis' rise in popularity, but admitted that Martin solidified his career through his mob relationships. "The mobsters tolerated Jerry, but they loved Dean; they courted him, seeking his company in saloons and casinos and on golf courses... Dean knew that the world for such men was a one-way arrangement; he was smart enough to never be disrespectful or insubordinate—asked to make an appearance, he usually complied—but he kept his distance and tried to maintain strictly professional relationships with any gangsters who wanted to get closer"—Shawn Levy. Lucky Luciano once lobbied Sinatra to induce Dean to play Luciano in a movie about his life. It never came to fruition; Dean begged off, he had his limits. During his declining years, La Famiglia restaurant owner Joe Patti would take Dean's dentures and hide them behind the bar. He preferred to drink without them. Dean entertained locals with endless stories, mostly about his golf exploits.

5. Jerry Lewis makes no mention of Mickey in his recent memoir. He did include New York boss Frank Costello, the Fischetti brothers, Gus Greenbaum, Willie Moretti, and Bugsy. He had admitted previously that Mickey might have arranged the Martin and Lewis debut, but denied Mickey's political assistance with the unions.

6. In return for favors and money, Mickey obliged the unions' suggestions, and was influential in controlling people who worked in and out of the entertainment business. The FBI watched and reported on Mickey's role in the show business unions, "They [Mickey's boys] were instructed to create as much disturbance as possible in order to discredit the strike. They were told to roust and slug persons in the picket lines and if apprehended they were to disclaim membership in any group…use dynamite and if necessary to kill anyone who interfered…"

7. Brenda Allen was one of the most successful madams in town; some referred to her as a prostitute, since she ran a stable with hundreds of girls. Her clients included movie stars and gangsters. Popular Allen had her name, picture, and telephone number printed in the Official Players Directory published by the Academy of Motion Picture Arts and Sciences. She had a stable of 114 girls, and it was not unusual for each girl to gross $1200 per day. Allen worked on a 50% split. She subscribed to doctors' and lawyers' telephone answering services, and made sure every cab driver, bartender, and bellhop had her direct line. Her Hollywood love-for-sale nests, as the newspapers called them, were an integral part of the social scene.

8. When things died down, *Newsweek* followed a social story about Mickey and his girlie friends. The sultry blondes, Vicki Evans and Lila Leeds, decked out in elegant outfits, posed for photographers. Lila draped a fancy fur stole, complete with the little mink's head, over her wide-lapelled jacket. The D.A. later charged her with membership in a call-girl setup. She, of course, denied the charges.

9. Many illegal abortion clinics existed throughout the United States until 1973, the year the Supreme Court legalized it. The costly illegal procedures often took place in unsanitary conditions with staffs of unqualified midwives and scam artists.

10. Other authors prefer a less popular version: later in the afternoon on a sunny California day, Mickey and henchman Frankie Niccoli waltzed into a restaurant across from Paramount Pictures, and then beat Utley.

Chapter 10 – Mickey and the Seven Dwarfs

1. Mickey made a foray into the oil business in Wichita Falls, Texas, but trouble with the Texas Rangers put a damper on his pursuits in the area.

2. Meltzer had come out west after his "New Joisey" pal Charlie "The Jew" Janowsky, a successful gambler, was ice-picked to death and left to drain. Since Meltzer knew Neddie, it was a natural to work for Mickey. Meltzer ran a jewelry store near Mickey's haberdashery.

3. So much graft filtered through the police department, that one officer had enough money to build a $100,000-dollar hotel.

4. Harry Grossman, of the Ruditsky Detective Agency, introduced Vaus to Mickey. Vaus worked for the police and Mickey at the same time—an undoubtedly favorable situation for Mickey. To make the initial switch, Mickey gave Vaus $300 in cash, a woman's diamond ring, chrome auto accessories, and suits and ties. Vaus exposed everything that he had done for the police to Mickey, including the location of his residential bugs.

5. Total bail estimates hit a high of $300,000 for Mickey and his gang. He posted $75,000 bonds for Frankie Niccoli and Davey Ogul. He had to collateralize his Brentwood home and cars to cover the bail. An FBI report stated that Mickey never reported income of more than $15,000 a year, causing agents to wonder how he came up with the bail money.

6. "Vice men have a bad public reputation. The public thinks we are just a bunch of bulls sneaking around to break up somebody's friendly Friday night poker game"—Captain Charles Stanley.

7. Garner was an established movie actress who began work as a child contemporary of Roddy McDowall. Her most famous theatrical work was her yearlong tour in *Bus Stop*, where she met and married leading man Albert Salmi. Her portrayal of Francis Nolan in Kazan's adaptation of the Betty Smith novel *A Tree Grows In Brooklyn* earned Garner a special juvenile Oscar.
8. Glaser had worked for the famous Music Corporation of America, a forerunner of MCA. MCA's impressive client list included Louis Armstrong and Billie Holiday.
9. Jim Richardson had originally asked Mickey to feed him occasional tips regarding anything newsworthy. The cordial relationship that developed instead helped sell millions of newspapers over an eighteen-year period.

Chapter 11 – Shootout on the Sunset Strip

1. *Laugh In* television producer George Schlatter was the "bagman" who transferred the Ciro's protection money to Mickey. His job was to take a bag, "a small, heavy, knotted white sack," from the nightclub's show producer, author Weller's Uncle Herman Hover, and walk it into the kitchen. One of Mickey's men would wait there with several of the haberdashery boxes from Mickey's store. Schlatter claims, "As far as I was concerned, I was legitimately buying boxes!" He did say that the boxes appeared devoid of garments.
2. Biscailuz would use Mickey as a focal point for reelection—Vote for me and I'll get rid of Cohen. Every night the sheriff's boys would frisk Mickey and anyone within a football field of the haberdashery or Continental Café on Santa Monica Boulevard. Since this part of the Strip and West Hollywood was still unincorporated, it fell under the larger jurisdiction of Sheriff Biscailuz, who was forever trying as hard as Mickey to maintain a favorable public image.
3. Ruditsky had opened a detective agency in Hollywood, and fancied himself an expert on the mob; Chief of Police Anderson of Beverly Hills questioned him after Bugsy's murder. Clients like Bugsy, Mickey, and Al Smiley had used him as a glorified bill collector. Ruditsky's exploits with partner Johnny Broderick became the hard-as-nails stuff of crime writers. Ruditsky died on October 18, 1962. Although a detective, his extensive obit outlined his almost fictional association with crime, culminating with consulting work on television and movies.
4. Stompanato had run gift, pet, furniture stores, and even sold cars.
5. Ballistic experts corroborated that the guns used in the Sherry's shooting were loaded with "heavy slugs," also called a .30-06 bullet, legal in some states for deer hunting, and consistent with Neddie and Mickey's injuries.
6. The whole setup smelled amateurish: a vacant lot was the worst choice to stage operations. Residents would later report that the escape route wasn't organized either. As the shooters raced down Hammond Street after pulling out of a dead-end, getaway cars nearly collided with the lookout car. Where were the shooters aiming? A better name for the L.A. mob, instead of "The Mickey Mouse Mafia," could be "The Gang That Couldn't Shoot Straight," a title once used by gonzo journalist Jimmy Breslin to describe the Crazy Joe Gallo wiseguys.
7. Another FBI memorandum half-heartedly tried to discredit Mickey and the attention directed toward him after the Sherry's shooting: "Cohen is commonly reputed to be a braggart who, at least until the recent past, was anxious to be esteemed as a notorious "tough" and it appears probable that the discrepancies between his admitted arrests and those reflected in his identification record arose from a feeble attempt on his part to deceive…agents as to his actual arrest record."
8. Mayor Bowron had summoned Worton, a retired major general in the Marine Corps, from San Diego when Chief Horrall suddenly took ill in the aftermath of the heated Brenda Allen events. Horrall resigned, content to collect his $572 monthly pension. Police Chief Reed also resigned after the final six-week grand jury inquiry into the corruption of the LAPD.

9. Recent versions of the Sherry's shooting do not always jibe with the newspapers or practical knowledge of mob operations. What appeared confusing in author Sheila Weller's delicious story about her family and Ciro's is the interpretation of "protection money." When referring to Mickey's local rackets she writes, "...he was extorting some kind of protection money from my uncle. (The protection money, however, didn't keep Cohen from getting shot in the shoulder outside Ciro's in 1949 by a rival gangster, who killed one of Cohen's lieutenants and wounded U.S. attorney general's agent, who was guarding Cohen after he'd 'flipped' to the feds' side in a mob prosecution.)" Her Uncle Herman didn't pay Mickey protection money so that *he* would protect Mickey. Most sources do not refer to Ciro's, today the Comedy Store, as the shooting location.

Chapter 12 – More Vicecapades

1. Underwood would hold the title of Hearst City Editor. Despite her popularity, the all-male Greater L.A. Press Club denied her membership.
2. J. Edgar Hoover was approximately in the middle of a forty-eight-year run as head of the FBI. His helpful prevailing attitude toward Mickey and the mob permeated the Bureau. He always maintained that organized crime was a local problem; he called the mob and Mafia "baloney" (in behind-closed-doors parlance, bullshit) and insisted that local crime was a function of lax police departments. He was a statistics nut, who loved to brag about his success with bank robberies, car thefts, kidnappings, and white-collar cases. The system under Hoover "...could pick and chose which cases you wanted to prosecute."—Curt Gentry. Hoover never picked Mickey, despite years of FBI underling work to nail him. When challenged, the FBI cited a lack of evidence.
3. J. Howard McGrath succeeded outgoing Attorney General Tom C. Clark. Both worked under President Harry S. Truman, and had to respect the president and Hoover's stand on Mickey.

Chapter 13 – Bad Boy Mickey

1. Mickey took full advantage of his continued celebrity. He kept his social lists and like the movie moguls sent out over 300 gift baskets for the holidays, mostly to poor families. His old card-playing pal Charlie Shuster, from the Jim Dandy supermarkets, saw to the gift-giving.
2. The 452 miles remained a patchwork, without any prior planning. When a piece of land became available, the city annexed it, increasing the sprawling and therefore uncontrollable urban expanse. Numerous tiny independent municipalities existed like Beverly Hills, little islands of land that fell under Los Angeles county jurisdiction, many easily manipulated by Mickey.
3. Addicted gambler Mike Todd, part owner of the track at Del Mar, married Elizabeth Taylor, and was tragically killed in a plane crash one year later.
4. Superior Court Judge Thomas Ambrose had ruled that Mickey's attorneys did not prove that Niccoli was dead. Dee David had found Niccoli's car at the municipal airport back in September. Ogul's car turned up at UCLA, where a student witnessed Ogul leave in another vehicle. The judge told Mickey that he would have ninety days to come up with information that is more pertinent. He also issued a warrant for Niccoli's arrest as a bond-jumper. Mickey could not help the court obtain any additional information, and therefore lost the money, guaranteed by the Massachusetts Bonding Company.
5. Detective Wellpott eventually retired because his wife received threatening phone calls for two years. Intelligence Squad Sergeant Jerry Wooters blamed Mickey for his ulcer.
6. The house was located at 513 Moreno, still a very chic address today, a kissing cousin of Beverly Hills and Bel-Air. The interior colors were lemon, mauve, and shocking blue. Ex-con Jim Vaus (J. Arthur Vaus), "King of the Wiretappers," and a future evangelist, installed a radar system to

warn of unwelcome guests, remote control garage door openers, and floodlights, for $3,000. The warning device signaled a buzzer located over the bar. The house also periodically had phone taps and bugs installed by either the Los Angeles police or the FBI, likely the first time by Vaus during initial repairs. Hidden microphones lined the walls of every room, including the swanky bathrooms.

7. Mickey often left town with $30,000 cash in tow. He traveled lavishly, and spent fifteen grand per trip, but in the process would pick up gambling markers totaling over $20,000. He could be nine grand short one moment and suddenly collect twenty-four the same day.

8. Mickey had called Moe Sedway at the Flamingo to patch up their differences, and call off the estrangement that had begun when they had fought years back. He knew that he couldn't isolate himself from Sedway, whom Lansky admired. He had asked Moe Sedway to help locate the gambler who owed the money. The FBI mentioned that Sedway caught the flu during this period and had spent a few days in the hospital—typical of the inconsequential details interspersed inside thousands of reports.

9. A Packard auto dealer founded KFI, one of the first television stations. It survives as a radio station, while its original Channel 9 slot has new call letters.

10. Dean Jagger, a former Ohio farm boy and schoolteacher, was famous for his roles in *Twelve O'Clock High* (which earned him an Oscar for his performance opposite Gregory Peck) and *Rawhide*.

11. "Attempting determine relationship between Cohen and officers in Wilshire Div..." was one of the FBI's many communications. The FBI ultimately did figure out that the Wilshire Division of the L.A.P.D. had employed Mickey and his torpedoes to intimidate Pearson. They concluded that the police had held a grudge against Pearson, and Mickey's role was to settle the score. Any further federal attempts to unravel Mickey's police relationships proved unsuccessful.

Chapter 14 – Federal Heat

1. During the Kefauver hearings, Kefauver established that Borden owed perhaps $4,000, and paid some of it back with a $1,000 check from *Ring* publisher Nat Fleischer and an equal amount from fight manager Al Weil. Borden told Kefauver that he was a "dear friend" of Mickey's, and suffered from suicidal spells. The FBI and Kefauver did not appear to share files.

2. A future delegate to the United Nations, Douglas would die in 1980. She was married to fabled actor Melvyn Douglas (Hesselberg).

3. The Knickerbocker, not far from Hollywood and Vine, and now a landmark for its distinctive period architecture, was home to many popular entertainers during their heyday, including Elvis Presley and Jerry Lee Lewis.

4. By most standards, Nixon was an anti-Semite. Perhaps Mickey was unaware of this, or more likely overlooked Nixon's leanings revealed as humor in verbal jousting. Columnist Drew Pearson once told Mickey that "Nixon was an anti-Jew guy" but Jewish attorney Chotiner reassured Mickey that it wasn't the case. "Richard Nixon did not like 'our Jewish friends' or 'New York Jews' or 'the fucking Jews'—phrases he regularly used in private..."—Richard Reeves. Nixon even embarrassed Henry Kissinger by calling him "Jew-boy" or "my Jew-boy," sometimes in front of foreign policy associates.

5. Samish would eventually do time in Alcatraz for tax evasion.

6. Nixon's personal habits were far from conservative. He liked his single-malt Scotch, and was liberal with his dosage of Seconal and Dilantin. He was also alleged to have been physically abusive to his wife Pat, according to Anthony Summers.

7. Cadillac enjoyed a worldwide reputation as the best car built in the United States. The technical specs on Mickey's armored limo were 900 V8, ohv, 96.8 mm bore, 92.1 mm stroke, 5440 cc, and 160 bhp at 3800 rpm.

Chapter 15 – Showtime

1. Estes Kefauver, the former Senator from Tennessee who liked to wear coonskin hats, was a Yale law school graduate. He was able to parlay his sudden fame into a 1952 run for president, but lost the nomination to Adlai Stevenson, who took Kefauver on as a running mate against the immensely popular Dwight Eisenhower. Stevenson chose Kefauver over young Senator John F. Kennedy.

2. On December 13, 1950, to the chagrin of mob bosses everywhere, Willie Moretti testified before the Senate investigators and appeared befuddled. He would not be around for long: he was shot at Joe's Elbow Room on Palisades Avenue in Cliffside Park, New Jersey. Moretti, along with several others, would years later join the list as the model for *Godfather* Don Corleone. Moretti helped advance Frank Sinatra's career; on one occasion he held a gun in Tommy Dorsey's mouth to persuade him to release Sinatra from his contract.

3. Milton Berle, like all entertainers, needed mob connections to survive; the syndicate controlled almost every supper club and elaborate show. Milton had his series of gangster run-ins, including death threats and a beating that required stitches. He once performed a free gig for a Mr. Brown at the Cotton Club in Cicero, Illinois. Mr. Brown was Al Capone, who, after the show, handed Milton a bunch of hundreds to show his appreciation. Dinner with New York Teflon Don John Gotti was routine for him. Milton loved to gamble and knew every bum at the racetracks. His world included everyone from bookies to white-collar criminals.

4. Marcello was born in Tunisia in 1910 as Calogero Minacore. He operated mainly out of New Orleans, and his extensive operations included a web of casinos, off-track horse-betting parlors, restaurants and food-processing companies. No criminal could break into Louisiana during his tenure. New Orleans was his office, and he had a reputation as an insular operator; anyone starting a business needed his permission. Marcello was openly racist, fought against the civil rights movement, liked the Ku Klux Klan, and theorists linked him to the Martin Luther King and JFK assassinations. He bribed the Italian Parliament with sacks of money when he was looking for a safe haven. Shortly banished to Guatemala, he returned through El Salvador and the jungles of Honduras, and eventually arrived by commercial airline in Miami. Marcello lived to the ripe old age of eighty-three, despite running one of the toughest crime families in the country.

5. A *New York Times* article the day before the hearing outlined a war between the California Crime Commission and the IRS. The article mentioned the strong bonds between the criminals and the authorities, including prostitution figure Dorothy A. McGreedy, who had partnered with IRS officer Ernest Schino.

6. *Life* magazine priced the home at $100,000; $120,000 according to a 1947 FBI report.

7. The Fischettis were two close friends of Frank Sinatra. They helped book him in places like the Fontainebleau Hotel in Miami during the late forties and early fifties.

8. When Sinatra had gotten wind of Kelley's intention to write his biography, his staff wrote hundreds of letters to friends and associates, warning them not to cooperate, and he pursued Kelly through his attorneys. When a *Daily Mirror* (London) reporter asked what her compensation was for the book, she replied, "A million dollars plus a choice of funeral gown to be laid out in."

9. Records indicate that Sinatra's testimony was likely behind closed doors, and actually took place on March 1, 1951, at Rockefeller Center in New York. The Kefauver committee had arrived in Los Angeles two times, once in November and once in February, according to the *New York Times*.

Chapter 16 – The Fighter Stumbles

1. Linny's Delicatessen was located on Beverly Drive, in Beverly Hills, near the Egyptian-designed movie theater. It became R. J.'s, and the theater, a bank. The only surviving deli is Nate 'n Al's.
2. The Sunset Strip locale featured the second of four Brown Derbys at the symbolic intersection of Hollywood and Vine. Broadway and Hollywood personality Wilson Mizner, Herb Somborn (Gloria Swanson's second husband), and Sid Grauman of Chinese theater fame, established the fabled hangout. The Cobb Salad took its name from Gloria Swanson's husband Bob Cobb, who managed the restaurant after two of the original partners died. The first Brown Derby opened its doors across from the Ambassador Hotel in 1926. When the Hollywood Brown Derby first opened on Valentine's Day in 1929, it had its own publicist, Maggie Ettinger. She was the first female power-wielder in Hollywood, and responsible for naming and introducing Technicolor to the world. When Mickey arrived in Los Angeles, a Brown Derby operated on the corner of famous Rodeo Drive and Wilshire Boulevard. The Derby stayed open all night. Waiters carried telephones to the booths, where everyone from producers to local business owners set up second offices. It was home to Mary Pickford, Louella Parsons, Loretta Young, Bing Crosby, Robert Taylor, Gary Cooper, George Burns, Walt Disney, and Cecil B. DeMille. Many Derby regulars sponsored their own Triple-A baseball team, the Hollywood Stars. Playboy, power attorney, and Mickey associate Gregson "Greg" Bautzer would bring his potpourri of dates to the Derby for dinner. Sally Cobb's coffee table book on the Derby, *The Brown Derby Restaurant*, has endless pictures of happy Hollywood luminaries, including the Sinatras and Reagans.
3. "I'm glad that Jim asked me to write this Foreword to the story of his life. It gives me a chance to say that I'm all for the work he has been doing since November 1949… The change that came into his life after that surprised a lot of us, but it was real… Well, I'm not a prophet, but I'll wager that anyone who reads his story will get plenty of good out of it"—Mickey Cohen.
4. Warren would become Chief Justice of the U.S. Supreme Court and head of the controversial Warren Commission, which underplayed Jack Ruby's criminal life, and temporarily put to rest any conspiracy theories involving JFK's assassination.

Chapter 18 – Starting Over

1. Authorities once arrested Farkas and Barrie Benson, the madam of a fancy Moorish castle on Schuyler Road, less than a mile above the Sunset Strip.
2. During 1956, Tony Accardo would hand over the national Italian reins to Sam Giancana; Frank Costello would head to prison for tax evasion; and Carlo Gambino, a future business partner of Frank Sinatra, received a promotion to underboss by Albert Anastasia.
3. FBI agents knew that Mickey had regained assets he had transferred or hid before his incarceration, yet the reports make no mention of him laundering cash through normal business channels. (According to Herman Hover, Ciro's forgave Mickey's tab during his prison stay.) The FBI estimated his stock portfolio at over $128,000. Mickey's Dow Jones collection didn't sound like much, considering the millions that went through his hands every week. What agents overlooked was the possibility that Mickey had several competent stockbrokers who looked out for his interests while he was in prison, and that would mean street-type accounts held by the broker, or simply accounts in other names. Plans for Mickey's brother to build a nine-story apartment building were in the works, and the FBI was certain that Mickey was financing the venture, but agents never ascertained a detailed business plan.
4. The Ambassador Hotel officially opened January 1, 1921, built on a dairy farm at the corner of Wilshire Boulevard and Seventh Street. The décor of the hotel club included actual props from Rudolph Valentino's famous silent movie *The Sheik*. Brooklyn-born Marion Davies (Douras),

famous for her relationship with William Randolph Hearst, rode a horse through the plush hotel lobby. Valentino made real-life use of the kasbah behind the pool with original vamp Pola Negri, and Norma Talmadge, who started work as a child actress in the Flatbush section of Brooklyn. The latter married future movie mogul Joseph Schenck and the pair made tons of money producing Talmadge's movies. The hotel's Coconut Grove was one of the most enduring hot spots and names in Hollywood, and featured acts like Bing Crosby and Sophie Tucker. Lansing Brown shot Grove bandleader Russ Colombo in a bizarre accident. Jean Harlow and William Powell enjoyed the pool cabanas for privacy. Harlow fiancé Paul Bern committed suicide, driven by her trysts or his impotency; his nude body was discovered next to his pool.

5. Mickey used many aliases, particularly for bank accounts, safety deposit boxes, and travel: Mickey Michael, Allen Weiner, C. Cain, Michael Cain, Frank Clark, Max Patterson, Michael Masters, Henry Jackson, Donald Duiz, M. Jones, Morris Kleinman, William Sterling, Jack Watson, and M. Weaver. Walter Winchell called him Michael Quinn. Mickey walked out of the Mocambo the night emcee Winchell invoked this nickname. He collected his mail from two stations in Beverly Hills and Hollywood, and used the Carousel or Bill Gray's Bandbox for important correspondence.

6. According to legend, the first unintentional Rat Pack meeting took place at the Las Vegas Desert Inn. A drunken entourage gathered to watch Noel Coward's 1955 opening. After one look at the glassy-eyed Sinatra, Judy Garland, David Niven, Bogart, agent Swifty Lazar, Martha Hyer, Jimmy Van Heusen, Mike Romanoff, and Angie Dickinson, Lauren Bacall quipped, "You look like a goddamn rat pack." Membership in the clan extended beyond the group glorified in movies like *Ocean's Eleven*. Bogart, composer Sammy Cahn, clothier Sy Devore, restaurateur Romanoff, Van Heusen, a Sinatra music friend, Eddie Fisher, Shirley MacLaine, and Elizabeth Taylor rounded out the core group of Sinatra, Martin, Lawford, Bishop, and Davis, Jr. The Holmby Hills Rat Pack would start out at the home of Ira and Lenore Gershwin, with vocalists like Judy Garland, Oscar Levant, and Kitty Carlisle. The entourage would be led by restaurant/raconteur Mike Romanoff to Bogart's house, where regulars included Ruth Gordon, her husband Garson Kanin, and Spencer Tracy, who occasionally brought Katherine Hepburn. The group had their own logo, a rat taking a bite out of a human hand, supplied by Robert Benchley's son Nathaniel. Members began to wear ruby-eyed rats' heads as lapel pins. Aristocratic Bogart would become the real Rat Pack leader, and Sinatra looked to him for social acceptance and friendship in the big leagues. Sinatra shadowed Bogart much in the same way as some writers claim that Mickey initially shadowed Bugsy. Ironically, the East-Coast polished Bogart acted and sounded like a mobster, but wasn't, and had no criminal aspirations. He and Sinatra were very close. In 1956, Sinatra, devastated by Bogart's illness, visited his friend regularly, despite his sickly appearance, bouts with depression, and the rumor of his (Sinatra's) two-year affair with Bogart's wife Lauren Bacall.

7. The Slate Brothers on La Cienega Boulevard was the site of the Rat Pack's famous intrusion on Sonny King's (Lou Schiavone) act. Dean Martin and Frank Sinatra doused the comedian with whiskey. They then proceeded to put on an impromptu show to the delight of the packed audience. The country had found a new pop culture phenomenon in the Rat Pack. "The Mount Rushmore of men having fun"—James Wolcott. "A wild iconoclasm that millions envy secretly....the innest in-group in the world"—Robert Legare.

Chapter 19 - Prime Time Mickey

1. Leon Marcus helped Sam Giancana run his legitimate bank businesses. When authorities indicted Marcus for embezzlement, he tried to blackmail Giancana, who had just completed changing the name of one of his new hotels from the River Road to the Thunderbolt. Giancana

sent Sal Moretti to take care of Marcus. Moretti left the $100,000 cash bill of sale for the Thunderbolt at the scene of the murder, so Giancana had him murdered, his pockets turned inside out, and a comb left on his body. Giancana hitmen got the message: crime scenes will be given a going over with a fine-tooth comb and that's all that can be left behind.

2.   J. Edgar Hoover routinely turned down requests from state attorneys general for assistance in tracking down crime bosses. He referred to such ventures as "fishing expeditions," and complained that the FBI had "...neither the manpower nor the time to waste on such speculative ventures."

3.   Costello, whose wife Loretta (née Geigerman) was Jewish, died peacefully in bed in 1973.

4.   Hamilton came from a rural background, and did not possess the aggressive, outgoing style of other officers. He had worked for the State Controller as an accountant. He switched to police training because it offered an increase of $38 in his monthly salary.

5.   Billy Graham was no friend to the Jews. He shared a regular anti-Jewish dialogue with Richard Nixon, and later supported Mel Gibson's film *The Passion of the Christ*, with its unflattering portrayal of Jews.

Chapter 20 – There's No Business Like Show Business

1.   Peter Lawford, whom Sinatra referred to as "Charley the Seal," may have been the most troubled Rat Pack member. Like Frank's mother, Peter's mother dressed him in girl's dresses as a child. His pimp relationship to Sinatra and JFK prompted, "The most startling dual relationship in the history of crime and politics"—William Safire. Sinatra's right-hand man George Jacobs often took Lawford on cocaine runs to Watts in the maid's old Chevy. Lawford was always falling in and out of favor. He once approached brother-in-law Attorney General RFK to lay off Sinatra pal Giancana. Toward the end of his Rat Pack tenure, Lawford felt excluded from plans for the popular movies, claiming that Sinatra had "turned Dean and Sammy and Joey against me..." Many wrote that Sinatra contributed to Lawford's mental downslide, spending years in and out of rehab. When the end neared, he holed up at the Playboy mansion alone, and communed with the squirrels. His last wife noted his fondness for electronic sex toys. "I had a fantasy ever since I visited my father on the set of *Ocean's Eleven* that one day my dad and I would work together and be able to have what I saw those guys have on that set. That never happened. The closest we got to that kind of intimate collaborative camaraderie was when he gave me a vial of cocaine for my twenty-first birthday"—Christopher Kennedy Lawford

2.   Racism was rampant in the nightclubs. Sammy Davis, Jr., was one of the first blacks to break into clubs. The Will Maston Trio was booked as a headliner at Ciro's for the 1952 Academy Awards night. The youngest member of the group was Sammy Davis, Jr. "The room was packed with Hollywood royalty, and Sammy and Company couldn't do enough. Dancing, singing, little comic bits, everything was a hit, nothing more so than Sammy's impersonations of such white stars as Jimmy Cagney, Cary Grant, and Humphrey Bogart"—Shawn Levy. "...no one had ever seen anything like it before...tap dancing, and then he did some impressions, and then he sang straight, and played every instrument in the band. And then he almost sang opera... And it went on and on"—George Schlatter. Sammy sang Jacques D'Iraque: "There's a guy named Jack from a country called Iraq..." "I had been on for over two hours... Herman Hover was walking onstage followed by every waiter, bus boy, every cook and kitchen helper in the club...they were singing to me [Auld Lang Syne]...led by the Chinese chef holding a long spoon for a baton. The audience fell apart"—Sammy Davis. "...he had more strikes against him than you could count—he was short, maimed, ugly, black, Jewish, gaudy, uneducated"—Levy. Sammy frequently had tax trouble. He once tried to stiff a Vegas furrier on two lavish coats.

3. By the end of 1959, Sammy had his hands full with May Britt, a Swedish star he met at the Fox studios. His racial problems never seemed to end. Sinatra had to act as the beard when May was shuttled around the Vegas hotels with Sammy. The Sands drained the swimming pool after Southern high rollers saw little Sammy taking a dip in their no-blacks-allowed cement pond.

4. Joseph "Doc" Stacher set up the Sands Hotel not far from the Flamingo after touring Tahoe and Reno looking for sites in his fancy Cadillac. He grew up in the New Jersey area, and by the time he was thirty his rap sheet showed extensive arrests. Stacher, pals with Bugsy, Louis "Lepke" Buchalter, and Jacob "Gurrah" Shapiro, was an experienced gambling operator who ran illegal casinos in upstate New York. When the Sands opened, Stacher was the boss (who incidentally couldn't sleep alone at night), although the mob produced a convoluted paper trail of partners, including Joe Fusco, Mack Kufferman, Mal Clarke, Ed Levinson, Meyer Lansky, Gerry Catena, Frankie Carbo, Abraham "Longie" Zwillman, Champ Segal, and Abraham Teitelbaum. The front men were Hyman Abrams, Carl Cohen, and Jack Entratter. Sinatra had at least two points in the Sands deal and created a "blood feud" in 1968, according to author Shawn Levy, when he switched to Caesars Palace while Dean Martin ended up at the Riviera. The groundbreaking Jack Entratter ran the show at the Sands. When he became the front man at the Sands, entertainers flocked to his side—Sinatra, Martin and Lewis, Danny Thomas, Lena Horne, Tony Bennett, Nat King Cole, Red Skelton, and Milton Berle. The Sands became the prototypical mob-run casino. Entratter had worked as a bouncer at the Stork Club in New York. He originally went to work for well-known Jules Podell at the Copa in 1940, and once threw a "thirty-third" birthday party for Sinatra at the Copa (Sinatra was older than thirty-three). He believed in high salaries and deluxe accommodations right above the club. He moved the Copa Girls concept to Vegas. He included unusual-for-Vegas performers like Edith Piaf, Tallulah Bankhead, Ezio Pinza, Señor Wences, Van Johnson, Robert Merrill, and Louis Armstrong. "We wouldn't go anywhere in Vegas but where Jack was"—Jerry Lewis.

5. At age sixty-nine, a chubby, bald Joe Schenck spotted actress Norma Jean Mortensen, and he was compelled to invite her to dinner. After some significant socializing, Schenck suggested that she leave his own company Fox and sign a six-month contract with Cohn at Columbia as Marilyn Monroe.

6. Liz Renay would write a book called *My Face for the World to See,* and continued stripping through the seventies. She received nearly $40,000 for her memoir. She had shared her varied talents drinking German beer at Burt Lancaster's Malibu Beach home, mixed rum drinks with Marlon Brando at Polynesian-themed clubs before nights at his apartment, and flew with Sinatra for romps in Atlantic City. According to her son, John McClain, she married seven times, divorced five, and was widowed twice. Her last marriage was to Tom Freeman, a multimillionaire who rented a $200-a-month apartment for her dogs. That marriage lasted longer than all the others combined. She acknowledged that her allegiance to Mickey ruined her show business aspirations.

    In January 2007, Renay died at Valley Hospital in Las Vegas of cardiopulmonary arrest, secondary to gastric bleeding. Her rebellious publisher, Lyle Stuart, had died seven months earlier; he had a home in Las Vegas once belonging to Renay. Her daughter Brenda, who toured with her, died in 1982 at age thirty-nine.

Chapter 21 - Who Dunnit?

1. During this period, Turner spent time with attorneys Geisler and Louis Blau. Blau helped her get rid of a nude movie taken of her in her bedroom.

2. The salacious scandal upped Turner's movie fee. In her first picture after the trial, *Imitation of Life,* she received fifty percent of the profits, over $2,000,000, surpassing million-dollar stars Elizabeth Taylor and Marlon Brando. She would date eccentric Howard Hughes, who liked to

remain in his hotel room before whisking her off to El Morocco in New York. Turner's other romantic links included handsome actor Tyrone Power and the movie Tarzan, Lex Barker.

Chapter 22 – I Want To Be in Pictures

1. "Her throat had been cut as well, but apparently only after she had been knocked unconscious with a heavy bottle. Newspapers and towels had been used to soak up the blood and keep it from staining the carpet... The Greenbaum killer had been most considerate"—Hank Messick.
2. Conservative columnist and celebrity Dorothy Kilgallen, famous for her popular stint on television's game show *What's My Line?*, was found dead on November 8, 1965, soon after interviewing Jack Ruby. She knew that Ruby had met with Bernard Weisman, who had placed the "JFK—Wanted for Treason" ad in Dallas newspapers, two weeks before the assassination. Ruby also knew slain officer J. D. Tippit. All three men had met at Ruby's Carousel Club in Dallas. Kilgallen had informed Israeli authorities about David Ferrie/Ferret Man's connections to Jack Ruby. Kilgallen died of an alcohol and barbiturate overdose, similar to Marilyn Monroe. She first broke the story of the Marilyn-JFK tryst. She was found fully clothed and sitting up in bed. All her JFK notes had disappeared. She had regularly appeared on *What's My Line?* with Bennett Cerf, Louis Untermeyer, Hal Block, Arlene Francis, Arlene's husband Martin Gabel, Steve Allen, Fred Allen, and host John Daly.
3. Lindy's was famous for its cheesecake, and the source material for the Sky Masterson/Nathan Detroit bet over cheesecake consumption. When Mickey pal Damon Runyon wrote the book for *Guys and Dolls*, he substituted Mindy's for Lindy's, and Nathan Detroit for Arnold Rothstein.
4. Before he was through, Meyer Lansky skimmed over $300,000,000 from gambling. By the early sixties, the Stardust Hotel alone threw off $400,000 per month. The skim extended to gambling enterprises in New York, Florida, Kentucky, Louisiana, Arkansas, Cuba, the Bahamas, England, and Beirut.
5. Folklore enjoys how the brass at Columbia Pictures insisted that the entire staff show up at mogul Harry Cohn's funeral or else look for new employment. When comedian Red Skelton saw the funeral throngs he remarked, "It just shows you that if you give the people what they want, they'll turn out for it."

Chapter 23 – Another Knockdown

1. Mickey's favorite hangout for meeting attorney Melvin Belli was Rondelli's, a popular Mickey-owned home-style Italian restaurant in the Valley's Sherman Oaks at 11359 Ventura Boulevard, less than fifteen miles northwest of the usual haunts. In addition to Errol Flynn and Belli, Liberace and his brother were part of the irregular clique. Mickey ate there several times a week.
2. The McClellan hearings, and its precursor, the McCarthy hearings, did not maintain consistent witness reimbursements, and when they did, the amounts for the most part were paltry. The Civil Rights Act, initiated by JFK and signed by Lyndon Johnson, was one of the first documents to include witness travel expenses.
3. "For years after [Jean] Harlow's death, he [Zwillman] was still boasting nostalgically about the various ways he'd once banged the actress"—Dennis McDougal.
4. Named for John Little McClellan, a career politician who had lost two sons in an auto accident and plane crash, the investigations lasted many years.
5. RFK had attained national attention when he worked for Roy Cohn during the anti-Communist McCarthy hearings; he sat on the far left of McCarthy. Fighting gangsters was a perfect fit for the altar boy turned pragmatic politician. Once fearless RFK had decided somebody was a gangster, he used his subpoena power to drive testimony, making the Fifth Amendment the choice of people with questionable character.

Chapter 24 – Mickey's World

1. Born in 1935, Candy (Juanita Slusher Dale Phillips Sahakian) had been around. She was already an ex-con and had worked a social gig with the powerful Marcello in Louisiana before meeting Mickey.

2. Landis was one of the perennials on the Strip. During the forties, he owned the Trocadero, switched to Jazz in the fifties, and with Gene Norman ran the Crescendo. Landis converted the well-known Hazan's Food Market into a fancy strip joint called the Largo, and renamed the Roxy in the early seventies. Mickey was a regular at the Largo. "I enjoyed it in the '40s and '50s. It was a coat-and-tie sort of thing, very formal... In the '60s, the hippies turned the Strip around... It was almost impossible to travel from Crescent Heights to Doheny. Business dropped overnight... If you weren't on the Strip, you weren't in the business, in the old days...but not anymore... You roll with the punches"—Chuck Landis.

3. Mickey exiled Candy and her child to Mexico City. Despite all attempts at sheltering her, she ultimately began a fifteen-year sentence, and that's when Mickey claimed that the relationship ended. Texas governor John Connolly would eventually pardon her after three and one-half years. Despite his regrets and denials, Mickey was always in Candy's corner, the last time to the tune of $60,000 for legal fees. At age forty-one, she posed nude for *Oui* magazine. She later shunned publicity, and died in 2005 in Victoria, Texas, at age seventy.

4. The centuries-old badger con consists of luring someone into a sexually compromising position with the intention of using the scenario for blackmail purposes. Before the advent of recording and audiovisual devices, a woman would visit the local physician, complaining of symptoms that would require a gynecological exam. During the exam, a husband, or partner, would burst into the room and accuse the doctor of impropriety. The woman would side with her accomplice.

5. Bloomingdale wanted no part of the FBI or any other negative publicity. He already had his own sexual agenda, a "mover and shaker" in the bedroom. His sexual escapades made greater news when his longtime mistress Vicki Morgan, was bludgeoned to death with a baseball bat. Her estate collected $200,000 in palimony from Bloomingdale.

6. The FBI had always watched Belli: "...sent greetings to the Soviet Union in support of the new Army's struggle against Nazi Germany...accused an insurance company of unethical practices...protested the prosecution of twelve communists... In 1951, Belli's name appeared on the letters of the 'Lawyers Against Test Oaths for the Bar'... In 1959, Belli received notoriety for defending racketeer Mickey Cohen..."

7. Desi Arnaz (Desiderio Alberto Arnaz y de Ahca, III), was born in Santiago, Cuba. He served as a staff sergeant in the U.S. Army Medical Corps for three years during WW II, according to FBI files. The bulk of the FBI files focus on his wife Lucy's possible Red connections and Arnaz's television clippings. Many FBI pages are devoted to Desilu Productions' fan mail from a ten-year-old. FBI agents were both fans and critics of *The Untouchables*, particularly its fictional embellishments. Arnaz often sent the scripts to Hoover personally for approval, with letters addressed "Dear Edgar." Actor Robert Stack's name appears in the files almost as often as Arnaz's. More "serious" issues involved the Communists who still lurked about in the entertainment industry and Arnaz's "Cuban connections"; he belonged to a political organization, and his father still lived in Cuba. He did run into trouble with the police on September 19, 1959; he wasn't walking a straight line on a Hollywood street. A drunken Arnaz resisted arrest. At the station house, when asked whom he would like to call, he insisted on J. Edgar Hoover or retired Sheriff Eugene Biscailuz. His file also contains one account of an assault charge—he beat up an actor. Sam Giancana supported the activities of the Federation of Italian-American Democratic Organization, which organized a boycott of Arnaz's *Untouchables* television show, and forced Chesterfield cigarettes to drop its advertising. "Millions of people all over the world see this show every fucking week. It's even popular in Italy. And what they

see is a bunch of Italian lunatics running around with machine guns, talking out of the corner of their mouths, slopping spaghetti like a bunch of fucking pigs. They make Capone and Nitti look like bloodthirsty maniacs... The guys that write that shit don't know the first thing about the way things were in those days. Eliot Ness, my ass. The tax boys got Al, not Ness. And what did he ever have to do with Frank Nitti?... Nobody pays attention to that shit. It's like a comic book, a joke... Jimmy [Fratianno], what I'm about to tell you has been decided by our family. The top guys have voted a hit. I've already talked to Bomp about it. We're going to clip Desi Arnaz, the producer of the show"—Johnny Rosselli. The solution fell in the lap of a depressed Frank Sinatra, who rented space for his production company at Desilu studios. He had just finished a gig at the Sands in Vegas, and despite his fatigue he continued on to the Fontainebleau in Miami, where he met with Sam Giancana. Giancana was also busy entertaining a hit on Fidel Castro. Sinatra returned to his beautiful home in Palm Springs, where George Jacobs, the longstanding and faithful houseman, catered to regulars Marilyn Monroe, Pat and Peter Lawford, Sammy Davis, Jr., May Britt, and Jimmy Van Heusen. "I'm going to kill that Cuban prick," Sinatra forewarned his guests. He drove with pretty actress Dorothy Provine, while Jimmy Van Heusen and a date followed, to the Indian Wells Country Club, where they would wait for Arnaz at his favorite watering hole. Before Arnaz arrived, Sinatra made it clear he was going to put him out of business. Van Heusen tried in vain to get Sinatra out of the restaurant. Arnaz arrived with a three-hundred-pound slab of muscle on each arm. Drunk Arnaz spotted Sinatra and yelled across the room loudly, "Hi ya Dago!" and then walked over to Sinatra, who told him that his Italian gangster friends didn't like *The Untouchables* because it made all Italians look like bad guys. Arnaz replied, "What do you want me to do—make them all Jews?"—a natural favorite of anti-Semites. "You want them all to be 'yous'?" is the other take. Sinatra argued, "I always know what I'm talking about. That's how I got where I am." Arnaz laughed it off and said, "Oh, yeah. I remember you when ju couldn't get a yob, Frankie, couldn't get a yob! So why don't you forget all this bullshit and just have your drinks and enjoy yourself? Stop getting your nose in where it doesn't belong, you and your so-called friends." Arnaz walked to the bar with his bodyguards. Sinatra said, "I couldn't hit him, we've been pals for too long." That night Sinatra destroyed a Norman Rockwell painting that hung in Van Heusen's home. He pulled his production offices out of Desilu. Arnaz died in 1986 of lung cancer after his second marriage.

8. The Formosa Café, built in 1925 from a trolley car, adjoined the United Artists lot, now Warner Hollywood Studio, near La Brea and Santa Monica boulevards. An entertainment business staple, the still popular Formosa, with its nondescript look and black-and-white striped awnings, likely kept a safe under the floor belonging to Mickey. It was easy to place a bet while dining or drinking there. Prostitutes always found the corner outside the building a safe haven at any time of day.

9. Sidney Korshak, from the shtetl-like Kosher Calcutta of Chicago, Lawdale, was the highest paid attorney in the country. He wasn't just another "hard-on with a suitcase." Korshak was friend to movie producers, CEOs, and high-level politicians. He represented Dinah Shore, Debbie Reynolds, and Tony Martin; he made them stars at the Riviera Hotel in Vegas. The labor editor of the Los Angeles *Herald Examiner* portrayed Korshak as a man "who seldom stops long enough in one place to get a wrinkle in his suit." "I was never afraid with Sam [Giancana], but Sid frightened me"—Judith Campbell Exner. After one meeting, Korshak told Exner that her FBI grievance was solvable. "Our informers have stated that Sidney Korshak, a lawyer in Chicago, Illinois, is often delegated to represent the Chicago gang, usually in some secret capacity"—FBI, July 25, 1942. Korshak's brother Marshall became an Illinois state senator and the city treasurer of Chicago. Without fearless and independent Korshak, a working relationship between management and casino employees would never have come to fruition in Vegas. Korshak joined the posh Beverly Hills Tennis Club, and hobnobbed with the wealthiest and

most celebrated people in town. He developed a reputation as the ultimate dealmaker, a man who could fix anything, even between sworn enemies. Former showgirls Bea Korshak and Barbara Sinatra remained close friends after marrying their powerful husbands. When the front desk denied comedian Alan King a suite in Vegas, one phone call to Korshak produced the best accommodations within seconds. His clients included Schenley, Diners' Club, the Chargers, the Dodgers, the Knicks, the Rangers, Seeburg, National General, Hyatt, Hilton, and a variety of racetracks, including Mickey's Santa Anita. He had the power to shut down Santa Anita or turn the lights on so the Dodgers could play at night. His close Hollywood friends included Debbie Reynolds, Kirk Douglas, Frank Sinatra, and David Janssen. Sinatra and Douglas were also members of the Beverly Hills Tennis Club. Korshak enjoyed high-priced call girls, while girlfriends included actress Stella Stevens. "And there was Sidney Korshak, the ultimate insider who never owned a single share of stock or attached his name to any movie, yet held more influence over the fortunes of the company than anyone other than Lew [Wasserman] and Dr. Stein"—Dennis McDougal. Aside from MCA Universal—Wasserman and Stein—Korshak was of counsel to Tony Accardo, Rosselli, and Giancana, linked to movie giants Charles Bluhdorn, Robert Evans (one of Korshak's greatest fans), and Kirk Kerkorian. Carl Sifakis pegged Korshak, who used the Bistro (owned by Kurt Niklas) in Beverly Hills as a second office, perfectly: "...ensconced at a corner table, flanked by two telephones that kept ringing, and in between calls he had private chats with friends and beautiful women who came by to give him a friendly kiss." Smartly, when a call came from Chicago, Korshak adjourned to a pay booth, armed with coins and the common sense to keep his old clients private. In late June 1976, Seymour Hersh exposed Korshak in a four-part series for the *New York Times*. He described him as a labor fixer, with ties to Capone, Nitti, Bioff, and Browne. Sidney Korshak lived to eighty-eight, despite a lifetime of unusual associations. "Their apologists assert that no proof can be found of Supermob lawbreaking. Pointedly, Sid Korshak was never convicted of so much as a parking violation. But the truth is Korshak and company constantly bent, folded, and—yes—broke the law... Without doubt, Sid Korshak played the most dangerous game of all his fellows..."—Gus Russo

Hollywood luminary Bob Evans, once boss at Paramount, loved to say that Korshak was Al Capone's consiglieri. Journeyman movie producer Berle Adams supported attorney Greg Bautzer's claim that Korshak was Capone's chauffeur. Folklore aside, Korshak likely catered to the Capone syndicate, and at an early age.

Chapter 25 – Let's Get Mickey

1. The Navarre became the Ritz Carlton, followed by the Inter-Continental, and a recent conversion to upscale residences.

Chapter 26 – Time Out for Politics

1. "I just got back from the conspiracy convention. Have you been? It's fun. Seven hundred conspiracy theorists all in one hotel, with the little name tags, 'Hello, my name is—none of your fucking business!'... In the lobby, I saw five people get off the elevator—what, you think that's a coincidence?"—Paul Krassner. "Little money can be had writing Marilyn Monroe was not killed by either or both the Kennedys"—Konstantin Sidorenko. "The only casualty is truth"—Gerald Posner. Some question the agenda of Posner's one-sided work, while others accept his professional rehabilitation of the Warren Commission Report.

2. JFK was the first president to sell major arms to Israel. "...architect of today's strong military alliance between Israel and the America"—Warren Bass. Eric J. Greenberg's review in the *Jewish Week* of Bass' recent book, *Support Any Friend: Kennedy's Middle East and the Making of the U.S.-Israel Alliance,* examines Kennedy's failed efforts to bring Egyptian President Nasser to the

negotiating table. JFK conflicted with Israeli Prime Minister David Ben-Gurion over the future of Israel's nuclear weapons. Kennedy suspected that the Dimona facility was strictly for nuclear weapons development. He threatened the peace process, but was able to reach an unhappy compromise with new Prime Minister Levi Eshkol. Palestinian newspapers wrote that the JFK assassination was a Zionist conspiracy and Oswald, Ruby, and even Lyndon Johnson were all working for the Jews. "Such squalid surmise—four decades before Gallup polls would reveal that millions of Arabs blamed the Mossad for [9/11]—remains a sobering reflection on the depths and distortions of anti-Israel animus in the Arab world"—Bass.

3. Nixon gave up via a televised statement at 3:10 a.m. from the Ambassador Hotel in Los Angeles. His wife Pat did not want him to concede. Sinatra had tried to call Nixon to urge him to give up, but the telephone operator at the hotel refused to put his call through. Nixon was no philo-Semite, but was ultimately pragmatic when it came to world politics concerning Israel.

4. The RFK-Monroe romance has become an accepted fact, appearing in the works of several reputable authors, including Anthony Summers, Seymour Hersh, and C. David Heymann. The authors rely on a variety of sources, including Hollywood detective Fred Otash, who had Peter Lawford's home wiretapped. The authors also cite an eyewitness, Jeanne Carmen, purported Monroe friend and neighbor. Sinatra employee and Marilyn confidant George Jacobs could never accept the fact that she had had sex with RFK, whom Jacobs called a "weasel."

5. Exner was born Judith Katherine Inmoor in 1934 to a successful architect father and former Bonwit's model mother. She spent her early adult life married to actor Billy Campbell. She would fall in love with prodigy singer Tony Travis, a handsome, wealthy Beverly Hills resident. Tony, as mentioned, was Travis Kleefeld, the son of a successful builder, and Kleefeld introduced Exner to a life of champagne and caviar. Travis also introduced her to the "big boys" at the Racquet Club in Palm Springs and the Beverly Hills Tennis Club. Their breakup found her at Beverly Hills shrink Dr. Sherman, whom she would continue to consult periodically. Exner became no stranger to Jewish business moguls on both coasts. She knew everyone of power in the mob, politics, and entertainment. She became a victim of FBI surveillance. "Campbell (Exner) did not know Giancana's real name. To her he was simply Sam Flood. Giancana once told Exner after she had complained of her difficulty securing a room at the Plaza Hotel in New York, 'Don't worry, when you get there, call Joe DiMaggio…he'll get you a room'"—Bill Adler. Sinatra introduced Desi Arnaz to Exner, and pimped her to Joe Fischetti and Jack Entratter. "Judy was a mob moll and the mistress of my brother-in-law, the president of the United States. In 1960, Judy, then twenty-three, an aspiring actress, became the consort of Jack Kennedy. What made Judy more than just another presidential girlfriend was the other company she kept, notably John "Don Giovanni" Rosselli and Salvatore Sam "Momo" Giancana, both members in good standing of organized crime, not to mention the Central Intelligence Agency. This is a lurid tale, and the more one probes it, the more lurid it becomes"—Peter Lawford. The Church Committee assigned Exner a lawyer from Sargent Shriver's law firm. Shriver was JFK's brother-in-law; his daughter is married to Governor Arnold Schwarzenegger of California. "The guy [Giancana] even proposed marriage but she turned him down and that's all she wrote. Sam ditched her. Kennedy got killed, the Feds were all over her, and she fell head first into the bottle… This was Judy Campbell's favorite bubble [Dom Perignon]. Do you realize that was only a dozen years ago? Seems like a million"—Johnny Rosselli. In 1999, Exner would die of breast cancer at age sixty-five. JFK had once given her a diamond and ruby broach, with thirty full-cut diamonds set in platinum. After the JFK assassination, Giancana and Sinatra ignored Campbell, including one conspicuous snubbing at the Key Club in Palm Springs.

6. On October 12, 1964, less than a year after JFK's assassination, Mary Pinchot Meyer, 43 years old, was mysteriously murdered on a towpath in Georgetown while going for a walk, sparking conspiracy theories.

7. Phyllis McGuire of the McGuire sisters dated both Giancana and comedian Dan Rowan. Giancana bugged Rowan's hotel room simultaneously with the CIA, who helped Giancana. He hired Arthur J. Balletti, who left all the equipment out on the bed during a lunch break, to the dismay of maids who phoned police. Giancana died in his basement—his head was full of twenty-two caliber bullets—while his home-cooked sausage and beans continued to fry nearby. He was shot once in the back of the head, and six times in the mouth.

8. JFK was instrumental to the production of the Sinatra movie *The Manchurian Candidate*. "That's the only way that the film ever got made. It took Frank going directly to Jack Kennedy"—Richard Condon. "I hope it pisses the shit of them [the Kennedys]"—Frank Sinatra. After the JFK assassination, the prophetic film became the center of attention. Producers yanked the movie from reruns, since it dealt with a programmed assassination. Condon discussed the brainwashing of Lee Harvey Oswald, while Truman Capote would later spout that RFK assassin Sirhan Sirhan was another Manchurian candidate. Sinatra always suspected that Oswald assassin Jack Ruby was programmable. When Sinatra's son was kidnapped eight days after the JFK assassination, the fabled crooner felt that the mob had sent him a message to remain silent about anything that could implicate the mafia in the assassination and its aftermath. "Kennedy glamorized politics and embraced danger, and Hollywood responded in kind… *The Manchurian Candidate*, in a sense, is an anthology of Cold War concerns that materialized at the height of the Cuban missile crisis to startle audiences with a baroque tale of mind control, assassination and conspiracy"—J. Hoberman. "…that concentration of ecstasy and violence which is the dream life of the nation"—Norman Mailer.

9. Giancana received free personal Rat Pack performances in Chicago anytime he asked. Sinatra and Dean Martin never refused Giancana's requests for free gigs, sometimes lasting as long as ten days.

Chapter 27 – Down for the Count

1. While RFK was instrumental in putting Mickey back in prison, Kennedy, the FBI, and local authorities couldn't stop the role of organized crime in Las Vegas' gargantuan development. The Justice Department had quickly assigned eighty-six investigators to Las Vegas when RFK took over. The first year of activity would bring only two convictions amongst 135 prostitution arrests. RFK's bold ambitions did not frighten the national organization.

2. When the 9th Circuit Court of Appeals rejected (two to one) attorney A. L. Wirin's request for bail on September 14, 1961, he vowed to take the case to the U.S. Supreme Court. Justice William O. Douglas was sympathetic, although cautious, since the United States District Court in Los Angeles and the United States Circuit Court in San Francisco had already said "no" to bail the first time around during the appeals process. Douglas instinctively felt that Mickey would not flee. The Justice Department announced a new indictment on September 16, including charges of concealing assets. On October 12, Justice Douglas granted Mickey his release on bail of $100,000. Mickey's sister and her husband had pledged their business as security, their only source of income, and had influenced the justice's bail decision. His mother had signed an affidavit pledging the trust deed on her home, and part of her equity in Carousel Ice Cream. The FBI had information that the bond company, run by old pal Abe Phillips, was actually Mickey's. A strip club owner, a Beverly Hills barber, and a restaurateur in San Francisco who owned Paoli, had supplied the rest of the bail money. Mickey cites Paoli as the major source for his release bond. The U.S. District Court in Los Angeles blocked his release. His attorneys, including Jack Dahlstrum, spent the entire day in court on October 16. Abe Phillips stood ready to deliver the bond papers to prison authorities. Judge Leon R. Yankwich had Mickey asked for additional money, and the Stuyvesant Insurance Co. in Newark supplied the

new bond. Justice Douglas eventually convinced Judge Yankwich to side with him and not hardball U.S. Attorney Thomas R. Sheridan.

3. The show business house was the former home of poker operator Morrie Kasoff, and later a famous-ten blacklisted screenwriter named Robert Adrian Scott, whose wife wrote the *Lassie* television series.

4. Problems arose, and Mickey relied on attorney A. L. Wirin. Chief U.S. Judge Pierson M. Hall entered the Valley Hospital for a three-day examination. Wirin had needed Hall to certify the appeal bond. Judges William C. Mathes and Yankwich got cold feet when asked to help, and insisted that U.S. Judge George Boldt, who had originally sentenced Mickey, was the only one who could certify the process, even though Boldt had told Judge William M. Byrne to permit Mickey's release, pending the Supreme Court's disposition. On a Friday, Wirin made a difficult long distance call to Mexico City to speak with vacationing Judge Boldt. Thirty minutes after the expensive telephone call the legal tumult had paid off and authorities released Mickey. "... The Supreme Court let Mickey Cohen go. You know why they gave him bail? Because he was going to go to the World Court if he didn't get it from them. And the Supreme Court didn't want him doing that. Because then the people of the United States would find out and say, 'What the hell's this World Court that is over the Supreme Court?'"—Drew Pearson.

Chapter 28 – Stripes But No Stars

1. Many of the inmate leaders were competitive with Mickey since most of them had never achieved his status or celebrity. It was obviously jealousy—Mickey was rich and powerful on the outside. However, many prison employees were enamored with Mickey's celebrity, and he received extra special attention from those impressed with books sent by Billy Graham, visits by Graham's father-in-law Dr. L. Nelson Bell, and letters from Sammy Davis, Jr.

2. The Democrats and Pearson did not release Mickey's full statement. Nixon lost again, without the Democrats smearing him with Mickey's recent detailed information. After the loss in California, fundraisers held a Lincoln Day Dinner at the St. George Hotel in Brooklyn for the defeated Republican warrior. The packed dais included Governor Nelson Rockefeller, U.S. Senator Jacob Javits, and Attorney General Louis Lefkowitz. Tickets were at a premium for the red carpet event. The Republican Party refused to give up on resilient Nixon.

3. Pearson made the original mob allegations on his radio program in 1956 and 1959—that Mickey had "collected money from the underworld" and gave it to Nixon. Pearson labeled attorney Murray Chotiner an organizer and front man for Nixon. Surprisingly, the Democrats did not release the new information that Mickey had supplied until 1968, when Pearson ran the story October 31 in his syndicated *Washington Post* column with even more evidence, one year before his own death.

4. Archaic Alcatraz finally relocated the remaining thirty-eight inmates and closed on March 21, 1963, after RFK gave the order.

5. During 1979, the government investigated Carlos Marcello and Sam Sciortino, a mobster from San Francisco, concerning the bribery of a federal judge and recordings of associates bragging about the mob's connection to the RFK assassination. Phillip Rizzuto, New Orleans operator and cousin to Sciortino, said, "Yeah, so we put him outa business," referring to RFK.

6. McDonald, from St. Stephen, South Carolina, was initially incarcerated for forgery, but later received ten years for assaulting a Leavenworth prisoner. He died in the early 1970s.

7. Flamboyant Melvin Belli was a multi-layered piece of work who drove a Rolls Royce and ultimately supported three homes, including one fancy Hollywood Hills home with a swimming pool. He was a popular television guest for many years, and was never shy about seeking publicity for his cases. Reporters lost count of his many wives; one Shinto marriage in Japan escaped records. Belli, also a pal of actor Errol Flynn, died in 1996 at age eight-eight.

8. Marcello, Trafficante, and Hoffa all receive honorable mentions when it comes to JFK's assassination. Johnny Rosselli was hardly a fan, either. There was no love lost between the mob and the Kennedys. Estimates on the contract to kill JFK were as high as $750,000.

9. Degenerate Ruby, who loved to brag about his mob connections, was the fifth of eight children. Surprisingly, he tried to stay in shape, and was not a big drinker or smoker. His father was a poor carpenter, and Ruby ended up in the Jewish Home Finding Society of Chicago. Eventually committed, Ruby's mother Fanny would "ramble and shriek in Yiddish, crochet compulsively, demand that others serve her meals...hit them and had delusions about having sex with them (her children)"—Seth Kantor. Ruby was a defiant, depressed, and frequently truant child. Before moving on to his career running seedy clubs, he worked with future boxer Barney Ross. The two men met Al Capone in 1926 at the Kit Howard Gymnasium in Chicago, and Ruby started delivering packages for him, while running with street gangs. Ruby, who suffered multiple head injuries during his life, loved to stand on stage, and act as master of ceremonies. "Yet Ruby also could present an apparently normal and jovial side, that of a club owner ready to ensure his patrons had a good time. He went out of his way to encourage Dallas policemen to visit his clubs, giving them reduced rates and free drinks"—Gerald Posner. Police arrested Ruby nine times during a fourteen-year run, for charges ranging from carrying concealed weapons to serving liquor after hours. "Ruby often resorted to violence with his employees, and lost the tip of his left index finger when one bit it off during a scuffle. He beat one of his musicians with brass knuckles, cracked another's head with a blackjack, knocked another's teeth out, and put the club's handyman in the hospital with a severe beating. To avoid paying the club's cigarette girl $50 in back wages, he threatened to throw her down the stairs until she relented... He was not above attacking people from behind, kicking men in the groin or face once he had them to the floor, or even striking women... He was often malicious, forcing beaten victims to crawl out of the club on hands and knees"—Posner. Jim Garrison, in painting his picture of a gay assassination cabal that included David Ferrie, Lee Harvey Oswald, and Clay Shaw, reminds us that Ruby was bisexual and frequented gay clubs. "...Jack Ruby, whose homosexuality is clearly established in almost forty instances in the Warren volumes... Oswald...was victimized by Ferrie in adolescence...(older men preying on teenage boys) included Jack Ruby..."—Lamar Waldron. In 1959, gunrunner Ruby made more than two trips to Cuba, arming Castro. "The smuggling of arms to Cuba was overseen by Norman "Roughhouse" Rothman, a burly associate of Miami's mob boss Santos Trafficante, who managed Trafficante's Sans Souci in Havana. At the same time Rothman reportedly was splitting Havana slot machines with Batista's brother-in-law... Ruby was part of the Rothman operation"—Jim Marrs. Rothman had signed the rental agreements for the airplanes that transported the guns. He also had an interest in the Biltmore Terrace Hotel in Miami. He threatened to sue when a friend of Richard Nixon, Dana C. Smith, ran up gambling debts of over $4,000 on a little junket with Nixon in 1952. "Rothman was a New York City bookmaker, who made it big in Cuba... Rothman began running guns to Castro...like most U.S. mobsters, figured that Castro would cut the mob in for an even bigger Cuban take, if he got guns and ammunition when he needed them"—Kantor. Ruby turned FBI informant. The Warren Commission overlooked his courier role for Rothman and Trafficante. Connections existed between Lansky's courier Jim Braden and Ruby. Braden was on parole for mail fraud and interstate transport of stolen property when he ended up in Dallas in late 1963, about the same time as Ruby. Braden may have met with David Ferrie, Oswald's acquaintance from his days in the Civil Air Patrol. Ruby also had connections to Sinatra's Reprise record company. Calls to Sinatra confidant Mike Shore coincided with a call to Irwin Weiner, an associate of Giancana, in Chicago. A few months before JFK's assassination, Giancana met with his connections in Dallas at Ruby's Carousel Club to discuss the bookmaking business. After Ruby shot Oswald, Ruby's brother Earl, who knew Shore when they were both children, called him to find an

attorney for his brother. Following his arrest, Ruby was kept in a windowless cell for thirty-two months, where some report that he often ranted incoherently. He would soon die of advanced cancer with metastasis all over his body.

10. Six years after Hecht's death, *Scanlan's Monthly*, a short-lived, somewhat radical periodical, published the remains of his writings about Mickey, and included humorous anecdotes of their vacations in which Mickey was always a fish out of water. The rare *Scanlan's* article was twenty pages, including photos. Columnist Leonard Lyons had predicted that the article would reach 25,000 words. Perhaps Hecht never got much more down on paper, or editor Sidney Zion had reduced the article size for publication. Zion had promised that *Scanlan's* would "… carry out an unreasonable editorial policy which would vilify the institutions so dear to the hearts of most investors." He also promised to jumpstart Hecht's literary renaissance.

11. Harry ran a dress shop in Simi, California, named Cathy-Rose Fashions.

12. Nixon curried favor with some of the most sullied people in America, and arranged deals that would have impressed the most ingenuous criminal. He slyly rose to power through a symbiotic relationship with mobsters, investment bankers, CEOs, and wealthy families. During the 1950s Meyer Lansky had the blessings of Cuba's Batista, who was the beneficiary of tons of cash. Then Vice-President Nixon embraced the Batista-Lansky gambling connection, and ignored Cuba's socio-economic problems. His lifelong pal Bebe Rebozo had shares in Lansky's Cuban gambling haven, a short flight from Miami. Another Havana partner was Moe Dalitz, someone Nixon had to ignore when making his Washington reports. Nixon was a heavy gambler, and received comps whenever he traveled to Cuba. Lansky wasn't alone; Rebozo associate Santos Trafficante and Johnny Rosselli shared in the largesse offered by upscale gambling in Havana. The Rebozo connection linked Nixon to mobsters all over the country. Nixon's Florida real estate holdings came as a courtesy of lenders who also did business with Jimmy Hoffa and Meyer Lansky. Watergate hush money suggested funneling from the coffers of gambling czar John Alessio, Howard Hughes, Carlos Marcello, and Tony Provenzano. Conspiracy theorists make the most out of Nixon's bad memory regarding his whereabouts at the time of the JFK assassination; he utilized several versions about how he had learned of JFK's death. He had been in Dallas at a Coca-Cola board meeting just before the shooting. Joan Crawford and Nixon bragged to local reporters how they didn't require Secret Service protection, perhaps embarrassing JFK into reducing his own security plans. Speculators loved to pin on Nixon the reason that JFK did not use a Plexiglas top on his limo. The Giancanas wrote about Nixon's life-long help with government contracts and even bailing Jack Ruby out of a jam. The authors claim that Sam Giancana spoke of the Lyndon Johnson and Nixon complicity in the JFK assassination. "When Nixon died I thought of the Shakespeare quote about the evil that men do living after them, and the good being interred with their bones. With Nixon the reverse was happening: They wanted the good to live on and the evil to be buried"—Anthony Summers. "If there was a candidate for the presidency whom the mob wanted elected, it was Richard Nixon. Since the earliest days of his political career in California, Nixon had seemed to walk hand in hand with the Mafia…"—John Davis. "Santos [Trafficante] viewed Nixon as a realistic, conservative politician who was not a zealot and would not be hard on him and his mob friends. The Mafia had little to fear from Nixon"—Frank Ragano. Many still argue that a vicious Democratic smear campaign tarnished Nixon's legacy, at least with regard to mobsters.

13. Pat Nixon was not fond of Chotiner or any of her husband's other shady connections. Richard Nixon had an agenda, an early architectural design for power, knew that the mob would always be helpful, and never heeded his wife's warnings. "But when she [Pat Nixon] voiced her disapproval, my father decided Chotiner's hard-line, street-smart political advice was more important to him than his wife's objections. So the subject of Murray became a non-subject"— Julie Nixon Eisenhower.

Chapter 29 – Things Change

1. In 1970 Marlon Brando-look-alike Marcello had his photo taken by Christopher R. Harris at a Louisiana State Senate Hearing in Baton Rouge. He never paid taxes on his extensive Louisiana businesses, while his mob controlled the entire state. The tight web of politics and organized crime coexisted in a world where jazz and well-prepared gumbo fronted for reality. Authors have linked Marcello to the Martin Luther King assassination.
2. Nixon's nefarious backers list compiled by author John Davis included Allen Dorfman, "mob-connected Teamsters financial 'consultant' from Chicago (who was murdered gangland style), Mafia-backed Teamsters vice-president Tony Provenzano, and southern California Mafia figure John Alessio" and Murray Chotiner, a "California mob attorney." Dorfman once told mafia attorney Frank Ragano that payoffs were made directly to President Nixon's aides to reduce Jimmy Hoffa's prison sentence.
3. "I am presently serving a sentence in the federal prison in Alcatraz. At my request, I asked for a meeting with a state law enforcement officer, and on October 9, 1962, Richard R. Rogan met with me in the visitor's room at Alcatraz. I informed Mr. Rogan that I wanted to discuss with him a question concerning the influence of persons engaged in gambling and bookmaking on the early political career of Richard Nixon. I first met Richard Nixon at a luncheon in the Goodfellow's Fisherman's Grotto on South Main Street in 1948. The meeting was arranged by Murray Chotiner, who asked me to meet Mr. Nixon, who was about to start his first campaign as a representative in Congress that year. I was asked by Nixon and Chotiner to raise some money for Nixon's campaign. In either 1948 during Nixon's second race for Congress or 1950 in his campaign for the senate, I was again asked by Murray Chotiner to raise funds for Nixon's campaign. During that time I was running most of the gambling and bookmaking in Los Angeles County. I reserved the Banquet Room in the Hollywood Knickerbocker Hotel on Ivar Street in Hollywood for a dinner meeting to which I invited approximately 250 guests who were working with me in the gambling fraternity. Among those who were present, whose names are well known by the law enforcement officers, were Joe and Fred Sica, Jack Dragna and George Capri. Also present was Hy Goldbaum, who is one of the pit bosses at the Stardust Hotel in Las Vegas, who also served a term of imprisonment at the federal prison at McNeil Island. Capri was one of the owners of the Flamingo Hotel in Las Vegas. Murray Chotiner told me I should have a quota of $25,000 for the campaign. During the course of the evening Nixon spoke for approximately 10 minutes. Chotiner spoke for half an hour. At this meeting my group pledged between $17,000 and $19,000 but this did not meet the quota set by Nixon and Chotiner and the group was informed they would have to stay until the quota was met. In addition to helping Mr. Nixon financially, I made arrangements to rent a headquarters for Nixon in the Pacific Finance Building at Eighth and Olive Streets in Los Angeles, which was the same building occupied by Attorney Sam Rummel. We posted Nixon signs and literature, and I paid for the headquarters for three to four weeks in that building. During the period that I ran the Nixon Headquarters, I contacted most of the gambling fraternity in Los Angeles County to tell them what their share of the contribution to the Nixon campaign would be. I have been asked by several newspaper persons and television employees of NBC during the 1956 presidential campaign to make these facts known, but until now I have refused to do so. In view of the fact that Mr. Nixon is now making speeches in his campaign for governor and stating that organized crime is active in California and that Eastern hoodlums were seeking a foothold in California to organize bookmaking, I have decided that the people of California should know the true facts with Nixon's entry into politics being based upon money raised by me and my associates in the gambling fraternity who started him off with $25,000. There have been no promises made to me of any kind or nature and the above statement has been given by me freely and voluntarily"—Mickey Cohen (Released for Publication in 1968). "What the gamblers got in

return is spelled out in the records of the Los Angeles County Court between 1949 and 1952, which show that Nixon's campaign manager, Murray Chotiner, and his brother, acted as attorney in 221 bookmaking and underworld cases. In almost all instances their clients got off with light fines or suspended sentences"—Drew Pearson. In a telephone conversation with the author on October 25, 2006, revisionist Nixon scholar and biographer Irwin Gellman mentioned how Nixonphobic biographers before him had too readily repeated the shady fundraising tales and smear campaign politics. Historian Gellman reported that in his exhaustive new research, including diaries, Nixon does not mention receiving money directly from Mickey Cohen; the connection relies too heavily on folklore.

Chapter 30 – Mickey's Back in Town

1. Attorney Sidney Korshak used his muscle on Kirk Kerkorian, the major shareholder of MGM, engaged in building the new Vegas hotel of the same name, and asked that he release Al Pacino from his contract to play Michael Corleone. A work stoppage at the hotel's construction site by powerful labor leader Korshak would have been costly to Kerkorian. Legendary producer Irwin Winkler had bought the theatrical rights to Jimmy Breslin's *The Gang That Couldn't Shoot Straight*. Winkler already had Al Pacino slated to play the lead when David Begelman, then managing Pacino, let Winkler know that there was a problem. Frank Rosenfelt, head of MGM, called Winkler personally to describe the Korshak phone call to Kerkorian. Winkler substituted Robert DeNiro in the lead role, which led to many further creative associations: *Raging Bull; New York, New York; Goodfellas; Guilty by Suspicion;* and *Night and the City*. (Begelman committed suicide in the chic Century Plaza Hotel after an evening with Sandi Bennett, former wife of fabled singer Tony.)
2. The headliners in the early seventies included Sammy Davis, Jr., Elvis, Liberace, Englebert Humperdinck, Rowan and Martin (Ciro's former bartender), Don Rickles (a Mickey favorite), Debbie Reynolds, Johnny Carson, Perry Como, Barbra Streisand, and Andy Williams. Attorney Sidney Korshak negotiated a famous one-million-dollar contract for Reynolds, and represented Barbra Streisand and Dean Martin.
3. Jay Sarno and Nate Jacobson ran Caesars Palace. Sarno later started Circus Circus. Dalitz, Morris Kleinman, and Sam Tucker operated the Desert Inn. Sidney Wyman, Al Gottesman, and Jake Gottlieb ran the Dunes. The Riviera elite were Ben Goffstein, Willie Alderman, and David Berman. Milton Prell started with the Sahara, and later resurrected the Tally-Ho, which became the Aladdin. Allen Glick fronted the Stardust, Fremont, Hacienda, and Marina hotels. "Dandy Phil" Kastel, under the auspices of Meyer Lansky, spearheaded the Tropicana. During the modern era, Arthur Goldberg (Park Place Entertainment), Sheldon Adelson (Sands), Steve Wynn (Mirage, Bellagio, Wynn), and Sol Kerzner (Sun City) would run casino complexes.
4. Mickey, who had no health insurance, paid thousands of dollars in cash before treatment. In addition, he paid $250 per day during his short-lived stays in the facility.
5. La Famiglia owner and ubiquitous Rat Pack host Joe Patti said that Mickey was involved during the application process, but despite later investigations, authorities could not link Mickey directly with the restaurant.

Chapter 31 – Mickey, the Elder Statesman

1. Matteo's was Sinatra's favorite restaurant. He knew the owners/brothers Mattie and Mike Jordan (who were on hand every night) from Hoboken. They named the annex next door to Matteo's, Little Taste of Hoboken. Sinatra's booth in the back of the main restaurant was only for him, and maître d's still refer to it to as "Sinatra's booth."

Chapter 32 – The Last Round

1. A plausible, but hardly ironclad case suggests that Nugent did have CIA affiliations. During one trip to Africa, authorities detained *Newsweek* writer Nugent and held him in custody on suspicion of being a CIA agent, who naturally was not welcome. He once wrote a detailed documentary for David Wolper about Stanley and Livingston's travails in Africa. During the Soviet invasion of Czechoslovakia, authorities suspected Wolper of CIA associations. Suspiciously absent in Mickey's book is any reference to the CIA; the index is CIA-blank. Three minor mentions of the FBI exist. FBI files avoid Mickey's relationship to Nixon, the Kennedys, Marilyn Monroe, or Sinatra's Rat Pack.

2. Audiences unknowingly watched actors perform high on television and in the movies. Business was booming for the drug traffickers; anyone in the drug business was raking in the dough. Mickey refused to discuss anything having to do with narcotics, and he always stuck to the same story—no drugs. The syndicate had spent decades organizing the flow of illegal drugs into the United States. After years of development, mostly in Europe, the drug trade became a permanent international enterprise. "The criminals who took part in the transformation of the international traffic in drugs by migrating to the manufacturing end represented a variant of modernity itself—they were relativistic, lurid, and urbane"—Alan A. Block. Mickey lived to see pharmacies dispense thousands of Quaaludes each month to 'lawful' prescription-carrying yuppies, who had received their triplicate narcotic drug forms—with directions to cooperative pharmacists—from "pain centers" organized all over the country, many in chic neighborhoods.

3. Frank Sinatra posed for one the most famous mob photographs of the era. All smiles, he took his place at the Westchester Premier Theater, a popular mob-run location, with Paul Castellano, Carlo Gambino, Richard Fusco, Jimmy Aladena Fratianno, Thomas Marson, Gregory De Palma, and Salvatore Spatola. Despite Hoover's hatred for Sinatra, not a single fact in Sinatra's monstrous FBI file would result in an indictment. The Friars Annual Testimonial Dinner finally got around to honoring him.

4. Rosselli, who married actress June Lang (Valasek) and produced movies, once took a beating by restaurant owner Kurt Niklas in his popular Beverly Hills Bistro Garden, now Spago. Attorney Sidney Korshak told Niklas to stay in a hotel overnight until he could reach Rosselli, who never returned to the restaurant. The Bistro Garden would close when business suffered after Niklas' son Christopher, who seated patrons, insulted a diner with anti-Semitic remarks.

Epilogue

1. Corpulent Herbie liked to hang out in Vegas, which still had its strong connections to Los Angeles. He was a lieutenant for Tony Spilotro, who ran the Hole in the Wall Gang, and had a nice run working for him until 1986, when someone buried Spilotro and his brother Michael alive in an Indiana cornfield after clubbing them unconscious. Nobody seemed to care about Herbie's activities, since he was hardly making a dent in the national syndicate. His regular source of income came from loan sharking and insurance fraud, and he operated out of his own auto repair shop. Robert Panaro from Buffalo conspired with locals Carmen Milano and Stephen Cino to take over Herbie's business. Herbie's last words were "Why me? What did I do?" before he was riddled with bullets in his Las Vegas residence. Authorities made a big deal out of his friendship with famous Las Vegas casino operator Teddy Binion, a popular gun-toting Texan who knew how to cater to the little man. Because of Herbie's "Vegas connections," prosecutors and federal investigators suggested that his downfall at age sixty-three signaled the end of organized crime in Los Angeles.

Index

Index

382

Index

Brad Lewis is a novelist, biographer, playwright, screenwriter, and former actor. He co-wrote the bestselling biography of Milton Berle, *My Father, Uncle Miltie,* with the actor's son William Berle, a candid look at an American television icon. Lewis' novel *Dysplasia* is a scalpel thriller centered on the sordid lives and weird sexual habits of "celebrity doctors," exposing the seamy side of high profile specialists who performed unnecessary surgery on their female patients.

An oral surgeon in Beverly Hills and New York, Lewis has written often about the Hollywood scene, and is no stranger to celebrities and celebrity doctors. His offices treated numerous luminaries, including Richard Nixon, Spiro Agnew, Frank Sinatra, Willie Mays, Diane Keaton, Hugh Downs, Henry Mancini, and Henry Kissinger. Lewis also treated several anonymous underworld "businessmen," who often sent their lady friends in for treatment. The experience with known mobsters contributed to Lewis' interest in the interconnection of gangsters, Hollywood, and Washington.

As an actor, Lewis appeared on *As the World Turns, Love of Life, The Guiding Light,* and trained at the prestigious H. B. Studios in Manhattan, with its founder Herbert Berghof and fabled acting teacher William Hickey. He appeared in many off and off-off Broadway productions. Lewis has degrees from CUNY (Psychology) and New York University; a fellowship at Columbia University, College of Physicians and Surgeons, and St. Luke's-Roosevelt Hospital. A popular talk show guest, he has appeared on numerous radio and television programs. He lives in Los Angeles.